P9-DTX-554

THE BIBLICAL RESOURCE SERIES

A Treatise on
The Use of the Tenses in Hebrew
And Some Other Syntactical Questions

S. R. Driver

WILLIAM B. EERDMANS PUBLISHING COMPANY
GRAND RAPIDS, MICHIGAN / CAMBRIDGE, U.K.

DOVE BOOKSELLERS
LIVONIA, MICHIGAN

First published 1874
© Oxford University Press, London

Third edition published 1892
Oxford University Press, London

This edition with new Introduction by W. Randall Garr
Published jointly 1998 by
Wm. B. Eerdmans Publishing Co.
255 Jefferson Ave. S.E., Grand Rapids, Michigan 49503 /
P.O. Box 163, Cambridge CB3 9PU U.K.
and by
Dove Booksellers
30633 Schoolcraft Road, Suite C, Livonia, Michigan 48150

Introduction © 1998
Wm. B. Eerdmans Publishing Co.

Printed in the United States of America

02 01 00 99 98   7 6 5 4 3 2 1

Library of Congress Cataloging-in-Publication Data

Driver, S. R. (Samuel Rolles), 1846-1914.
A treatise on the use of the tenses in Hebrew and some other
syntactical questions / by S. R. Driver. — 4th ed.
p.   cm.
Includes bibliographical references and index.
ISBN 0-8028-4160-0 (pbk. : alk. paper)
1. Hebrew language — Tense.   2. Hebrew language — Syntax.
I. Title.
PJ4659.D75   1998
492.4′82421—dc20   95-44053
                                                          CIP

PREFACE

—◆—

THE present small volume was designed originally—in 1874—as an attempt to supply what had for long appeared to me to be needed in England by the student of Hebrew—a systematic exposition, upon an adequate scale, of the nature and use of the Hebrew tenses. The subject is an important one, and is beset by many and peculiar difficulties. In Hebrew, as in most other inflexional languages, the verb is a flexible and elastic instrument, the smallest movement of which alters the character of the scene or fact which it pourtrays; and hence, without a vivid sense of the difference between its principal parts, the full power and beauty of the language can be but imperfectly appreciated. At the same time, Hebrew has but two tenses at its disposal: each of these therefore has practically to cover the ground occupied in an Aryan language by half a dozen or more distinct formations, every one denoting a fresh relation of time or mood. With an instrument of such limited resources, it might be expected that insuperable difficulties would arise: but such is the skill with which it is handled, that to the reader who has mastered the principles of its use, and perceives it to be regulated by law, the ceaseless variation of tense, instead of being a cause of confusion, will seem a most telling and expressive feature. Indeed the capacity for rapid transitions thus produced constitutes an element of force almost peculiar to Hebrew: and though doubtless there are passages on which some degree of uncertainty must rest, the conditions imposed by the context, interpreted in the light of parallel constructions, will usually reduce it within narrow limits.

There are, however, many obstacles to be overcome before the true nature of the tenses can be realized. In the first place there is the influence of our own language. This has been familiar to us from childhood; it constitutes the framework of our thoughts; it has determined for us the forms under which ideas present themselves to our mind; it has impressed upon us its own distinctions and lines of demarcation, at the same time silently ignoring those established by other languages. On the agreement of a verb with its subject in number, a point to which in certain cases the ancient Hebrew attached no importance whatever, we are ourselves sensitive and precise: on the other hand, the difference between *being* and *becoming*, *seyn* and *werden*, εἰμὶ and γίγνομαι has never been fully appropriated or naturalized in English. Accordingly 'I am convinced' has to do duty for πείθομαι as well as for πέπεισμαι, for 'ich *werde* überzeugt' as well as for 'ich *bin* überzeugt;' ἔπειθον differs indeed essentially from ἔπεισα, but so cumbrous is the mechanism which has to be set in motion in order to express the difference, so palpable is the strain to which our language is subjected in the process, that we feel irresistibly tempted to discard and forget it. Similarly, on the distinction of tense, which in Hebrew is fundamental, English, except in the more obvious cases, is comparatively indifferent: and thus we are predisposed to underrate its importance, if not to neglect it altogether.

Secondly, there are the intrinsic difficulties offered by the language itself. Each tense, and particularly the imperfect, seems to unite in itself incompatible meanings, which the reader too often finds resist all his efforts to reconcile with one another, or to derive from a common origin; and the complications superinduced when either is brought within range of the potent but mysterious *waw*, increase his perplexity. And yet it is impossible, if we are right in supposing language to be the reflex and embodiment of reason, that anomalies such as these can be ultimate and inexplicable: some hidden link of connexion must exist, some higher principle must be operative, the discovery of which will place us at the true centre of vision, and permit the confused and incoherent figures to fall into their proper perspective and become consistent and clear. The difficulties arising from the causes here indicated I had felt forcibly myself, as well as the practical inability to surmount them with the aids usually available by the student; and this treatise was designed in the hope that, whether by contributing towards their solution, or by directing attention to what might otherwise pass unobserved, it might promote, if possible, an intelligent appreciation of the language of the Old Testament. The favourable notice which it has received, both on the Continent and in England, has much exceeded what I had ventured to anticipate; and students of Hebrew have frequently expressed to me their obligations for the assistance which they have derived from it.

The original plan of the work was somewhat enlarged in the second edition (1881) by the addition of a chapter on the Participle, as well as of two fresh Appendices, one treating of an important principle of Hebrew Syntax (Apposition), which had not at that time received generally the prominence that it deserves, the other dealing with two or three other questions, which seemed to offer scope for fresh illustration. The present edition does not differ substantially from the second edition. It is not, however, a mere reprint of it: in numerous places improvements, more or less important, have been introduced[1]; several additional notes have been

---

[1] The sections in which the improvements have been most material are §§ 39 *a, β* (chiefly in arrangement), 161–162, and especially §§ 172–175, 178 (in particular, pp. 228–232), and 190–191 (with the *Obss.*). The notes also have in many cases been enlarged. (I am indebted to Prof. H. L. Strack, of Berlin, for calling my attention to several oversights and misprints.)

inserted[1]; the references have frequently been revised, and, where necessary, more fully explained; while throughout notice has been taken of the fresh exegetical literature of the last ten years. I have also paid more attention to questions of text in the passages cited, than I gave to them in my previous editions. The question, to what extent Hebrew grammar has been artificially complicated by a corrupt text, is one which sooner or later cannot but force itself upon the student's notice. And the more minutely I study the Massoretic text of the Old Testament, the more fully am I persuaded that it presents in many places anomalies of form or construction which cannot be legitimately explained in accordance with the principles of Hebrew (or Semitic[2]) grammar. In some cases it is only the vocalization, in others it is the consonantal text itself, which appears to be at fault. Most of the difficulties connected with the use of the jussive form can, I now believe (§§ 172–175), be overcome, if it be granted that the Massoretic vocalization does not represent the intention of the original authors. In my previous edition, I was induced, by the authority of Philippi, to extend the principle of Apposition to cases where its application becomes forced and unreal; and I do not question now (cf. §§ 190 *Obs.*, 191 *Obs.* 1, 2), that in all these cases we are dealing with a corrupt text (as indeed, in several instances, is attested independently by the LXX)[3]. The aim which I have set myself throughout has

---

[1] E.g. §§ 120 *Obs.* 2, 198 *Obs.* 1, 199 *Obs.* § 209 is also new. The Index of Texts has likewise been considerably augmented, and includes now, I hope, all passages to which any particular difficulty or interest attaches.

[2] I say Semitic, because a grammatical phenomenon, though isolated in Hebrew, is not necessarily wrong, if it be supported by the analogy of one of the other Semitic languages.

[3] My principles of textual criticism are exemplified more fully than in the present volume in my *Notes on the Hebrew Text of the Books of Samuel* (Oxford, 1890): comp. also my review of Workman's *Text of Jeremiah* (1889) in the *Expositor* for May, 1889, pp. 321–337. The Ancient Versions,

been to produce a trustworthy manual, which may be of service as a supplement to the grammars ordinarily used by learners. Had I been writing it now for the first time, I should probably have endeavoured to state the rules more succinctly: but my first edition was published at a time when no satisfactory treatment of the subject existed in English, and tolerably full explanations appeared to be needful. If nevertheless some points should still seem to have been dwelt on too diffusely or repeatedly, I must crave the reader's indulgence on another ground: experience shews me that there are departments of Hebrew syntax in which inexactness and looseness of thought so speedily creep in that it is impossible to be too explicit and particular.

In the selection of proof-passages, my object has been to illustrate and distinguish the varieties of Biblical usage as accurately as possible : but it will of course be understood that there are instances in which a different opinion may legitimately be held respecting either the construction generally, or the precise force of a given tense[1]. To the student who may be interested in tracing a particular use, the number of examples will not probably appear excessive ; and others also may be glad sometimes to have the opportunity of judging for themselves how far an alleged custom extends, whether it is really common or only exceptional. Moreover,

---

rightly used, are often of great value in the restoration of corrupt or defective passages; occasionally also conjecture, if applied discreetly, may be legitimately resorted to. A selection of the best and most probable restorations, which have received the approval of modern scholars, may be found in the *Variorum Bible* (see p. xv) : though it was not in accordance with the plan of this work for the editors to introduce such various readings only as commended themselves absolutely to their own judgment, none were admitted which did not appear to them to deserve consideration beside the existing Massoretic text, and the majority were deemed by them to be decidedly preferable to it.

[1] In cases where commentators are divided, authorities for the rendering adopted have frequently been cited.

a rule is more firmly grasped when it has been seen repeatedly exemplified : and (as has been observed) it may even happen that, in virtue of the common point of view attained by the comparison of numerous instances, passages and constructions appear for the first time in their true light.   Another advantage is on the side of textual criticism.   On the one hand, an isolated expression, which perhaps excited suspicion, may be justified by parallels thus discovered : on the other, it may be shewn to conflict with some principle established by an extensive induction, to presuppose a signification at variance with the *consistent* usage of the language.   Certainly, it is the province of the grammarian to explain (if possible), and not to emend ; but in the latter case, a consideration of the text is forced upon him.   Instances will be furnished from time to time by the following pages ; but, though I have done this more frequently in the present than in the previous editions, I have still not felt it incumbent upon me to inquire uniformly into the textual accuracy of particular citations.

My obligations to previous writers were indicated in the Preface to the first edition.   It will be sufficient here to say that, while Gesenius still retains his place as the master of Hebrew lexicography[1], Ewald by his originality and penetration was the founder of a new era in the study of Hebrew grammar ; and there is probably no modern Hebraist who is not, directly or indirectly, indebted to him.   In the treatment of details, Ewald was indeed liable to be arbitrary and inattentive ; but he excelled in the power of grouping the broader

---

[1] The speculative character of Fürst's philological principles and the boldness with which he puts them to a practical use, render his *Hebrew and Chaldee Lexicon* an untrustworthy guide.   Nor can Mühlau and Volck's editions of Gesenius' *Handwörterbuch* (the latest, 1890) be trusted implicitly ; for they contain many questionable etymologies, and often assign arbitrary or hypothetical meanings to the Arabic words quoted.

features of language, and of recognizing the principles which underlie and explain its phenomena. From the numerous exegetical works of Hitzig[1] all may learn: when he is not led astray by a vein of misplaced subtlety—always, happily, visible on the surface—no one has a clearer or truer perception of the meaning of a Hebrew sentence. As a grammarian, Hitzig stands on a level not inferior to that of Ewald; and his writings are the source of much that is best exegetically in more recent commentaries[2]. The few lines which Delitzsch devotes to his memory, in the Preface to the second edition of *Hiob*, p. vi, are a graceful and cordial testimony to his exegetical skill. And by sobriety, fulness of information, and scholarship combined Delitzsch has succeeded in making his commentaries[3] indispensable to every student of the Old Testament. The commentaries of Dillmann[4] are also

[1] *Jesaja* (1833), *Die Sprüche Salomo's* (1858), *Die Psalmen* (1863–5), *Hiob* (1874); and in the 'Kurzgefasstes Exegetisches Handbuch,' *Jeremia* (ed. 2, 1866), *Ezechiel* (1847), which still retains an independent value by the side of the Commentary of Rud. Smend, which took its place in the same series in 1880, *Die Kleinen Propheten* (ed. 3, 1863, ed. 4, substantially unaltered, ed. by Steiner, 1881), *Das Hohe Lied* (1855), *Der Prediger Salomo's* (1847,—largely excerpted, though without signs to indicate the passages retained, in Nowack's second edition of the Commentary on this book in the same series, 1883), *Daniel* (1850).

[2] Let the reader who makes use of the *Variorum Bible* (p. xv) observe how frequently the combinations 'Hi. De.,' 'Hi. Ke.' occur.

[3] *Genesis* (ed. 5, 1887), *Isaiah* (ed. 4, 1889), *The Psalms* (ed. 4, 1883), *Proverbs* (1873), *Job* (ed. 2, 1876), *Song of Songs* and *Ecclesiastes* (1875). These are all translated into English, that on the Psalms being published by Hodder and Stoughton, those on the other books by T. and T. Clark. The translation of Job is, however, based on the *first* German edition (1864), and consequently lacks many improvements introduced by the author into his second edition.

[4] In the 'Kurzgefasstes Exegetisches Handbuch;' viz. *Genesis* (ed. 3, 1886), *Exodus and Leviticus* (1880), *Numbers, Deuteronomy, and Joshua* (1886), *Isaiah* (1890), *Job* (ed. 2, 1891).

The 'Speaker's Commentary,' on the other hand, is to be frequently distrusted, especially in matters of philology: several of the contributors,

exceedingly complete and valuable, their author being distinguished both for calm and sober judgment and for sound scholarship. In the exegetical and critical works of my colleague Professor Cheyne[1], though they rest uniformly upon a basis of exact philology, it frequently happens that the philological element, as such, is not the most prominent feature : but the watchful student will not overlook the many fruitful notes on either text or interpretation which his volumes always contain[2].

S. R. D.

CHRIST CHURCH, OXFORD,
  March, 1892.

---

for instance, have not yet learnt such a simple principle of Hebrew syntax, as that a noun, in the construct state, does not take the article : see the notes on Ex. 3, 15. Dt. 20, 9. Josh. 10, 12 (ii. p. 56). 1 Chr. 10, 2.

[1] The principal are *The Prophecies of Isaiah* (ed. 3, 1884); *Jeremiah and the Lamentations* in the 'Pulpit Commentary' (exegetical part), 1883, 1885; *Job and Solomon, or the Wisdom of the Old Testament*, 1887; *The Book of Psalms*, 1888; and *The Origin and Religious Contents of the Psalter in the light of Old Testament Criticism and the History of Religions*, 1891.

[2] See, for instance, the 'Critical Notes' in *The Book of Psalms*, p. 369 ff., and the study on 'The Linguistic Affinities of the Psalms' in *The Origin of the Psalter*, p. 461 ff., as well as various notes in other parts of the volume.

In questions of Semitic philology, the guidance of Nöldeke, where it can be obtained, is invaluable : comp. below, pp. 159 *n.*, 219 *n.*, 220 *n.*, 243 *n.*; and add to the references there given, *ZDMG.*, 1886, p. 148 ff. (on W. R. Smith's *Kinship and Marriage in early Arabia*), 1887, p. 707 ff. (on Wellhausen's *Reste Arabischen Heidentumes*), 1888, p. 470 ff. (on Baethgen's *Beiträge zur Semitischen Religionsgeschichte*); also his interesting studies on the use of אַל and אֱלֹהַּ in the various Semitic languages in the *Monatsberichte der Kön.-Preuss. Akademie der Wissenschaften zu Berlin*, 1880, p. 760 ff., and in the *Sitzungsberichte* of the same Academy, 1882, p. 1175 ff.; on the Old-Aramaic Inscriptions from Tema, *ibid.*, 1884, p. 813 ff.; and the philological notes contributed by him to Euting's *Nabatäische Inschriften*, 1885; etc. On the late Dr. Wright's *Comparative Grammar of the Semitic Languages*, comp. below, p. 219 *n.*

CONTENTS

List of principal Works referred to by Authors' Names only, or by Abbreviations.

Böttcher, Fr., *Ausführliches Lehrbuch der Hebr. Sprache,* 1866.

Comprises the accidence ('Formenlehre') only. A monument of industry, and valuable for occasional reference, but inconvenient for general use.

Ewald, H., *Lehrbuch der Hebräischen Sprache,* ed. 8, 1870.

The *Syntax,* invaluable to the advanced student, has been translated by J. Kennedy, Edinburgh, 1881.

Ges.-Kautzsch (or Ges.-K.), the 25th edition of Gesenius' *Hebräische Grammatik,* enlarged and greatly improved, especially in the syntax, by E. Kautzsch (1889).

An English translation of this grammar, which is now abreast of the present state of philological knowledge, will, it is expected, appear before very long. In the parts covering the same ground, numerous references have been introduced, derived apparently from the previous edition (1881) of the present work.

GGA.=Göttingische Gelehrte Anzeigen.

GGN.=Göttingische Gelehrte Nachrichten.

König, F. E., *Historisch-kritisches Lehrgebäude der Hebr. Sprache,* i. 1881.

Vol. ii, containing the treatment of the noun, and the syntax, has not yet (March, 1892) appeared. Especially useful on account of the full discussions of anomalous forms.

Olshausen, Justus, *Lehrbuch der Hebr. Sprache,* i. 1861.

A masterly work, but lacking the syntax, which the author did not live to complete.

QPB.[3] = *Queen's Printers' Bible* (also called the *Variorum
Bible*), ed. 3, 1888, published by Eyre & Spottis-
woode, being *The Holy Bible* (A.V.) *edited with
Various Renderings and Readings from the best
authorities,*—the Old Testament by Prof. T. K.
Cheyne and the present writer.

Stade, B., *Lehrbuch der Hebr. Grammatik*, i. 1879.

> Convenient and useful. More comprehensive (so far as it goes)
> than Gesenius-Kautzsch, but not so elaborate as Olshausen or
> König. The syntax has not yet appeared.

ZATW. = *Zeitschrift für die Alttestamentliche Wissenschaft*,
edited by B. Stade.

ZDMG. = *Zeitschrift der Deutschen Morgenländischen Gesellschaft.*

For Commentaries, see above, pp. xi, xii, and add—

> Graf, K. H., *Der Prophet Jeremia erklärt*, 1862.
> Hupfeld, H., *Die Psalmen übersetzt und ausgelegt*, ed. 3, bearbeitet
> von W. Nowack, 1888.
> Nowack, W., *Die Sprüche Salomo's* (in the 'Kurzgefasstes Exegeti-
> sches Handbuch'), 1883.
> Strack, H. L., *Die Sprüche Salomo's* (in Strack and Zöckler's
> 'Kurzgefasster Kommentar'), 1888.

ADDITIONS AND CORRECTIONS.

P. 33, line 4: *for* 13, 20 *read* 2 Ki. 13, 20.

P. 37, § 33. Add Hos. 13, 11 אתן־לך מלך באפי ואקח בעברתי, where the repeated change of dynasty in the northern kingdom is indicated by the tense employed.

P. 44, note 2, line 2, 2 Chr. 2, 7 has been overlooked (2 Chr. 18, 15 is, of course, merely a transcript of 1 Ki. 22, 16).

P. 49, note 1, line 2: *prefix* ברוך *to* ויאמר.

P. 71, note 3. For the comparison of the Phoenician with the Hebrew vocabulary, A. Bloch's *Phoenicisches Glossar* (Berlin, 1890)—substantially an Index to the Inscriptions published prior to that date—is useful.

P. 77, line 19. It is possible, however, that in Qoh. 5, 14 שֶׁיֹּלֵךְ (assuming the punctuation to be correct) may be intended as a real jussive, with the sense 'which he *might* carry away in his hand' (on the analogy of the more usual construction with וְ, § 64); so Ew. § 235ᶜ, Hitzig (though he prefers himself to read שֶׁיֹּלַךְ), Del., König, i. p. 445.

P. 77, note 2. In the parallel 2 Chr. 5, 2 אָז יַקְהִיל. It must, however, remain an open question whether the punctuation is here correct (cf. § 174), and whether the original pronunciation was not יַקְהֵל, יַקְהִל: the shorter form is found nowhere else after אז (see Ex. 15, 1 and Nu. 21, 17 אָז יָשִׁיר, Dt. 4, 41 אָז יַבְדִּיל, 1 Ki. 11, 7 אז יבנה, etc.).

P. 100, note. The reader who is interested in the subject may consult also the learned and elaborate study of Ad. Büchler, *Untersuchungen zur Entstehung und Entwickelung der Hebr. Accente,* 1. Theil (1891).

P. 127, (4) *a*, line 6: *for* והיו *read* והיה.

P. 141, line 2 from bottom. The passages from Malachi (all ואמרתם) should perhaps rather be referred to § 120, or even to § 133.

P. 157, § 129. Add Qoh. 8, 16 f. (כאשר . . . . . וראיתי).

P. 157, note. The 11th edition of Delitzsch's *Hebrew New Testament,* embodying the author's final corrections and improvements, has just appeared (March, 1892).

P. 163, note, lines 1–2. *Dele* the reference to Dan. 8, 12. The perfects here belong rather to line 1 of the same note (p. 162); cf. § 174 *end.*

P. 213, § 171. An anomalous instance of a jussive appears to occur in Qoh. 11, 3 יְהוּא (for יְהוּ, from הָוָה: Ges.-K., § 75 rem. 3ᵉ): but perhaps יְהֵוֶא (cf. Dan. 2, 41) was intended by the author (Olsh. p. 511). Grätz, however, suggests plausibly שָׁם הוּא (cf. Job 39, 30).

FURTHER CORRECTIONS

P. xiv, line 4: *for* 1866 *read* i. 1866, ii. 1868.

P. xiv, line 10: *for* 1881 *read* 1879, 1881, 1891.

P. xiv, line 21. *Dele. Read NGGW. = Nachrichten von der Georg-Augusts-Universität und der Königlichen Gesellschaft der Wissenschaften zu Göttingen.*

P. xiv, lines 22-26: Vol. ii appeared in 1895, and vol. iii in 1897.

P. xiv, after line 26: Add Add *Luth. Zeitschrift = Zeitschrift für die gesammte lutherische Theologie und Kirche.*

P. 56, last line of main text: *for* 55,3.18 *read* Ps. 55,3.18.

P. 119, line 19: *for* וַיְכֵנִי *read* וַיְכֻנִי.

P. 246, line 14: *for* GGAN. *read* NGGW.

DRIVER'S *TREATISE* AND THE STUDY

OF HEBREW: THEN AND NOW*

W. Randall Garr
University of California, Santa Barbara

0. *Orientation.* A *Treatise on the Use of the Tenses in Hebrew* launched the career of Samuel Rolles Driver (October 2, 1846–February 26, 1914).[1] The reason is simple. "It was the first attempt in English to expound the principles of Hebrew syntax on lines at once philosophical and scientific. . . . All modern study of Hebrew has been founded on the *Tenses*: it remains perhaps the most interesting and original book that Driver wrote."[2] Its final edition was hailed as the best single study of the Hebrew verbal

---

*Wherever possible, the citation style in this essay imitates Driver's, with the following exceptions. References to the *Treatise* are generally cited internally, in parentheses, and by page number. When the edition is unspecified, references are cited according to the third edition, reprinted here; earlier editions are cited with an initial superscripted numeral (e.g., [1]v or [2]viii). Finally, references to sections within this essay are marked by their corresponding sign (§).

[1] For an excellent biography of Driver, see G. A. Cooke in *The Dictionary of National Biography Founded in 1882 by George Smith, 1912-1921* (ed. H. W. C. Davis and J. R. H. Weaver; London, 1927), pp. 162-163. For an accessible bibliography, see G. R. D[river] in *The Ideals of the Prophets. Sermons: together with a Bibliography of his published Writings* (ed. Cooke; Edinburgh, 1915), pp. 213-234.

[2] Cooke in *Dictionary of National Biography*, p. 163. See also idem, *Harvard Theological Review*, ix, 1916, pp. 249, 250.

system.[3] Even its critics conceded it to be an exciting and brilliant work that shaped the future discussion of the Hebrew and Semitic verb.[4] The *Treatise* placed Driver at the forefront of Hebrew grammar and biblical studies.

0.1. In his original study of 1874, Driver was guided by two analytic principles. One was syntactic. According to Driver, the Hebrew verbal system is subsumed under the larger framework of Hebrew syntax (see ix). His analysis of the verb, then, involved syntactic issues that usually lay in other grammatical arenas: e.g., accents, conjunctions, hypotheticals, and circumstantial clauses. The other analytic principle was morphological or, more precisely, inflectional. In his investigation of the Hebrew verbal system, Driver originally restricted himself to two classes of finite verb forms: the suffixed forms and the inflectionally distinct prefixed[5] forms (v, 1; see also 6-12). Accordingly, Driver devoted separate and extensive discussions to each verb form that participates in one of these two grammatical patterns.

Consistent with Driver's focus on syntax, the later editions aptly carry an expanded title: *A Treatise on the Use of the Tenses in Hebrew and Some Other Syntactical Questions.* Their contents were also broadened and refined. The expansion itself occurred in the second edition of 1881 (vii), in which Driver added studies of several other syntactic phenomena, such as apposition and casus pendens. More importantly, he included a new chapter on the participle — a verb form that is inflectionally unrelated to the

---

3 See Baumgartner, *Orientalistische Literaturzeitung*, xl, 1937, col. 686.

4 "Als die umfassendste Leistung auf diesem Gebiete gilt mit Recht die Monographie von S. R. Driver, *regius Professor* des Hebräischen in Oxford: „Über den Gebrauch der Tempora im Hebräischen", ein glänzendes und geistvolles Buch, dessen Resultate nicht nur in die meisten unserer hebräischen Grammatiken übergegangen sind, sondern, wie es scheint, die Anschauungen über die semitischen Tempora überhaupt stark beeinflusst haben" (H. Bauer, *Beiträge zur Assyriologie und semitischen Sprachwissenschaft*, viii/1, 1910, p. 23).

5 Cf. n. 60, below.

suffixed and prefixed verb forms (cf. §2.1) but completes the aspectual system that Driver had begun to define with the other two "tenses" (see §2.3). This new chapter in the second edition signaled Driver's recognition that, in addition to syntax and inflectional pattern, a third analytic principle organizes the Hebrew verbal system: aspect. Thereafter, in the third and final edition of 1892, Driver inserted several paragraphs, refined a number of sections, and provided more complete explanations (vii-viii). As he modestly noted, the third edition was "revised and improved."

0.2. Even though the *Treatise* itself changed throughout its three editions, Driver's purpose did not. "The present small volume was designed originally . . . as an attempt to supply what had for long appeared to me to be needed in England by the student of Hebrew — a systematic exposition, upon an adequate scale, of the nature and use of the Hebrew tenses" (v). Originally, too, Driver supplied a candid elaboration of this introductory statement of purpose.

> Upon most of the points connected with Hebrew grammar, the student can from more sources than one . . . acquire a minute and accurate acquaintance with the language: but in their treatment of the verb, and especially its two leading forms, they all from one cause or another seem suddenly to withdraw their assistance and fail. The merely empirical treatment is inadequate and unsatisfying; and that which essays to be something more is obscure, abstract, and hard. ([1]v)

Later, Driver was more generous. "[M]y first edition was published at a time when no satisfactory treatment of the subject existed in English, and tolerably full explanations appeared to be needful" (ix). "The aim which I have set myself throughout has been to produce a trustworthy manual, which may be of service as a supplement to the grammars ordinarily used by learners" (viii-ix).[6]

---

[6] R. H. Kennett, however, felt that the "learners" targeted by Driver were still somewhat advanced. Accordingly, Kennett aimed at the true beginner:

The need felt in 1874 was satisfied, at least in part, by 1892.[7] Beginning in 1882, Müller's Hebrew grammar[8] was accessible to the English reader in the form of James Robertson's abbreviated English translation.[9] More importantly, an English translation of parts of Ewald's monumental biblical Hebrew grammar[10] appeared in 1879.[11] Driver had once predicted that "the *Lehrbuch*, unless it met with an exceptionally skilful translator, would probably be disappointing in an English form . . . ; to our ears, its nomenclature would be strange and unfamiliar, its massive and involved sentences repellent and obscure" ([1]xi-xii). But after James Kennedy's translation became available, Driver all but retracted his prediction; he was "now . . . glad to see" that "Ewald's syntax . . . is accessible in English" ([2]viii). Yet Driver was undaunted. He remained determined to present a "trustworthy manual . . . in English" of the Hebrew verbal system (ix).

0.3. Given his sentiment that "no satisfactory treatment of the subject existed *in English*" (italics added), it is unsurprising that Driver acknowledged almost no debt to his English predecessors.

To English books (except Dr. Kalisch's Hebrew Grammar,[12]

"The present volume is an attempt to give an account of the nature and use of the Tenses in Hebrew in a form suitable for those who have but recently begun the study of the language, and who have not attained to such proficiency as will enable them to use with advantage Professor Driver's indispensable book" (*A Short Account of the Hebrew Tenses* [Cambridge, 1901], p. vii). See also A. Müller, *Luth. Zeitschrift*, xxxviii, 1877, pp. 199-200.

7 See, in this context, W. G. Ballantine, *Hebraica*, ii, 1885, p. 53.

8 Müller, *Hebräische Schulgrammatik* (Halle, 1878).

9 *Outlines of Hebrew Syntax* (tr. and ed. J. Robertson; Glasgow, 1882; 2nd ed., 1883; 3rd ed., 1888; 4th ed., 1894).

10 H. Ewald, *Ausführliches Lehrbuch der hebräischen Sprache des Alten Bundes* (8th ed.; Göttingen, 1870).

11 *Syntax of the Hebrew Language of the Old Testament* (Edinburgh, 1879). This translation was reissued in 1881 and 1891.

12 M. M. Kalisch, *A Hebrew Grammar, with Exercises*, i (London, 1862). ii (1863). A second edition of the *Grammar* appeared in 1875 and, again, in 1884-1885.

and Professor Wright's Arabic Grammar,[13] which are indispensable to every student) I am under no obligations whatever: I could wish that the case had been otherwise, but, at least in questions of scholarship, the majority of English writers upon the Old Testament seem to me to be incapable of offering an opinion of any value that has not been derived from some foreign source. ([1]xiii)

In later editions, though, Driver mollified this position by deleting it altogether.

With regard to previous non-English scholars, Driver was aware of his "obligations" (x; see also xi-xii). But "[t]o define the exact extent of my indebtedness to each and all of the writers named [in part, on x-xii] would be impossible: where it is special and direct some acknowledgment or indication of it has generally been given" ([1]xiv-xv). "First and foremost" among them was Ewald, about whom Driver waxed rhapsodic. He was, after all,

the brilliant and distinguished scholar who may be truly called the father of rational Hebrew grammar. . . . [T]o the originality and penetration of Ewald is to be ascribed the foundation of a new era in the study of the language. Arbitrary at times and impetuous — when is genius not so? — Ewald is one of those thinkers who seem to move in a different plane from ordinary men: possessing in a rare degree the power of seizing the right clue for unravelling a tangled web, and of recognising the true principle that underlies and is presupposed by an isolated fact, he applies to whatever he touches a fresh and unconventional mode of treatment, is never at a loss for a fruitful and suggestive combination, and can always bring to bear upon his subject luminous and appropriate conceptions.[14] ([1]x-xi)

---

[13] C. P. Caspari, *A Grammar of the Arabic language* (tr. and ed. W. Wright; London/Edinburgh, 1862).

[14] Cf. Müller, *Luth. Zeitschrift*, xxxviii, 1877, pp. 198-199.

"[T]here is probably no modern Hebraist who is not, directly or indirectly, indebted to him" (x). Driver was no exception. He owed his overall taxonomic scheme to Ewald (see x-xi), and his terminology was largely Ewald's as well (see §1.5). To paraphrase Müller, Driver honed Ewald's taxonomy into an organized system that was both replete with examples[15] and conceptually, grammatically, and textually precise.[16]

Other non-English predecessors to Driver did not fare as well. Gesenius, "the father of modern Hebrew grammar,"[17] got only a perfunctory nod (x; see also [1]x and [2]xi). The work of Böttcher,[18] whose semantic and syntactic analyses foreshadowed Driver's,[19] received diminishing applause: "a monument of industry, and invaluable as an exhaustive collection of fact and forms . . .

[15] At first, Driver was somewhat apologetic for the number of proof texts he presented.

> If their number should in some cases seem excessive, it must be recollected that it is often of the first importance to know how far an alleged custom extends, whether it is really common or only exceptional; and that, in days when strange assertions are sometimes met with respecting Hebrew idioms, it is desirable to give the reader every facility for testing each statement for himself. ([1]xv-xvi)

In later editions, Driver was more confident.

> To the student who may be interested in tracing a particular use, the number of examples will not probably appear excessive; and others also may be glad sometimes to have the opportunity of judging for themselves how far an alleged custom extends, whether it is really common or only exceptional. ([2]ix; [3]ix)

[16] Müller, *Luth. Zeitschrift*, xxxviii, 1877, p. 201. See also Cooke, *Harvard Theological Review*, ix, 1916, p. 249. Cf. B. K. Waltke and M. O'Connor, *An Introduction to Biblical Hebrew Syntax* (Winona Lake, 1990), §§29.3l-m.

[17] W. L. Moran in *The Bible and the Ancient Near East: Essays in Honor of William Foxwell Albright* (ed. G. E. Wright; Garden City, 1961), p. 54.

[18] F. Böttcher, *Ausführliches Lehrbuch der hebräischen Sprache*, i (ed. F. Mühlau; Leipzig, 1866). ii (1868).

[19] See, e.g., C. Brockelmann, *Grundriss der vergleichenden Grammatik der semitischen Sprachen*, ii (Berlin, 1913), §74b; and Bauer, *Beiträge zur Assyriologie*, viii/1, 1910, pp. 23-24.

which deserves to be more widely known and used in England" ([1]xii); "a monument of industry and invaluable for purposes of reference . . . has also been of service to me" ([2]xii); "[a] monument of industry, and valuable for occasional reference, but inconvenient for general use" ([3]xiv). Olshausen,[20] though, languished unacknowledged until the final edition, where his grammar was pallidly characterized as "[a] masterly work, but lacking the syntax, which the author did not live to complete" (xiv). Unacknowledged, too, was the near identity between Driver's formal and aspectual classification of the Hebrew verb and that of Olshausen.[21] Despite his statement to the contrary, then, Driver actually underplayed the "obligations" owed to his German forerunners — except for Ewald.

0.4. Just as Driver's purpose was unchanged throughout the different editions of the *Treatise*, he was consistent in other areas, too. His analytic principles remained constant, though they were somewhat expanded (see §0.1). The major grammatical influences on Driver — Gesenius,[22] Olshausen, Böttcher, and Ewald[23] — all predated 1874. In several important ways, the

---

[20] J. Olshausen, *Lehrbuch der hebräischen Sprache* (Braunschweig, 1861).

[21] Müller, *Luth. Zeitschrift*, xxxviii, 1877, p. 201.

[22] Specifically, W. Gesenius' *Ausführliches grammatisch-kritisches Lehrgebäude der hebräischen Sprache: mit Vergleichung der verwandten Dialekte* (Leipzig, 1817) and *Gesenius's Hebrew Grammar* (ed. E. Rœdiger, tr. B. Davies; London, 1869). The latter was a hybrid edition. "This new edition of Gesenius's Hebrew Grammar is from the 20th edition of the German, but it may be regarded as a translation from the 21st, Dr. Rœdiger having made arrangements for its appearance in advance in English" (p. viii). The twenty-first edition of the grammar appeared some three years later (*Wilhelm Gesenius' Hebräische Grammatik* [ed. E. Rödiger; Leipzig, 1872]).

In 1892, however, Driver also utilized the "enlarged and greatly improved . . . 25th edition of Gesenius' *Hebräische Grammatik*" (ed. E. Kautzsch; 1889) (xiv), which is cited below according to the subsequent and very similar *Gesenius' Hebrew Grammar* (ed. E. Kautzsch and A. E. Cowley; 2nd English ed.; Oxford, 1910).

[23] *Kritische Grammatik der hebräischen Sprache* (Leipzig, 1827); *Grammatik der hebräischen Sprache des A.T.* (rev. ed., 1828; 2nd ed., 1835); *Gram-*

author of the first edition was the same as the author of the third, some eighteen years later.

Constancy, however, can have its limitations. After 1874, a body of grammatical information on Akkadian ("Assyrian") slowly emerged,[24] culminating in Delitzsch's *Assyrische Grammatik* of 1889.[25] Almost immediately thereafter, this information was applied to problems of Hebrew grammar. For example, in 1890, Wright observed that several Semitic languages, Akkadian included,[26] use the jussive form to express past or aorist meaning: Arabic *(lam) yaqtul,* Hebrew *"vâv conversive,"* and Akkadian *iškun.*[27] A few years later, Lambert took the comparison a step further.[28] Guided by the semantic range of the Akkadian prefixed form *(iprus),* Lambert hypothesized that the Hebrew jussive and "prefixed perfect" may have originally been identical.[29] Driver, though, thought otherwise. The mounting grammatical evidence to the contrary notwithstanding, he rejected the similarity of the

---

matik der hebräischen Sprache des Alten Testaments (3rd ed., 1838); *Ausführliches Lehrbuch der hebräischen Sprache des Alten Bundes* (5th ed., 1844; 6th ed., 1855; 7th ed.; Göttingen, 1863; 8th ed., 1870).

[24] For a bibliography of Akkadian studies published prior to 1874, see A. H. Sayce, *An Assyrian Grammar for Comparative Purposes* (London, 1872), pp. 18-23.

[25] F. Delitzsch, *Assyrische Grammatik mit Paradigmen Übungsstücken Glossar und Litteratur* (Berlin/London, 1889). For an evaluation, see W. von Soden and W. R. Mayer, *Grundriss der akkadischen Grammatik* (3rd ed.; Rome, 1995), §3a.

[26] See already Delitzsch, *Assyrische Grammatik,* §93.1 in conjunction with §145.

[27] Wright, *Lectures on the Comparative Grammar of the Semitic Languages* (ed. W. R. Smith; Cambridge, 1890), pp. 191-193.

[28] Cf. Brockelmann, *Zeitschrift für Phonetik und allgemeine Sprachwissenschaft,* v, 1951, p. 146; and G. R. Driver, *Problems of the Hebrew Verbal System* (Edinburgh, 1936), p. 93, who credited this discovery to Bauer (*Beiträge zur Assyriologie,* viii/1, 1910, p. 25). Cf., in this context, M. Sprengling, *ZDMG.* lxx, 1916, pp. 542-545.

[29] M. Lambert, *Revue des Études Juives,* xxvi, 1893, pp. 49-50 with n. 2. See also F. Philippi, *Beiträge zur Assyriologie,* ii, 1894, p. 373.

jussive and imperfect consecutive as "one of those *accidental coincidences* not unknown to language" (78) and ultimately attributed the nonjussive meaning of the jussive form to textual corruption. "Most of the difficulties connected with the use of the jussive form can, I now [March, 1892] believe . . . , be overcome, if it be granted that the Massoretic vocalization does not represent the intention of the original authors" (viii; see also 215-216; cf. x). In other words, the problem was textual (cf. §6.2). Apparently disregarding the grammatical progress achieved since 1874, Driver maintained in this case a more conservative,[30] biblical focus.[31]

1. *Method.* In keeping with his German predecessors, particularly Ewald, Driver's method was primarily taxonomic. "Each tense, indeed, but especially the imperfect, exhibits a singular flexibility: at the same time it will be clear that this flexibility does not overreach the limits prescribed by the most rigorous logic" (47; see also [1]ix). Though each verb form is "flexible and elastic" (v), "some hidden link of connexion must exist, some higher principle must be operative, the discovery of which will place us at the true centre of vision, and permit the confused and incoherent figures to fall into their proper perspective and become consistent and clear" (vii; see also x). Driver sought to order the chaos[32] of the Hebrew verb.[33]

1.1. And toward this end, Driver was indefatigable. He formu-

---

[30] See Cooke, *Harvard Theological Review*, ix, 1916, pp. 251-252, on Driver's conservative leanings.

[31] Cf. the approach of G. R. Driver, *Problems of the Hebrew Verbal System*, as described by J. A. Montgomery, *Anglican Theological Review*, xix, 1937, p. 210; and H. Birkeland, *Archiv für Orientforschung*, xiii, 1939, p. 79.

[32] In the first edition, Driver expressed a sense of despair as well. The preceding quotation continued: "The difficulties arising from the phenomena alluded to I have felt forcibly myself, and also the *hopelessness* of being able to surmount them without further assistance than is usually accessible to the student" ([1]x [italics added]). In the later editions, he moderated his tone, replacing "hopelessness (of being able)" with "practical inability" ([2]vii; [3]vii).

[33] Müller, *Luth. Zeitschrift*, xxxviii, 1877, p. 201.

lated phonological rules (see §6.1) and catalogued cases of unusual pausal forms (110-113). He classified the Hebrew verbal
system according to the two inflectional patterns of its finite
verbs (see §0.1). More practically, he constructed most chapters
of the *Treatise* around discrete formal categories. Driver held a
particular interest in negations, too (e.g., 207). He noted instances where a single verb form is governed by multiple negations (in addition to 207, see, e.g., 54 [on the jussive and אַל/לֹא])
and deduced significance from such constructions (e.g., 275 [on
the infinitive construct governed by לֹא and אֵין]). Negations,
though, exemplified another taxonomic focus of Driver's: com-
binatory patterns (see §7.5). Hence Driver listed the various verb
forms that can precede the perfect consecutive (124-129). So too,
in the chapter on hypotheticals, Driver classified the conditional
sentence into its different types, and within each type according
to the different combinations of verb forms in the protasis and
apodosis (e.g., 174-177). Driver applied his taxonomic method
whenever and wherever the verb was concerned: on the word-
level, clause-level, and beyond.

1.2. Driver was also sensitive to the different ways that clauses
combine with one another. In hypothetical sentences, an apodosis may be represented by a syndetic or asyndetic clause (see,
e.g., 191-192). Similarly, a circumstantial clause may be explicitly
connected to the preceding discourse by וְ, or it may be "entirely
disconnected" (196). Driver therefore recognized two basic components of paratactic combination — coordination and apposition — and offered numerous examples of each.

Of these two components, coordination was the more important and problematic for Driver. Even the simple conjunction was not simple but could have multiple interpretations,
including *sub*ordination (see 197). "Sentences must be connected in the simplest manner possible: co-ordination must
often take the place of subordination" (265).[34] That is, Driver

---

34 See also Ewald, *Syntax of the Hebrew Language,* §339a; Müller, *Outlines*

recognized the difference between grammatical marking and rhetorical relation.

He also realized that the entire system of consecutive verb forms is bound up with the conjunction. When compounded with the imperfect or perfect, the conjunction alters the verbal stem in a number of classifiable ways (see §§6, 7). The conjunction also compounds the "intrinsic difficulties offered by the language itself. Each tense, and particularly the imperfect, seems to unite in itself incompatible meanings, which the reader too often finds resist all his efforts to reconcile with one another, or to derive from a common origin; and the complications super-induced when either is brought within range of the potent but mysterious *waw*, increase his perplexity" (vi; see also the stronger statement in [1]ix-x). According to Driver, the conjunction does not merely join the consecutive verb form with its context (see 196; cf., e.g., §6.4). It does something else, too. Hence, Driver sought to "enquire more closely into the nature of the relation in which an action thus introduced [by a consecutive form] may stand towards the preceding portion" of the discourse (80; see, e.g., §6.3). Its rhetorical interpretation may be highly fluid (e.g., 80-83), yet the *waw* is not rhetorically or exegetically limitless. It abides by certain context-sensitive principles (e.g., 93).

1.3. For Driver, the two consecutive verb forms do not have the same prefixed "strong waw" ([1]xix; [2]xiii). That of the perfect consecutive is quite different and, despite its form and apparent meaning, is not the ordinary copula or "weak waw . . . simple waw" ([1]xix; [2]xiii). "In fact, the *waw* possesses really in this connexion a demonstrative significance, being equivalent to *then* or *so*" (117). This demonstrative *waw*, however, underwent change (for the following, see 150). In some cases, "the stronger and

---

of Hebrew Syntax, §149; and Kennett, *A Short Account*, pp. 24-29, 38; as well as Olshausen, §224b (obliquely); and S. A. Thompson and R. E. Longacre in *Language typology and syntactic description*, ii (ed. T. Shopen; Cambridge/London, 1985), p. 176 (more generally).

more decided sense is still evidently retained." But in most cases, it has generally weakened in two incremental stages. Either "the earlier meaning has to be assumed" though "the conscious re-collection of it was probably as much forgotten in practice by the ancient Hebrew as it is disregarded by the modern reader in translation"; for Driver, this stage appears in the *waw* consecu-tive[35] and, especially, in the perfect consecutive (see also §7.1). Or "its force is equivalent to that of the copulative conjunction — 'the heavens, *then* the earth', being identical with 'the heavens *and* the earth.'" Stated generally, Driver grounded his interpreta-tion of the perfect consecutive in historical and developmental argument.

He also invoked comparative evidence.

> The Arabic language possesses two forms of the copulative, فَ *fa* as well as وَ *wa*: the latter being the *mere* copulative, the former carrying the stronger meaning *then, so,* οὖν etc., and being employed generally in all those cases which correspond to the *first* class just mentioned. It lies near to conjecture that both *wa* and *fa* (cf. the Heb. אַף) are but modifications of the same original labial stem,[36] that in Arabic the two words once existed side by side as by-forms, but that, in process of time, a differentiation was effected, in consequence of which *fa* was reserved for emphatic occasions, while in Hebrew *fa* as such fell out of use, and the single form *wa* had to do double duty. And that a demonstrative signification is not foreign to the syllable *fa,* may be inferred from the adverbs פֹּה *here,* אֵיפֹה *where?* (formed from פֹּה, like אֵי־זֶה from זֶה), or אֵפוֹ אֵפוֹא *then, so,* δή. Upon the whole, then, we seem sufficiently justified in assigning a *demonstrative* origin to the Semitic וֹ:

---

[35] In the imperfect consecutive, Ewald derived the prefix וַ· from the conjunction וְ and demonstrative אָז 'then' (Ewald, *Syntax of the Hebrew Language,* §231a). At first, Driver simply reported this opinion (¹75 n. 1; ²85). Later, he rejected it (³72 n. 1).

[36] See also the conjunction *-ma,* as noted by Montgomery, *Anglican Theological Review,* xix, 1937, p. 211 n. 1.

the conclusion suggested, if not necessitated, by the usages of
Hebrew syntax receiving independent confirmation from the
analogies offered by the Aryan family of speech.[37] (150-151)

But these appeals to comparative and even historical evidence
were unusual for Driver. "The discovery of the origin of a
grammatical form is of the highest value to the comparative
philologist, or the student of primitive modes of thought; it does
not of necessity throw fresh light directly upon the meaning
borne by it in practice, particularly if the period of formation
be long anterior to that in which the examples of its use actually
occur" (10). Just as he had resisted applying Akkadian grammar
to the problems of Hebrew, Driver was generally adverse to the
historical-comparative method.[38] But sometimes it was necessary or otherwise unavoidable, as in the case of וֹ. At those times,
Driver acquiesced, privileging Arabic among the known Semitic
languages (e.g., 219-245, esp. 237-242).

The non-Semitic languages, though, were something else.
Driver was not at all adverse to invoking classical languages, and
within this context he privileged Greek. Greek, in fact, provided
the linguistic underpinnings for Driver's aspectual analysis and
classification of the Hebrew verb (see 3 n. 1).[39] Greek also furnished Driver with ready comparisons to Hebrew usage.[40] The
Hebrew perfect, for example, was "equivalent to the Greek aorist" and "[l]ike the Greek perfect" (13).[41] Driver compared the
ingressive and iterative functions of the imperfect (27-28) to
those of the suffix -σχ (28 n. 1). He even named a specific
function of the participle after a classical Greek prototype.

[37] Cf. Böttcher, i. §530e.

[38] Cf. Cooke, *Harvard Theological Review,* ix, 1916, pp. 249-250.

[39] Brockelmann, *Hebräische Syntax* (Neukirchen, Kreis Moers, 1956),
§40b. See also idem, *Zeitschrift für Phonetik,* v, 1951, p. 135; and the references
in n. 19. Cf. V. DeCaen, *Zeitschrift für Althebraistik* ix, 1996, pp. 142-144.

[40] Cf. Müller, *Luth. Zeitschrift,* xxxviii, 1877, p. 206 n. **.

[41] Cf. Ballantine, *Hebraica,* ii, 1885, p. 55.

If we compare a sentence such as 1 Ki. 13,20 with one like *v.* 23, we shall at once see that the participial clause הֵם יֹשְׁבִים in the former is, in position and force, the precise counterpart of the adverbial clause אַחֲרֵי אָכְלוֹ וג׳ in the latter; and that like it, it notifies a circumstance strictly subordinate to the main narrative, in a manner exactly reproducible in Greek by the use of the gen. abs. (LXX καὶ ἐγένετο αὐτῶν καθημένων κ.τ.λ.). . . . [F]rom the analogy of the corresponding expressions in the classical languages, it may be appropriately termed *the participle absolute.* (208)

In the case of the participle, too, Driver's comparison was prescient.[42]

1.4. The breadth and depth of his inquiry into the Hebrew verbal system can blur Driver's fundamental purpose in writing the *Treatise:* "to supply . . . a systematic exposition, upon an adequate scale, of the nature and use of the Hebrew tenses" (v). Yet despite his many forays into attendant issues, Driver did devote the bulk of the *Treatise* to his two stated goals. Toward one goal, he described the literal, stable meaning of a particular verb form; he defined its "nature" or, in current terminology, its semantic content (see §2.3). Toward the other goal, he delineated and systematically arranged the context-driven, variable interpretations of a verb form (see, methodologically, [1]ix or [3]48); he accounted for the "use," or pragmatic inferences, that a verb may assume.[43] Within his own tax-

---

[42] See the discussion of "absolutive" clauses by Thompson and Longacre in *Language typology and syntactic description,* ii. pp. 200-203.

[43] See, for example, the case of perfect consecutive: "it does not occur *promiscuously.*" Therefore, "when a writer abandons a construction which he employs in nine cases out of ten in favour of another, . . . it is, at least, reasonable to infer that he means *something* by the change" (143). Cf. F. R. Blake: "It is useless to attempt, as is often done, to explain contradictory syntactical usages by assuming delicate shades of meaning between them; it is most likely that such contradictions are due to differences in dialect, temporal, technical, or social" (*A Resurvey of Hebrew Tenses* [Rome, 1951], p. 79).

onomic method, then, Driver consciously focused on semantic
and pragmatic analyses.[44]

1.5. Unfortunately, Driver lacked the necessary, appropriate,
and specific terminology to execute these analyses. He retained
the analytic and formal labels of his predecessors but, at the
same time, seemed aware that the terminology available to him
was insufficient and inexact. Even the title of his book posed a
terminological problem for Driver.

> The Hebrew language, in striking contrast to the classical lan-
> guages, in which the development of the verb is so rich and
> varied, possesses only two of those modifications which are
> commonly termed 'tenses.' These tenses were formerly known
> by the familiar names of *past* and *future,* but inasmuch as the
> so-called *past* tense is continually used to describe events in
> the future, and the so-called *future* tense to describe events in
> the past, it is clear that these terms, adapted from languages
> cast in a totally different mould from the Hebrew and other
> Semitic languages, are in the highest degree inappropriate and
> misleading. (1)

Driver nonetheless yielded to expedience. He not only used
"tense" as the equivalent of inflectional pattern, he also adopted a
tense-based taxonomic framework.[45] Such concessions, though,
were not unique to Driver.[46] Böttcher and Ewald certainly paved
the way. They simultaneously rejected a temporal analysis of the
Hebrew verbal system while retaining its terminology[47] and taxonomic framework.[48] Admittedly, "[i]t would probably have been

44 See, in this context, Cooke, *Harvard Theological Review,* ix, 1916, pp.
250-251.

45 See Müller, *Luth. Zeitschrift,* xxxviii, 1877, p. 200.

46 See also Lambert, *Revue des Études Juives,* xxvi, 1893, pp. 47-48; and,
differently, idem, *Traité de grammaire hébraïque* (Paris, 1946), §679 with n. 2,
on terminological conservatism.

47 E.g., "zeiten" in Ewald, *Lehrbuch,* 8th ed., §134. See also "Tempus-
formen" in Böttcher, i. §589.

48 Compare, for example, Driver's treatment of the perfect (13-24) with

better if Driver omitted the term 'tenses' altogether in his work."[49]
Driver, however, followed the convention set by his predecessors.

After discussing "tense," Driver introduced the basic terminology of his analytic framework: perfect and imperfect.[50]
But the latter term was problematic as well.

> It will appear hereafter that the term *imperfect* does not in
> strictness correspond to a primary but to a derived charac-
> teristic of the tense called by that name. Böttcher in his *Ausf.*
> *Lehrbuch der Hebr. Sprache*,[51] it must be admitted with greater
> precision, gives to the imperfect the name of *fiens:*[52] but in-
> asmuch as what is *incipient* is also necessarily *imperfect,* the
> latter term may be fairly held to express a fundamental at-
> tribute of the tense. No sufficient ground therefore seems to
> exist for abandoning the now usual nomenclature in favour of
> the new and peculiar term preferred by Böttcher. (1-2 n. 1)

Driver thereby confessed that part of his basic, aspectual terminology was not entirely satisfactory. Nevertheless, once again,
he conceded to established usage.

---

those of Böttcher, ii. §939; Ges.-Rœdiger, 20th ed., §§126.1-4 (see Ges.-
Kautzsch-Cowley, §§106b-o); and Ewald, *Syntax of the Hebrew Language,*
§135. See also Müller, *Outlines of Hebrew Syntax,* §§1-3.

[49] L. McFall, *The Enigma of the Hebrew Verbal System: Solutions from
Ewald to the Present Day* (Sheffield, 1982), p. 76.

[50] For the terminological background, see Ewald, *Grammatica Critica
Linguae Arabicae cum Brevi Metrorum Doctrina,* i (Leipzig, 1831), §195 (correct, accordingly, the references in idem, *Lehrbuch,* 8th ed., p. 350 n. 1; and
idem, *Syntax of the Hebrew Language,* p. 3 n. 1). For additional discussion,
see Böttcher, ii. §944; and Brockelmann, *Zeitschrift für Phonetik,* v, 1951,
p. 135. Cf. DeCaen, *Zeitschrift für Althebraistik* ix, 1996, pp. 134-136.

[51] Böttcher, i. §587.IIa.

[52] Cf. P. T. Daniels (in G. Bergsträsser, *Introduction to the Semitic Languages: Text Specimens and Grammatical Sketches* [tr. and aug. Daniels;
Winona Lake, 1983], p. 10 n. r; followed by Waltke and O'Connor, *An Introduction to Biblical Hebrew Syntax,* p. 348 n. 14), who incorrectly attributed
the term to Benno Landsberger (*Monographs on the Ancient Near East,* i/4,
1976, p. 8 [64]).

The imperfect, however, was fundamentally important for Driver's analysis, and he tried to describe its semantic contents with care, diligence, precision, and correctness. Toward this end, using all the vocabulary, terminology, and descriptions he could muster, Driver bombarded the reader with terminological alternatives: e.g., beginning, developing, evolving, inchoative, incipient, and nascent;[53] liable, possible, and potential; uncertain; or incomplete, indefinite, and indeterminate. With the help of technical and nontechnical terms, Driver offered a theoretically consistent, though scattered and dizzying, array of descriptive terms. But Driver's effort may have been self-defeating. Though a sympathetic reader might appreciate Driver's struggle for clarity and precision,[54] most reviewers did not. For them, Driver's terminology confused rather than clarified (see, e.g., §4).[55]

1.6. Terminology, however, can be explicated. Driver, after all, reflected the linguistic sophistication of his day. Yet in the time since the three editions of the *Treatise* were published, much more grammatical, historical, and comparative linguistic information has become available for the study of the Hebrew verbal system. Linguistics, too, has developed into a mighty discipline. It is likely, then, that scholarship subsequent to the *Treatise* may be able to clarify what Driver struggled to convey.

The following discussion is intended to provide some of this clarification. After providing an overview of Driver's analysis (§2), the discussion follows Driver's taxonomic scheme. It is restricted, though, to finite verb forms (§§3-7). But it also exceeds Driver's presentation by including the imperative (§5.2),

[53] See McFall, *The Enigma of the Hebrew Verbal System,* pp. 62-63. Contrary to McFall, however, Driver did not characterize the imperfect as "egressive" (11; cf. 2 n. 1).

[54] As did Müller, *Luth. Zeitschrift,* xxxviii, 1877, p. 200.

[55] See, e.g., Ballantine, *Hebraica* ii, 1885, pp. 54-55. See also J. Strong, *Hebraica,* ii, 1886, p. 229; DeCaen, *Zeitschrift für Althebraistik* ix, 1996, pp. 144-146; and the discussion in §4, below.

which Driver omitted. Its overall goal is selective elucidation.[56] In some instances, only terminological decipherment and explanation is required (e.g., §4). In others, the *Treatise* may benefit from updating (e.g., §3).[57] At times, however, a particular analysis may require reconfiguration (e.g., §6). If successful, the following discussion should therefore bring Driver closer to realizing his goal of providing "a systematic exposition, upon an adequate scale, of the nature and use of the Hebrew tenses" (v).

2. *Overview of the Hebrew Verbal System* (1-12). Following Olshausen, Böttcher, and Ewald,[58] Driver classified the Hebrew verbal system into two inflectionally distinct categories.[59] "Hebrew has but two tenses at its disposal" (v): the perfect, whose subjective pronouns are suffixed to the verbal stem; and the imperfect, whose subjective pronouns are prefixed[60] to the stem (see 7). The Hebrew verbal system is morphologically binary.

2.1. Though Driver described another, semantic distinction in the Hebrew verbal system (see §2.2), Wright characterized this second difference in terms of form. He recognized, albeit obliquely, that the "tenses" also have distinct stems. For example, in the simple, nonderived conjugation, the perfect stem is bivocalic:[61] **qatal*, **qatil*, or **qatul*, depending on the semantic and phonological composition of the underlying root. The corre-

---

[56] See also Kennett, *A Short Account*, p. vii, as quoted in n. 6.

[57] See, in this context, Müller, *Luth. Zeitschrift*, xxxviii, 1877, p. 208 n. *.

[58] Olshausen, §§18c-d, 226b-c; Böttcher, i. §587.IIa; and Ewald, *Lehrbuch*, 8th ed., §137a.

[59] See also B. Stade, *Lehrbuch der hebräischen Grammatik* (Leipzig, 1879), §382b; and Wright, *Comparative Grammar of the Semitic Languages,* p. 179.

[60] See §4.1, below. Technically, however, the subjective pronouns of the imperfect are circumfixed, since its inflectional elements precede *and* follow the verbal stem (e.g., Olshausen, §18d; Brockelmann, *Grundriss der vergleichenden Grammatik der semitischen Sprachen,* i [Berlin, 1908], §260Ba).

[61] Wright, *Comparative Grammar of the Semitic Languages,* p. 165.

sponding imperfect stem is monovocalic:[62] **qtul,* **qtal,* or **qtil,* depending again on semantic and phonological criteria.[63] Each Hebrew "tense," then, has its own verbal stem, in addition to its own inflectional pattern.[64] Formally, the two "tenses" of the Hebrew verbal system are doubly distinct.

Driver used both diagnostic features to align almost every Hebrew verb form with one or the other "tense." According to these features, the majority of forms are affiliated with the imperfect: the cohortative (50-51), jussive (51-52), imperfect consecutive (76-77; cf. §6.1), and even the imperative (see 52; cf. §5). Driver associated the infinitive construct with the imperfect as well, since their verbal stems are often identical (see 7; cf. §4.1).[65] Under the rubric of the imperfect, then, Driver included both finite and nonfinite verbs.

The perfect also constitutes a formal, taxonomic rubric within the Hebrew verbal system, though its members are fewer in number: the perfect consecutive (e.g., 117-118); and, less obviously, the participle (7). Here too, Driver did not offer formal support for this latter association. But Wright did.

> Of the active participle there would appear to have been originally three forms, corresponding to the three forms of the

---

[62] Cf. the *bi*vocalic imperfect stem in Akkadian and Ethiopic, on which see §7.1, below.

[63] Wright, *Comparative Grammar of the Semitic Languages,* p. 180 (the "shorter" stem). Cf., e.g., Philippi, *Zeitschrift für Völkerpsychologie und Sprachwissenschaft,* x, 1878, pp. 266-267; and, on the imperative, von Soden in *Babylonien und Israel. Historische, religiöse und sprachliche Beziehungen* (ed. H.-P. Müller; Darmstadt, 1991), p. 468. See also the references and discussion in nn. 116 and 117.

[64] Based on the theory that accent may be phonemic in the Semitic languages and Hebrew, each stem has also been subdivided on accentual grounds. See §§7.1-2, for the two proposed bivocalic stems. And, for the phonemically distinctive accent in the jussive and imperfect consecutive, see n. 240.

[65] See n. 117; as well as Olshausen, §227a; Ges.-Rœdiger, 20th ed., §46.1; and, somewhat differently, Böttcher, i. §587.IIIα.

perfect, viz. *ḳatal, ḳatil,* and *ḳatul.* The first of these, however, is actually known to us only as a verbal adjective, e.g., חָכָם, יָשָׁר, חָדָשׁ. . . . The other two actually occur as participles: יָגוֹר . . . , יָשֵׁן, גָּדֵל; מָלֵא, רָעֵב, etc.[66]

Like the infinitive construct, then, the participle retains only one (vestigial) feature of its parent "tense." And like the imperfect, the perfect includes both finite and nonfinite relatives.

2.2. The nonfinite member of each "tense" in turn motivated Driver's semantic interpretation of the perfect and imperfect. From its formal identity to the noun-like participle, Driver inferred that the perfect stem has a fundamental, concrete meaning (7).[67] And from the formal identity between the imperfect and the infinitive construct, Driver concluded that the imperfect stem has a basic, abstract meaning (7; see also 274).[68] For Driver, then, morphological identity implies semantic identity.

2.3. At the end of the twentieth century, semantic analysis of the verb is conventionally separated into three component parts: tense, mood, and aspect. In temporal analysis, a situation is located in time, whether relative to the moment of speaking or relative to another situation in context.[69] In modal analysis, an utterance is assessed in terms of speaker belief, certainty, and knowledge or, alternatively, speaker attitude and will.[70] And in aspectual analysis, the focus shifts to "different ways of viewing

---

[66] Wright, *Comparative Grammar of the Semitic Languages,* p. 196. See also Ges.-Rœdiger, 20th ed., §44.1 with n. 1.

[67] See Olshausen, §§18c, 227a. See also, in greater detail, Wright, *Comparative Grammar of the Semitic Languages,* pp. 161, 165.

[68] See Olshausen, §18d; and, less directly, Ges.-Rœdiger, 20th ed., §47.1 (= Ges.-Kautzsch-Cowley, §47a).

[69] For an accessible and detailed study of tense, see B. Comrie, *Tense* (Cambridge/London, 1985). See also R. I. Binnick, *Time and the Verb: A Guide to Tense and Aspect* (New York/Oxford, 1991), pp. 3-132.

[70] For a current, standard discussion, see F. R. Palmer, *Mood and Modality* (Cambridge/London, 1986).

the internal temporal constituency of a situation";[71] a situation may be viewed as a single whole, or in its (sub)phases and internal structure.[72]

In the late nineteenth century, these three analyses were also available to Driver, though not necessarily in their later form, terminology, or characteristics. "Hebrew . . . possesses no forms specifically appropriated to indicate date" (3-4). "[T]he tenses mark only differences in the kind of time, not differences in the order of time:[73] i.e. they do not in themselves determine the *date* at which an action takes place, they only indicate its *character* or kind" (3). With these words, Driver[74] explicitly rejected a temporal analysis of Hebrew ("order of time")[75] and embraced aspect ("kind of time") as his principal analytic method (5).[76] He also utilized modal analysis. Despite his misuse of the term itself (3; cf. 21),[77] Driver adduced modal characteristics in his discussion of various verb forms (see, e.g., §§3.3, 5.1). Hence, Driver adopted a double-barreled semantic approach to the Hebrew verbal system: aspect, first; and mood, second.

Even though he did not set forth his theory of Hebrew mood, Driver did present and illustrate his aspectual theory.

---

[71] Comrie, *Aspect: An Introduction to the Study of Verbal Aspect and Related Problems* (Cambridge/London, 1976), p. 3.

[72] Ibid., p. 16; and C. S. Smith, *The Parameter of Aspect* (Dordrecht/Boston/London, 1991), p. 6.

[73] See also Stade, §382a Anm. 2. Cf., recently, R. Hendel, *Zeitschrift für Althebraistik* ix, 1996, pp. 156-168.

[74] See also Kennett, *A Short Account*, pp. vii-viii.

[75] Cf., e.g., Ballantine, *Hebraica*, ii, 1885, p. 54; B. Douglass, *A Letter to Professors, Scholars and Friends of the Holy Tongue, Criticising "Driver's Hebrew Tenses" as founded on the three Pairs of Texts given in Chapter one, Section three* (Chicago, 1885); Bergsträsser, *Hebräische Grammatik*, ii (Leipzig, 1929), §3a; and, on Ewald, Strong, *Hebraica*, ii, 1886, pp. 228-233.

[76] McFall, *The Enigma of the Hebrew Verbal System*, pp. 61-62. Cf. DeCaen, *Zeitschrift für Althebraistik* ix, 1996, pp. 129-151.

[77] In this context, see Ballantine, *Hebraica*, ii, 1885, p. 54.

[A]n action may be contemplated, according to the fancy of the speaker, or according to the particular point which he desires to make prominent, either as *incipient,* or as *continuing,* or as *completed;* the speaker may wish to lay stress upon the moment at which it begins, or upon the period over which it extends, or upon the fact of its being finished and done . . . the three phases just mentioned, those namely of incipiency, continuance, and completion, being represented respectively by the imperfect, the participle, and the perfect. (2-3)

In Driver's view, the two "tenses" represent particular subevents of a situation: "[O]ne is calculated to describe an action as *nascent* and so as imperfect; the other to describe it as *completed* and so as perfect" (5). That is, the subevents are initial and terminal, respectively.[78] The intermediate, ongoing event, however, is represented by the participle:[79] "the participle admits of being used where neither of the two special 'tenses' would be suitable, in the frequently recurring cases, namely, where stress is to be laid on the *continuance* of the action described" (165).[80]

2.4. For Driver, this tripartite aspectual classification reverberates in the morphology, too. The special semantic status of the participle correlates with its inflectional pattern that, uniquely among verbs, inflects like an adjective. The characteristics of incipience and nascency pervade all forms that inflect like the imperfect, with pronominal prefixes (e.g., 71-72). Conversely, those verb forms that are inflected like the perfect, with pronominal suffixes, are completive in meaning (e.g., 117). Since, in Driver's opinion, morphological identity implies semantic identity, all finite Hebrew verb forms are aligned with one of two

[78] See the discussion in Böttcher, ii. §944.3.

[79] Cf. Douglass: "Having degraded the two tenses which are peculiar to the Hebrew and to all primitive languages, [Driver] would, volens nolens, introduce a third, viz. the participle" (*A Letter to Professors, Scholars and Friends,* p. 5).

[80] Olshausen, §18b; in conjunction with Böttcher, ii. §944.3,6; and Ewald, *Lehrbuch,* 8th ed., §168c.

formal and semantic categories: the incipient imperfect or the completive perfect.[81]

3. *Perfect* (13-26). Driver began his analysis of individual verb forms with one of the prototypical "tenses," the perfect. Though he arranged the presentation around temporal referent (cf. 5; see §1.5 with n. 48) and other pragmatic embellishments (e.g., 24-25), the analysis itself was primarily aspectual. Specifically, Driver favored a phasal interpretation of the perfect, suggesting that the perfect form connotes completed action[82] or, more particularly, the final phase of a situation.[83] For example, the perfect can "denote an action completed and finished at a definite moment in the past" (13). Even in counterfactual conditions, "the pf. is employed to denote events appertaining to past time, which *might have happened* but *did not happen,* which are therefore only for the moment conceived as having occurred, under conditions not actually realized" (23-24).[84] Throughout its many applications, Driver's perfect expresses completed aspect.

3.1. Subsequent scholarship has shown, however, that Driver's characterization is too narrow and places undue stress on the terminal phase of a situation.[85] For instance, as Driver admitted, the situation expressed by the perfect may "itself extend over a considerable period" (e.g., Nu. 9,23 'the Lord's mandate שָׁמָרוּ they kept'[86]) (13; cf. §4.3).[87] Sometimes, too, a perfect is accom-

---

[81] See the references in n. 58. Cf. Landsberger, *Monographs on the Ancient Near East,* i/4, 1976, p. 7 [63].

[82] See also Ges.-Rœdiger, 20th ed., §125; Ewald, *Syntax of the Hebrew Language,* §§135a-c; Stade, §382a; and Kennett, *A Short Account,* pp. 2-4.

[83] Böttcher, ii. §§939-941. See also Ges.-Kautzsch-Cowley, §106a.

[84] Cf. Kennett, *A Short Account,* pp. 8-9; in conjunction with §3.3, below.

[85] Comrie, *Aspect,* p. 18.

[86] Cf., e.g., J. Milgrom, *Numbers: The Traditional Hebrew Text with the New JPS Translation* (Philadelphia/New York, 1990), p. 72.

[87] See, in this context, Ges.-Rœdiger, 20th ed., §126.3a. Cf. Müller, *Luth. Zeitschrift,* xxxviii, 1877, p. 208 n. *.

panied by an adverbial phrase of temporal duration (e.g., 1 Ki. 15,2 שָׁלֹשׁ שָׁנִים מָלַךְ 'he reigned three years'). These examples do not prove that the perfect form expresses completed terminative aspect.

Others, in fact, seem to disprove this analysis. For instance, Driver claimed that the perfect can "describe the immediate past, being generally best translated by the present" (e.g., 2 Sa. 17,11 יָעַצְתִּי 'I advise'. 16,4 הִשְׁתַּחֲוֵיתִי 'I bow low') (15).[88] But the situations represented by these perfects are, in no way, past or completed; they coincide with the speaker's present. Driver also maintained that the perfect may express a situation that "lies indeed in the future, but . . . may be spoken of as having actually taken place" (e.g., Gen. 23,11 'the field נָתַתִּי I give you'; see also Ez. 21,9 הִכְרַתִּי 'I will wipe out') (17-18).[89] At the very least, though, his interpretation is implausible; for in this scenario, a seemingly terminative verb form would represent a prospective event. Like Nu. 9,23 and 1 Ki. 15,2, these examples of the perfect undercut Driver's thesis that the perfect form expresses completed aspect.

Yet they do suggest a more fitting and organic interpretation of the perfect. 2 Sa. 17,11 and 16,4 are particularly significant in this regard, for their perfect verb forms express acts or situations whose temporal location coincides with the speaker's present moment.[90] In 2 Sa. 17,11, the coincidence is exact, for the act named is performed by and identical to its utterance. The performative act, then, can be considered "momentaneous, . . . i.e. at each point in the utterance of the sentence there is coincidence

---

[88] See Ewald, *Syntax of the Hebrew Language,* §135b; and Kennett, *A Short Account,* pp. 2-3. See also Müller, *Outlines of Hebrew Syntax,* §2.1; and, differently, Ges.-Rœdiger, 20th ed., §126.3b. Cf. Ges.-Kautzsch-Cowley, §106g.

[89] See Ges.-Rœdiger, 20th ed., §126.4 (= Ges.-Kautzsch-Cowley, §106i); Ewald, *Syntax of the Hebrew Language,* §223b; and Stade, §383a.1-2. Cf. §3.3, below.

[90] See Waltke and O'Connor, *An Introduction to Biblical Hebrew Syntax,* §30.5.1d.

between the present moment with regard to the utterance and the present moment with regard to the act in question."[91] But in 2 Sa. 16,4, the utterance is a report "of an ongoing series of events" and is "simultaneous with the situation being described."[92] Thus the perfect form can represent both a momentaneous performative and simultaneous report.[93] Further, the perfect in these passages "presents the totality of the situation referred to . . . without reference to its internal temporal constituency: the whole of the situation is presented as a single unanalysable whole, with beginning, middle, and end rolled into one; no attempt is made to divide this situation up into [its] various individual phases."[94] Rather than pinpoint the terminal phase of a given situation, then, the perfect presents its situation as a single complete undifferentiated whole.[95] In 2 Sa. 17,11 and 16,4, as also in Gen. 23,11 and Ez. 21,9, the perfect does not represent a situation as complet*ed* but simply as complete.[96] According to Driver's own examples, then, the perfect form expresses the perfective aspect.[97]

[91] Comrie, *Tense*, p. 37.

[92] Ibid.

[93] Cf. Waltke and O'Connor, subsuming both categories under the heading "instantaneous" (*An Introduction to Biblical Hebrew Syntax*, §30.5.1d). This designation, however, is misleading since it reflects a different taxonomic category. In current usage, instantaneousness is a feature of semelfactives (e.g., *tap, knock*) and achievements (e.g., *win the race, reach the top*), as opposed to durativity, which is inherent to states (e.g., *know the answer*), activities (e.g., *stroll*), and accomplishments (e.g., *build a house*) (Smith, *The Parameter of Aspect*, p. 6).

[94] Comrie, *Aspect*, p. 3.

[95] See ibid., p. 24.

[96] See Ballantine: "The Perfect is often defined as connoting 'finished' or 'completed' action. These words are misleading. They can only fairly be used to mean action viewed comprehensively" (*Hebraica*, ii, 1885, p. 55). See also Kennett, *A Short Account*, p. 1; and, equivocally, Müller, *Outlines of Hebrew Syntax*, §1.

[97] E.g., Waltke and O'Connor, *An Introduction to Biblical Hebrew Syntax*, §30. Cf. DeCaen, *Zeitschrift für Althebraistik* ix, 1996, pp. 131-132.

3.2. In keeping with his focus on aspect, Driver recognized that the perfect form also has a second aspectual meaning. It can "denote an action . . . in the past, but with the accessory idea of its consequences continuing up to the time at which the words are uttered: it is thus employed to describe an action resulting in a *state*" (e.g., Gen. 4,6 'and why נָפְלוּ has your face fallen [i.e., why are you now sad]?'.[98] Isa. 1,4 עָזְבוּ 'they have forsaken the Lord, נִאֲצוּ spurned the Holy One of Israel, נָזֹרוּ turned back') (13-14). The perfect form has the same meaning in stative verbs. "In verbs like these, expressive of a state or condition, whether physical or mental, which, though it may have been attained at some previous time, nevertheless continues to exist up to the moment of speaking" (e.g., Gen. 18,13 זָקַנְתִּי 'I have and am now aged'. Ex. 10,3 'How long מֵאַנְתָּ do you refuse?')[99] (16).[100] Driver concluded that "the perfect in the original really indicates a result or consequence" (124). That is, the perfect form can express the perfect aspect,[101] "indicat[ing] the continuing present relevance of a past situation."[102]

3.3. In addition to perfective and perfect aspects, Driver was aware that the perfect form has a modal value. Ewald had already provided an explanation by drawing an explicit connection to the form's aspectual meaning. "[The perfect] is used of actions, which, though really neither past nor present, are, through the inclination or lively fancy of the speaker, regarded as being already as good as finished; these are, accordingly, stated as if

---

[98] See, e.g., A. Dillmann, *Genesis Critically and Exegetically Expounded,* i (tr. W. B. Stevenson; Edinburgh, 1897), p. 187.

[99] Cf. G. R. Driver, *Problems of the Hebrew Verbal System,* pp. 87-88, on the latter passage.

[100] See, e.g., Ges.-Rœdiger, 20th ed., §126.3a (= Ges.-Kautzsch-Cowley, §106g); and Ewald, *Syntax of the Hebrew Language,* §135b. Cf. Ballantine, *Hebraica,* ii, 1885, p. 55, on קָטֹנְתִּי in Gen. 32,11.

[101] Kennett, *A Short Account,* p. 2; and Ges.-Kautzsch-Cowley, §106g.

[102] Comrie, *Aspect,* p. 52.

they were quite unconditional and certain."[103] For Ewald, then, the perfective perfect entails modal certainty. Driver concurred. But for him, modal certainty was more than a semantic inference; modal certainty constituted another axis for describing the perfect. In a clear example, Driver dubbed the prophetic perfect the "perfect of certitude" (19, 116):[104] It "imparts to descriptions of the future a forcible and expressive touch of reality, and reproduces vividly the certainty with which the occurrence of a yet future event is contemplated by the speaker" (e.g., Isa. 5,13 'Assuredly גָּלָה will my people go into exile') (18; see also 20).[105] Another context, though, prompted Driver to extend this modal characterization of the perfect. In a number of texts, he explained, "[i]t is used to express general truths known to have actually occurred, and so proved from experience" (e.g., Ps. 39,12 'in punishment for his sin יִסַּרְתָּ you chastise a man') (17).[106] In this broader description, the perfect expresses truth, knowledge, experiential proof, as well as actual occurrence. Or, in Driver's words, the perfect is a "statement of *a fact*" (21);[107] reports "[t]he *mere* occurrence of an event" (28);[108] and is definite, real, and concrete (114; see also §2.2; cf. 23-24). The perfect not only

---

[103] Ewald, *Syntax of the Hebrew Language,* §135c. See also Böttcher, ii. §939.IIIf; and Ges.-Rœdiger, 20th ed., §126.4. Cf. Ges.-Kautzsch-Cowley, §106p.

[104] See also Kennett, *A Short Account,* p. 5 n. 1.

[105] See also ibid., p. 52; and Müller, *Outlines of Hebrew Syntax,* §3b. Cf. Douglass, *A Letter to Professors, Scholars and Friends,* pp. 6-7; and, differently, Hendel, *Zeitschrift für Althebraistik* ix, 1996, p. 171; as well as the references in n. 245, below.

[106] See also Ges.-Rœdiger, 20th ed., §126.3b (= Ges.-Kautzsch-Cowley, §106k); Böttcher, ii. §940.3; Ewald, *Syntax of the Hebrew Language,* §135b; Müller, *Outlines of Hebrew Syntax,* §2.2; Stade, §383a.4; and Kennett, *A Short Account,* pp. 4-5, 4 n. 1.

[107] See also Ballantine, *Hebraica,* ii, 1885, p. 53.

[108] See also C. F. Burney, *The Journal of Theological Studies,* xx, 1919, pp. 211-212. Cf., e.g., the references in n. 103, assigning a pragmatic value to this perfect.

expresses perfective and perfect aspects but speaker certainty and knowledge as well.

4. *Imperfect* (27-49). The other prototypical "tense," the imperfect, afforded Driver the opportunity to illustrate the extent to which "the verb is a flexible and elastic instrument" (v). According to his aspectual premise, the imperfect "indicates action as *nascent*, as evolving itself actively from its subject, as developing" (27; see also 73).[109] But Driver was also sensitive to the implications of such a description. "An idea . . . like that of *nascency, beginning*, or *going to be* is almost indefinitely elastic" (29).

None of this was well-received. Driver's interpretation of the imperfect was denounced: "Perhaps I cannot do better than . . . to show the fallacy and inadequacy of Mr. Driver's chief point"[110] — that the imperfect expresses incipience (or incompleteness).[111] The logic of his interpretation was queried: "every action, whether incomplete or complete, is in some sense nascent or emergent, *i.e.* it has arisen out of certain precedent conditions that will have been described by a preceding verb in the narration of the story."[112] Or, as an example of his aspectual analysis generally, Driver's interpretation of the imperfect was considered just too flexible and elastic: "the new 'principles' which he now advocates will furnish sceptics, scoffers and infidels with all the material they want, to take all the life out of the Old Testament, and make it mean anything or nothing, as they

---

[109] See also Ewald, *Syntax of the Hebrew Language*, §136b; Kennett, *A Short Account*, p. 10; and, less directly, Böttcher, ii. §§942-943; and Müller, *Outlines of Hebrew Syntax*, §4.

[110] Strong, *Hebraica*, ii, 1886, p. 108.

[111] See also McFall, *The Enigma of the Hebrew Verbal System*, pp. 72-73; and Waltke and O'Connor, *An Introduction to Biblical Hebrew Syntax*, §29.3m.

[112] G. R. Driver, *Problems of the Hebrew Verbal System*, p. 86, with additional arguments on pp. 86-87.

please";[113] "[t]he detailed working out of this aspect theory, however, has resulted in a hopeless confusion of forms and meanings, and too many fanciful explanations to account for differences in form. The whole treatment presents a picture strongly characterized by complexity, obscurity and artificiality, a system which is it difficult to imagine as developing and existing in the minds of any language group";[114] or "Drivers These sich nur durch z. T. sehr gekünstelte Interpretationen des Textes durchführen ließ."[115] The criticism, both contemporary and subsequent, was unrelenting.

4.1. Whereas Driver claimed that the imperfect is a basic, prototypical "tense," formal criteria do not support this notion. They suggest, instead, that it is derived. For example, unlike its morphologically simpler relatives, the masculine singular imperative[116] and the infinitive construct[117] (see §§2.1-2), the im-

---

[113] Douglass, *A Letter to Professors, Scholars and Friends,* p. 3.

[114] Blake, *A Resurvey of Hebrew Tenses,* p. 1.

[115] Brockelmann, *Hebräische Syntax,* §40c.

[116] For the morphological identity of the masculine singular imperative and stem of the imperfect, see, e.g., Olshausen, §18e; and the references in n. 63. Cf., however, their apparent disparity in several, פ״א *qal* roots (e.g., 1 Sa. 9,24. 1 Ki. 18,41 etc. אֱכֹל 'eat'. Gen. 3,14. Ex. 13,6 etc.: תֹּאכַל 'you shall eat'; Gen. 45,17. Ex. 6,6 etc. אֱמֹר 'say'. 3,14. Lev. 17,8 etc. תֹּאמַר 'you will say'; and Ex. 16,23 אֵפוּ 'bake'. ibid. תֹּאפוּ 'you may bake'; see also Ex. 4,4. 2 Sa. 2,21 וֶאֱחֹז 'and grasp'. Job 18,9 יֹאחֵז 'it grabs', in contrast to Qoh. 7,18 תֶּאֱחֹז 'you hold'. Jud. 16,3. 1 Ki. 6,10 וַיֶּאֱחֹז 'he grasped, it held'). It has been suggested, though, that this difference is phonological rather than morphological (for references, see W. R. Garr, *Biblica,* lxvi, 1985, p. 578 n. 47).

[117] For the identity of the imperfect stem and infinitive construct see, in this context, Philippi, *Zeitschrift für Völkerpsychologie,* x, 1878, p. 264; Bergsträsser, *Hebräische Grammatik,* ii. §11b; G. R. Driver, *Problems of the Hebrew Verbal System,* p. 9; and the references in n. 65, below. These forms can, however, differ. Most visibly, a recurrent difference appears in the *qal* infinitive construct. For when this construct appends objective pronominal suffixes, a number of changes take place that differentiate it from both the imperfect stem and nonsuffixed infinitive construct: a vowel harmonic with the stem vowel is inserted between the first and second radicals; the stem

perfect is modified by prefixed inflectional pronouns that agree with or mark the grammatical subject. The prefix may specify person (i.e., in second person forms), person and number (in first person forms), or person and gender (in third person forms). Nevertheless, the pronominal prefix of the imperfect is in each case augmentative, modifying the underlying stem in its own person-specific way(s). By these formal considerations, the imperfect is not a basic verb form. Rather, it is augmented, modified, and derived.

In addition to the augment that precedes the verbal stem, the imperfect has an augment that follows the stem. This latter augment takes two forms. One is only sporadically attested in Hebrew: the paragogic *nun* in יִקְטְלוּן, whose Arabic cognate is the indicative ending -*na* in *yaqtulûna* (240). The other form of the augment, however, is not overtly attested in Hebrew. It has been lost due to phonological change yet has left its phonological imprint on certain classes of verbs (e.g., Dt. 20,19 לֹא תַשְׁחִית 'you

---

vowel is largely deleted; and the third radical is spirantized when phono-logically possible (see, e.g., Jer. 36,25. 27 שְׂרֹף 'to burn, burning'. Ex. 2,15. 32,12 etc. לַהֲרֹג 'to kill'. 19,13. Josh. 6,5 בִּמְשֹׁךְ 'when it is sounded', in contrast to Amos 2,1 שָׂרְפוֹ 'his burning'. Ex. 5,21 לְהָרְגֵנוּ 'to kill us'. Ps. 10,9 בְּמָשְׁכוֹ 'while he pulls', respectively; see also Josh. 8,16. 2 Sa. 20,7.13 לִרְדֹּף 'to pursue' and Dt. 11,4 בְּרָדְפָם 'while they pursued'). It is unlikely, however, that the suffixed forms reflect an underlying bivocalic infinitive construct form (cf., e.g., T. Nöldeke, *ZDMG*. xxv, 1871, p. 667; and J. Barth, *Die Nominalbildung in den semitischen Sprachen* [2nd ed.; Leipzig, 1894], pp. 99-100; see also Ges.-Kautzsch-Cowley, §46a). Rather, the change from nonsuffixed to suffixed infinitive construct can be formulated in phonological terms and is, hence, a sound change (see Bergsträsser, *Hebräische Grammatik*, i [1918], §23d; cf. J. L. Malone, *Tiberian Hebrew Phonology* [Winona Lake, 1993], p. 49 [on which, cf. H. M. Orlinsky, *Journal of the American Oriental Society*, lxvii, 1947, pp. 107-126]). Furthermore, the same change occurs between nonsuf-fixed and suffixed forms of the masculine singular *qal* imperative (e.g., Jud. 8,20 הֲרֹג 'kill'. Ps. 36,11 מְשֹׁךְ 'draw out'. Gen. 44,1. 1 Sa. 30,8 רְדֹף 'pursue', in contrast to Nu. 11,15 הָרְגֵנִי 'kill me'. Cant. 1,4 מָשְׁכֵנִי 'draw me'. Ps. 34,15 וְרָדְפֵהוּ 'and pursue it', respectively). This change, too, may be phonologically con-ditioned (e.g., Olshausen, §61; and, differently, Stade, §96a).

shall not destroy' [see also Lev. 19,27]; cf. Dt. 9,26 אַל־תַּשְׁחֵת 'do not destroy' [jussive]). Driver, however, insisted on describing the difference between תַּשְׁחִית and תַּשְׁחֵת in strictly phonological terms — syllable shortening (51-52; cf. §6.1).[118] But as his predecessors and contemporaries understood, the Arabic counterparts of these two verb forms prove that the difference is morphological: *yaqtulu* indicative; and *yaqtul* jussive, respectively.[119] And of these two Arabic verb forms, *yaqtulu* is the augmented and modified form.[120] The Arabic cognates demonstrate, then, that the imperfect is not a basic verb form. Neither יִקְטֹל nor יִקְטְלוּן is morphologically basic. They are, in fact, doubly augmented, by pronominal prefixes and inflectional suffixes.

4.2. This formal analysis also raises a question about Driver's semantic characterization of the imperfect. If the imperfect is formally not basic and prototypical, it is unlikely that the semantic features attributed to the imperfect are basic and prototypical either. On the one hand, the imperfect itself was traced to an underlying abstract stem (§2.2) that recurs in the imperative and the infinitive construct (§4.1). On the other hand, the inflectional pattern of the imperfect showed the form to be nonbasic and derived (§4.1). It is unlikely, then, that the imperfect is itself the prototypical verb form that Driver had claimed. Indeed, according to its specific, bilateral inflectional pattern, the imperfect appears to be idiosyncratic and unique — morphologically and, hence, semantically.

4.3. Driver's semantic analysis of the imperfect, just as that of the perfect, was primarily aspectual. And as with the perfect, here also Driver offered a phasal interpretation — that the imperfect connotes the initial phase of a situation. In his own

---

[118] See also Ewald, *Syntax of the Hebrew Language,* §224; Müller, *Luth. Zeitschrift,* xxxviii, 1877, p. 207; and Ges.-Kautzsch-Cowley, §48f.

[119] Olshausen, §228a; Wright, *Comparative Grammar of the Semitic Languages,* pp. 192-193; and Lambert, *Revue des Études Juives,* xxvi, 1893, pp. 51-52. See also Ges.-Rœdiger, 20th ed., §48.2 (= Ges.-Kautzsch-Cowley, §48b).

[120] See Bauer, *Beiträge zur Assyriologie,* viii/1, 1910, p. 11.

words,[121] the situation expressed by the imperfect is "nascent,"
"ready or about to take place" (27), "beginning" (29), "incipient,"
and "inchoative" (119; see §1.5). The imperfect, then, expresses
ingressive aspect.[122]

But in his effort to emphasize this ingressive character, Driver
overemphasized it. For, as is well known, the imperfect has
several standard noningressive meanings, too. A typical noningressive imperfect, for instance, expresses "a frequentative, to
suggest the reiteration of the event spoken of" (30). Such an
imperfect can express a customary or habitual situation (e.g.,
1 Sa. 9,9 יִקָּרֵא 'he used to be called') (34). It can express an
ongoing situation that lasts for a period of time (e.g., 21,12 יְעַנּוּ
'they sing') (34). It can express a string of separate, repeated
events as well (e.g., perhaps, Ps. 106,43 'time and again יַצִּילֵם he
saved them') (see 36). Clearly these situations are not ingressive;
they are habitual, continuous, and iterative, respectively.[123]

These different functions of the imperfect can nevertheless be
united under one aspectual rubric.[124] As Driver conceded, for
example, the phase-initial imperfect does not always express the
actual inception of a situation. It may represent, *inter alia,* a
situation that "has not yet begun to take place at all, but its
beginning to do so is contemplated in the future — nearer or
more remote, as the context and sense demand" (e.g., Gen. 49,1
'that I may tell you what יִקְרָא is to befall you in the days to
come'. 2 Ki. 13,14 'the illness of which יָמוּת he was to die') (33,
44). In these cases, the situations represented by the imperfect
are anticipated but not initiated.[125] Their inception is also not

---

[121] Italics have been removed from the following five quotations.

[122] In addition to the references in n. 109, see Müller, *Outlines of Hebrew Syntax,* §6.1. Cf. Strong, *Hebraica,* ii, 1886, pp. 231-232.

[123] See Ges.-Rœdiger, 20th ed., §127.4b (= Ges.-Kautzsch-Cowley, §§107b, e-i); Ewald, *Syntax of the Hebrew Language,* §136c; and Müller, *Outlines of Hebrew Syntax,* §6.3. See also Böttcher, ii. §942b,f.

[124] For a linguistic model, see Comrie, *Aspect,* pp. 24-40.

[125] See Ewald, *Syntax of the Hebrew Language,* §136a; Müller, *Outlines of*

real, much less sharp or distinct. In terms of the initial phase of these situations, then, the imperfect seems to reflect something indistinct, ill-defined, and fuzzy.[126]

When it represents the final phase of a situation, the imperfect has a similar aspectual character. Whether habitual, continuous, or iterative, this imperfect expresses situations that lack a distinct, well-defined, and clear end point. Each of these "frequentative" imperfects is open-ended (to different degrees). The imperfect can "express a characteristic of an individual" (e.g., Isa. 56,2 'happy is the man יַעֲשֶׂה who does this, the person יַחֲזִיק who holds fast to it') (37-38). Or, "expressing as it does a general truth, [the imperfect] is sometimes found attached to a substantive, the relative being omitted, to denote a general attribute belonging to it: under these circumstances it almost degenerates into an adjective" (e.g., Hos. 4,14 וְעָם לֹא־יָבִין 'a people without understanding'. Job 9,26 כְּנֶשֶׁר יָטוּשׂ 'like an eagle swooping on prey') (38-39). In each case, the terminal phase represented by the imperfect is not sharply demarcated (see, e.g., 1 n. 1, 47).[127] The phase-final imperfect, then, is very much like its phase-initial counterpart. The end points of a situation, whether initial or terminal, are represented as indistinct, ill-defined, and fuzzy.

The imperfect can also be used to describe a situation intermediate between its two end points. As Driver pointed out, this situation may be represented as in motion and in progress[128] (e.g., Gen. 37,15 מַה־תְּבַקֵּשׁ 'what are you looking for?') (27; see

Hebrew Syntax, §7.2a; and, differently, Ges.-Kautzsch-Cowley, §107o (on which, see below, §4.4).

[126] See Ewald, *Syntax of the Hebrew Language,* §136b.

[127] In addition to the references in n. 123, see, e.g., Olshausen, §18b; Ewald, *Syntax of the Hebrew Language,* §§134a-b; and Stade, §382a. Cf. Böttcher, i. p. 386.

[128] See also Ewald, *Syntax of the Hebrew Language,* §136b; Ges.-Kautzsch-Cowley, §107d; and Kennett, *A Short Account,* p. 11. Cf. Strong, *Hebraica,* ii, 1886, p. 107.

also 30).[129] It may be characterized as prolonged (e.g., Ps. 95,10 'for forty years אָקוּט I loathed that generation'; see also 1 Ki. 3,4 'a thousand burnt offerings יַעֲלֶה did Solomon offer') (see 35).[130] Further, the situation represented by the imperfect frequently has internal structure and complexity (e.g., Ex. 19,19 '[while] Moses יְדַבֵּר was speaking, and God יַעֲנֶנּוּ was answering him';[131] see also Jer. 52,7 'all the soldiers יִבְחֲרוּ fleeing, וַיֵּצְאוּ left . . . וַיֵּלְכוּ and went') (cf. 35). The imperfect can even frame another situation within it[132] (see also 2 Sa. 15,37 'Hushai, the friend of David, entered the city as Absalom יָבֹא was entering Jerusalem') (see 206).[133] A situation represented by the imperfect can therefore be viewed from an internal perspective.

All these examples suggest a single aspectual characterization of the imperfect — one that soundly contrasts with the perfect. Whereas the perfect portrays a situation from an external viewpoint, as a single undifferentiated whole ("a single picture") (see §3.1 with n. 95), the imperfect portrays a situation from an internal viewpoint, as an unfolding series ("a cinematographic representation") (see 4).[134] Because of these characteristics, the perfect is an aspectually completive verb form.[135] The imperfect, in contrast, is noncompletive:[136] Representing a situation with

---

[129] See also Driver's interpretation of Ps. 7,16b (31 with n. 1).

[130] In addition to the references in n. 123, see Müller, *Outlines of Hebrew Syntax,* §5.2.

[131] With, e.g., B. Baentsch, *Exodus-Leviticus-Numeri* (Göttingen, 1903), p. 174; and B. S. Childs, *The Book of Exodus. A Critical, Theological Commentary* (Philadelphia, 1974), pp. 343, 341.

[132] See Ewald, *Syntax of the Hebrew Language,* §136c; and Müller, *Outlines of Hebrew Syntax,* §6.2b.

[133] For the dependent and backgrounding nature of the imperfect, see Ewald, *Syntax of the Hebrew Language,* §136a; and §4.6, below.

[134] For the metaphors, see Kennett, *A Short Account,* p. 10. Cf., in this context, the syntactic statement by Landsberger, *Monographs on the Ancient Near East,* i/4, 1976, p. 7 [63].

[135] See §3.1 in conjunction with the references in nn. 82 and 83.

[136] See the references in n. 127.

internal structure and complexity, the noncompletive imperfect
lacks clear, distinct, and well-defined end points. When Driver
concluded, then, that the imperfect is the aspectual opposite of
the perfect, he was right. But the imperfect is not a nascent verb
form. According to his own examples and discussion, the imperfect expresses the imperfective aspect.

4.4. Driver noted the modal implications of his aspectual
analysis of the imperfect.

> [S]ince the imperfect expresses an action not as *done*, but only
> as *doing*, as possessing consequently an element of uncertainty
> and indeterminateness, not already fixed and defined but
> capable of assuming any form, or taking any direction that
> may be impressed upon it from without, it is used after con-
> junctions such as לְמַעַן, בַּעֲבוּר, פֶּן, precisely as in Latin the
> corresponding terms are followed not by the indicative, the
> mood of certainty, but by the subjunctive, the mood of con-
> tingency. . . . The imperfect, then, may characterize action as
> *potential*; but this potentiality may be expressed either (1) as a
> substantive and independent fact, i.e. the tense may appear as
> *indicative*; or (2) as regulated by the will of a personal agent,
> i.e. the tense may appear as *voluntative* (optative); or (3) as
> determined by some antecedent event, i.e. the tense may ap-
> pear as *subjunctive*. (29-30)

In Driver's opinion, the imperfect is a modal wildcard.[137]

Within this modal panorama, the imperfect expresses speaker
uncertainty.[138] The degree of uncertainty, though, was left rather
vague ("an element"). But according to Driver's pragmatic analysis and accompanying examples, this degree can be specified.
The imperfect can express a situation that is contemporary with

[137] See Böttcher, ii. §943c; Ges.-Rœdiger, 20th ed., §127.3; Ewald, *Lehrbuch*, 8th ed., §§136e-f; and Müller, *Outlines of Hebrew Syntax*, §7.2a. See
also *Zeitschrift für Althebraistik* ix, 1996, pp. 169-171.

[138] See also Strong, *Hebraica*, ii, 1886, p. 107; and Böttcher, ii. §942.IIe.

the speaker's present and is therefore known to the speaker (e.g., 1 Sa. 21,15 'Look, תִּרְאוּ you see the man is raving'; see also Jer. 6,4 'Woe to us: the day has waned [perfect], the shadows of evening יִנָּטוּ lengthen') (see 33). Similarly, the imperfect can denote other situations that are quite certain to the narrator or speaker (e.g., Isa. 6,2 'with two יְכַסֶּה each covered its face, with two יְכַסֶּה each covered its legs, and with two יְעוֹפֵף each flew'. Ex. 6,1 'Now תִּרְאֶה you shall see what אֶעֱשֶׂה I will do') (see 36). Examples like these also support Driver's contention that "[t]he imperfect is found . . . [a]sserting facts of definite occurrence — within a longer or shorter period, as the case may be" (e.g., Ps. 71,17 'until now אַגִּיד I proclaim') (37). If the imperfect expresses uncertainty, then, the degree of uncertainty seems rather low.

When the imperfect refers to a future situation, as is often the case (28, 33), that situation is not yet real but is merely envisioned. Represented by the imperfect, it is not known with absolute certainty or confidence (e.g., Gen. 12,12 'but you יְחַיּוּ they will let live'). Yet the imperfect can refer to future situations that are still relatively certain. For instance, the imperfect can appear when a speaker expresses confidence about a future situation (e.g., Ps. 5,8 'but I, through your abundant love, אָבוֹא will enter your house; אֶשְׁתַּחֲוֶה I will bow down toward your holy temple') (cf. 41). It can express a speaker's strong belief (e.g., Isa. 38,11 לֹא־אֶרְאֶה 'I will not see Yah . . . לֹא־אַבִּיט nor gaze upon humanity any longer'). The imperfect can have many pragmatically emphatic interpretations too, including promise (e.g., Ex. 3,17 אַעֲלֶה 'I will take you up') and curse (e.g., Gen. 3,14 'on your belly תֵלֵךְ shall you go, and dust תֹּאכַל shall you eat') (see §4.7). The imperfect, then, indeed represents future and unreal situations. They are not, however, completely unknown or uncertain. According to their discourse and exegetical contexts, the imperfect in these passages expresses "the definite expectation" that something will or will not happen.[139]

---

[139] See Ges.-Kautzsch-Cowley, §107o.

All told, the imperfect expresses reasonable, though not absolute, certainty on the part of the narrator or speaker. Because
it is an imperfective verb form, the imperfect does not represent
a situation as a totality. Hence, as Driver recognized, the speaker
does not know the situation completely. The speaker can, however, claim to know a particular phase of a situation (e.g., 1 Sa.
21,15). Using the imperfect, the speaker can formulate a gener-
alization (e.g., Isa. 56,2); its truth, though, cannot be absolutely
guaranteed but only reasonably inferred (see also 6,2). Even
when "[a]sserting facts of definite occurrence," a speaker pro-
jects beyond personal experience (e.g., Ex. 13,15 'but every first-
born among my sons אֶפְדֶּה I redeem'). Like the future-oriented
imperfect of "definite expectation," the imperfect generally represents a situation as likely and reasonably certain. But, unlike
the perfect, it does not express absolute certainty or knowledge.
The imperfect is modally qualified, possessing a small element
of doubt.

4.5. In addition, Driver recognized that the imperfect has a
predictive value. This value, however, was rather indeterminate.
"An idea . . . like that of *nascency, beginning,* or *going to be* is
almost indefinitely elastic: on the one hand, that which is in the
process of coming to pass is also that which is *destined* or *must*
come to pass (τὸ μέλλον); on the other hand, it is also that which
can or *may* come to pass" (29). For Driver, the imperfect expresses a number of predictive judgements, ranging from
(strong) necessity (see 44) to (weak) potentiality (30, 41); the
intermediate area is occupied by possibility (114) and liability
(38).[140]

But the modal value of the imperfect is not as indeterminate
as Driver claimed. For instance, though the imperfect "corresponds to *may* as a term indicating indefiniteness" (42), there is
no evidence that this meaning is inherent in the verb. Driver's

---

[140] See also Böttcher, ii. §942.IIIhβ; Stade, §383b.2-3; and, less directly,
Ballantine, *Hebraica,* ii, 1885, p. 54.

examples, in fact, suggest that it is not (e.g., Ex. 8,23 'as יֹאמַר he may command us'. 2 Ki. 12,5b 'any money which a man יַעֲלֶה may bring'). In Ex. 8,23, the modal reading of the verb may be attributable to the comparative relative 'as' (כַּאֲשֶׁר). And in 2 Ki. 12,5b, it may be traced to the relative particle and its indefinite antecedent 'any' (e.g., כָּל . . . אֲשֶׁר; cf. *v.* 5a). In both cases, the modal reading of the imperfect cannot be separated from its grammatical and semantic context (see also 174 [on conditions]). Similarly, Driver's examples of an indefinite imperfect "in past time" are not always compelling (e.g., Jud. 17,8 'to take up residence wherever יִמְצָא he could'; see also Ex. 34,34 'what יְצֻוֶּה he had been commanded'). In these cases too, the interpretation of the imperfect cannot be detached from the indefinite object of the verb or from the verb's subordinate construction. These examples do not prove that the imperfect form *per se* expresses either modal indefiniteness or potentiality.[141]

Other passages listed by Driver suggest that the imperfect expresses predictive likelihood[142] or, more forcefully, "definite expectation" (e.g., 1 Sa. 14,43 'Here I am, אָמוּת ready to die'. Ps. 18,30 'for with you אָרֻץ I rush a troop; with my God אֲדַלֶּג I leap over a wall'; see also Gen. 49,1. 2 Ki. 13,14). In 1 Sa. 14,43, Jonathan is both resigned and willing to face his future fate.[143] In Ps. 18,30, the speaker is confident that his actions will be successful (see *vv.* 21.25.29). Accordingly, the predictive value of the imperfect in these texts is high.

When the imperfect has a directive interpretation (see §4.7), it likewise expresses the speaker's confidence and positive attitude toward the predicted situation. The imperfect may function as a demand (e.g., Ex. 10,26 'our livestock, too, יֵלֵךְ must go with

---

[141] Cf. Ges.-Rœdiger, 20th ed., §127.3d.

[142] In this context, see Kennett, *A Short Account,* p. 18 n. 1.

[143] So, e.g., H. P. Smith, *A Critical and Exegetical Commentary on the Books of Samuel* (Edinburgh, 1899), pp. 122-123; and, in greater detail, Driver, *Notes on the Hebrew Text and the Topography of the Books of Samuel* (2nd ed.; Oxford, 1913), p. 118.

us—לֹא תִשָּׁאֵר there shall not remain a hoof, for נְקַח we must choose from it') (see 43). Or, it may have a much stronger reading (e.g., 20,13-16 לֹא תִרְצָח לֹא תִנְאָף לֹא תִגְנֹב לֹא־תַעֲנֶה 'You shall not murder. You shall not commit adultery. You shall not steal. You shall not bear false witness against your neighbor.'). These interpretations, however, are modally consistent with those of Isa. 38,11 and Ps. 5,8, in which the imperfect expresses "the definite expectation" that something will or will not happen (§4.4). In each case, the imperfect possesses a relatively high epistemic value and, hence, a correspondingly high predictive value. Thus, despite Driver's claims, the unqualified imperfect does not express weak potentiality, mere possibility, or modal indefiniteness. As an expression of reasonable certainty, the imperfect expresses predictive likelihood and reasonably strong predictive judgment.

4.6. The preceding modal analyses caution against equating the imperfect with an unqualified indicative mood (cf. 30). They do, however, favor the interpretation of the imperfect as a semantic subjunctive[144] — a modal form that registers greater likelihood, speaker confidence, and certainty, though falling short of unqualified. Morphology and grammar confirm this subjunctive interpretation, too (cf. 30 n. 1).[145] In Akkadian, for example, the cognates of the imperfect are syntactically restricted; *iprus-u* and *iprusū-ni* (Assyrian) specifically mark the predicate of a subordinate clause.[146] Arabic also employs *yaqtulu*

---

[144] See Ges.-Rœdiger, 20th ed., §§127.3,5.

[145] See, in this context, Olshausen, §228a. Cf. Müller, *Luth. Zeitschrift*, xxxviii, 1877, p. 208.

[146] E.g., Delitzsch, *Assyrische Grammatik*, §92; D. O. Edzard, *Orientalia*, xlii, 1973, p. 129; von Soden and Mayer, *Grundriss der akkadischen Grammatik*, §83a*; and, more forcefully, von Soden, *Zeitschrift für Assyriologie und Vorderasiatische Archäologie*, lxiii, 1973, pp. 56-57. See also E. Hincks, *Specimen Chapters of an Assyrian Grammar* (London, 1866), p. 15; and Sayce, *An Elementary Grammar; with Full Syllabary and Progressive Reading Book, of the Assyrian Language, in the Cuneiform Type* (London, [1875]), p. 65 (= 2nd ed. [1877], p. 65).

and *yaqtulûna* to form "a secondary, subordinate clause, expressing the state . . . in which the subject of the previous perfect found himself, when he did what that perfect expresses."[147] Both Akkadian[148] and Arabic[149] evidence, then, suggest that the ancestor of the imperfect is a subjunctive.[150] Moreover, the imperfect itself retains traces of its subordinative origin.[151] For example, it regularly follows the temporal conjunctions (בְּ)טֶרֶם 'before, not yet' and (אֲשֶׁר) עַד 'until' (cf. 32). It also appears after final conjunctions such as (אֲשֶׁר) לְמַעַן, בַּעֲבוּר, and פֶּן (see 29).[152] In each case, the conjunction explicitly subordinates the following clause and introduces a situation which the speaker cannot know with absolute certainty. Thus form, grammar, and semantics agree. The imperfect is the formal heir of a subjunctive verb form, appears in dependent and qualified contexts (see 42),[153] and expresses slightly qualified semantic certainty, knowledge, and confidence (see 30).

4.7. Driver's modal description of the imperfect also included a second component that pertained to speaker will.

> If the subject of the verb . . . be the speaker, i.e. if the verb be in the first person, that which is about to come to pass will be commonly that which he himself *desires* or *wishes* to come to pass; if, however, the verb be in the second or third person, it naturally expresses the wishes of the speaker *as regards some*

---

[147] Caspari, *A Grammar of the Arabic Language,* ii (tr. and ed. Wright, rev. W. R. Smith and M. J. de Goeje; 3rd ed.; Cambridge, 1951), §8e.

[148] Cf. Edzard, in von Soden, *Zeitschrift für Assyriologie,* lxiii, 1973, p. 57, rejecting the term "subjective" on linguistic grounds. These very grounds, however, disprove Edzard's conclusion. See A. Goetze, *Journal of the American Oriental Society,* lviii, 1938, p. 294; and, more generally, Palmer, *Mood and Modality,* p. 22.

[149] In Arabic, however, "subjunctive" properly refers to the *yaqtula* form.

[150] See, e.g., Baumgartner, *Orientalistische Literaturzeitung,* xl, 1937, col. 687; and R. M. Voigt, *Journal of Semitic Studies,* xxxii, 1987, p. 17.

[151] See Strong, *Hebraica,* ii, 1886, p. 108 with n. *.

[152] Ges.-Rœdiger, 20th ed., §127.3a.

[153] See Ballantine, *Hebraica,* ii, 1885, p. 54.

one else, and so conveys a more or less emphatic *permission* which imperceptibly passes, especially in negative sentences, into a *command.* (29; see §4.5)

Driver gave an analogy. "The imperfect . . . expresses not merely simple futurity (I shall, thou wilt, he will), but is equivalent further to the same auxiliaries in their other and more emphatic capacity as the exponents of volition (I will, thou shalt, he shall)" (41; see also 33-34 n. 3, 50). According to Driver, then, the imperfect has the same modal range as its English translational equivalents. In Hebrew, though, the volitional sense of the imperfect must be inferred — by grammar, logic, and pragmatic context.

Within the sphere of volition, Driver rightly mentioned several conspicuous readings of the imperfect. It may be interpreted as a desiderative (e.g., Dt. 18,6 'if יָבֹא a Levite wants to leave'),[154] permissive (e.g., Gen. 42,37 'my two sons תָּמִית you may kill if'. Dt. 12,20 תֹּאכַל 'you may eat meat'), prohibitive (e.g., Ex. 20,13-16), or command (e.g., Dt. 19,7 'therefore, I command you, "three cities תַּבְדִּיל you shall set apart" '; in the negative, Josh. 6,10 'Joshua commanded, לֹא תָרִיעוּ וְלֹא־תַשְׁמִיעוּ "you shall not shout or let your voices be heard" '). Driver also noted a related volitional interpretation of the imperfect: in combination with וְ, the imperfect can denote purpose (e.g., Gen. 1,9 וְתֵרָאֶה 'that the dry land appear'; see also Ex. 14,15 'tell the Israelites וְיִסָּעוּ to go forward') (64). For Driver, then, the imperfect can be used to express volition.

Though Driver attributed the volitional quality of the imperfect to pragmatic inference,[155] others assigned it to the semantic level. Ewald[156] and Gesenius-Kautzsch,[157] for example, claimed

---

[154] On Driver's analysis of Dt. 32,20 (29), cf. Ges.-Kautzsch-Cowley, §108a n. 2.

[155] See also Kennett, *A Short Account,* pp. 17-18.

[156] See Ewald, *Syntax of the Hebrew Language,* §§136g, 223c.

[157] Ges.-Kautzsch-Cowley, §§107m-n,s. See also Ges.-Rœdiger, 20th ed., §§127.3b-c.

that volition is an intrinsic semantic feature of the imperfect. Driver, however, is apparently correct. In contrast to the semantic features of imperfectivity, likelihood, and reasonable certainty, which recur throughout all the attestations of the imperfect (see §§4.3-4), its volitional reading is far more limited. This reading may follow a volitional head, whether it be a conjunction (e.g., לְמַ֫עַן or פֶּן), grammatical construction (e.g., Gen. 1,9 יִקָּווּ 'let the water collect . . . וְתֵרָאֶה that the dry land appear'),[158] or even verb (e.g., Lam. 1,10 'whom צִוִּ֫יתָה לֹא־יָבֹ֫אוּ you commanded not to enter') (see 44). In the latter instance, the volitional interpretation is explicitly provided by the text itself (see also, e.g., Dt. 19,7. Josh. 6,10). Or, when absent, this reading may be derived from interpretative fiat (e.g., Job 36,10 וַיֹּ֫אמֶר כִּי־ יְשֻׁבוּן, 'and he commands that they return'). In any event, the volitional quality of the imperfect does not appear to be intrinsic. On the contrary, it seems to be imposed by a variety of sources and is pragmatically driven.[159]

5. *Volitional Forms* (50-63). Whereas the volitional sense of the imperfect is pragmatically construed, in other forms it is semantically inherent.[160] Driver discussed two such volitional forms,

---

[158] On the latter, see S. E. Fassberg in שִׁי לחיים רבין. *Studies on Hebrew and Other Semitic Languages* Presented to *Professor Chaim Rabin on the Occasion of his Seventy-Fifth Birthday* (ed. M. Goshen-Gottstein, S. Morag, and S. Kogut; Jerusalem, 1990), pp. 273-294 (in Hebrew); and idem, *Studies in Biblical Syntax* (Jerusalem, 1994), pp. 103-112 (in Hebrew). According to his statistics, וְלֹא יִקְטֹל in complementary clauses is most frequently governed by the perfect consecutive or the imperfect (pp. 277-279 and p. 104, respectively). In contrast, פֶּן יִקְטֹל is governed most often by the imperative or a verb form negated by אַל (pp. 282-283 and p. 109, respectively). In other words, the lexically volitional פֶּן יִקְטֹל can be correlated with grammatically explicit volitional verb forms. וְלֹא יִקְטֹל cannot. For an interpretation of these data, see Kennett, *A Short Account,* p. 29.

[159] Ibid., p. 14.

[160] E.g., Böttcher, i. §587.IIb. ii. §951; Müller, *Luth. Zeitschrift,* xxxviii, 1877, p. 206; and Kennett, *A Short Account,* p. 24.

both of which he deemed to be modifications of the imperfect (see 50, xiii). One was the cohortative. Derived from the imperfect by the addition of ‫ה‬ָ-, the cohortative is largely restricted to the first person (51). The other was the jussive. Putatively derived from the imperfect by the subtraction or shortening of its final syllable (where possible) (51-52; cf. §4.1), the jussive is largely restricted to the second and third persons. For Driver, the distinction between these two volitional derivatives of the imperfect is formal as well as grammatical.

There are, however, three volitional forms in Hebrew. Speaker desire is expressed by three grammatically distinct forms: the cohortative, the imperative, and the jussive.[161] These three volitional forms are also not derived from the imperfect.[162] Formal criteria already suggested that the imperfect is itself an augmented and modified verb form whose stem recurs in the masculine singular imperative and infinitive construct (§4.1). Further, of these two simple relatives, it is most likely the masculine singular imperative that underlies the cohortative and jussive. Like the cohortative and jussive, it is partially finite[163] and semantically volitional. Moreover, it shares an optional ending with the cohortative (‫ה‬ָ-, in the long imperative),[164] its shortened form with singular jussives (see 52), and its inflectional endings with the jussive/imperfect. According to this formal, grammatical, and semantic evidence, the three volitional verb forms share a single underlying stem that is identical to the masculine singular imperative.[165]

---

[161] In addition to the references in the preceding note, see Ewald, *Syntax of the Hebrew Language*, §§224-228.

[162] Cf., especially, ibid., §223c.

[163] For the scale of finiteness in verbs, see Palmer, *Mood and Modality*, p. 162.

[164] For the identity of ‫ה‬ָ- in the long imperative and cohortative, see Olshausen, §228c.

[165] Cf. Böttcher, i. §587.IIb.2. ii. §956m.1; and Stade, §482a, suggesting a subtractive derivation of the imperative.

5.1. For Driver, the cohortative is clearly a modal verb form. It "is used . . . to express an intention or desire on the part of the speaker" (50).[166] But it does not merely express general volition; it "marks the presence of a strongly-felt inclination or impulse" (53).[167] Consequently, the volitional force of the co-hortative is strong, for it "mark[s] with peculiar emphasis the concentration of the will upon a particular object" (e.g., Gen. 27,41 וְאַהַרְגָה 'then I will kill') (51).

Driver acknowledged that the meaning of the cohortative depends, to a certain extent, upon the speech context. When the speaker's cohortative "is accompanied by the ability to carry the wished-for action into execution, we may, if we please, employ *I, we will . . .* in translating" (e.g., 22,5 נֵלְכָה 'we will go') (53). As this passage indicates, the cohortative can function as an an-nouncement of firm intent.[168] But the speaker is not always able to execute the expressed desire.[169] In which case, "we must re-strict ourselves to some less decided expression, which shall be better adapted to embody a mere proposal or petition" (e.g., Jud. 12,5 אֶעְבְּרָה 'I would like to cross'. Ps. 39,5 אֵדְעָה 'let me know') (53). For as Ps. 39,5 suggests in particular, the cohortative can be interpreted as a prayer.[170] Depending on context, then, the co-hortative can range from a strong assertion to a weak wish.[171]

Of these two polar readings, Driver regarded the former as the literal meaning of the cohortative.[172] The cohortative is, for

[166] See also, e.g., Böttcher, ii. §§954, 962; Müller, *Outlines of Hebrew Syntax,* §9; Ges.-Kautzsch-Cowley, §48e; and Kennett, *A Short Account,* p. 22.

[167] See also Ewald, *Syntax of the Hebrew Language,* §§224, 228.

[168] See C. Westermann, *Genesis 12–36: A Commentary* (tr. J. J. Scullion; Minneapolis, 1985), p. 359. See also Böttcher, ii. §962A.I.1; and, somewhat differently, Ges.-Kautzsch-Cowley, §108a.

[169] See also Kennett, *A Short Account,* pp. 22-23.

[170] For a discussion of this passage, see H.-J. Kraus, *Psalms 1-59* (tr. H. C. Oswald; Minneapolis, 1993), p. 418.

[171] See Böttcher, ii. §962A.I.1-4; and Ges.-Rœdiger, 20th ed., §§128.1a-b (= Ges.-Kautzsch-Cowley, §§108b-c).

[172] See n. 167. Cf. Müller, *Luth. Zeitschrift,* xxxviii, 1877, p. 205.

W. RANDALL GARR.

Driver, a self-statement of strong speaker desire. Any other reading is a pragmatic inference derived from and dependent on the particular social and/or discourse context (e.g., Isa. 27,4 אֶפְשְׂעָה 'I would march' [wish]).

Interestingly, the cohortative is occasionally dependent in other ways, too.[173] It may be governed by a subordinating conjunction, whether the conjunction be lexically desiderative (e.g., לְמַעַן Ps. 9,15 לְמַעַן אֲסַפְּרָה 'so that I may recount') or not (e.g., עַד Pr. 12,19 וְעַד־אַרְגִּיעָה 'but until I wink'). The cohortative may also follow the subordinator כִּי (e.g., Ps. 71,23 כִּי אֲזַמְּרָה 'when I sing'; cf. *v.* 22); in this case, אזמרה concretely illustrates the evaluative clause that precedes it, תְּרַנֵּנָּה שְׂפָתַי 'my lips will be jubilant' (cf. 59). Likewise, the cohortative may synonymously restate the principal verb (e.g., Pr. 7,7 וָאֵרֶא . . . אָבִינָה 'and I saw . . . , observed') or be backgrounded in some other way (e.g., 2 Sa. 22,38 אֶרְדְּפָה . . . וָאַשְׁמִידֵם '[after] I pursued . . . I destroyed them') (see 58). In each example, the cohortative is either grammatically or rhetorically dependent.

The grammatical, rhetorical, and pragmatic evidence suggests that Driver's semantic characterization of the cohortative is essentially correct, though in need of modification and slight expansion. As Driver understood, the cohortative is a modal verb form that expresses strong speaker desire. It is a volitional self-statement. But it is also a subordinate verb form, grammatically and contextually. Thus the cohortative has two intersecting modal components: volitionality and dependency.[174] It would appear, then, that the cohortative is a specifically volitional subjunctive verb form[175] that is, for the most part, restricted to the first person (cf. imperfect).

---

[173] Böttcher, ii. §962B; and Ges.-Kautzsch-Cowley, §§108d-f.

[174] See Böttcher, ii. §951, equating the cohortative with modal dependence.

[175] For the morphologically identical Arabic subjunctive, see n. 149; and the analysis in Caspari-Wright, *Grammar of the Arabic Language,* ii (3rd ed.), §§15a-d.

5.2. Whereas the cohortative is a volitional self-statement, the imperative is a volitional direct address (see 69).[176] Their respective addressees are different. In the cohortative, the addressee is the speaker (singular) or speaker-inclusive group (plural). In the imperative, the addressee is distinct from yet proximate to the speaker. Whereas the cohortative is a specifically first person volitional verb form, the imperative is specifically second person.[177]

There is a common misunderstanding of the imperative's semantic and pragmatic character. Müller exemplified this misunderstanding when he described the imperative as "the *mood of command*. . . . To express a *positive* injunction, the *imperative* is used for the *second* person" (e.g., Ex. 20,12 כַּבֵּד 'honor your father and your mother').[178] And besides "real commands,"[179] but nonetheless functionally similar, the imperative can denote, *inter alia,* supplication (e.g., Ps. 4,2 חָנֵּנִי 'have mercy on me'), permission (e.g., Isa. 21,12 בְּעָיוּ 'inquire'), and even advice (e.g., Pr. 4,1 שִׁמְעוּ 'heed').[180] In each case, the speaker voices "a desire regarding what is to be done."[181]

But the imperative need not be construed so narrowly. It does not always express a command, nor is it always task-oriented. For example, the imperative may denote urgency (e.g., Gen. 19,22 מַהֵר 'hurry'), well-wishes (e.g., 1 Sa. 20,42 לֵךְ לְשָׁלוֹם 'go in peace'), or warning (e.g., 2 Ki. 6,9 הִשָּׁמֶר 'beware'). In these instances, the imperative does not express the speaker's desire

---

[176] For the volitional quality of the form, see Böttcher, ii. §951; and Ewald, *Syntax of the Hebrew Language,* §226. See also Olshausen, §18b.

[177] See Müller, *Outlines of Hebrew Syntax,* §8.1; and Kennett, *A Short Account,* p. 24.

[178] Müller, *Outlines of Hebrew Syntax,* §§8-8.1. See also Ges.-Kautzsch-Cowley, §110a.

[179] Ges.-Kautzsch-Cowley, §110aa.

[180] See, e.g., Böttcher, ii. §957C.3,5,2, respectively; and Müller, *Outlines of Hebrew Syntax,* §8.2.

[181] Ewald, *Syntax of the Hebrew Language,* §226.

W. RANDALL GARR.

"regarding what is to be *done*" (italics added). Rather, it expresses the speaker's desire regarding the addressee's future.[182] Driver would have agreed. For according to his examples, the imperative can be interpreted as promise (e.g., Gen. 12,2 'I will bless you . . . וֶהְיֵה [I want that] you be a blessing'), purpose (e.g., 42,18 'do this וֶחְיוּ and live'), assurance (e.g., Isa. 54,14 רַחֲקִי 'be far'), challenge/prediction (e.g., 8,9 רֹעוּ 'band together . . . וָחֹתּוּ and be shattered'[183]), or disgrace (e.g., 23,4 בֹּושִׁי 'be ashamed') (see 54 n. 2, 60, 69, 191).[184] Like the imperatives of urgency, well-wishes, and warning, these imperatives are also not task-oriented. The imperative, then, denotes more than "real commands." It expresses a speaker's desire, directed at a second person addressee, regarding that addressee's future.

5.3. The jussive is the third Hebrew form that expresses speaker desire (see 50).[185] And like the other volitional forms, the jussive has multiple pragmatic interpretations. For example, it may denote a command or injunction (e.g., Gen. 1,3 יְהִי 'let there be'. Ex. 16,19 אַל־יֹותֵר 'let no one leave over'), consent (e.g., 2 Ki. 2,10 יְהִי 'let it be'), advice (e.g., Gen. 41,33 יֵרֶא 'Pharaoh should find'), suggestion (e.g., 1 Ki. 1,2 יְבַקְשׁוּ 'let someone look for'), request (e.g., 1 Sa. 19,38 יַעֲבֹר 'let him cross'), prayer (e.g., 1,23 יָקֵם 'may the Lord fulfill'), wish (e.g., 1 Ki. 20,32 תְּחִי 'would that, please, my life be spared'), etc. (54-55).[186] Driver did not, however, specify the semantic character of the jussive with similar precision. He only noted its general volitional nature.

This character can be deduced from grammar. In affirmative

---

[182] In addition to the references in nn. 176 and 177, see Böttcher, ii. §957C.

[183] For the text and discussion, see H. Wildberger, *Isaiah 1-12: A Commentary* (tr. T. H. Trapp; Minneapolis, 1991), pp. 349-350, 352-353.

[184] See Böttcher, ii. §957C; and Ges.-Rœdiger, 20th ed., §130.1.

[185] In addition to the references in nn. 160 and 161, see Böttcher, ii. §961; and Ges.-Kautzsch-Cowley, §109a.

[186] E.g., Böttcher, ii. §961A; and, in less detail, Ges.-Kautzsch-Cowley, §109b; and Müller, *Outlines of Hebrew Syntax*, §8.2; as well as Kennett, *A Short Account*, pp. 23-24.

utterances, the three volitional forms correspond principally to the three grammatical persons: cohortative/first, imperative/second, and jussive/third. That is, the addressee of the speaker's desire is formulated differently in each. In the cohortative, the addressee is identical to or includes the speaker. In the imperative, the addressee is distinct from the speaker; yet, as a direct address, the addressee is nonetheless proximate. But in the jussive, the addressee is distant from the speaker. Represented in the third person, the addressee is grammatically distant. Further, the addressee can be physically (e.g., 2 Sa. 19,38) or metaphorically (e.g., Gen. 41,33. 44,33) distant from the speaker. It may even be altogether absent (e.g., 1,3).[187] Of the three volitional verb forms, then, the addressee of the jussive is the most distant and remote from the speaker — in terms of grammar, conception, physical reality, and pragmatic function.

When the jussive is compared to the cohortative alone, a further, terminological conclusion emerges. As mentioned above, their respective addressees are contrastive: in the cohortative, the addressee is closest to the speaker; in the jussive, it is farthest. The cohortative is a direct self-statement, whereas the jussive is an indirect utterance that invokes a third party. The cohortative is a volitional subjunctive, the jussive more remote. The jussive clearly contrasts with the cohortative. According to internal and comparative evidence, the jussive is therefore an optative verb form.[188]

6. *Imperfect Consecutive* (70-99). As its name would suggest,[189] Driver derived the imperfect consecutive from an underlying imperfect verb form: e.g., וַיָּבוֹא 'he came' < יָבוֹא 'he comes, will come' (see 73).

---

[187] See, in this context, P. J. Hopper and S. A. Thompson, *Language,* lvi, 1980, pp. 276-277, on negated clauses.

[188] See Lambert, *Revue des Études Juives,* xxvi, 1893, p. 51. Cf., in this context, Müller, *Luth. Zeitschrift,* xxxviii, 1877, p. 204.

[189] For terminological background, see Böttcher, ii. pp. 192-194.

> The principle upon which the imperfect is here employed will
> not . . . be far to seek. The imperfect represents action as *nas-*
> *cent:* accordingly, when combined with a conjunction connect-
> ing the event introduced by it with a point already reached by
> the narrative, it represents the *continuation* or *development* of
> the past that came before it. וַיֹּאמֶר is thus properly not *and he*
> *said*, but *and he proceeded-to-say*. (71-72)

In Driver's opinion, the verbal core of the imperfect consecutive
is the imperfect of nascency (see §2.4; cf. §4.3)[190] or movement
(see §4).[191]

The imperfect consecutive has a second underlying component, the *waw consecutive* (וַ־). This prefix is not only inextri-
cably fused to its verbal stem (cf. §6.2), but for Driver it also
produces phonological changes that are characteristic of the new
verb form: accent retraction (e.g., יֹאכַל > וַיֹּאכַל 'he ate'),[192]
vowel or syllable shortening (e.g., יַשְׁבִּית > וַיַּשְׁבֵּת 'he destroyed,
ended') (see §4.1), and apocopation (e.g., יַעֲשֶׂה > וַיַּעַשׂ 'he did,
made') (76-78). Driver attributed to the prefix a number of the
verb's pragmatic readings as well: e.g., most prominently, succession (e.g., 4,1 וַתַּהַר וַתֵּלֶד 'she conceived and bore')[193] and
consequence (e.g., 12,19 וָאֶקַּח 'so that I took her') (80; see also
71-72 n. 4).[194] The prefix is crucial to the phonological shape
and functional description of this narrative verb form (see
§1.3).[195]

6.1. There are problems with each part of Driver's analysis. In
the first place, his semantic analysis of the verbal stem is self-

---

[190] Ibid., §976.

[191] Ewald, *Syntax of the Hebrew Language*, §231a; and Müller, *Outlines of
Hebrew Syntax*, §16. See also Ges.-Kautzsch-Cowley, §111n.

[192] E.g., Olshausen, §229b.

[193] See ibid.; Böttcher, ii. §§975D, 976; Kennett, *A Short Account*, pp. 38,
41.

[194] See also Müller, *Outlines of Hebrew Syntax*, §149b; Ges.-Kautzsch-
Cowley, §§111a, 49b and n. 1; and n. 213, below.

[195] In this context, see also Ewald, *Syntax of the Hebrew Language*, §231a.

contradictory (see §4). For in its "consecutive" form, the underlying ingressive or incompletive imperfect would express "the
idea of a *fact done*" (94), that is, a completive preterit (see 73).[196]
The verbal core of the imperfect consecutive, however, is not the
imperfect. As Wright and Lambert noted in the 1890s,[197] and as
all modern researchers now assume,[198] the imperfect consecutive does not descend from **yaqtulu* but from **yaqtul* (§0.4; see
also §6.2). In formal and semantic terms, the verbal stem of the
imperfect consecutive is not the imperfect.[199]

Driver's understanding of the prefixed ־וְ is also problematic.
In particular, the phonological effects of this prefix are either
incorrect or ill-defined. For example, Driver incorrectly attributed the apocopation of וַיַּעַשׂ to the prefix ־וְ. The apocopation is, rather, attributable to the phonological effect of its underlying **yaqtul* form (e.g., תְּהִי 'let there be' [jussive] and וַתְּהִי
'it, there was') (see §4.1).[200] Likewise, the vowel shortening that
can occur in the final syllable of consecutive forms also occurs
in the jussive (e.g., תּוֹצֵא and וַתּוֹצֵא; cf. תּוֹצִיא [imperfect]). It,
too, is attributable to the underlying **yaqtul* form and not, as
Driver claimed, to the conjunctive prefix (cf. 52 and 78).[201] In
another phonological realm, accent retraction, Driver's analysis
is overly morphological; in his opinion, the accent shift is cata-
lyzed by the "heavy prefix." But it is not. Other heavy prefixes,
such as the definite article, have no effect on accent position[202]

---

[196] G. R. Driver, *Problems of the Hebrew Verbal System*, pp. 86-87. Cf.,
e.g., P. P. Saydon, *Biblica* xxxv, 1954, pp. 44-46; and Landsberger, *Monographs
on the Ancient Near East*, i/4, 1976, p. 8 [64]. For a discourse-based solution,
see Kennett, *A Short Account*, p. 49.

[197] See nn. 27 and 29.

[198] See Waltke and O'Connor, *An Introduction to Biblical Hebrew Syntax*,
§§29.4e-i.

[199] E.g., G. R. Driver, *Problems of the Hebrew Verbal System*, p. 95.

[200] See Böttcher, ii. §969.1.

[201] See Olshausen, §60.

[202] G. R. Driver, *Problems of the Hebrew Verbal System*, p. 85 n. 3.

(cf. the examples on 77 with n. 2). Still, Driver's morphological description can be reformulated in phonological terms, with satisfying results (see 74 n. 2).[203] The accent shift occurs in the imperfect consecutive when three syllabic[204] conditions are present: a closed heavy ultima, an open heavy penult,[205] and a closed antepenult (e.g., 11,5. 12,10 etc. וַיֵּרֶד '[and] he went down'; cf. Ex. 3,8. Dt. 9.15. 10.5. Jer. 18,3 וָאֵרֵד '[and] I went down').[206] Further, and necessarily, the form must have a particular prosodic character (e.g., Gen. 25,34. 31,15 etc. וַיֹּאכַל '[and] he ate, consumed' [context]; cf. 3,6. 27,25. 2 Sa. 12,20 וַיֹּאכַל 'and he ate' [pause]) (see §7.4).[207] •וַ, then, does not affect the accent shift because of its morphological status as a heavy prefix. Rather, it satisfies a phonological condition of the shift — a closed heavy antepenult — in contextual position.

6.2. Another problem for Driver's analysis is the sporadic preservation in Hebrew of *yaqtul preterit, the ancestor of the imperfect consecutive. Lacking the prefix •וַ, the preterit can be formally identical to the jussive (e.g., Hos. 6,1 יַךְ 'he struck' [preterit]. 14,6 וְיַךְ 'he shall strike' [jussive]) (cf. 96-98, 212-218).[208] But when distinguishing phonological conditions do not obtain, it can resemble the imperfect as well (e.g., יִשְׁמַע Ps. 18,7 'he heard' [preterit]. 2 Ki. 19,4 'he will hear' [imperfect]. 1 Sa. 26,19 'may my lord the king hear' [jussive]; cf. 2 Sa. 22,7 וַיִּשְׁמַע 'he heard') (see 31). In other words, the written form of the simple preterit is often deceiving and, without a comparative-

---

[203] See Olshausen, §229b. For a morphophonological compromise, see R. Hetzron, *Journal of Semitic Studies*, xiv, 1969, pp. 13-14.

[204] A fourth, nonsyllabic condition requires that the underlying vowel of the ultima be high (i.e., *i or *u) (see, in this context, Olshausen, §§242a, 243b).

[205] Cf. Philippi, *Deutsche Litteraturzeitung*, xix, 1898, cols. 1678-1679.

[206] E. J. Revell, *Vetus Testamentum*, xxxviii, 1988, p. 424.

[207] Olshausen, §230.2. See also Philippi, *Beiträge zur Assyriologie*, ii, 1894, p. 374 n. ††; and F. Praetorius, *Über den rückweichenden Accent im Hebräischen* (Halle, 1897), pp. 68-69.

[208] See Böttcher, ii. §973.5.

historical perspective, suspectible to grammatical misinterpretation (see 78).

Driver confronted this problem of homography directly. "[G]rammarians have been driven sometimes to the adoption of strange expedients in order to overcome the disagreement existing between the meaning apparently forced upon them by the form, and that which the context seems to demand" (212). Ironically, Driver fell victim to his own criticism. He did not adopt a comparative-historical solution but reconciled this disparity between form and function by proposing a phonological compromise (cf. §0.4): despite their appearance, these forms with preterit meaning are, in fact, imperfect consecutives whose consecutive prefix has been deleted (96-97, 213-214).[209] Hence, imperfect- and jussive-looking forms are ultimately identical to the imperfect consecutive. And ultimately they are, though not as Driver had envisioned.

6.3. Whereas Driver derived the simple preterit from the compound consecutive, most scholars propose the opposite development. It is the imperfect consecutive that is the derived form. Its underlying preterit acquired, at an early developmental stage, the coordinating conjunction *wa* which eventually became fused to the verbal stem:[210] that is, *wa-yaqum* > *wayyaqum*[211] > וַיָּקָם 'he got up'. The new compound participated in phonological change (74-78), while its conjunction explicitly marks the syntactic relation between the compound and its preceding context (71-72 with n. 4).[212]

---

[209] See, descriptively, ibid.; Ewald, *Syntax of the Hebrew Language,* §233a; and Müller, *Outlines of Hebrew Syntax,* §22 Rem. *a.*

[210] E.g., Philippi, *Beiträge zur Assyriologie,* ii, 1894, pp. 373-374 n. ††; and, differently, Bauer, *Beiträge zur Assyriologie,* viii/1, 1910, pp. 26-27. See also Ges.-Kautzsch-Cowley, §49b.

[211] For early phonological statements, see, e.g., Olshausen, §229b; Ges.-Rœdiger, 20th ed., §49.2 Rem. (= Ges.-Kautzsch-Cowley, §49f); and, somewhat differently, Stade, §134f.

[212] This statement has been questioned on phonological as well as mor-

The difficulty, however, lies in the interpretation of this connective element (see §1.2). It may signify a relation of simple chronological succession ('and') or consequence ('and so'). It may even be interpreted as a relation of contrast ('and yet'), climax ('so, thus'), and others as well (80-83). Although Driver recognized these various interpretations, he followed the opinion of his predecessors, that the prefixed •וַ denotes a consecutive relation.[213] For Driver, 'and' yields to '(and) then' (see §1.3).

But Driver's examples and discussion undercut his conclusion. For instance, among the texts cited in support of the consequential reading of the imperfect consecutive, one is nonconsequential (Isa. 36,9 'how could you turn away . . . וַתִּבְטַח relying'). The consecutive form here has a circumstantial reading.[214] More importantly, Driver explicitly acknowledged that the imperfect consecutive often carries no consequential function (see 81-83). It may be introductory (e.g., 1 Ki. 7,13 וַיִּשְׁלַח 'King Solomon sent for and brought Hiram'), explanatory (e.g., Ex. 2,10 'she named him Moses, וַתֹּאמֶר saying'), elaborative (e.g., 40,17b-18 'the Tabernacle was erected: וַיָּקֶם Moses erected the Tabernacle, וַיִּתֵּן placing . . . , וַיָּשֶׂם setting . . . , וַיִּתֵּן placing . . . , וַיָּקֶם and erecting its columns'), summarizing (e.g., Gen. 5,5 וַיִּהְיוּ 'all the days . . . numbered'), or appositional to a nominal (e.g., 36,14 'these were בְּנֵי אָהֳלִיבָמָה the sons of

---

phological grounds. Phonologically, the gemination that bridges the two parts of the imperfect consecutive has been attributed to the assimilation of an underlying consonant, as in the derivation of the consecutive prefix from וְאָז* (see n. 35). Morphologically, the analysis of the prefix has been challenged, too. Instead of representing the conjunction, the prefix has been characterized as a remnant of the Semitic verb "be" (e.g., היה*, הוה*), a non-Semitic existential copula (e.g., *iw), or one of several particles (for details, see Böttcher, ii. pp. 193-194; and McFall, *The Enigma of the Hebrew Verbal System*, pp. 217-219 n. 13-2).

[213] See, e.g., Böttcher, ii. §968.II; and Ewald, *Syntax of the Hebrew Language,* §230.

[214] See also Müller, *Outlines of Hebrew Syntax,* §149.

Oholibamah . . . : וַתֵּלֶד she bore'). It may even be backgrounding (e.g., 1 Sa. 14,1 וַיְהִי הַיּוֹם 'one day, Jonathan said'; see also,
perhaps, Ex. 9,12 וַיְחַזֵּק 'the Lord hardened'). In none of these
cases is the imperfect consecutive pragmatically consecutive.[215]

Driver also stated that the imperfect consecutive can denote
concomitance. "Where . . . a transaction consists of two parts
closely connected, a Hebrew author will often state the principal
fact first, appending the concomitant occurrence by help of וְ־"
(81). But the order of verbs may be less relevant than their
relation. The situation represented by the imperfect consecutive
may be simultaneous[216] or, more generally, synchronous[217] with
its antecedent (e.g., 1 Sa. 25,5 וַיִּשְׁלַח 'David sent ten young men,
וַיֹּאמֶר and David said to the young men'). This synchronous
imperfect consecutive may follow another imperfect consecutive, as in 1 Sa. 25,5 (see also 1 Ki. 19,6 וַיֹּאכַל וַיֵּשְׁתְּ 'he ate and
drank'). It may follow other verb forms as well, both finite (e.g.,
Job 14,10 'but mortals יָמוּת die וַיֶּחֱלָשׁ and languish'[218]) and
nonfinite[219] (e.g., 1 Ki. 8,7 'the cherubim פֹּרְשִׂים spread their
wings . . . וַיָּסֹכּוּ and screened'[220]). In each of these examples,
the imperfect consecutive signifies a situation occurring at the
same time as its antecedent (see also, e.g., 2 Ki 19,26 חַתּוּ וַיֵּבֹשׁוּ
'they are dismayed and confounded').[221]

---

[215] See A. B. Davidson, *Hebrew Syntax* (3rd ed.; Edinburgh, 1901), §47
(= *Davidson's Introductory Hebrew Grammar ~ Syntax* [ed. J. C. L. Gibson;
4th ed.; Edinburgh, 1994], §78).

[216] P. Jöuon, *A Grammar of Biblical Hebrew*, ii (tr. and rev. T. Muraoka;
Rome, 1991), §118k.

[217] See Davidson, *Hebrew Syntax*, §47 (= *Davidson's Introductory Hebrew
Grammar ~ Syntax*, 4th ed., §78).

[218] See, in this context, M. H. Pope, *Job* (3rd ed.; Garden City, 1973),
p. 108. For the function of the imperfect here, see above, §4.3 with n. 132.

[219] Davidson, *Hebrew Syntax*, §50a (= *Davidson's Introductory Hebrew
Grammar ~ Syntax*, 4th ed., §83); and Jöuon, *A Grammar of Biblical Hebrew*,
ii. §118l.

[220] For the discourse function of the participle, see §1.3.

[221] Böttcher, ii. §979.2β. Cf. S. A. Kaufman in *Solving Riddles and Untying*

6.4. According to the foregoing discussion, the imperfect consecutive is not an "imperfect," either formally or semantically. Nor is it pragmatically "consecutive." The imperfect consecutive is, instead, a compound verb form whose morphological components are the preterit and coordinating conjunction. The former element suitably accounts for the form's narrative function, since the imperfect consecutive is "capable of being generally employed in historical narrative" (73). Yet its other element, the coordinating conjunction, is functionally uncertain. In a pragmatic analysis, at least, the prefix •ַו has a number of diverse, but not diagnostic, readings (see 150). The meaning of the prefix •ַו remains unclear.

In somewhat backhanded fashion, Driver offered a suggestion.

> [I]nasmuch as the [morphologically compound] formula became one of the commonest and most constant occurrence, it is probable that a distinct recollection of the exact sense of its component parts was lost, or, at any rate, receded greatly into the background, and that the construction was used as a whole, without any thought of its original meaning, simply as a form *to connect together* a series of past events into a consecutive narrative. (73 [italics added])

With these words, Driver proposed that the prefix •ַו may have a grammatical meaning in the imperfect consecutive (cf. §1.2). The prefix *connects* its verb to the preceding discourse.[222] In this way, the "consecutive" prefix serves the same grammatical role as its etymon, the conjunction *wa*, and its descendent, the simple or weak conjunction וְ (see 72). The consecutive prefix and weak *waw* both link their constituent to the preceding dis-

---

Knots: Biblical, Epigraphic, and Semitic Studies in Honor of Jonas C. Greenfield (ed. Z. Zevit, S. Gitin, and M. Sokoloff; Winona Lake, 1995), p. 98 n. 4.

[222] See also Ges.-Rœdiger, 20th ed., §129.1; and Müller, *Outlines of Hebrew Syntax*, §21.

course, and they both have a number of contextsensitive readings.[223] Fundamentally, however, they both *coordinate.* Even their different forms may be explicable, since the unusual form of the consecutive prefix is not unparalleled elsewhere in Hebrew.[224] Accordingly, the inseparable prefix may serve a grammatical, conjunctive function. When attached to the preterit, it marks the verb as coordinated or conjoined.[225]

7. *Perfect Consecutive* (114-157). Just as the imperfect consecutive is morphologically complex, so too is the perfect consecutive. At first glance, its verbal stem is the perfect, and its second component is the prefixed וֹ (cf. §7.1). And together, these two elements combine to create a new verb form.[226] As Driver observed, "it is essentially the *union* of the verb with the conjunction which produces, and conditions, the special signification assumed by the formula as a whole" (115). The whole exceeds the sum of its parts.

For Driver, the perfect consecutive differs from the perfect in striking and even paradoxical ways. Whereas the perfect denotes an absolute statement, the perfect consecutive is relative and contingent (see 120-121).[227] The perfect represents a situation as

[223] For details, see F. Brown, S. R. Driver, and C. A. Briggs, *A Hebrew and English Lexicon of the Old Testament* (corrected ed.; Oxford, 1953), pp. 252a-253b; in conjunction with D. Schiffrin, *Discourse Markers* (Cambridge, 1987), pp. 128-190. See also Thompson and Longacre in *Language typology and syntactic description,* ii. p. 174.

[224] In addition to the references in n. 211, see T. O. Lambdin in *Near Eastern Studies in Honor of William Foxwell Albright* (ed. H. Goedicke; Baltimore/London, 1971), pp. 325-326 with nn. 16,17; and Malone, *Tiberian Hebrew Phonology,* pp. 47-48. For the significance of this unusual form of the consecutive prefix, see Palmer, *Mood and Modality,* p. 5; in conjunction with P. J. Hopper and E. C. Traugott, *Grammaticalization* (Cambridge, 1993), p. 149.

[225] See also Kennett, *A Short Account,* pp. 44-46; and Müller, *Zeitschrift für Althebraistik,* iv, 1991, p. 156.

[226] Olshausen, §229a.

[227] See also Ewald, *Syntax of the Hebrew Language,* §342a.

definite, real, and concrete (see §§2.2, 3.3), while the perfect
consecutive represents it as indefinite, indeterminate, and abstract (see 137). For Driver, these two, related verb forms are also
aspectual opposites.[228] Unlike its basal, completive perfect, the
consecutive derivative can express a situation as "in process, but
not complete" (145 n. 1) or "as *advancing to completion*" (117).[229]
In addition, "the most noticeable use of the perfect and *waw*
consecutive, though the one least likely to attract attention, is *as
a frequentative*" (142-143). Despite its morphological background, then, the perfect consecutive is the semantic analogue
of the imperfect (114, 140).

Driver described other dissimilarities between the perfect and
the perfect consecutive. For example, the perfect consecutive is
a single entity; unlike the perfect with the nonconsecutive, weak
waw (see 158-163), "when its connexion with ‍ו is broken, [the
perfect consecutive] lapses regularly into the *imperfect*" (114).[230]
The perfect and perfect consecutive are therefore not interchangeable. In a similar vein, the perfect and perfect consecutive
appear in syntactically different contexts. The perfect consecutive can continue, among others, an imperative, imperfect, or
future-oriented participle (124-128); the perfect can not, nor can
the perfect with weak *waw* (see 159). Again, the perfect and
perfect consecutive are not interchangeable. Finally, there is an
overt phonological sign of their dissimilarity: differential accent
patterns, especially that of the perfect consecutive. For in the
consecutive form, the accent is "essentially dependent upon
union with *waw*, of which union the change of tone (where not
hindered from taking place by external or accidental causes) is
the inseparable criterion and accompaniment: dissolve this
union," and the distinctive accent disappears (117 in conjunction

---

[228] See ibid., §234a.

[229] See Olshausen, §229a. For an evaluation, see McFall, *The Enigma of
the Hebrew Verbal System*, pp. 75-76.

[230] Olshausen, §229a.

with 116). From all of these perspectives, the perfect and perfect consecutive are dramatically different.

But Driver also acknowledged that this difference is not restricted to the perfect consecutive and simple perfect. "However difficult it may appear to find a satisfactory explanation of this waw consecutive with the perfect, one thing is perfectly clear, and ought most carefully to be borne in mind: a *real difference* of some kind or other exists between the use of the perfect with simple *waw*, and the use of the perfect with waw consecutive" (115). The perfect consecutive, then, is different from both the simple perfect and the perfect with weak, conjoining *waw*.

7.1. For Driver, the difference resides in the nature of the consecutive *waw* (see §1.3). It is this *waw*, and no other, that affects the accent shift (e.g., Dt. 13,15 וְשָׁאַלְתָּ 'and you shall ask' [perfect consecutive]; cf. 1 Ki. 3,11 וְשָׁאַלְתָּ 'but you asked' [conjoined perfect]).[231] This *waw* also has, for Driver, a limiting function. "[B]y a pointed reference to some preceding verb, it *limits* the possible realization of the action introduced by it to those instances in which it can be treated as a direct consequence of the event thus referred to" (117-118).[232] More generally, "the *waw* limits its occurrence to such occasions as fall within the scope of the preceding dominant verb" (119). Thus the *waw* accounts for the relative or contingent reading of the perfect consecutive (see above). In Driver's opinion, "the *waw* possesses really in this connexion a demonstrative significance, being equivalent to *then* or *so*" (117).

Lambert, for one, disagreed. In his opinion, the distinctive character of the perfect is not attributable to the prefix but to the stem.[233] For just as the semantic difference between the imperfect and imperfect consecutive reflects an underlying mor-

---

[231] See ibid.; and Böttcher, ii. §968.II.

[232] See also Böttcher, ii. §977; and Ges.-Kautzsch-Cowley, §112a.

[233] Lambert, *Revue des Études Juives*, xxvi, 1893, pp. 52-53. See also G. R. Driver, *Problems of the Hebrew Verbal System*, pp. 88-97.

phological difference, Lambert reasoned that the semantic disparity between the perfect and perfect consecutive can also be located in the underlying morphology. The perfect for Lambert is derived from *qatál* (past), whereas the perfect consecutive is derived from *qátal* (future). Other languages, too, would preserve this future *qátal*: Ethiopic, in indicative *yə-qátəl* (*yəqáttəl*);[234] and Akkadian, in its present-future *i-paqqid* (< *i-páqid*).[235] According to Lambert, then, the stems of the perfect and perfect consecutive are morphophonologically distinct.

7.2. In current scholarship, both these theories are rightly ignored. They are speculative at best and lack any historical, comparative, or internal support. For example, *qátal* is not established by the alleged Ethiopic and Akkadian cognates. These latter forms exhibit a grammatically determined, geminate second consonant: *yəqáttəl*;[236] and *ipaqqid*,[237] respectively.[238] And since this gemination is not phonologically conditioned,[239] the structure of these cognates inherently differs from that of the perfect consecutive.[240] Conversely, there is no evidence that the

---

[234] Praetorius, *Aethiopische Grammatik mit Paradigmen, Litteratur, Chrestomathie und Glossar* (Karlesruhe/Leipzig, 1886), §§58-59.

[235] See Delitzsch, *Assyrische Grammatik,* §90a in conjunction with §53a; and, with a comparison to Ethiopic, Sayce, *An Elementary Grammar,* p. 65 (= 2nd ed., p. 65). In this context, see also Landsberger, *Monographs on the Ancient Near East,* i/4, 1976, pp. 7 [63], 8 [64]. Cf. Wright, *Comparative Grammar of the Semitic Languages,* pp. 180-181.

[236] See Voigt, *Journal of Semitic Studies,* xxxv, 1990, pp. 11-12.

[237] See von Soden and Mayer, *Grundriss der akkadischen Grammatik,* §87j. Cf. I. J. Gelb, *Sequential Reconstruction of Proto-Akkadian* (Chicago/London, 1969), p. 205.

[238] See also the inflectional process mentioned by von Soden in *Babylonien und Israel,* pp. 469, 486, on Ethiopic and Akkadian, respectively. For an early statement, see Dillmann, *Grammatik der äthiopischen Sprache* (Leipzig, 1857), §92 (= Dillmann and C. Bezold, *Ethiopic Grammar* [tr. J. A. Crichton; 2nd ed.; London, 1907], §92).

[239] Cf. the references in nn. 234 and 235.

[240] Like Lambert, Hetzron has suggested a morphophonological distinction between *yaqtul* preterit (imperfect consecutive) and jussive. For him,

waw in the perfect consecutive is morphologically unique. As Gesenius recognized, this *waw* "shares its various vocalization" with the simple conjunction (e.g., Ex. 6,7 וְיָדַעְתֶּם . . . וְלָקַחְתִּי 'I will take you . . . and you shall know'. 2 Sa. 15,36 וּשְׁלַחְתֶּם 'and you can send'. 1 Ki. 17,12 וַאֲכַלְנֻהוּ וָמָתְנוּ 'we shall eat and die'). Accordingly, it is internally justified to conclude that "[t]his *wāw* is in form an ordinary *wāw copulative.*"[241] Therefore, the demonstrative *waw* and the future **qátal* do not exist.

7.3. Unlike these morphological theories, a syntactic account of the perfect consecutive is currently in vogue. Moran led the way with his recognition that a construction identical to the perfect consecutive is attested in the Amarna letters. There, the conjunction *u* 'and' and perfect have future reference "in sentences which are implicitly or explicitly conditional."[242] Gordon added another construction to the inventory when he noted that the Ugaritic conjunction *w* 'and' and perfect can also behave like a perfect consecutive.[243] Here, too, the only persuasive examples appear in conditional sentences, and more particularly only in apodoses.[244] And in both languages, there is no evidence of a

---

the underlying preterit is **yáqtul,* whereas the jussive is the accentually different **yaqtúl* (Hetzron, *Journal of Semitic Studies,* xiv, 1969, p. 3; and, in this context, Z. Zevit, *Hebrew Studies,* xxix, 1988, p. 28). But, like Lambert, Hetzron is wrong. Any accentual discrepancy between the jussive and imperfect consecutive devolved from a late phonological rule governing the contextual accent shift (see §6.1). The distinctive accent in the imperfect consecutive is phonologically induced and is not traceable to an underlying accentual feature of **yaqtul* preterit (see R. L. Goerwitz, *Journal of the American Oriental Society,* cxii, 1992, pp. 198-203).

[241] Ges.-Kautzsch-Cowley, §49h; and, almost identically, Ges.-Rœdiger, 20th ed., §49.3. See also Olshausen, §229a Anm.; and Kennett, *A Short Account,* p. 53.

[242] Moran in *The Bible and the Ancient Near East,* p. 65.

[243] C. H. Gordon, *Ugaritic Textbook, Grammar* (Rome, 1965), §13.29. See also D. Sivan, *A Grammar of the Ugaritic Language* (Leiden/New York/Köhl, 1997), p. 98.

[244] M. S. Smith, *The Origins and Development of the* Waw-*Consecutive: Northwest Semitic Evidence from Ugarit to Qumran* (Atlanta, 1991), pp. 8-11.

compound consecutive verb form; the "consecutive" reading is derived from the perfect verb form in the apodosis of conditional sentences.[245]

According to the available historical-comparative evidence, the perfect consecutive may be far less different from the perfect than Driver or Lambert thought. In the Amarna letters and in Ugaritic, the "consecutive" perfect is a context-specific reading of the perfect. Hence, the perfect consecutive and perfect seem to be, in origin, morphologically identical. Further, this consecutive reading apparently originated in logically consequential clauses or apodoses. From this perspective, the Hebrew perfect consecutive may represent a grammaticalized form of the perfect, originally marking a particular type of dependent relation.[246]

7.4. The ultimate identity of the perfect and perfect consecutive is supported by Hebrew evidence as well. For example, the accent shift in the perfect consecutive is not as distinctive as it first appears. In first person plural forms, the accent position is identical in the perfect and perfect consecutive (e.g., Dt. 3,4. Jud. 21,22. Amos 6,13 לָקַחְנוּ 'we took'. Gen. 34,17. Jud. 20,10 וְלָקַחְנוּ 'we will take', respectively); this very form of the perfect consecutive does not participate in the accent shift (122). In other forms, the accent shift may be "very fluctuating" (e.g., Zech. 13,7 וַהֲשִׁבֹתִי יָדִי 'I shall turn my hand', yet Amos 1,8 וַהֲשִׁבוֹתִי יָדִי 'I shall turn my hand') (123).[247] Or the shift may be "hindered from taking place by external or accidental causes" (117), as in

---

[245] Cf., e.g., Moran in *Bible and the Ancient Near East*, p. 65, on Amarna; H. L. Ginsberg, *Orientalia*, v, 1936, p. 177, on Ugaritic; and, more generally, Lambert, *Revue des Études Juives*, xxvi, 1893, p. 50. On their theory of an underlying precative or optative perfect, cf. §3.3.

[246] Cf. T. Fenton in *Ugarit and the Bible: Proceedings of the International Symposium on Ugarit and the Bible, Manchester, September, 1992* (ed. G. J. Brooke, A. H. W. Curtis, and J. F. Healey; Münster, 1994), pp. 84-85. For a possible phonological effect of this grammaticalization, see §7.4, end.

[247] Some of the oxytone forms cited by Driver, however, may be explained phonologically. See Olshausen, §229a; and Böttcher, i. §410b.

third person *hiphil* forms (e.g., Josh. 7,9 וְהִכְרִיתוּ 'and they will wipe out'; see Jud. 4,24 הִכְרִיתוּ 'they wiped out'), certain forms of geminate roots (e.g., Isa. 34,3. Mic. 1,4 וְנָמַסּוּ 'they will melt'; see Ps. 97,5 נָמַסּוּ, 'they melt'), and certain final weak forms (e.g., Gen. 17,4. 24,41 etc. וְהָיִיתָ '[then] you shall be'; see 40,13. Dt. 5,15 etc. הָיִיתָ 'you were') (122-123). As these examples demonstrate, the accent shift is by no means an "inseparable criterion and accompaniment" of the perfect consecutive (cf. 117).[248] Moreover, when it does not occur, the perfect consecutive is phonologically identical to the simple perfect.

Driver attributed the absence of the consecutive accent shift to "external or accidental causes." On the contrary, however, the causes are internal and conditioned. For example, prosody is a major conditioning factor: whereas the shift takes place in contextual position, when the perfect consecutive is clause-initial or -medial, it does not occur in pausal position, when the perfect consecutive is clause-final (e.g., Gen. 32,19. 44,4 etc. וְאָמַרְתָּ 'you will say' [context]; cf. Isa. 14,4 וְאָמָרְתָּ 'you will say' [pause]) (see 110, 122).[249] In addition, the pausal variant of the perfect consecutive has the same accent pattern as the simple perfect (e.g., Jud. 4,8 וְהָלָכְתִּי 'I will go' [pause]. Jer. 2,23. Ps. 26,1. Job 31,5. Ruth 1,21. Neh. 2,16 הָלָכְתִּי 'I have gone'. Gen. 35,3 הָלַכְתִּי 'I have gone'; cf. Lev. 26,24.28. Jud. 1,3 etc. וְהָלַכְתִּי '[then] I will go' [context]). In pause, then, the accent of the perfect consecutive remains on the same syllable as in the perfect. Otherwise, under a conditioned, Hebrew-internal prosodic rule, the accent of the perfect consecutive can shift in contextual forms.

These prosodic variants can be anchored in the phonology as well. For the most part,[250] accent in Hebrew is sensitive to several

[248] See below with n. 259.
[249] E.g., Olshausen, §230.2; Böttcher, i. §497.5; Ges.-Roediger, 20th ed., §49.3 Rem. (= Ges.-Kautzsch-Cowley, §49m); and Ewald, *Lehrbuch,* 8th ed., §234d.
[250] Cf. n. 204.

syllabic factors, namely, syllable position, syllable closure, and syllable weight.[251] According to one rule, the accent is paroxytone when the ultima of a Hebrew form is open *and* its penult is (super-)heavy. This phonological rule holds true throughout the language, regardless of morphological category (e.g., Josh. 1,18. Jud. 13,12 etc. דְּבָרֶיךָ 'your words' [nominal]. Ez. 7,19 יַשְׁלִיכוּ 'they shall throw' [verb]. Job 21,18. 27,20 גְּנָבַתּוּ 'it has carried, carries him off' [verb-objective suffix]. חָלִילָה 'far be it' [particle]). It also applies to perfect and perfect consecutive forms that are accented identically, on the penultimate syllable: e.g., (ו)לקחנו, (ו)נמסו, and (ו)היית.[252] When the ultima is open and the penult is (super-)heavy, the Hebrew form is generally accented on the penult.[253]

But when these same phonological conditions appear in forms with both pausal and contextual variants, only one variant has the expected paroxytone accent. For example, pausal אָנֹכִי 'I' is paroxytone (e.g., Gen. 3,10. 4,9), whereas contextual אָנֹכִי is oxytone. Pausal עָתָּה 'now' (e.g., Gen. 32,5. Ex. 9,18) and עַתָּה (e.g., Gen. 46,34. Jud. 11,7) are paroxytone; contextual עַתָּה is oxytone. Or, as expected, אָנִי 'I' (e.g., Gen. 27,24.34.38), ולא יָכֹלוּ 'but they were unable' (Ex. 8,14. 2 Ki. 3,26. Jon. 1,13), and תְּדַבֵּרִי 'you (will) speak' (Isa. 29,4. Job 2,10) are pausal as well as paroxytone. The pausal variant, then, conforms to the phonological rule: when a form has an open ultima and (super-)heavy penult, the accent is assigned to the penultimate syllable, which, in pausal and contextual variants, coincides with that of the paroxytone pausal alternant. According to this rule of accent assignment, the pausal accent is therefore phonologically primary; the contextual alternant, phonologically secondary.[254]

---

[251] This broad formulation is sufficient for the present purposes. A more precise formulation, however, would consider underlying historical factors, which in turn would account for many apparent exceptions.

[252] Cf. Lambert, *Revue des Études Juives,* xx, 1890, pp. 76-77.

[253] See Revell, *Journal of the American Oriental Society,* civ, 1984, p. 438.

[254] E.g., Praetorius, *Über den rückweichenden Accent im Hebräischen,* pp.

So too in the perfect consecutive, when the ultima is open and the penult is (super-)heavy, the accent generally falls on the penultimate syllable. For example, וְלָקְחֻנוּ, וְנָמֹסוּ, and וְהָיִ֫ית are paroxytone for the same reason that their perfect counterparts are paroxytone: they conform to the accent rule. Similarly, in those perfect consecutive forms that have prosody-sensitive variants, only the pausal variant conforms to the rule: e.g., וְאָמָ֫רְתְּ and וְהָלַ֫כְתִּי.[255] The contextual variant does not; forms such as וְאָמַרְתְּ and וְהָלַכְתִּ֫י are oxytone and violate the phonological rule. Like other pausal variants throughout the language, the pausal form is phonologically primary in the perfect consecutive.[256]

In contrast, the phonologically secondary contextual variant results from a combination of prosodic, phonological, and morphological conditions. The phonological conditions, however, cannot be formulated with certainty,[257] because this accent shift is "not consistently carried out."[258] There are numerous and recurrent lexical exceptions.[259] Further, the accent shift is morphologically specific: It occurs only in the perfect consecutive; and within the perfect consecutive, some forms participate in the shift (first person singular and second person masculine singular), though another, structurally identical form does not (first

---

60-63; Philippi, *Deutsche Litteraturzeitung* xix, 1898, col. 1678; and J. Cantineau, *Bulletin d'études orientales,* i, 1931, p. 88.

[255] See Cantineau, *Bulletin d'études orientales,* i, 1931, p. 95; in conjunction with idem, *Bulletin d'études orientales,* ii, 1932, p. 141. See also J. Blau, *Israel Oriental Studies,* i, 1971, p. 22 n. 15.

[256] E.g., Kennett, *A Short Account,* p. 55; and Revell, *Journal of the American Oriental Society,* civ, 1984, pp. 440, 444.

[257] In addition to the references cited earlier in this section, see Gordon, *Journal of Biblical Literature,* lvii, 1938, pp. 319-325; and Revell, *Hebrew Annual Review,* ix, 1985, pp. 277-300.

[258] Ges.-Kautzsch-Cowley, §49k. See also Ges.-Rœdiger, 20th ed., §49.3 Rem.

[259] Cf. Lambert, *Revue des Études Juives,* xx, 1890, pp. 76-77; and, differently, Gordon, *Journal of Biblical Literature,* lvii, 1938, pp. 320, 323, 325.

person plural). In the perfect consecutive, then, the accent shift is inconsistently executed and depends on very specific morphological input.[260] This particular context-induced accent shift does not, strictly speaking, appear elsewhere in biblical Hebrew.

But the distinct contextual accent of any form, the perfect consecutive included, is secondary. As such, the morphology-specific sound change that affects certain contextual perfect consecutive forms would not, by definition, recur beyond the perfect consecutive. Nor does the sound change prove or disprove that the perfect and perfect consecutive are underlyingly different. In fact, the contextually conditioned accent is irrelevant. Only the pausal variants of the perfect consecutive are relevant to the comparison. They are phonologically primary, as well as regular and predicted by rule. They are also phonologically identical to the simple perfect. Rather than suggesting a difference between the perfect and perfect consecutive, the accentual evidence therefore suggests the opposite conclusion: with the exception of the idiosyncratic and developmentally secondary accent shift in the perfect consecutive, the perfect and perfect consecutive are ultimately identical.[261]

7.5. As Driver recognized, the perfect and perfect consecutive also share a semantic feature: resultative aspect (124 and 149, respectively). As an aspectual perfect, the perfect form inherently expresses "the continuing present relevance of a past situation."[262] The resultative perfect (perfect of result), in turn, is a subset of this aspectual value. "In the perfect of result, a present state is referred to as being the result of some past situation: this is one of the clearest manifestations of the present relevance of a past situation."[263] Thus the cases of the aspectual perfect (§3.2)

---

[260] Cf. Revell, *Hebrew Annual Review*, ix, 1985, pp. 289-290, 296-299.

[261] See also, in this context, Bauer, *Beiträge zur Assyriologie*, viii/1, 1910, pp. 30-35; and Müller, *Zeitschrift für Althebraistik*, vii, 1994, pp. 166-167.

[262] See n. 102.

[263] Comrie, *Aspect*, p. 56.

more particularly illustrate the resultative perfect aspect of the perfect verb form.[264] The resultative perfect consecutive is similar. It expresses a situation that results from a preceding situation or discourse context (e.g., Nu. 4,19 'do this for them וְחָיוּ and [as a result] they will live'. Jer. 48,26 'make him drunk . . . וְסָפַק and [as a result] Moab will vomit';[265] see also Isa. 6,7 'this has touched your lips, וְסָר your guilt will depart'. Gen. 2,24 'therefore a man leaves his father and his mother וְדָבַק and clings to his wife, וְהָיוּ becoming one flesh'. Ex. 21,12 'he who smites a man וָמֵת fatally') (see 118).[266] As a resultative construction, the perfect consecutive "is also found without being attached to any preceding verb from which to derive its special signification" (139) (e.g., Ex. 6,6 'I am the Lord. וְהוֹצֵאתִי I will bring you out').[267] Further, the resultative meaning of the perfect consecutive is functionally compatible with apodoses; for like its Amarna and Ugaritic ancestors, the perfect consecutive can introduce consequential clauses (e.g., Gen. 18,26 'if I find . . . וְנָשָׂאתִי I will forgive'. 43,9 'if I do not bring him back . . . וְחָטָאתִי I shall be guilty'; see also 1 Ki. 13,31 'when I die, וּקְבַרְתֶּם you should bury me'. Gen. 44,22 וְעָזַב 'were he to leave his father, וָמֵת he would die') (149, 153).[268] As these examples indicate, the perfect and perfect consecutive semantically overlap. One is a resultative perfect, the other a resultative construction.

While the perfect and perfect consecutive are semantically alike, they are also different. For example, Driver recognized that the two verb forms express different degrees of modal certainty.

---

[264] See ibid., pp. 56-58.

[265] See W. L. Holladay, *Jeremiah 2: A Commentary on the Book of the Prophet Jeremiah Chapters 26–52* (Minneapolis, 1989), p. 360.

[266] In addition to the references in n. 232, see Ewald, *Syntax of the Hebrew Language*, §342a; Müller, *Outlines of Hebrew Syntax*, §149; and, perhaps, Kennett, *A Short Account*, pp. 60-61.

[267] See Ewald, *Syntax of the Hebrew Language*, §344b.2.

[268] Ges.-Rœdiger, 20th ed., §126.6 Rem. 1b (= Ges.-Kautzsch-Cowley, §§112ff-kk). See also Müller, *Outlines of Hebrew Syntax*, §§26, 28.

Whereas the perfect expresses unqualified certainty (see §3.3), the perfect consecutive expresses substantially less. The perfect consecutive can "express what is not certain to happen, but is only probable, and so, perhaps, feared" (e.g., 20,11 'there is no fear of God in this place, וַהֲרָגוּנִי and they might kill me'. 34,30 וְנֶאֶסְפוּ 'should they unite against me וְהִכּוּנִי and attack me, וְנִשְׁמַדְתִּי I and my house will be destroyed'; see also 44,22) (see 141). As further support, Driver noted the many cases where the perfect consecutive follows an imperfect (or jussive) that "is preceded by various particles" (129). Among these particles Driver listed אוּלַי 'perhaps', אַל 'don't', בַּל/לֹא 'not', and פֶּן 'lest'; that is, the antecedent imperfect or jussive may be negated. The antecedent may be qualified by an interrogative (e.g., אֵיךְ 'how?', הֲ '?', הֲלֹא *nonne?*, לָמָה 'why?', and מָתַי 'when?'). It may also be preceded by a particle, whether modally conditional or functionally desiderative (e.g., אִם 'if', לוּ 'if [only]', and מִי 'would that') (130-136). Each of these particles, however, performs the same function: It qualifies the verb in modal terms, adding a layer of semantic uncertainty. The perfect consecutive, then, can follow a number of qualified imperfects and jussives that register, through their accompanying particles, greater uncertainty. Accordingly, the perfect and perfect consecutive are indeed modally unalike:[269] The perfect expresses certainty; the perfect consecutive expresses uncertainty. Stated broadly, the perfect and perfect consecutive are both the same (resultative perfect aspect) and different (modal [un]certainty).

8. *Conclusion.* When the *Treatise* is evaluated against its stated goals — "to supply . . . a systematic exposition, upon an adequate scale, of the nature and use of the Hebrew tenses" (v) — it must be considered a success. It is indeed a systematic exposition, taxonomically and formally arranged, of almost every Hebrew verb form. Its scale is not only adequate but remarkable;

---

[269] Cf. Kennett, *A Short Account,* pp. 53-55.

Driver provided more than sufficient examples and discussion both to evaluate his analysis and, when necessary, to enable a reanalysis. Further, despite his many diversions into related topics, the *Treatise* does concentrate on its two foci: the semantic nature and the pragmatic use of the individual verb forms. From this perspective alone, then, Driver accomplished what he set out to do.

8.1. He provided a basic semantic outline of the Hebrew verbal system, the principal component of which is aspect. For Driver, the entire verbal system is classified according to three aspects: incipience (imperfect), continuousness (participle), and completion (perfect). But upon reanalysis of the finite verb forms, this classification seems too narrow. Instead, the finite verb forms express perfectivity (perfect) (§3.1), imperfectivity (imperfect) (§4.3), as well as the perfect aspect (perfect; see also perfect consecutive) (§§3.2 and 7.5, respectively).

For Driver, mood is the other semantic component expressed by the Hebrew verb. On the one hand, some forms express speaker certainty and knowledge, as in the perfect (absolute certainty) (§3.3) and perfect consecutive (uncertainty) (§7.5). The imperfect belongs to this modal category as well, expressing reasonable certainty (§4.4). On the other hand, other verb forms express speaker attitude and especially will: the cohortative, imperative, and jussive (§5). In this latter series, each volitional form corresponds grammatically to the addressee's relative distance from the speaker: zero; proximate; and remote, respectively.

8.2. In addition to the nature of the Hebrew verb forms, Driver amply illustrated their individual use. For example, the perfective, certain perfect can be interpreted as a performative perfect (see §3.1) or as a "prophetic" perfect (§3.3). The imperfective imperfect can denote, *inter alia,* habituality, continuousness, and iterativity (§4.3); the reasonably certain imperfect can even have a volitional reading (§4.7). Among semantically volitional verbs, a range of interpretations is also possible. For example, the cohortative can be read as a statement of intention or as a weak proposal (§5.1). Similarly, the jussive has a wide pragmatic range, from command to wish (§5.3). In each case, the pragmatic reading correlates with the semantic meaning, varying with the discourse context.

The use of the consecutive verb forms shows, too, that they are pragmatically different from the simple verbs. Formally compound, they consist of a verbal stem and initial morpheme 'and'. This conjunction serves the grammatical function of connecting its verb with the preceding discourse (§6.4; see also §§7.2-3). This connective element can have a number of pragmatic readings, particularly in the case of the imperfect consecutive: e.g., succession and consequence, or introduction and explanation (§6.3). Further, these readings are no different from those of the conjunctive *waw* attached to any other word in Hebrew. Thus the readings of the consecutive prefix are united by a common grammatical feature — coordination — and are attested beyond the verbal system *per se* (see §1.2).

8.3. From this perspective, the study of the Hebrew verb intersects with the study of Hebrew syntax. The intersection can be morphological and grammatical as well as pragmatic. But Driver long recognized this convergence (§0.1) and also knew that, at times, the two cannot be separated. The full title of his book makes this point very clear indeed.[270]

---

[270] I thank John Huehnergard and Laura Kalman for their critical reading of this manuscript. I also thank Alan Cooper, Charles Jones, Tremper Longman III, and Cynthia Miller.

A TREATISE

ON

THE USE OF THE TENSES IN HEBREW.

— ◆ —

CHAPTER I.

Introduction.

1. THE Hebrew language, in striking contrast to the classical languages, in which the development of the verb is so rich and varied, possesses only two of those modifications which are commonly termed 'tenses.' These tenses were formerly known by the familiar names of *past* and *future*, but inasmuch as the so-called *past* tense is continually used to describe events in the future, and the so-called *future* tense to describe events in the past, it is clear that these terms, adapted from languages cast in a totally different mould from the Hebrew and other Semitic tongues, are in the highest degree inappropriate and misleading. It will be better therefore to acquiesce in the names now generally employed by modern grammarians, and deduced from real and not fictitious or accidental characteristics of the two forms in question, and to call them by the terms *perfect* and *imperfect*[1] respectively.

2. For if we adopt these designations, we shall be continually reminded of the fundamental[2] character of the two

---

[1] These words are of course employed in their etymological meaning, as signifying *complete* and *incomplete*: they must not be limited to the special senses they have acquired in Greek and Latin grammar.

[2] It will appear hereafter that the term *imperfect* does not in strictness

'tenses,' and be thereby enabled to discern a rational ground for such phenomena as those alluded to, § 1, which, especially to persons who are perhaps more familiar with the languages of modern or classical times, appear when approached for the first time so inexplicable, so contradictory, not to say so absurd. In order properly to understand this fundamental character, we shall have to revert to a distinction which, though not unknown in other languages, has not, until recent years, obtained from Hebrew grammarians the recognition and prominence which it deserves. I allude to the distinction between *order* of time and *kind* of time. In the first place, a particular verbal form may exhibit a given action as prior or subsequent to some date otherwise fixed by the narrative: this is a difference in the order of time. But, secondly, an action may be contemplated, according to the fancy of the speaker, or according to the particular point which he desires to make prominent, either as *incipient*[1], or as *continuing*, or as *completed*; the speaker may wish to lay stress upon the moment at which it begins, or upon the period over which it extends, or upon the fact of its being finished and done: these are differences in the kind of time. Thus, for example, ἔπειθε and πείθει differ in the order or date, not in the kind of action specified: each alike expresses a continuous action, but the one throws it into the past, the other places it in the present. On the other hand, πεῖσαι and πείθειν, μὴ πείσῃς and μὴ πεῖθε differ in kind, not in date; in each the date is equally indeterminate, but the aorist indicates a momentary act, the

---

correspond to a primary but to a derived characteristic of the tense called by that name. Böttcher in his *Ausf. Lehrbuch der Hebr. Sprache*, it must be admitted with greater precision, gives to the imperfect the name of *fiens*: but inasmuch as what is *incipient* is also necessarily *imperfect*, the latter term may be fairly held to express a fundamental attribute of the tense. No sufficient ground therefore seems to exist for abandoning the now usual nomenclature in favour of the new and peculiar term preferred by Böttcher.

[1] Or, viewed on the side of its subject, as *egressive*.

present one that is continuous. Now in Hebrew the tenses
mark only differences in the kind of time, not differences in
the order of time : i. e. they do not in themselves determine
the *date* at which an action takes place, they only indicate its
character or *kind*—the three phases just mentioned, those
namely of incipiency, continuance, and completion, being
represented respectively by the imperfect, the participle, and
the perfect [1].

3. Thus the 'tenses' in Hebrew, at least as regards what
they do *not* express, are in their inmost nature fundamentally
distinct from what is commonly known in other languages
by the same name : indeed they might almost more fitly
be called *moods* [2]. Certainly the difference between various
kinds of time is clearly marked in Greek : but then it exists
side by side with a full recognition and expression of the
other difference, which in our eyes is of paramount importance (as regards *kind* of time we are mostly less sensitive),
and which, nevertheless, Hebrew seems totally to disregard.
And this is just the novelty with which we are here so struck,
—the position occupied in the language by the one distinction
that it appreciates, with the consequences which follow from
it ; and the fact that Hebrew, unlike Greek and most other
languages, possesses no forms specifically appropriated to

---

[1] The distinction here drawn between the two relations, under which
every action may present itself, is also insisted on, and further illustrated,
by G. Curtius, in his *Elucidations of Greek Grammar* (translated by
Abbott), pp. 203–212.

[2] This was the term employed formerly by Ewald ; and Hitzig to the
end spoke of the perfect as the *first mood,* and of the imperfect as the
second mood. And in so far as each of the two forms in question seizes
and gives expression to a particular phase of an action, 'mood,' suggestive as it is of the idea of *modification,* might seem the preferable term
to adopt. Since, however, as we shall see, the Semitic languages developed for the imperfect special modal forms, which still exist in
Hebrew, though not in the same perfection they exhibit in Arabic, and
as it is convenient to have a separate name for the *genus,* of which these
modal forms are the *species,* the more customary titles may be retained.

indicate date, but meets the want which this deficiency must have occasioned by a subtle and unique application of the two forms expressive of kind. Only, inasmuch as an action may of course be regarded under either of the three aspects named above, whether it belong to the past, the present, or the future—a writer may e. g. look upon a future event as so certain that he may prefer to speak of it in the perfect as though already *done*—an ambiguity will arise as to which of these periods it is to be referred to, an ambiguity which nothing but the context, and sometimes not even that, is able to remove. The tenses in Isa. 9, 5 are identical with those in Gen. 21, 1–3: it is only the context which tells us that in the one case a series of events in the future, in the other one in the past is being described. On the other hand, יֵרֵד Ex. 33, 9 refers to the past, 19, 11 to the future, although the tense does not vary; and יָסוּר שָׁמָּה relating, 2 Ki. 4, 10, to the future, is used two verses previously to describe what happened in the past.

4. This peculiarity, however, is only an extension of what meets us, for instance, in Greek. We are sufficiently familiar with the distinction between ἐλάλησαν (as Acts 16, 32) and ἐλάλουν (as 19, 6): we are apt to forget that a similar distinction may appertain to events in the future as well as in the past. And, further, has not the *exact* date of both the actions quoted to be fixed from the context? Within what limits of time did the action ἐλάλησαν take place? and does ἐλάλουν signify 'they *used* to talk' (over a long period of time), or 'they *were* talking' (at the moment arrived at by the history, or when the writer came upon the scene), or 'they *began and continued* talking' (as consequent upon some occurrence previously described)? 'The imperfect,' it has been said, 'paints a scene:' true, but upon what part of the canvas? upon a part *determined by the whole picture*. And what has just been said we shall find to be pre-eminently true of the tenses as employed in Hebrew.

5. The tenses, then, in so far as they serve to fix the date of an action, have a relative not an absolute significance. It will, however, be evident that, since it is more usual, especially in prose, to regard a past event as completed, and a future event as uncompleted, the perfect will be commonly employed to describe the former, and the imperfect to describe the latter; but this distinction of usage is not maintained with sufficient uniformity to justify the retention of the old titles *past* and *future*, which will now clearly appear to express relations that are of only secondary importance, and only partially true. It is, on the other hand, of the utmost consequence to understand and bear constantly in mind the fundamental and primary facts stated above: (1) that the Hebrew verb notifies the character without fixing the date of an action, and (2) that, of its two forms with which we have here more particularly to deal, one is calculated to describe an action as *nascent* and so as imperfect; the other to describe it as *completed* and so as perfect. Upon these two facts the whole theory of the tenses has to be constructed; and the latter fact, at any rate, will be most readily remembered by the use of terms which at once recall to the mind the distinction involved in it.

6. The use of the Hebrew tenses will be better understood and more thoroughly appreciated if we keep in mind some of the peculiarities by which Hebrew style, especially the poetical and prophetical style, is characterized. One such peculiarity is the ease and rapidity with which a writer *changes his standpoint*, at one moment speaking of a scene as though still in the remote future, at another moment describing it as though present to his gaze. Another characteristic is a love for variety and vividness in expression: so soon as the pure prose style is deserted, the writer, no longer contenting himself with a series, for instance, of perfects, diversifies his language in a manner which mocks any effort to reproduce it in a Western tongue; seizing each individual detail he invests it with a character of its own—you see it perhaps emerging into the light, perhaps standing there with clearly-cut outline before you—and presents his readers with a picture of surpassing brilliancy and life.

Obs. 1. With what has been said above, compare the opinion expressed, from a very independent point of view, by Bishop Patteson :— ' I wish some of our good Hebrew scholars were sound Poly- and Melanesian scholars also. I believe it to be quite true that the *mode of thought* of a South Sea islander resembles very closely that of a Semitic man. . . . The Hebrew narrative viewed from the Melanesian *point of thought* is wonderfully graphic and lifelike. The English version is dull and lifeless in comparison' (*Life*, by Miss Yonge, 1874, ii. p. 475 f.). Again, ' An Englishman says, "When I get there, it will be night." But a Pacific islander says, "I am there, it is night." The one says, "Go on, it will soon be dark;" the other, "Go on, it has become already night." Any one sees that the one possesses the power of realizing the future as present or past; the other, *now*, whatever it may have been once, does not exercise such power' (p. 189). And so, ' the Hebrew's mind (and his speech) moved on with his thought, and was present with the whole range of ideas included in the thought' (p. 505). The time is ' not inherent in the *tense* at all' (p. 476).

Obs. 2. It does not fall within the scope of the present work to discuss at length the origin and structure of the two forms; though some indication of the principal opinions that have been held may not be out of place. The subject is discussed by Dietrich, *Abhandlungen zur Hebr. Grammatik* (1846), pp. 97 ff. (specially on the imperfect); Turner, *Studies Biblical and Oriental* (1876), pp. 338 ff.; Sayce, *The Tenses of the Assyrian Verb* (in the *Journal of the Royal Asiatic Society*, Jan. 1877); and especially by Dr. Wright, *Comparative Grammar of the Semitic Languages* (1890), pp. 164 ff.; and on the other side (so far as the imperfect is concerned), by Philippi, *ZDMG.* xxix. 1875, pp. 171–174. In the perfect the resemblance of the third pers. masc. to an adjectival or participial form is evident and generally recognized: the oldest ending of the 3 sing. fem. -*at* is closely akin to that of the ordinary fem. of Arabic nouns: the 3 pl. -*û*[1] is, perhaps, only modified from

---

[1] The form in ‏ן‎, found thrice in the O. T. (Dt. 8, 3. 16. Isa. 26, 16), is hardly old: it appears, in fact, to be a *secondary* formation (see Nöldeke, *ZDMG.* 1884, p. 410 f.), found occasionally in Syriac and Mandaic, and more frequently in later dialects, as that of the Palest. Targums,

the usual pl. form -*ûna* by the omission of the final -*na* (which is dropped also in the st. c. of nouns). In the third person, therefore, the subject is not expressly represented, nor are there any *distinctively* verbal forms: in the second and first persons, on the contrary, the subject is regularly marked by a formative element appended to the base, the pronominal origin of which can hardly be mistaken (-*tā*, -*tem*, evidently akin to אַתָּה, אַתֶּם: and the old Semitic -*kū*, -*nā*, doubtless connected with the -*kī* and -*nū* of אֲנֹכִי, אֲנוּ, אֲנַחְנוּ)[1].

In the imperfect, the first and second persons are formed pretty plainly by the aid of pronominal elements, though no longer affixed, as in the perfect, but prefixed, and not attached to a base bearing a concrete signification (participial), but to a base with one that is *abstract*[2], —mostly, indeed, agreeing in form with the infinitive. The origin of the third pers. is not so clear, and two divergent views have found their supporters. The old explanation, which derived the preformative י from הוא, pronounced 'tolerably satisfactory' by Gesenius in his *Lehrgebäude* (1817), p. 274, and accepted by Ewald until 1844, must indeed for valid reasons (Dietrich, 122–126; Turner, 371 f.) be rejected, though voices are still occasionally heard in its favour (see J. Grill, *ZDMG.* xxvii. 434; F. E. König, *Lehrgebäude der Hebr. Spr.* i. (1881) pp. 156–9). The later theory of Ewald (*Lb.* § 191[a]) that the י is 'weakened from *l* or *n*' (the latter being the regular Syriac form) is likewise open to objection: but the view that a pronominal element still lies hidden in the prefix, alike in Syriac and in the other dialects, is capable of being

---

the Jerus. Talm., the *Midrashim*, the *Evangeliarium Hierosolymitanum* (5th–6th cent. A.D.), published by Miniscalchi Erizzo; but mostly quite as an exceptional form. Examples: from Syriac, Acts 28, 2 ܡܛܪ̈ܐ (see also Hoffmann, § 53. 3; Merx, *Gramm. Syr.* p. 333; Nöldeke, *Syr. Gramm.* §§ 158 D. 176 E); from the Pal. Targs., the Jer. Targ. of Ex. 16, 1 אתון. Nu. 20, 21 סתון, הוון. 29 חמון, הימינון, בכון. Dt. 32, 16 אקנון. 30 ארגזון, *al.*, Ps. 53, 5 סערון. 54, 5 קמון. 69, 2 איציקון. 76, 7 דמכון. 77, 17 רתיתון. 78, 58 אקנון. 106, 20 פרגון, *al.*; and esp. in verbs ל"א, as 48, 6. 58, 9 חמון; 60, 9. 62, 10 הוון; 106, 11 חפון; 107, 30 חדון, etc.; from Samaritan, Gen. 19, 2 ואמרון (also the imper. וביתון). 3 ואכלון; 32, 23. In the *Ev. Hier.* there are two instances (*ZDMG.* xxii. p. 491), ܬܕܚܠܘܢ and ܬܫܟܚܘܢ. Under the circumstances, the three isolated forms in the O. T. can hardly be original: had the form been in actual use in ancient Hebrew, it is difficult not to think that instances would have been more frequent.

[1] See more fully Dr. Wright's *Comp. Gr.* pp. 164 ff.
[2] A genuine Semitic construction: comp. below, § 189.

placed upon a more defensible basis ; and it is accordingly asserted by
Dillmann, *Aeth. Gramm.* § 101. 2, and, in particular, by Philippi,
ZDMG. l. c., who points, for example, to the traces of old demonstrative
roots *ya* and *na* existing in the different Semitic languages [1], and whose
arguments are well worthy of consideration. Many recent grammarians
have, however, given their assent, more or less pronounced, to the
powerful reasoning by which Dietrich, in the Essay referred to above,
advocates the originally nominal character of the third person. The
line of argument pursued by him may be stated very briefly as follows.
Dietrich starts with the remark that it would only be natural to find in
the imperfect the two peculiarities observed in the perfect, the presence
in it, viz., of a *double mode* of flexion—the first and second persons
being compounded with pronouns, the third being formed and declined
on the analogy of a noun—and the fact that the ground-form of the
tense, the third masc., is not distinguished by any special sign of
the person : he next calls attention to the features in which the third
imperfect, especially in Arabic, resembles and is treated as a noun—
features recognized and noted by the native Arabic grammarians (Wright,
Arab. Gr. i. § 95), and doubtless forming a strong argument in favour
of the theory : in the third place, he collects (pp. 136–151), from Hebrew
and the other dialects, numerous examples of the nominal form ילקוש,
יצהר ,יריב ,יקום, etc., which, though in some cases even identical with
the tense-form, still cannot as a class be derived from it (on account of
their varying vocalization, their appearance in Syriac, and for other
reasons), but must be regarded as an independent though parallel formation. This form is in use to represent sensible qualities or attributes,—
originally, it would seem, as purely mental conceptions, i. e. as abstract
(cf. יען ,יתור), but in practice restricted mainly to the representation of
the quality as manifested in some concrete object : hence, as a rule, it
designates an object under a specially active or conspicuous attribute,
being often employed adjectivally to denote a striking bodily peculiarity
or defect, or to provide a name for some plant or animal from a characteristic feature [2].

---

[1] As in אני=*'an* + *ya :* cf. Wright, *Comp. Gr.* p. 99.
[2] The *transition* of meaning indicated above is essential to Dietrich's
own view of the parallelism between the noun and the tense; the imperfect, with him, denotes primarily an action or state, not (like the perfect)
as objectively realized, but as subjectively *conceived*—as assumed, for
example, by the speaker, or as desired or viewed by him as conditional
or dependent : its concrete application, though predominant, is deduced
and secondary.

Dietrich now advances, but with greater reserve (p. 155, *ohne mehr als die Stelle einer Muthmaassung in Anspruch zu nehmen*), a similar explanation for the third fem. As תקטל is not distinguished from יקטל by the usual mark of the feminine, the first step is to shew that cases exist in which the Semitic languages give expression to a difference of gender, not by the normal change of termination, but by having recourse to a different derivative (e. g. masc. *akbaru*, fem. *kubra*ᵞ). Next, he collects, as before, instances of the substantives created by prefixing ה, pointing out the close resemblance between the various groups of these and the groups formed with י, and indicating the reasons which forbid their being treated as themselves derivatives from the imperfect (pp. 139, 165-171), while at the same time they are plainly parallel to it. The characteristic of this class is to represent an action under the most abstract relation possible : it is thus strongly contrasted with the previous class exhibiting י, and is adapted, in accordance with the principle just established, to mark the opposite gender,—its appropriation for this purpose being probably facilitated by the resemblance of the prefix ה to the ordinary sign of the feminine (cf. Turner, p. 374; Sayce, p. 30; Stade, § 505). In a word, according to Dietrich, out of the double group of nouns, analogous in form, but contrasted in signification, one of uniform formation was selected from each—of course, at a remote period, when both forms were, so to say, more *fluid* than they subsequently remained—and set apart to mark the two opposite genders of the nascent tense. And, in conclusion, the Syriac imperfect in נ is shewn to be capable of an explanation in complete agreement with the same theory, being similarly related to a corresponding nominal form in נ, existing both in Syriac itself and also in Hebrew.

This hypothesis of the origin of the third pers. is accepted substantially by Böttcher, § 925 (the י not a mark of the person, but of the tense); Merx, p. 199 f.; Koch, *Der Semitische Infinitive* (1874), p. 7 ; Turner, p. 373 f.; Sayce, *l. c.*, pp. 23–27, 30–32 ; and Stade, *Lehrbuch der Hebr. Grammatik* (1878), § 478ᶜ. While agreeing on the whole, however, these scholars differ as to details : thus Böttcher expressly disconnects, § 927, the ה of the fem. from the nominal ה, § 547ᵈ, and Stade also considers that it is difficult. Mr. Turner, again, lays no stress on Dietrich's first, or abstract, stage; and Prof. Sayce appears disposed to identify unduly (pp. 29, 33) the form of the third pers. with the base of the first and second. Olshausen, *Lehrbuch* (1861), § 226ᶜ, regarded the explanation of the third pers. as 'still obscure;' Kautzsch, in the 25th ed. of Gesenius' Grammar (1889), § 47. 2, and Aug. Müller, in his *Schulgrammatik* (1878), § 171ᵃ, express themselves in similar terms, although the latter inclines towards Dietrich's view in the case of the masc.

(§ 174ª). Dr. Wright, however (*Comp. Gr.* pp. 179, 182), thinks that the prefix *ya* must be of pronominal origin = 'one who,' though he is apparently dissatisfied with the parallels cited by Philippi, and admits that he cannot explain it etymologically. The ‍ח‍ of the fem. he supposes (p. 184) to be the same mark of the fem. gender which appears at the end of the oldest form of the 3 sing. fem. in the perfect.

The discovery of the origin of a grammatical form is of the highest value to the comparative philologist, or the student of primitive modes of thought ; it does not of necessity throw fresh light directly upon the meaning borne by it in practice, particularly if the period of formation be long anterior to that in which the examples of its use actually occur. In the case before us, either view must be regarded at present as conjectural : the cognate languages do not exhibit the imperfect tense in a form so diverse from the Hebrew as to enable us to perceive, either immediately or by a conclusive inference, the elements of which it is composed ; there are probable arguments in abundance, but no crucial fact appears to have been yet produced. The utmost that can be done is to appeal to analogy. Much has been said, for instance, on the originally *abstract* character of the third imperfect : and in favour of the assumption languages such as Turkish are cited, in which certainly the third pers. of the past tense appears to be an abstract substantive ; still before we can build with safety upon the analogy, we ought to possess some practical acquaintance with the languages in question, both as regards their general character and (if possible) their history. Otherwise the comparison may be superficial or unreal. Again, in the particular form which the theory takes in Dietrich's hands, it should be remembered that it depends upon a coincidence,—upon the agreement between an assumed transition of meaning in the noun and an assumed derivation of significations in the tense. And in applying it to the purpose immediately before us, there is an additional difficulty in the fact that it postulates a *triple* structure for a single tense. The perfect is formed homogeneously throughout : the imperfect, on the contrary, presents one formation for the third masc., another for the third fem., a third for the other persons (for Philippi is certainly right in maintaining, against Koch, that these cannot be naturally explained as contracted from *ta-yaktul, a-yaktul*, etc.—the pronominal element being prefixed to the form of the third pers. *yaktul*) : which of these three, now, is to be regarded as expressing the fundamental character of the tense ? The second fem., not being a primary formation, may indeed be set aside : but with which of the other two are we to start in our exposition *à priori* of the meaning conveyed by it ? Perhaps, however, it may be fair to assume that the third pers. masc. gave the *type* of the tense, to which the other persons, though constructed out of different elements, were then made conformable, the external parallelism of form being symbolical of the internal unity of signification thereby secured to the entire tense. This being so, its representative power will be ana'ogous to that of the corresponding nominal form : i. e. (if we confine ourselves to what is the predominant signification of the noun) it will depict an act or attribute, not as a quiescent fact, but as the manifestation of an energy residing in the subject, or as ' a stream evolving itself from its source :' the subject will be conceived as exerting itself in the production of an activity, the action as egressive (cf. Turner, pp. 376 f., 383-385). יראה, ישמח, there is the faculty of seeing, the capacity of joy, realizing itself in the subject ; the processes of seeing, of rejoicing, are not represented to us as completed (as by the perf., ' in einem nach allen Seiten hin begränzten und erfasslichen Bilde,' Dietrich, p. 113), but as being actively manifested by the subject ; in other words, he *sees, rejoices*. Here the alternative theory of the nominal origin of the third pers. is represented in its simplest form. Fortunately, however, the view thus obtained of the primary idea of the tense hardly differs materially from that which has been already expressed in these pages ; for such terms as *incipient, nascent, progressive*, §§ 2, 21, 43 (understood in connexion with the context), do not convey an appreciably different conception from that which now occurs to me as fairly embodying the other opinion (at least as held by Mr. Turner), viz. *egressive*. As the latter makes prominent what after all is the fundamental fact, namely, the objective relation of the action to the subject which exhibits it, I have not scrupled to introduce it, together with a few other modifications, into the text of this and the third chapter.

It may be worth while to add that analogies exist in other languages for the substantival character of the verb, which must certainly be allowed in the case of the third pers. of the Semitic perf., and which is postulated by Dietrich's theory for the third pers. impf. There was doubtless a time when ' noun ' and ' verb' were as yet indistinguishable (cf. Curtius, *Das Verbum der Griech. Sprache*, i. p. 13), and Schleicher has shewn in a lucid and valuable Essay, *Die Unterscheidung von Nomen und Verbum in der lautlichen Form* (extracted from the *Abhandlungen der phil.-hist. Classe der Kön.-Sachs. Gesellschaft der Wissenschaften*, iv. 1865), that the clearness and decision with which the Aryan family of speech has expressed the distinction of noun and verb, is far from being a general characteristic of other languages. In Indo-Germanic, ' words which have or had a case-suffix are nouns, those which have or had a personal suffix are verbs :' but the third pers. of the Semitic perf. at once reveals to us that the separation of the two parts of speech is by no means here so complete. Semitic, in this respect, resembles rather, for instance, Finnish, in which (p. 530) *saa* being ' accipere,' and *saa-va* ' accipiens,' the third pl. pres. is *saa-va-t* ' accipiunt,' lit. ' accipientes :' or Samoyedic, where an adjective, and even a substantive, may be used and conjugated exactly as a verb (pp. 537, 539); and where the possessive suffixes to the noun and the personal suffixes in the verb bear the closest resemblance to each other (so also pp. 527, 535, 542); or Mexican (p. 568), where there are no ' true verbs ' (cf. Steinthal, *Characteristik*, pp. 216–218),—the plural of the verb being formed in the same manner as that of the noun [1]. The agreement of the third pers. with a nominal form, and the absence from it of any personal sign is in fact, he remarks (p. 515), a phenomenon often meeting us in other languages [2], particularly where the verb is no verb in the Indo-Germanic sense of the word, but rather a noun : in such cases, the pronoun of the third pers. calls for no special designation, being understood of itself, and it is only the other persons which require to be separately indicated. Though we must not place Semitic on a level with the Polynesian Dayak (respecting·which, see Steinthal, p. 165, or Sayce, *Principles of Comparative Philology*, p. 281, ed. 1), we may admit, with Dietrich (p. 136) and Turner (p. 366), no less than with Schleicher, that the distinction between noun and verb does not find in it, formally, the same clear expression as in the languages of our own Aryan family [3].

---

[1] Schleicher's thesis, ' that no grammatical categories exist in the consciousness of the speaker which do not find formal expression in sound,' is doubtless enunciated in terms which are too general, and cases may readily be imagined in which it does not apply (see, above all, Bréal, *Sur les idées latentes du langage*, in his *Mélanges de Mythologie et de linguistique*, pp. 300 f., 308 ff., 312 ff.); but he is right in refusing as a rule to credit a people with a sense of grammatical relations which find no expression in their speech, and in protesting against the assumption— often unconsciously influencing us—according to which all languages are framed on the same model, expressing the same distinctions, and possessing the same resources, as those with which we happen to be ourselves familiar.

[2] Instances from Magyar (p. 527), and from the Mongolian Buriat (p. 546), in which ' the third perf., in form and signification alike, is a noun.'

[3] Comp. further, on the subject of the preceding note, J. Barth, *Die Nominalbildung in den Semitischen Sprachen* (1889–91), pp. 228, 279 f., 484 f.

CHAPTER II.

The Perfect alone.

N. B. Throughout the present volume, in every pointed word quoted without its proper accent, the tone is *always on the ultima* (milra'), *unless specially marked otherwise* by ⌣. Attention to the position of the tone is of importance for a right understanding of the language; and the necessity of observing it cannot be too emphatically inculcated. By acquiring the habit of doing this regularly, the eye will become trained so as to notice it instinctively and without effort, and will be at once arrested by any deviation a word may present from the customary rule.

7. THE perfect tense, in accordance with its fundamental character, as stated § 2, is used—

(1) As equivalent to the Greek aorist, to denote an action completed and finished at a definite moment in the past, fixed by the narrative; as Gen. 1, 1. 3, 16 unto the woman אָמַר *he said.* 10, 8 יָלַד. 25, 30 קָרָא. 32, 11 *I passed over.* 49, 30 f. Ps. 18, 5. 6. 9. 30, 3. 32, 4 *was turned.*

Even though the action indicated by the verb should itself extend over a considerable period; as Ex. 1, 7 פָּרוּ. 12, 40. Nu. 9, 23. Dt. 2, 14. 1 Ki. 15, 2 three years מָלַךְ *he reigned.* Ps. 35, 13 f.; or even though it be repeated, as in 1 Sa. 18, 30[1].

8. (2) Like the Greek perfect, to denote an action completed in the past, but with the accessory idea of its conse-

---

[1] Whether in cases like these the pf. or impf. is employed, depends naturally upon the *animus loquentis*: if the speaker does not desire to lay any special stress on the frequency or continuance of an event, the simplest and most obvious way of designating it will be by the employment of the perfect.

quences continuing up to the time at which the words are uttered: it is thus employed to describe an action resulting in a *state*, which may be of longer or shorter duration, according to the context.   Thus Gen. 4, 6 why נפלו *hath* thy face *fallen?* 32, 11 *I have become* (LXX γέγονα) two camps. Isa. 1, 4 *have forsaken* Yahweh. 5, 24ᵇ. Ps. 3, 7. 5, 11. 10, 11 הסתיר. 16, 6. 17, 5 בַּל נָמֹוטוּ *have* not *tottered.* 11. 18, 37. 22, 2. 31, 15 *have trusted.*

Where the consequences of such an action continue into the present we may sometimes render by the present tense, although, if idiom permits it, it is better to preserve the perfect.   Amos 5, 14 as *ye say.* Ps. 2, 1 why do the peoples rage? (*have raged*—an action which the context shews has not ceased at the moment of the poet's writing).   38, 3–9 *are* filled, *am* benumbed, etc. 88, 7–10. 14. 16–19. Isa. 21, 3 f. Job 19, 18–20.

Obs. It is of importance to keep the aoristic and perfect senses of this tense distinct, and also to ascertain upon every occasion which of the two is meant, whether, in other words, the action or state described by the tense is one which has ceased, or one which still continues.   There is frequently some difficulty upon this point, especially in the Psalms: and unless care be taken in translation, the sense of a passage may be much obscured.   For instance, Ps. 31, 7 f. (Heb. 8 f.) in the English Versions, is only intelligible by the side of *v.* 10, if the perfects are explained according to § 14.   This is possible, but it is more natural to suppose that the two cohortatives express a wish or prayer rather than an intention, and that ראית, ידעת are aoristic, relating to a former condition of things now come to an end.   The English 'thou hast considered' in no way suggests the possibility of such a termination: and the sense of the Hebrew is only properly represented by 'sawest . . . tookest notice of,' etc. (so Cheyne).   Similarly, 32, 4 (*was*, not *is;* the context shews that the period of depression is past); but 35, 15 f. 21 ('rejoice, gather,' etc.: the petition *v.* 17 is an indication that the persecution described does not belong wholly to the past): 39, 3 *was* dumb, but *v.* 10 *am* dumb.

The same doublesidedness of the perfect will explain Lam. 3, 55–58: the pff. in these verses are aoristic, describing a state of things *anterior* as well to *vv.* 52–54 as to *vv.* 59–61 (ראיתה *v.* 59 exactly as Ps. 10, 14.

35, 22: the change from *v.* 54 to *v.* 55 is not more abrupt or unprepared than the very similar one between Job 30, 31 and 31, 1). In Lam. 4, 7 (*were*). 8 (*is*), the two senses occur side by side.

9. (3) In cases where in English the perfect *has* is used idiomatically to describe an action occurring in the past at a moment which the speaker is not able or not desirous to specify more closely; as 1 Sa. 12, 3 whose ox לָקַחְתִּי *have I taken?* [or *did I* (ever) *take?*]. 4[1]. Ps. 3, 8 thou hast smitten (on some previous occasion). 4, 2. 7, 4. 21, 3. 37, 35[2]. 44, 2. Pr. 21, 22 (cf. Qoh. 9, 14 f.). Job 4, 3. 9, 4. 30, 25. 31, 5 etc. 33. 34, 31. 37, 20 did a man ever say (=intend *or* command) that he should be annihilated? Jer. 2, 11[a].

In these cases, the limits of time within which the action must lie are obvious from the context: passages like Gen. 4, 1 קָנִיתִי. 10 מֶה עָשִׂיתָ *what hast thou done* (a few moments ago)? or *what didst thou do?* (just now; but the former is the English idiom). 32, 27. 31. 41, 28. Ex. 2, 18. Nu. 22, 34. Ps. 2, 7[c]. 30, 4. 48, 4 נוֹדַע hath made himself known; and the common phrase כֹּה אָמַר יְהֹוָה Ex. 4, 22 etc. lead us on to the next usage.

10. (4) Here the perfect is employed to describe the immediate past, being generally best translated by the present; as Gen. 14, 22 הֲרִמֹתִי *I lift up* (have this moment, as I speak, lifted[3]) my hand to heaven. 1 Sa. 17, 10 חֵרַפְתִּי I reproach. 2 Sa. 16, 4 I bow myself down. 17, 11 I advise. 19, 30 I say. 1 Ki. 1, 35 ואתו צויתי and him do I appoint to be prince over Israel, etc. 2 Chr. 2, 12 (in a letter[4]) I send.

11. (5) Closely allied to (3) is the use of the perfect with such words as יָדַעְתִּי Gen. 4, 9. 21, 26 *I have* not *known=I*

---

[1] Cf. Thucyd. 5, 103 οὐ καθεῖλεν, *never ruined.*

[2] Comp. Sophocles, Ajax 1142 (aorist), 1150 (perfect).

[3] Compare in Greek the so-called 'aorist of immediate past,' so common in the tragedians, e. g. Aesch. Choeph. 423. Soph. El. 668 ἐδεξάμην (*I welcome*) τὸ ῥηθέν. 677 etc.

[4] Cf. 2 Cor. 8, 18. Acts 23, 30.

do not *know;* זָכַרְנוּ Nu. 11, 5 *we remember;* כַּאֲשֶׁר אָהֵב Gen.
27, 9 as *he loveth.* In verbs like these, expressive of a state
or condition, whether physical or mental, which, though it may
have been attained at some previous time, nevertheless continues to exist up to the moment of speaking, the emphasis
rests so often upon the latter point, that the English *present*
most adequately represents the force of the original perfect.

To the verbs already cited may be added, as belonging to
the same class, the following, which are selected from the list
given by Böttcher, *Ausf. Lehrbuch*, § 948: by this grammarian they are not inaptly termed *verba stativa* or 'statives,'
אֻמְלַל *to languish;* בטח *to trust* Ps. 26, 2 etc.; נבה *to be high*
Isa. 55, 9; גָּדֵל *to be great* Ps. 92, 6; דָּמָה *to be like* Ps. 144,
4; זקן *to be old* Ruth 1, 12; חָסָה *to take refuge* Ps. 7, 2 etc.;
טהר *to be clean* Pr. 20, 9; יָכֹל *to be able* Ps. 40, 13; מֵאֵן *to
refuse* Ex. 10, 3; מאס *to despise* Job 7, 16; מלא *to be full* Ps.
104, 24; צדק *to be just* Job 10, 15. 34, 5; קָטֹן *to be small*
Gen. 32, 11; רבב *to be*[1] *many* Ps. 104, 24; שמח *to rejoice*
1 Sa. 2, 1; שָׂנֵא *to hate* Ps. 5, 6; add היה Gen. 42, 11. Isa.
15, 6; חפצתי Ps. 40, 9 etc.[2]

It will be understood, however, that many of these verbs
are found also as aorists, i. e. with the emphasis not on the
continuance of the state described, but on its commencement, or upon the fact of its existence generally at some
period in the past; e. g. Gen. 28, 16 לא ידעתי *I knew* it not.
37, 3. 1 Sa. 10, 19. 22, 22. Ps. 39, 3 (p. 14). 41, 10. In
itself the perfect enunciates simply the completion of an act:
it is by way of accommodation to the usage of another language that, eliciting its special force from the context, we

---

[1] ' To *become* many,' i. e. be multiplied, is רָבָה.

[2] Cf. μέμαα, πέφυκα, πέποιθα, οἶδα, ἔρρωμαι, etc. *We* commonly denote a state by the use of the present: the Greek, in verbs like these,
' conceives it as the result of the act necessary for attaining it, and therefore denotes it by the perfect.'

make the meaning more definite by exhibiting it explicitly, as occasion demands, under the form of an aorist, a perfect, or a present.

12. (6) It is used to express general truths known to have actually occurred, and so proved from experience: here again the idiomatic rendering in English is by means of the present[1]: Isa. 1, 3ᵃ. 40, 7. 8. 23. Ps. 7, 16 כָּרָה he *hath dug* or *diggeth* a pit and holloweth it out. 10, 3. 33, 13 f. 34, 11. 37, 23. 39, 12. 84, 4 מָצְאָה, שָׁתָה[2]. Pr. 22, 12. 13. Jer. 10, 13ᵇ. Qoh. 8, 14 (*has taken* place, or *takes* place). Comp. 1 Sa. 20, 2 Kt.

13. (7) The perfect is employed to indicate actions the accomplishment of which lies indeed in the future, but is regarded as dependent upon such an unalterable determination of the will that it may be spoken of as having actually taken place: thus a resolution, promise, or decree, especially a Divine one, is frequently announced in the perfect tense. A striking instance is afforded by Ruth 4, 3, where Bo'az, speaking of No'ŏmi's determination to sell her land, says, מָכְרָה נָעֳמִי lit. *has sold* (has resolved to sell: the Engl. idiom would be *is selling*). Gen. 23, 11 *I give* thee the field; 13, Abraham replies, נָתַתִּי *I give* thee the value of the field (although the money does not actually pass till *v.* 16). 15, 18 to thy seed *I give* this land; similarly 1 Ki. 3, 13. Isa. 43, 14. Jer. 31, 33; Jud. 15, 3 נְקֵיתִי, referring to the contemplated

---

[1] Though in particular cases a perfect may be used.

Both the pf. and aorist (the 'gnomic' aorist) are similarly used in Greek: Xen. Mem. 4, 2. 35 πολλοὶ δὲ διὰ δόξαν καὶ πολιτικὴν δύναμιν μεγάλα κακὰ πεπόνθασιν (preceded by three *presents*); cf. the aorist Plato Rep. 566 D. E. in the description of the conduct of the τύραννος, also Il. 9, 320. 13, 62. 243. 300. 14, 217. 18, 309 etc.

In the gnomic aorist (which is sometimes found coupled with the present, as Il. 17, 177 ὅστε καὶ ἄλκιμον ἄνδρα φοβεῖ, καὶ ἀφείλετο νίκην Ῥηϊδίως·) 'a fact of the past is exhibited as a rule for all time.'

[2] Not *may lay* (A.V.), which would be תשׁית: the word states a fact, exactly as מצאה does.

act of violence. 1 Sa. 15, 2. Ez. 21, 9 (cf. 8) הִכְרַתִּי. Lev. 26,
44 nevertheless, when they are in the land of their enemies,
לֹא מְאַסְתִּים *I do not reject them.* Ps. 20, 7 now know I that
Yahweh *is sure to save* his anointed. Nu. 32, 19 בָּאָה (*mil'el,*
and so pf., not ptcp.[1]). 2 Chr. 12, 5 עזבתי.

Here also may be noticed the use of the pf. in Jer. 4, 13
Woe to us, for שֻׁדָּדְנוּ : *we are undone!* (at the prospect of the
invader's approach : comp. ὄλωλα, and such phrases as Il. 15,
128 μαινόμενε, φρένας ἠλέ, διέφθορας). Isa. 6, 5. Ps. 31, 23.
Lam. 3, 54. Nu. 17, 27.

14. (8) But the most special and remarkable use of the
tense, though little more than an extension of the last idiom,
is as the *prophetic perfect:* its abrupt appearance in this
capacity imparts to descriptions of the future a forcible and
expressive touch of reality, and reproduces vividly the certainty
with which the occurrence of a yet future event is contemplated by the speaker[2]. Sometimes the perfect appears thus

---

[1] It may be worth while here to remind the reader that in verbs ע"ו
the pf. fem. בָּאָה is *mil'el,* the ptcp. fem. בָּאָה *milra';* (הַשָּׁבָה, therefore,
Isa. 51, 10, according to the punctuation, is the perfect, although preceded by the article; see, however, on this and similar passages, the
writer's *Notes on the Hebrew Text of Samuel,* p. 58, or Ges.-Kautzsch,
ed. 25, § 138, 3ᵇ). This distinction may be easily borne in mind, if it
be recollected that in each case the position of the tone depends simply
upon the particular application of a *general* rule : on the one hand, all
fem. adjectives in ָה are regularly accented on the ultima, e. g. קְטַנָּה;
on the other hand, all *tense-forms* ending in ָה, וּ, ִי, with a *vowel*
(not *shwa'*) before the last radical, except in certain special cases, take
the tone upon the penultima, e. g. וְנָהֲרוּ, הַבִּישׁוּ, קוּמִי, אֵשֹׁובָה. We are
now further in a position to understand how upon exactly the same
principle נֶאֱמָנָה Ps. 19, 8 must be the ptcp., and נֶאֱלָמָה Isa. 53, 7 the
pausal form of the perfect.

[2] The Greek aorist is similarly used, at least in the apodosis, to
'express future events which must certainly happen' (Jelf, § 403, 2);
and even coupled with a future, Il. 4, 161 ἔκ τε καὶ ὀψὲ τελεῖ, σύν τε
μεγάλῳ ἀπέτισαν. 9, 413 (see further below, § 136 γ). Compare also
its force in such descriptive passages as Il. 9, 7 (ἔχευαν). 15, 626. 16,
299–300. 20, 497. Phaedrus 245 A (ἠφανίσθη). 251 A. B. 254 B. etc.

only for a single word; sometimes, as though nothing more than an ordinary series of past historical events were being described, it extends over many verses in succession: continually the series of perfects is interspersed with the simple future forms, as the prophet shifts his point of view, at one moment contemplating the events he is describing from the *real standpoint* of the present, at another moment looking back upon them as accomplished and done, and so viewing them from an *ideal position* in the future.

It will be best to classify under distinct heads the various modes in which this perfect of certitude, or prophetic perfect, may appear.

(*a*) The description of the future scene may *begin* with the perfect, whether the verbs following (if there be any) fall back into the future or not: Nu. 24, 17 a star דָּרַךְ *hath proceeded* out of Jacob, and *shall* etc. Jud. 4, 14 hath he not gone out before thee? Isa. 5, 13 Therefore גָּלָה *hath* my people *gone* into captivity (although the captivity is only *anticipated*). 25 על כן חרה etc. 8, 23. 9, 1–6 the people that walked in darkness *have seen* a great light etc. 10, 28–31 (of the march of the Assyrian) he *is come* to 'Ayyâth etc. 21, 1 בא. 12 אתא. 24, 4–12 (except 9). 28, 2 הניח (the prophet sees Samaria already laid low on the ground). 30, 5. 33, 3. 42, 17. 45, ₊16 f. 46, 1 f. (the fall of Babylon and its idols spoken of as *achieved:* for the parallel ptcp. cf. Jer. 5, 6). Jer. 2, 26 הבישו. 5, 6 הכם (where observe that the impf. and ptcp. follow: in each of the three parallel expressions the prophet seizes upon a fresh aspect of the scene). 13, 26 חשפתי. 28, 2 (in 4, the impf. אשבר). 32, 24 f. 46, 14–16. 23 f. 51, 8. 41. Ez. 3, 25. 24, 14ᵇ etc. Amos 5, 2. Zeph. 3, 18. Ps. 22, 22. 30 all the fat ones of the earth *have eaten* and worshipped. 26, 12 my foot *standeth* in a level land. 30, 12. 36, 13 (the Psalmist sees the wicked already fallen). 41, 4. 71, 24. 85, 11 etc. Compare Jer. 6, 15ᵇ. 49, 8. 50, 31 (עֵת פְּקַדְתִּיו).

It thus occurs (exceptionally) after oaths or other strong

asseverations; as אִם לֹא Jer. 15, 11 (22, 6 etc. with the impf.);
כִּי אִם 2 Ki. 5, 20 (1 Sa. 26, 10. 2 Sa. 15, 21, the impf.; cf.
§ 115).

(β) It frequently appears after כִּי, the reason for an assertion or a command being found in some event the occurrence
of which, though still future, is deemed *certain*, and contemplated accordingly by the writer; Isa. 11, 9 they will do no
destruction in all my holy mountain, for the earth *is filled* with
the knowledge of Yahweh (at the time alluded to *has been*
filled). 15, 6ᵇ. 8. 9. 16, 8. 9 נפל. 23, 1. 4. 14 howl, for your
stronghold *has been wasted!* 24, 18. 23 מלך. 29, 20. 32, 10
כלה. 14. 34, 2. 35, 6. 60, 1. Jer. 25, 14. 31, 6. 9ᵇ. 11. 25.
Mic. 1, 9. 12. 16. Zeph. 1, 11. Zech. 11, 2. Ps. 6. 9 f. שָׁמַע.
28, 6. 31, 22 (prob.). 56, 14. 59, 17[1]. Gen. 30, 13 I am in
luck, for the daughters אִשְּׁרוּנִי *are sure to call* me lucky!

Without כי, Isa. 21, 2 השבתי. 14 (reason for 13). 33, 14.
34, 14ᵇ. 15ᵇ. 16ᵇ. 35, 2. Zeph. 2, 2 like chaff *hath* the day
(the time of delay before לדת חק) *passed by!* 3, 14 f. Lam. 4, 22.

(γ) But the pf. is also found (without כי) where, in a
description of the future, it is desired to give variety to
the scene, or to confer particular emphasis upon individual
isolated traits in it; it may in this case appear in the midst
of a series of imperfects, either ἀσυνδέτως, or connected with
what precedes by the copulative, *provided that the* ן *is separated*

---

[1] In some of the passages from the Psalms we may not perhaps feel
assured that the perfects are to be understood in this sense, as representing the certainty and confidence felt by the writers as regards the events
they anticipate. It is no doubt *possible* that they may simply describe
past facts or former experiences (like 4, 2. 31, 6 etc.) which the writer
desires to refer to: so, for example, 28, 6. 31, 22. 36, 13. But the
'perfect of certitude' is of such frequent and well-established occurrence,
and at the same time so much more forcible and appropriate to the context than the more common-place 'perfect of experience,' that we need
not scruple to interpret accordingly. Such sudden turns as those in 6, 9.
28, 6. 30, 12 are no less effective and emphatic than the abrupt introduction of a new and dissimilar key in a piece of music.

from the verb by one or more intervening words (if this be not the case, i. e. if the conjunction is *immediately* followed by the verb, the imperfect tense with ·**וְ** is of course employed: see below, § 82). For instance, without *waw:*—

Isa. 5, 28. 30 חָשַׁךְ. 8, 8. 13, 10[b]. 16, 10. 17, 11[b] (if נֵר be a verb). 19, 6[b]. 7[b]. 24, 14[b]. 25, 8 בִּלַּע he hath swallowed up death for ever! (contrast 7 וּבִלַּע). 30, 19 עָנָךְ as soon as he heareth, he *hath answered* thee! 33, 5[b] *hath* filled, etc. 47, 9. 49, 17. 51, 11[b] נָסוּ יַשִּׂיגוּן[1]. Jer. 25, 38. 31, 5[b]. 47, 3. Joel 2, 10. 4, 15. Zech. 9, 15 הָמוּ. Ps. 37, 20. Job 5, 19 f. in six troubles he will deliver thee, and in seven evil will not touch thee; in famine פָּדְךָ *he hath redeemed* thee from death, and in war from the power of the sword!

Obs. After an imperative,—the poet, by an abrupt transition, picturing what he desires as already achieved, Isa. 21, 14. Ps. 68, 31[b] (cf. 29[a]). Many commentators, to be sure, prefer to punctuate the verbs in question as imperatives; but the alteration has a weakening effect, and does not appear to be necessary: cf. Ezek. 24, 5[b].

With *waw :*—

Isa. 5, 27[b] (a particular feature in their approach described as though *present to the eye*). 11, 8 הָדָה . . . וְ. 18, 5 הֵסִיר הֵתַז: 19, 8[b]. 25, 12. 30, 32. Jer. 48, 33[b]. Job 5, 23. 22, 28[b]. And similarly in descriptions of the present, Ps. 7, 13 (we see the bow *already drawn*). 11, 2 כּוֹנְנוּ. Job 41, 20. Compare also Ps. 38, 17; Job 5, 11. 28, 25 and he *regulateth :* in all these passages there is a change of construction, the writer passing suddenly from an expression of *modality* to the statement of *a fact*[2].

---

[1] In the parallel passage 35, 10 we have the smoother, less forcible יַשִּׂיגוּ וְנָסוּ: the change is curious and instructive; it appears to have arisen from the tail of the וְ becoming accidentally shortened, or a copyist in doubt preferring the more ordinary construction, as the LXX in 35, 10 as well as 51, 11 have ἀπέδρα (which they are unlikely to have gone out of their way to choose, had they read וְנָסוּ).

[2] I have been led to give a large number of examples of this use of the

15. Sometimes the perfect is used in order to give emphatic expression to a predicate, conceived as being immediately and necessarily involved in the subject of the verb[1]: thus Pr. 8, 35 Qri, he that finds me *has* (in that very act) *found* life. 14, 31. 16, 26. 30. 17, 5. 27, 16; cf. 22, 9.

16. (9) The perfect is used where we should employ by preference the pluperfect, i. e. in cases where it is desired to bring two actions in the past into a special relation with each other, and to indicate that the action described by the pluperfect was completed before the other took place. The function of the pluperfect is thus to throw two events into their proper perspective as regards each other: but the tense is to some extent a superfluous one—it is an elegance for which Hebrew possesses no distinct form, and which even in Greek, as is well known, both classical and Hellenistic, is constantly replaced by the simple aorist. Gen. 2, 2 God blessed the works which עשה *he had made*, LXX ἃ ἐποίησε; 6, 1. 19, 28 and behold the smoke עלה *had ascended* (had begun to ascend before Abraham looked). 20, 18 for *he had shut* up etc. 28, 11 בא. 31, 34 and Rachel *had* taken (before Laban entered into the tent, *v.* 33). 34, 5. 38, 15. Dt. 9, 16. Jud. 6, 28. 1 Sa. 28, 20 for לא אכל he *had* not *eaten* bread. 30, 12. 2 Sa. 18, 18. 1 Ki. 1, 6. 41 (they *had finished* eating when they heard). 2 Ki. 9, 16. Isa. 6, 6; after a conjunction like כַּאֲשֶׁר Gen. 7, 9. 18, 33. 20, 13 etc.

Or, somewhat differently, when it may be wished to indicate explicitly that a given action was anterior to another action named immediately afterwards (not, as in the first case, named previously), Ps. 30, 7. 8 (where by rendering אמרתי, העמדתה by the plupf. we bring them into distinct relief as *anterior* to the following הסתרת). 31, 23. Job 32, 4

---

perfect, not only on account of its intrinsic importance, but also for a reason which will appear more fully in Chap. VIII.

[1] Cf. Rom. 13, 8 ὁ γὰρ ἀγαπῶν τὸν ἕτερον, τὸν νόμον πεπλήρωκε, and Winer, § 40. 4[b].

but Elihu *had waited*, for they were older than he. 42, 5 by hearing of the ear *had I heard* of thee, but now hath mine eye seen thee.

17. (10) Similarly, in the description of future events, it is often convenient in English to exhibit more distinctly the relation of two actions to one another by substituting for the Heb. perfect the future perfect, or 'paullo-post-futurum;' but this is by no means always obligatory, or even desirable. Thus after כִּי=*for:* Lev. 14, 48 נִרְפָּא. 19, 8 they that eat it shall bear their own sin, for (if any one eats it) he *will have profaned* what is holy to Yahweh.   1 Sa. 14, 10. 20, 22 if I say thus, go; for שְׁלָחַךְ Yahweh *will* (in that case) *have sent* thee away.   2 Sa. 5, 24 כִּי אז (אז omitted in 1 Chr. 14, 15). Ez. 3, 21 for (in that case) נִזְהָר (pf. *in pausa*) he *will have been warned* and THOU *wilt have delivered* thy soul; in a relative clause, Gen. 48, 6 which thou *shalt have* begotten (not *mayest* beget, which would be תּוֹלִיד).   1 Sa. 1, 28 all the days אֲשֶׁר הָיָה *which he shall have been.* Jer. 8, 3 (24, 9 הַדַּחְתִּים אַדִּיחֵם); after conjunctions, such as אַחַר Lev. 14, 43 אַחַר חִלֵּץ after that *he has taken away* the stones. 25, 48; עַד 2 Ki. 7, 3 עַד עֵת יוֹלֵדָה: till we *are dead.* Ez. 34, 21. Mic. 5, 2 עַד עֵת יוֹלֵדָה יָלְדָה until the time when she that beareth *shall have* borne; עַד אֲשֶׁר אִם Gen. 28, 15 until *I have done* etc. Nu. 32, 17. Isa. 6, 11†; עַד אִם 30, 17. Gen. 24, 19. Ruth 2, 21†; כִּי אִם אמרתי לך 2 Ki. 4, 24 except I bid thee; כִּי Isa. 16, 12 it shall come to pass, כִּי נִרְאָה when Moab *has appeared* (cum apparuerit) etc. Ps. 138, 4. 1 Chr. 17, 11 when thy days מָלְאוּ *have been* fulfilled (in 2 Sa. 7, 12 יִמְלְאוּ). Dan. 11, 36; אִם (=when), Isa. 4, 4: cf. § 138.

18. (11) The use of the perfect in both the protasis and apodosis of certain forms of hypothetical propositions will be illustrated below: see Chap. X. A few cases, however, may be noticed here in which the pf. is employed to denote events appertaining to past time, which *might have happened* but *did not happen*, which are therefore only for the moment conceived as having occurred, under conditions not actually realized. In Greek the existence of such conditions is (though not universally[1], Jelf, §§ 858 f. Winer, § 42. 2ᵇ) noted by ἄν in the apodosis: we observe therefore that the Heb. perfect corresponds not merely to the Greek aorist by itself, but to the Greek aorist with ἄν, that in other words it expresses the *contingent* as well as the *actual* occurrence of an event—the sense of the reader, or the tone in which the words are spoken, readily determining to which category the event is to be referred. So after כִּמְעַט Ps. 73, 2. 119, 87. Pr. 5, 14; כַּאֲשֶׁר Zech. 10, 6ᵇ. Job 10, 19 I ought to have been (§ 39 β) as though לא הייתי I *had not been* born. Ob. 16 וְהָיוּ כְּלוֹא הָיוּ. See further §§ 139, 141, 144.

19. (12) The perfect is used rather singularly in *questions:* 1. after עַד מָתַי Ex. 10, 3 until when מֵאַנְתָּ *wilt* thou *have* refused? Ps. 80, 5; or עַד אָנָה Ex. 16, 28, and with an impf. in the parallel clause Hab. 1, 2. Pr. 1, 22. Cf. Jer. 22, 23 מַה־נֵּחַנְתְּ (contrast 4, 30. 13, 21).

And 2. to express astonishment at what appears to the speaker in the highest degree improbable:—

Gen. 18, 12 הָיְתָה. Jud. 9, 9. 11. 13 *am I to have* lost my fatness וְהָלַכְתִּי and go? etc. 2 Ki. 20, 9 הָלַךְ *iveritne*? Nu. 17, 28 shall we ever have finished dying? Pr. 24, 28; and possibly Ps. 73, 11. Job 22, 13.

Gen. 21, 7 who[3] *could have* said to Abraham? Nu. 23, 10. 1 Sa. 26, 9 מִי שָׁלַח ... וְנִקָּה who *is to have* put forth his hand ... and be guiltless? LXX τίς ἐποίσει (quite different from

---

[1] And compare the use of the indicative in Latin, e. g. Hor. Carm. 2. 17, 27 Me truncus illapsus cerebro *Sustulerat* nisi Faunus ictum Dextra levasset.

[2] Where, accordingly, there is no occasion (with Hitzig on Ps. 11, 3) to change the punctuation and read הָלַךְ.

[3] Cf. Ephrem Syrus III. p. 59 if painters cannot paint the wind ܠܚܡ ܟܡ ܘܐܢ whose tongue *can have* described the Son of God? for which in str. 18 we have the impf. ܢܣܘܪ.

Dt. 5, 23. Lam. 3, 37. Pr. 30, 4. Job 9, 4 who ever hardened himself against him וַיִּשְׁלָם: and escaped whole? as is clear from both the sense of the passage and the difference in the *tense* of the second verb: see above, § 9, and Chap. VIII). Ps. 11, 3. 60, 11.

20. (13) Is there a *precative* perfect in Hebrew? or does the perfect in Hebrew, as in certain cases in Arabic, serve to give emphatic enunciation to a wish? The affirmative was maintained by Ewald, § 223[b], who cited Isa. 26, 15. Ps. 10, 16. 31, 6. 57, 7. 116, 16. Job 21, 16. 22, 18. Lam. 1, 21. 3, 57-61 and the 'old form of speech' preserved Ps. 18, 47; and by Böttcher, §§ 939[g], 947[g], who, accepting out of Ewald's instances only Ps. 116, 16. Job 21, 16. 22, 18. Lam. 3, 57-61, added to the list Isa. 43, 9. Mic. 1, 10 Kt. Ps. 4, 2. 7, 7. 22, 22. 71, 3. 141, 6 f.[1] In any case, if the usage exists, it is but an extension of the same manner of speech which has been already explained, § 14, viz. the perfect of certitude; the prominent position of the verb—in Arabic[2], to avoid misconstruction, it all but universally stands first in the sentence—aided by the tone of voice with which it is uttered, being sufficient to invest the conviction or hope, which is all that the tense employed in itself expresses, with the character of a wish. But the fact is that the evidence for this signification of the pf. is so precarious, the passages adduced in proof of it[3]

---

[1] Two other passages quoted, Jer. 50, 5. Joel 4, 11, do not belong here, the verb in each being attached to וְ.

[2] For the Arabic usage see Ewald, *Gramm. Arab.* §§ 198, 710; Wright, *Arabic Gramm.* ii. p. 3. Even the fact that in Hebrew the position of the verb is neglected ought to excite suspicion: in Arabic it is just the position which gives to the tense that interjectional force, upon which, in Ewald's words, its peculiar significance entirely depends.

[3] E. g. Ps. 4, 2. 116, 16 are quite naturally explained by § 9; 7, 7. 71, 3 resemble substantially רָאִיתָה Ps. 10, 14. 35, 22; Lam. 3, 57 ff. has been discussed already; Isa. 26, 15 are words spoken from the standpoint of the future, and 43, 9 the tenses, if נִקְבָּצוּ be a perf. (so König, *Lehrgebäude*, i. p. 184), are similar to those in 41, 5 (Ew. Hitz. Del. Dillm. and Ges.-K. § 51 Rem. 3 [doubtfully], however, treat נקבצו as

admitting of a ready explanation by other means, that it will be safer to reject it altogether[1].

---

an imperative).   As regards Ps. 22, 22 it is to be noticed that the words in question stand on the border-ground between the petition for help and the thanksgiving for its approach : it might almost be said that the poet began with the intention of saying : וּמִקַּרְנֵי רֵמִים עֲנֵנִי, but that, as he wrote, the prospect of the deliverance burst upon him so brightly as to lead him to speak of it as an accomplished fact עֲנִיתַנִי, which he then makes the key-note of the following verses 23–32.   Compare further Hupfeld's note on Ps. 4, 2.   Delitzsch would confine the use to such 'interjectional exclamations' as the one contained in the two verses from Job; but even there it is questionable whether it is necessary or legitimate to have recourse to it : Hitzig sees in רחקה only an earnest protestation of innocence, and translates by the present indicative.

[1] The same conclusion is defended, with additional reasons, by Prof. August Müller, in his review of the present work, pp. 202 f. (the precative perfect not used at all in Arabic to express concrete, personal petitions, such as would be contained in most of the passages referred to : in the other passages, no exegetical necessity for having recourse to it) : it is adopted also by Ges.-Kautzsch, § 106. 3[b] *note.*

CHAPTER III.

The Imperfect alone.

21. IN marked antithesis to the tense we have just discussed, the imperfect in Hebrew, as in the other Semitic
languages, indicates action as *nascent*, as evolving itself
actively from its subject, as developing. The imperfect does
not imply *mere* continuance as such (which is the function
of the participle), though, inasmuch as it emphasizes the
process introducing and leading to completion, it expresses
what may be termed *progressive* continuance; by thus seizing
upon an action while nascent, and representing it under its
most striking and impressive aspect (for it is just when a
fresh object first appears upon a scene that it exhibits greater
energy, and is, so to speak, more aggressive, than either
while it simply continues or after it has been completed),
it can present it in the liveliest manner possible—it can
present it in *movement* rather than, like the pf., in a condition
of rest. The action thus exhibited as *ready* or *about to take
place* may belong to the past, the present, or the future; but
an event ready and so capable of taking place would be
likely and liable to occur more than once; we thus find the
imperfect employed to denote *reiterated* actions—'a mist
יַעֲלֶה *used to go up*' (upon repeated occasions; but וְנָהָר יֹצֵא
'and a river *was* (unintermittently) *proceeding* out of the
garden')[1]. In strictness, יעלה expresses only a *single* event

---

[1] Cf. the English 'apt,' properly = fitted, suited, adapted, but also
used in the phrase '*to be apt* to do so and so,' in a frequentative significa-

as beginning or ready to take place; but an action of which this may be predicated is in the nature of things likely to happen more frequently, and thus the additional idea of ' recurrency' would be speedily superinduced upon the more limited original signification of the imperfect [1].

22. The same form is further employed to describe events belonging to the *future;* for the future is emphatically τὸ μέλλον, and this is just the attribute specially expressed by the imperfect. The idea of reiteration is not prominent in this case, because the occurrence of the event spoken of is by itself sufficient to occupy and satisfy the mind, which does not look beyond to reflect whether it is likely to happen more than once: on the other hand, when a *past* event is described by the impf. the attention is at once arrested by the peculiarities of the tense—original and derived—which are *not* explained if a *single* action alone be assumed. The *mere* occurrence of an event is denoted by the perfect; the impf., therefore (unless its appearance be attributable solely to chance), must have been chosen in order to suggest some

---

tion = ' *to be liable, accustomed,* or *used* to do so and so :' we here see how an expression indicating simply *readiness* or *capacity* may so extend its original connotation as to acquire in addition the power of connoting *recurrence.*

[1] The connexion between the ideas of *incipiency* and *reiteration* may be illustrated by the use of the element -σκ- in Greek, which in words like γηράσκω, ἡβάσκω (cf. senesco, pubesco, cresco, etc.), possesses an inchoative force, while in the Homeric and Ionic forms ναιετάασκε, εἴπεσκε, ἐλάσασκε, etc., it appears as an affix expressing iteration. 'The gradual realization and the repetition of an action are regarded by language as nearly akin' (Curtius, *Elucidations*, p. 143) : εἴπεσκε, then, meaning properly ' he was *on the point* of saying,' very quickly becomes ' he *would* or *used to* say.'

In most of the verbs ending in -σκω, the original inchoative force is no longer traceable at all, in others it is only traceable after reflection, e. g. in γιγνώσκω, μιμνήσκω, θνήσκω, στερίσκω—another example of a form preserved by language, even after its distinctive meaning had been lost. Cf. Curtius, *Das Griech. Verbum,* i. 269, 285.

additional feature characteristic of the occurrence, which, in
the case before us, is the fact (or possibility) of its repetition.

23. An idea, however, like that of *nascency, beginning*, or
going to be is almost indefinitely elastic : on the one hand,
that which is in the process of coming to pass is also that
which is *destined* or *must* come to pass (τὸ μέλλον) ; on the
other hand, it is also that which *can* or *may* come to pass.
If the subject of the verb be also the speaker, i. e. if the verb
be in the first person, that which is about to come to pass
will be commonly that which he himself *desires* or *wishes*
to come to pass; if, however, the verb be in the second
or third person, it naturally expresses the wishes of the
speaker *as regards some one else*, and so conveys a more
or less emphatic *permission* which imperceptibly passes,
especially in negative sentences, into a *command*. אֶרְאֶה Dt.
32, 20 *I will* or *am about to look*, I should like to look ;
תֹּאכֵל *thou mayest eat* Gen. 2, 16, but, in the injunctions for
the passover, Ex. 12, 11 *ye are to* or *shall* eat it ; לֹא תֹאכֵל
Gen. 2, 17 *thou mayest, shalt,* or *must,* not eat it ; יִהְיֶה *it is
about to be,* or, if spoken by a person with power to bring
it about, *it shall be*, לֹא יִהְיֶה *it is not to be.*

24. But again, since the imperfect expresses an action not
as *done*, but only as *doing*, as possessing consequently an
element of uncertainty and indeterminateness, not already
fixed and defined but capable of assuming any form, or
taking any direction which may be impressed upon it from
without, it is used after conjunctions such as פֶּן, בַּעֲבוּר, לְמַעַן,
precisely as in Latin the corresponding terms are followed
not by the indicative, the mood of certainty, but by the
subjunctive, the mood of contingency.   And, in accordance
with the principle stated above that the Hebrew 'tenses' do
not in themselves specify the period of time within which
a given action must have happened, any of the *nuances* just
assigned to the imperfect will retain their force in the past as
well as in the present, the same tense is competent to express

both *is to* and *was to, may* and *might, can* and *could, will* and *would, shall* and *should,* in all the varied positions and shades of meaning which these auxiliaries may assume. Our English *will* and *would,* as commonly used to describe a custom or habit, correspond probably most closely to the Hebrew tense in this application ; but obviously these terms would not be suitable to represent it always, and recourse must therefore be had to other expressions.

25. The imperfect, then, may characterize action as *potential;* but this potentiality may be expressed either (1) as a substantive and independent fact, i. e. the tense may appear as *indicative;* or (2) as regulated by the will of a personal agent, i. e. the tense may appear as *voluntative* (optative); or (3) as determined by some antecedent event, i. e. the tense may appear as *subjunctive*[1].

26. We may now proceed to arrange the various senses in which the imperfect is employed.

In the description of past occurrences it is used in two different ways, as explained above : 1. to represent an event while nascent (γιγνόμενον), and so, by seizing upon it while in movement rather than while at rest, to picture it with peculiar vividness to the mental eye ; and 2. as a frequentative, to suggest the reiteration of the event spoken of. In which of these senses it is on each occasion to be understood is left to the intelligence of the reader to determine; and this will not generally lead him astray. In cases where any doubt remains, it may be inferred either that the decision is immaterial, or else that the requisite data for forming one no longer exist as they must have done when the passage was written—a con-

---

[1] It will be observed that this tripartite division is not maintained in what follows. The fact is that Hebrew, unlike Arabic, possesses no distinctive terminations to mark the subjunctive mood : although therefore the imperfect fulfils the functions which elsewhere belong to a subjunctive, distinguishable as such, it is sufficient to notice the fact generally, without pausing to enquire upon each occasion whether the tense is indicative or subjunctive.

sideration which will of course account for much of the obscurity that rests upon the interpretation of ancient documents in all languages.

27. (1) This usage is naturally most frequent in a poetical or elevated style : but in prose equally the imperfect, if describing a single action and so not capable of explanation as a frequentative, operates by bringing into prominence the process introducing it and preliminary to its complete execution (as in Greek κατεδύετο, *was in course of sinking*). Here it may sometimes be rendered in English by the '*historical present*,' the effect of which is to present in strong relief and with especial liveliness the features of the scene which it describes : but in fact, the idiom is one of those which our language is unable to reproduce : the student must *feel* the force of the tense in the Hebrew, and endeavour not to forget it as he reads the translation in English.

(*a*) First of all, in the language of poetry or prophecy ; Ex. 15, 5 the depths יְכַסְיֻמוּ *covered them !* 6. 7. 15. Nu. 23, 7 and he took up his parable and said, From Aram Balaq יַנְחֵנִי *bringeth me !* Dt. 32, 10 יִמְצָאֵהוּ he *found* him (or *findeth* him) in a desert land! (contrast Hos. 9, 10 מְצָאתִי). Jud. 5, 8. 26. 29 (vivid pictures of Jael *stretching out* her hand, and the princesses in the act of *answering*). Isa. 43, 17. 45, 4 אֲכַנְּךָ. 5. 51, 2 Sarah תְּחוֹלֶלְכֶם who *bare* you. Hab. 3, 3. 7. Job 3, 3 perish the day אִוָּלֶד בּוֹ I *was being* born in ! (contrast Jer. 20, 14 אֲשֶׁר יֻלַּדְתִּי בּוֹ). 11 why did I not *go on to* die (at once die) from the womb? 4, 12. 15 f. 10, 10 f. 15, 7. 38, 8[b]. Ps. 7, 16 and falleth into the pit : יִפְעָל *he is* or *was making*[1]. 18, 4[2]. 7. 21. 30, 9 (Hitz. Del.). 32, 5[a]. 80, 9[a]. 104, 6–8. 116, 3 f. 6. Lam. 3, 8 when I *would fain* cry : see further § 85.

---

[1] Not, as A. V., *made ;* the impf. shews that the writer thought of the process as not completed—while *engaged upon carrying out* his design, the destruction overtakes him.

[2] 'In lebhaft erregter Rede die Vergangenheit wie Gegenwart geschaut' (Hitzig).

(β) In prose this use of the impf. is only common after אָז or טֶרֶם, which introduce or point to an ensuing event, and are accordingly constantly followed by this tense. Thus, for example, after אָז Ex. 15, 1 אָז יָשִׁיר *then sang* Moses (*proceeded, went on* to sing). Dt. 4, 41. Josh. 8, 30. 10, 12 etc.; after טֶרֶם or בְּטֶרֶם all but uniformly, Gen. 2, 5. 19, 4. 24; 45. 1 Sa. 3, 3. 7ᵇ etc.[1] The impf. is also found occasionally with reference to past time after עַד or עַד אֲשֶׁר *until;* but here the indefiniteness inherent in this conjunction being at times more perceptibly felt may have co-operated in the adoption of the impf. in preference to the perfect. Thus Josh. 10, 13 עַד יִקֹּם. Jon. 4, 5. Ps. 73, 17. Qoh. 2, 3. 2 Chr. 29, 34[2].

(γ) The following instances are of an exceptional character: Jud. 2, 1 אַעֲלֶה I *brought you up* out of Egypt etc. (setting forth the occurrence in bright relief)[3]. 1 Ki. 21, 6 כִּי אֲדַבֵּר (perhaps frequentative). 2 Ki. 8, 29 (=9, 15: in 2 Chr. 22, 6 the pf.); and preceded by the conj. וְ (cf. § 85 *Obs.*). Gen. 37, 7 והנה תסבינה and behold *they began to* move round (Joseph represents the sheaves as being in *motion;* conceive סבו in place of 'ת, and how lifeless the image becomes!). Ex.

---

[1] או is, however, also frequently found with the pf., Gen. 4, 26. Ex. 4, 26. 15, 15. 1 Ki. 22, 50 etc.: but טרם only very rarely, Gen. 24, 15 (contrast *v.* 45 above). 1 Sa. 3, 7ᵃ (contrast 7ᵇ); and בטרם Ps. 90, 2. Pr. 8, 25. Comp. the use of the impf. in Syriac, after ܡܛܠ ܕ Gen. 13, 10. Dt. 33, 1. 1 Sa. 9, 15. *Acta S. Pelagiae* (Gildemeister), 5, 21; ܥܕ ܡܛܠ ܕ John 17, 5; ܚܠܦ 2 Ki. 6, 32. Jer. 1, 5 al.

[2] With the *perf.*, Dt. 2, 14. 9, 21. Josh. 2, 22 etc. It will be remembered how *antequam, priusquam,* and *donec* may be followed indifferently by a subjunctive or indicative, according to the mode in which the occurrence of the event is conceived by the writer.

[3] The impf., as used in this *prose* passage, of past time, is no doubt unexpected and peculiar: hence some scholars suspect the text to be defective, and would restore ויאמר [פקר פקדתי אתכם] וַאֹמַר (Ex. 3, 16) 'ויאמר [פקר פקדתי אתכם וָ]אַעֲלֶה or אעלה וג (Böttcher; Doorninck, *Bijdrage tot de Tekstkritiek van Richt.* i–xvi, 1879, p. 13; Budde, *Theol. Lit.-zeit.* 1884, col. 211: notice in the first suggestion the ὁμοιοτέλευτον): but it is doubtful if such expedients are necessary.

8, 20. 2 Sa. 15, 37 ואבשלום יבוא (*went on to enter;* the actual entry is recorded later, 16, 15 בָּא). 23, 10. 1 Ki. 7, 8[b]. 20, 33. 13, 20. Jer. 52, 7. Ezra 9, 4 וְאֵלַי יֵאָסְפוּ *came gathering to me.*

In poetry also it sometimes occurs immediately after a pf., in which case it indicates the rapid or instantaneous manner in which the second action is conceived as following the first: Ex. 15, 12. 14. Hab. 3, 10. Ps. 37, 14 f. 46, 7. 69, 33 (cf. 1 Sa. 19, 5). 74, 14. 77, 17[1].

28. But the impf. is also used in the same way of a single action in the *present* time, in order to express it with force, Gen. 37, 15. Nu. 24, 17 אֶרְאֶנּוּ *I see* him, but not now! 1 Sa. 21, 15 תִּרְאוּ. Jer. 6, 4 the day *hath turned* (pf.), and the shadows of evening יִנָּטוּ *are beginning to* lengthen. Hos. 1, 2[b] (or freq. *plays* the whore). Hab. 3, 9. 12. Job 4, 5. 32, 19 יִבָּקֵעַ *is ready to burst* (A.V.). Ps. 2, 2. 17, 12 he is like a lion יִכְסוֹף (*that is*) *eager* for prey (at the moment when he is eager). In poetry, after לְעֵת Dt. 32, 35[2]. בְּעֵת Job 6, 17. יוֹם Ps. 56, 4[a].

29. More frequent is the use of the impf. as equivalent to the *future*—a use which is clearly only an extension of that noted in § 28: there the action is conceived to be taking place (but not completed) as the words are uttered; here it has not yet begun to take place at all, but its beginning to do so is contemplated in the future—nearer or more remote, as the context and sense demand. Numerous instances may readily be found, e.g. Gen. 12, 12[b]. 16, 12. 49, 1. Ex. 6, 1. 9, 5 etc.[3]

---

[1] Ps. 66, 6. 104, 6 (where a word is interposed) are different. The same ἀσύνδετον is a favourite idiom with Hosea, 4, 7. 5, 10. 8, 3. 9, 6[a] (see § 154). 7, 9 (cf. *v.* 15): see also 2 Chr. 12, 7.

[2] This and the two following passages might also be explained by § 33. The infin. is the usual construction after עת or יום.

[3] In the *first* pers. *I shall*, Gen. 15, 8. Jud. 13, 22. 15, 18. Isa. 38, 11. Jer. 4, 21[a]. Job 17, 10: but most usually *I will*, 1 Ki. 2, 30. Ruth 1, 17. Gen. 2, 18. 6, 7. 8, 21. 12, 2 etc. Ps. 12, 6. 22, 26 etc. *I shall* is the

If the future is close at hand, the verb may be rendered almost indifferently by a present or future : 1 Ki. 1, 42 תְּבַשֵּׂר annunciaturus es, *announcest* or *wilt announce*, art on the point of announcing. Ps. 2, 2. 59, 9.

30. (2) So much for the impf. as denoting a single act. By what steps it in addition assumes a frequentative signification has been explained above : it only remains to give instances of its use.

(*a*) In past time : Gen. 6, 4 יָבֹאוּ (LXX rightly οὗ ἐὰν εἰσεπο-ρεύοντο[1]). 30, 38 תָּבֹאןָ. 42 *would* not put them in (LXX οὐκ ἐτίθει). 31, 39 I אֲחַטֶּנָּ *used to bear* the loss of it. Ex. 1, 12 in proportion as they *afflicted* it, so it *multiplied*, and so it *spread abroad*. 19, 19. 40, 36. 38 (*used to be*). Nu. 9, 16–23[a] (describing what the Israelites *used constantly* to do in the desert : *v.* 23[b] the whole is summed up, and stated generally as a single fact, in the pf. שמרו). Dt. 32, 16. 17. Josh. 23, 10 (*would* often pursue). Jud. 2, 18 (*would* repent). 6, 5 (*would* come up). 17, 6 = 18, 25 יעשה. 1 Sa. 2, 22. 9, 9 יִקָּרֵא. 18, 5. 21, 12 הֲלוֹא לָזֶה יַעֲנוּ is not this he of whom *they kept singing?* (on the well-known occasion 18, 6. 7). 2 Sa. 1, 22 the sword of Saul לא תשוב ריקם *never returned* (*was not wont* to return) empty. 12, 18 כי כן תלבשנה. 1 Ki. 3, 4. 5, 28 a month יהיו *would they be* etc. 6, 8. 7, 26 יָכִיל (*used to* or *would* contain). 38. 10, 5. 16 f. Isa. 1, 21 ילין *used* to dwell. 6, 2. 7, 23 (where the freq. and the fut. senses of the impf. meet in a single

---

pure and simple future—German *ich soll*, *I am to* or *must;* the speaker's own inclinations are dormant, and he regards himself as the passive creature of circumstances : *I will*, on the contrary, is the exponent of a purpose or volition, and the *personal* interest of the speaker makes itself strongly felt. We may, if we please, substitute *I shall* for the more expressive *I will*, without materially altering the sense: the opposite change can, of course, not be made with impunity.

[1] On the frequentative force of ἐάν, ὅταν, ἡνίκα ἄν, etc. with the indic., in Hellenistic Greek, see Winer, *Gramm. of N. T. Greek*, § xlii. 5 (where, in the note, *this* passage is wrongly treated as an exception).

verse). 23, 7 etc. Ps. 42, 5. 55, 15 נְהַלֵּךְ . . . נַמְתִּיק סוֹד *used to walk in the throng.* 95, 10. 99, 6 f. (with *v.* 7 comp. Nu. 9, 23). 106, 43 (cf. Neh. 9, 27). Job 4, 3 f. 29, 2. 3. 7. 9. 12 f. 16 f. etc. 2 Chr. 24, 11. 25, 14.

31. The passages quoted will suffice amply to shew that when occurring in the historical books the impf. *always* expresses a deal more than the mere pf.: how far more picturesque, for example, is the scene Jud. 6, 5 rendered by the choice of יַעֲלוּ than it would have been had the writer simply used the pf. עָלוּ! No more, then, need be said on the necessity of discriminating the impf. from the pf.; but a few words must be added to guard against the error of confusing it with the participle.

The only species of continued action to which the impf. can give expression is the introductory process which may culminate in the finished act, §§ 27 γ, 28; and even here its use is limited: *mere* continuance in the sense of duration *without progress* is never expressed by the impf.; wherever this seems to be the case, closer examination will shew that the apparently continuous action is not really indivisible, but consists of a number of separate acts which, following one another in rapid succession, present the appearance of perfect continuity, and may be actually treated as such by language. But the fact that the same series of events may be treated under two aspects must not lead us to confuse the form which gives expression to the one with the form that gives expression to the other. The participle is the form which indicates continued action. 'Forty years long *was I grieved* with this generation:' the English is ambiguous; it may correspond either to an original participle or to an original impf. As a fact it corresponds to the latter: 'forty years long אָקוּט *was I grieved*,' i. e. upon repeated occasions, not of necessity continuously. Similarly, מֹשֶׁה יְדַבֵּר (Ex. 19, 19) is 'Moses *kept speaking*:' 'Moses *was speaking*' would be expressed by the part. מֹשֶׁה מְדַבֵּר (see 1 Ki. 1, 25. 42 etc.).

Thus while the impf. multiplies an action, the participle pro-longs it. Sometimes the two forms are found in juxtaposi-tion, as Ps. 99, 6; but however closely they may seem to resemble each other in meaning, and even where they would admit of an interchange without material alteration or detri-ment to the sense, it must not be forgotten that they are still quite different, and that each seizes upon and brings into view a different phase of action.

The difference between the impf. and the part. is most clearly displayed in passages like Gen. 29, 2 רבצים *were lying*, ישקו *used to water*. 1 Sa. 2, 13 f. 1 Ki. 10, 22. Isa. 6, 2 (*were standing*, at the period of the vision—*used to* cover, fly). At other times, on the contrary, the separate units of which the series actually consists are lost from sight and replaced by a continuous line[1]: e. g. Gen. 39, 6 אוכל (contrast 2 Sa. 12, 3 תאכל). 23 (contr. Ps. 1, 3. 1 Sa. 14, 47). 1 Ki. 17, 6 מביאים (but also ישתה). 2 Ki. 4, 5. Ps. 37, 12. 21. 26.

32. (β) In present time. It may be well here, in order to avoid confusion, to remind ourselves of an ambiguity existing in the English present tense. The present tense in English, besides declaring single and isolated facts, is used also to express general truths, to state facts which need not necessarily take place at the moment at which the assertion is being made, but which either *may* occur at *any* time or do *actually* occur periodically: in other words, the present tense appears as a *frequentative:* it *multiplies* an action, and distri-butes it over an indefinite number of potential or actual realizations. And, in fact, this use of the present in English to denote acts which may be or are repeated, is more

---

[1] Accordingly the participle, filling up the intervals which the impf. leaves open, is adapted to magnify or exaggerate any circumstance: cf. 1 Ki. 10, 24 f. Ex. 18, 14 (where observe how in this way Jethro repre-sents Moses as being more fully and continuously occupied than the latter in his reply is willing to admit). Esth. 3, 2 and the reversal of the picture in 8, 17[b]. 9, 3.

common than any other.　But it is just this frequentative or
distributive force which the Hebrew impf. possesses, asserting, as it does, facts which either *may be* realized at any time,
or *are* realized repeatedly.　Our present, therefore, and the
Hebrew impf. agree in a remarkable manner in being able
to specify actions which though not in themselves appertaining to any particular period of time whatever, *may* nevertheless make their appearance at any or every moment.　This
distinction between the two senses of our present tense it is
important here to keep in mind : because the Hebrew impf.,
while but rarely found in one sense, is extremely common
in the other.　When, therefore, it is said that this tense
corresponds to the English 'present,' it is necessary to have
a clear and precise view of what this statement really means.

33.　The imperfect, then, is found—

(*a*) Asserting facts of definite occurrence—within a longer
or shorter period, as the case may be : Ex. 13, 15 אֶפְדֶּה *I
redeem* (am in the habit of redeeming).　18, 15 the people יָבֹא
cometh to me (keep coming).　Gen. 10, 9. 22, 14 therefore
יֵאָמֵר *it is said;* so יאמרו Nu. 21, 27. 2 Sa. 5, 8ᵇ; Nu. 17, 19
where אִוָּעֵד לָכֶם *I meet you.*　Josh. 7, 12. Gen. 50, 3 כִּי כֵּן יִמְלְאוּ
for so *are wont to be* fulfilled.　Jud. 14, 10 for so young men
are accustomed to do.　1 Sa. 9, 6. 2 Sa. 11, 20 how they *shoot.*
Isa. 1, 23. 3, 16ᵇ. 5, 11. 23. 14, 8 *doth not come up* (never
cometh up, where notice how *never* distributes the verb). 27,
3. 40, 20 יְבַקֵּשׁ. 41, 6 (a graphic verse). 44, 17. 59, 11. Jer.
9, 3. 20, 8. Hos. 4, 12 f. Ps. 3, 6 יִסְמְכֵנִי *sustaineth* me. 10,
5. 8–10. 11, 2. 12, 3. 16, 4. 17, 9. 18, 29 because THOU
dost lighten. 22, 3. 8. 18ᵇ. 23, 2 f. 35, 11 f. 41, 7 f. 42, 2ᵇ.
46, 5. 64, 5–7. 71, 17 till now *do I keep declaring* thy
wonders. 94, 4–6. Job 9, 11 he *goeth* by me, and I *see* him
not. 23, 8 f. ; after מִדֵּי *as often as,* Jer. 20, 8 (elsewhere the
infinitive).

To express a characteristic of an individual : Ps. 1, 2
Happy is the man who . . . יֶהְגֶּה *meditateth.* 15, 4 who יְכַבֵּד

honoureth etc. 17, 14. 38, 14^b. 52, 9 יָשִׂים (contrast 40, 5 שָׂם).
58, 6. 91, 5–6. Isa. 40, 26 he *calleth.* 28 f. 41, 2 f. 56, 2.

Obs. Frequent as the idiom כֹּה אָמַר יי is in the prophets, the *impf.*
יֹאמַר יי, introduced parenthetically, is exceptional and should be noticed:
the call is not a single, momentary one, it is repeated, or at least continuing. The instances are Isa. 1, 11. 18. 33, 10 (Ps. 12, 6). 40, 1. 25.
41, 21. 66, 9: and similarly Jer. 51, 35. Pr. 20, 14. 23, 7.

(*b*) Asserting facts, which are not conceived as definitely
occurring within stated or implied limits of time, but as liable
to occur at any period that may be chosen: e. g. in the enunciation of general maxims or truths, Ps. 1, 3 which *giveth* (is
always ready to give, in the habit of giving) its fruit in due
season, and its leaf *doth* not *fade,* and all that *he doeth* he
maketh to prosper, 4 *driveth away,* 5 *do not stand* or *endure* in
the judgement (are not in the habit of doing so), 6 *perisheth*
('will' perish, i. e. either as a pure future, however sure it may
seem to appear for a time, it will in the end perish; or as a
frequentative, implying what may be expected to occur,
wherever there is a דֶּרֶךְ רְשָׁעִים). 1 Sa. 16, 7 יִרְאֶה. 24, 14.
Isa. 32, 6 A.V. the vile person *will* speak villainy (where
'will' expresses the habit, just as Pr. 19, 6. 24. Jer. 9, 4. 5
[Heb. 3. 4]). 40, 31. Hos. 4, 11. Ps. 5, 5–7. 7, 9 *judgeth*
nations (a *general* attribute, forming the ground for the
petition which follows). 10, 14. 11, 4. 17, 2^b thine eyes *behold* (ground of 2^a). 18, 26–28. 39, 7. 48, 8. 49, 11. 65, 9.
68, 20. 104, 11–17. 22; in the Proverbs constantly, the
perfect (§ 12) being less usual, 10, 1. 2. 3. 4 etc. 26, 14 the
door *turns* upon its hinge, and a sluggard upon his bed. Job
4, 19. 5, 2. 6. 7^b. 12. 14. 18 etc.; regularly also in similes,
where a *habit* or *custom* is referred to, as Ex. 33, 11 כַּאֲשֶׁר
יְדַבֵּר as a man *speaketh* with his neighbour. Nu. 11, 12. Dt. 1,
44. 28, 49. Isa. 9, 2. 31, 4. 55, 10. 65, 8 etc.

34. This form of the verb, expressing as it does a general
truth, is sometimes found attached to a substantive, the relative being omitted, to denote a general attribute belonging to

it: under these circumstances it almost degenerates into an adjective. Thus Gen. 49, 27 Benjamin is זְאֵב יִטְרָף a *ravening* wolf (lit. a wolf (that) ravens). Isa. 40, 20 לֹא ירקב. 51, 12 אֱנוֹשׁ יָמוּת *mortal* man. 55, 13 an *indestructible* sign. Hos. 4, 14 a people לֹא יָבִין *without understanding*; cf. Ps. 78, 6 בָּנִים יִוָּלֵדוּ (22, 32 the ptcp.). And in comparisons, to define more closely the *tertium comparationis*, whether it be regarded as expressing pictorially a particular act (§ 28), or as describing a general attribute: Dt. 32, 11. Ps. 42, 2 like the hind, *as* it desires (or, *which* desires) the water-brooks. 83, 15. 92, 13[b]. Job 7, 2 as a servant יִשְׁאַף צֵל *that longeth* (or *longing*) for the shade. 9, 26[b] like a vulture יָטוּשׁ עֲלֵי אֹכֶל *as it darts* upon the prey. Isa. 61, 10–11. 62, 1[b] כְּלַפִּיד יִבְעָר as a *burning* lamp[1]. Or it is attached to another verb, so as to qualify it almost in the manner of an adverb, Isa. 30, 14 bruising לֹא יַחְמֹל *unsparingly*[2]. 42, 14[a][3]. Ps. 17, 3 *without finding* (qualifying צְרַפְתַּנִי). 26, 1 I have trusted לֹא אֶמְעָד *without wavering* (Hitz. Del.). Job 31, 34.

35. It appears from what has been said that both the perf. and the impf. alike, though upon different grounds, may be employed to designate those permanent relations which constitute on the one hand personal habits or attributes, on the other general truths. A permanent relation of this sort may, firstly, be viewed as a completed whole, and, as such, be denoted by the perfect; but inasmuch as a state or condition most commonly declares itself by a succession of acts —more or less numerous, as the case may be—its existence may, at the same time, with equal propriety, be indicated by the impf. as well. It is accordingly at once intelligible upon what principle we frequently find the two tenses alternating—

---

[1] At other times, naturally, the perf. is more appropriate: Jer. 23, 9. Job 11, 16 כְּמַיִם עָבְרוּ as waters that *have passed by*. 13, 28[b].

[2] If with Baer we read כְּתֹת, לֹא יַחְמֹל will qualify וּשְׁבָרָהּ.

[3] The 'synchronistic' imperfect (אַחֲרִישׁ and אֶתְאַפָּק being *synchronous* with the preceding הֶחֱשֵׁיתִי מֵעוֹלָם): cf. below, §§ 162, 163.

for example in the two members of a verse—when used in this way; the interchange being naturally encouraged by the agreeable variety and relief thereby afforded to the ear. Sometimes the change of tense may be retained in English: at other times it will be simpler and less pedantic—a minor grammatical distinction, unless absolutely indispensable for the sense, must be given up if its preservation involve stiffness or sound unnatural—to render both tenses by what is here, in English, the idiomatic equivalent of both, viz. the present. Yet, however we translate, it must not be forgotten that a difference still exists in the words of the original, and that each tense possesses a propriety the force of which is still perceptible, even where it cannot be reproduced; it is simply the imperfection, in this respect, of our own language, its deficiency in delicacy that necessitates our obliterating the lights and shades which an otherwise constructed instrument is capable of expressing.

Thus Isa. 5, 12ᵇ. 26, 9ᵃ. 33, 7. 40, 19. 44, 12–18. Hos. 7, 1ᵇ. Joel 2, 3ᵃ. 6. Hab. 3, 3. Ps. 2, 1 f. 5, 6 (*cannot stand ... thou hatest*). 6, 7 (the pf., as *v.* 8, expressing the Psalmist's completed state of exhaustion; the impff. his repeated acts). 7, 13 f. (he *hath* prepared instruments of death: his arrows he *maketh* (or *is making*) flaming!). 11, 5. 7 the upright *behold* his face. 16, 9 יֵשֵׁב (parallel to שָׂמֵחַ) *dwelleth* or *can dwell.* 22, 16. 23, 5. 26, 4. 5. 38, 12. 62, 5. 65, 14. 73, 7–9. 27. 74, 1. 84, 3. 93, 3. 102, 15. 109, 3 f. Pr. 4, 17. 12, 12. 28, 1. Job 3, 17. 11, 20. 12, 20 f. etc.[1]

36. It will now, moreover, be apparent how the impf., especially if suddenly introduced ἀσυνδέτως, may be effectively employed by prophets and poets in the description of a scene or series of events not merely to vary the style of narrative, but to throw into what would otherwise have been a motion-

---

[1] Cf. Lev. 11, 4–6, where the ptcp., impf., and pf. are employed in succession to describe, from different points of view, the same attribute.

less picture the animation and vigour of life. Thus, for
example, Isa. 2, 8 and the land is filled with idols, to the
work of their own hands יִשְׁתַּחֲווּ *they bow down!* 3, 16ᵇ (designed to make the reader realize forcibly the image presented
by וַתֵּלַכְנָה). 5, 15ᵇ (in *v.* 15ᵃ. 16 the prophet is describing the
future in terms of the past [see § 82]; in 15ᵇ he confers a
passing vividness upon a particular feature in the scene). 9,
10ᵇ and his enemies *he armeth* (notice in 10ᵃ the *past* tense
וַיְשַׂגֵּב). 16. 17. 18ᵇ. 19ᵇ the people has become as fuel for fire,
none *spareth* (or *is sparing*) his brother! 10, 4. 28. 14, 10
(after the pff. in *v.* 9). 15, 2ᵇ. 3ᵇ. 4ᵇ. 24, 9 etc. Joel 2, 3 ff.
Nah. 2, 5 f.

37. The imperfect, as we saw above, expresses not merely
simple futurity (I shall, thou wilt, he will), but is equivalent
further to the same auxiliaries in their other and more emphatic capacity as the exponents of volition (I will, thou shalt,
he shall). We saw further that it possesses a potential and
concessive force, corresponding to *can* and *may*. In past
time or in oratio obliqua, these auxiliaries naturally suffer in
English a change of tense, becoming respectively *should,
would, could,* and *might*. Some instances of the impf. occurring with these significations will now be given: it is
noticeable, however, that frequently we are by no means
restricted to a single equivalent in translating[1].

(*a*) Gen. 41, 15 תִּשְׁמַע thou *canst* understand a dream (or
simply *dost* understand; and similarly in the other passages).
Ex. 4, 14. Nu. 35, 33 יְכֻפַּר. 1 Ki. 3, 8. 8, 27 *cannot* or *will
not* contain thee. 2 Ki. 6, 12 Elijah *can* tell. Ps. 5, 8². 18,

---

[1] The senses which follow I have arranged simply with reference to
the auxiliaries as they are met with in English, without stopping to
enquire, except incidentally, how far any of the latter may bear equivocal
meanings.

[2] Cf. Delitzsch: 'die Futt. *v.* 8 besagen was er thun darf und thun
wird: durch die Grösse göttlicher Gnade *hat er Zugang* zum Heilig-
thum.' Comp. Isa. 26, 13.

30; in questions, Isa. 49, 15ª *can* (or *will*) a woman forget, etc. Ez. 28, 9. Job 8, 11. 13, 16 (see Del.). 38, 34 f. 40, 25 f.; and with מִי, Ps. 15, 1. Isa. 33, 14. Ex. 4, 11ᵇ who *maketh* (or *can make*) dumb? etc. Pr. 20, 9 מִי יֹאמַר זִכִּיתִי לִבִּי.

(β) 1 Ki. 8, 5 oxen לֹא־יִסָּפְרוּ that *could* not be counted. Hos. 2, 1 (=innumerable). Jer. 24, 2 figs that *could* not be eaten (=uneatable). Ez. 20, 25 statutes which they *could* not live in. 1 Ki. 18, 10 that לֹא־יִמְצָאֶכָּה he *could* not find thee (not לֹא־מְצָאֶךָ׃ *had not found thee*). Job 38, 31 couldst thou bind? 39, 19 f.

38. (*a*) Gen. 2, 16 ye *may* eat. 42, 37 thou *mayest* (or *shalt*) kill my two sons, if etc. Ex. 19, 13ᵇ. Nu. 35, 28 the slayer *may* return. Lev. 22, 23. Dt. 5, 21 we see God *may* speak with a man, and he (yet) live. 12, 20 תֹּאכַל. Jud. 16, 6 wherewith thou *canst* (or *mightest*, A.V.) be bound. Isa. 40, 30 *may* weary. 49, 15ᵇ (cf. Ps. 91, 7). Ps. 30, 6. Job 14, 21. 21, 3ᵇ.

Sometimes in a defiant sense: Ps. 12, 9. 14, 6 תָּבִישׁוּ ye *may* put to shame (if ye like! it matters not). 46, 4. 91, 13. 109, 28 *they* may curse, but do *thou* bless! Mal. 1, 4.

In the preceding instances the impf. is equivalent to *may* in its permissive or concessive capacity; in those which follow, it corresponds to *may* as a term indicating indefiniteness. In the former case, therefore, the tense expresses an independent idea (*licet*, ἔξεστιν), and is consequently indicative; in the latter, it conveys the notion of dependency, and accordingly assumes the position and force of a true subjunctive.

Ex. 5, 11. 8, 23 we will sacrifice כַּאֲשֶׁר יֹאמַר as he *may* command us (see 10, 26). 9, 19 אשר ימצא LXX ὅσα ἐὰν εὑρεθῇ. 2 Ki. 12, 5. Pr. 4, 19.

(β) And in past time: Gen. 2, 19 πᾶν ὃ ἐὰν ἐκάλεσεν. Ex. 34, 34 whatever he *might* be commanded. Dt. 4, 42 LXX τὸν φονεύτην ὃς ἂν φονεύσῃ τὸν πλήσιον αὐτοῦ. Josh. 9, 27 which he *might* choose. Jud. 17, 8. 1 Sa. 23, 13 ויתהלכו באשר יתהלכו

and they went about, wherever they went about, LXX καὶ
ἐπορεύοντο οὗ ἐὰν ἐπορεύοντο[1] (in this, as in some of the other instances, the impf. *combines* the ideas of repetition and indefiniteness, and its force may be nearly represented by the English
'-ever:' on οὗ ἐάν, comp. p. 34 *note*). 2 Sa. 15, 6 יָבֹא (or *used
to come*). 1 Ki. 5, 8 יהיה. 2 Chr. 2, 11 (qui aedificaret). Ez. 1,
12 οὗ ἂν ἦν.

39. (*a*) Expressing a command: Gen. 3, 14. Ex. 21, 12
מוֹת יוּמָת he *shall* be put to death. 14. 15 etc. Nu. 15, 14 as
ye do, כֵּן יֵעָשֶׂה so *shall* he do. 36, 7. 9 יִדְבְּקוּ; and regularly in
prohibitions (which indeed can be expressed in no other
way), Gen. 2, 17. Ex. 20, 3–17 etc.

With a different *nuance:* Ex. 22, 26 in what (else) יִשְׁכָּב *is*
he *to* lie? Nu. 23, 8 how אֶקֹּב *shall* I (or *can I, am I to*) curse?
Job 9, 29 אָנֹכִי אֶרְשָׁע I *must* (or *am to be*) guilty (viz. in the
judgement of another). 10, 15 לֹא אֶשָּׂא רֹאשִׁי I *am not to* lift up
my head. 12, 4 אֶהְיֶה. 17, 6. 19, 16[b]: comp. Hitzig (who cites
1 Sa. 20, 5 MT. to-morrow I *ought* to sit. 28, 1[b] תֵצֵא[2]). 2 Ki.
20, 9 or יָשׁוּב *shall* it return ten degrees? Gen. 4, 7 וְאַתָּה
תִּמְשָׁל בּוֹ *shouldest* or *must* rule over him. 20, 9 deeds אֲשֶׁר
לֹא יֵעָשׂוּ that *should* or *ought* not to be done. 34, 7. Lev. 4,
13 אֲשֶׁר לֹא תֵעָשֶׂינָה. Job 15, 28 in cities לֹא יֵשְׁבוּ לָהֶם which
should not have inhabitants (lit. which should not sit for themselves: for the idioms see Is. 13, 20, and Ew. § 315[a], Ges.-K.
§ 119. 3[c], 2); and in dependent sentences, as Ex. 3, 3. 10,
26 we do not know מַה־נַּעֲבֹד how we *shall* (or *are to*) serve
Yahweh, till etc. 18, 20. 1 Ki. 8, 36. Ps. 32, 8.

(β) And in past time:—Gen. 43, 7 הֲיָדוֹעַ נֵדַע *were* we
possibly *to* know? (or *could* we know?). Jud. 5, 8 *was* there

---

[1] On the *idem per idem* construction in this passage, see the author's
Notes on Samuel, ad loc.; and comp. 2 Sa. 15, 20. Ex. 4, 13. 16, 23.
33, 19. 2 Ki. 8, 1. Ez. 12, 25. Zech. 10, 8, as also Ex. 3, 14 אֶהְיֶה אֲשֶׁר
אֶהְיֶה *I will be that I will be*, on which see *Studia Biblica*, i. (Oxford,
1885), p. 15 ff., with the references.

[2] On 1 Sa. 14, 43 see *Notes on Samuel*, p. 292.

to be seen? 1 Ki. 7, 7 (=οὗ ἔμελλε κρίνειν). 2 Ki. 13, 14 the sickness אשר ימות בו which he *was to* die of. Jer. 51, 60: and involving the idea of an obligation, 2 Sa. 3, 33 *was* Abner *to* die as a fool dieth? (Germ. *sollte* A. *sterben* . . .?), in our idiom (the result anticipated *not* being realized), *ought* A. *to have* died . . .? (יָמוּת, quite different from הֵמַת *did* A. die?). 2 Ki. 3, 27 A.V. his eldest son אשר ימלך that *was to reign* (i. e. *that ought to have reigned*) in his stead. Job 10, 18ᵇ.אגוע verhauchen *hätte ich gesollt* = I *ought to have* expired. 19 ¹.אהיה . . . אובל. And in the oratio obliqua, as Gen. 2, 19 to see מה יקרא what he *would* call them. 43, 7 .כי יאמר 25 for they heard כי שם יאכלו לחם that they *would* (or *were to*) eat bread there. 48, 17 וירא יוסף כי ישית אביו that his father *was putting* etc. Ex. 2, 4. Nu. 15, 34. 24, 11 I said (that) I *would* honour thee. 1 Sa. 22, 22. Isa. 48, 8; 2 Ki. 17, 28 he taught them אֵיךְ יִרְאוּ how they *ought to* fear Yahweh. Further, with אֲשֶׁר or² כִּי, after טוב, as 2 Sa. 18, 3 it is better כִּי־תִהְיֶה־לָּנוּ *that thou shouldest be* (ready) to help us from the city. Ruth 2, 22. Job 10, 3. 13, 9. Qoh. 5, 4 (אשר). 7, 18 (אשר)³; and also after words expressive of a desire or command, though mostly only in the later prose, where the earlier language would use a *direct* expression⁴, as Neh. 2, 5. 7, 65 (=Ezra 2, 63). 8, 14 f. 13, 1. 19. 22. Dan. 1, 8. Esth. 2, 10. Job 36, 10; cf. *v.* 24. 37, 20ᵇ. In poetry (without כי or אשר), Lam. 1, 10: so, in inferior prose, Ezra 10, 8. Dan. 1, 5. Esth. 9, 27 f.⁵

(γ) Moreover, in questions after לָמָה (or לָמָה), מַדּוּעַ, אֵיךְ, instead of the outspoken, categorical perf., the impf. as more

---

¹ Where A.V. R.V. *should have been* must be taken in the sense of *ought to have been:* 'should have . . . ,' as expressing merely a contingent *result*, would correspond to the Heb. perfect (see Job 3, 13 : and §§ 39, 141).

² אשר in the sense of כי is chiefly (though not quite entirely) a late usage (Neh. Esth. Qoh. Dan. [but *not* Chron.]).

³ The *inf.* is more usual with טוב: Gen. 2, 18. Jud. 18, 19 etc.

⁴ *E.g.* in Esth. 2, 10 לאמר לא תגידי. Contrast especially 1 Chr. 21, 18 with 2 Sa. 24, 18.

⁵ Cf. Lev. 9, 6. 2 Sa. 21, 4 (perhaps); also Jer. 5, 22. Ps. 104, 9. Pr. 8, 29.

courteous, more adapted to a tone of entreaty or deprecation, is often preferred[1]: thus Gen. 44, 7. Ex. 2, 13 why תַכֶּה *shouldest* thou smite thy neighbour? 5, 15 (addressing a superior). 32, 11. 1 Sa. 21, 15. Ps. 11, 1. Job 3, 20[2]. Similarly, the less direct form of question (תָּבֹא (תְּבֹאוּ) מֵאַיִן (or אֵי־מִזֶּה) *whence may you be coming?* appears to have been adopted from a sense of its greater politeness as the conventional greeting, in preference to the perfect (which indeed occurs but twice, Gen. 16, 8. 42, 7); e.g. Josh. 9, 8. Jud. 17, 9. 19, 17. Job 1, 7 etc.[3]

(δ) Ex. 3, 11 qualis sum כִּי אֵלֵךְ *ut adeam?* 16, 7. Nu. 11, 12. Job 3, 12. 6, 11. 7, 12 etc. 2 Ki. 8, 13 what is thy servant, the dog (2 Sa. 9, 8), that he *should* do this great thing? Isa. 57, 11. Ps. 8, 5 and in the parody Job 7, 17.

Obs. The analogous idiom with the *perfect* likewise occurs: Ruth 1, 12 that *I should have said*, I have hope. Gen. 40, 15 that they *should have put me*. 1 Sa. 17, 26[b]. Isa. 43, 22. Ps. 44, 19 f. that thou *shouldest have crushed us*; while in Isa. 29, 16 we find both tenses side by side. And with the ptcp., 1 Sa. 20, 1. 1 Ki. 18, 9. Ez. 24, 19. The perf. in such cases denotes the action as *completed*; the ptcp., as still in progress.

40. For the impf., as signifying *would* in the apodosis, and generally for its use in hypothetical propositions, see Chap. XI.

41. Lastly, the imperfect is used after *final* conjunctions, as בַּעֲבוּר ,לְמַעַן (אֲשֶׁר), *in order that*, Gen. 27, 4. 10. 19. 25 etc. פֶּן־ *lest*, 3, 22; further, after אוּלַי *perhaps*, אִם *if*, אֲשֶׁר *whoso*, and other similar words. לְבִלְתִּי also, though construed with

---

[1] And of course when the speaker desires to avert or deprecate an action which is only impending, or not finally completed, as Nu. 27, 4. 1 Sa. 19, 5. 17. 2 Sa. 16, 9; cf. also Gen. 44, 34. Ps. 137, 1 how *shall* (or *can*) we sing? Jer. 47, 7. 1 Sa. 20, 2 why *should* he hide? Contrast the pf. Gen. 26, 9. 2 Sa. 1, 14.

[2] Contrast the different language, 2 Sa. 16, 10. 1 Ki. 1, 6.

[3] So Dietrich, *Abhandlungen*, p. 111. Compare in Greek the modest expression of an opinion, or request, by the opt. with ἄν, e.g. Gorgias 449 B ἆρ᾽ οὖν ἐθελήσαις ἄν, ὦ Γοργία, κ.τ.λ.

the infinitive by preference, is twice followed by the impf., Ex. 20, 20 לְבִלְתִּי תֶחֱטָאוּ. 2 Sa. 14, 14; and מֵן occurs similarly once, Dt. 33, 11 מֵן יְקוּמוּן *that they rise not* again (= מְקוֹם=מֵאֲשֶׁר יְקוּמוּן, which would be the normal construction, Gen. 16, 2. 31, 29. Isa. 24, 10. Job 34, 30). For additional instances the reader is referred to § 115.

Obs. Two or three times פֶּן is found with a perfect, 2 Sa. 20, 6. 2 Ki. 2, 16 (followed by וּ·), the result feared being conceived as having possibly already taken place (exactly as Thuc. 3, 53 νῦν δὲ φοβούμεθα μὴ ἀμφοτέρων ἅμα ἡμαρτήκαμεν); cf. 10, 23. Thrice also, Jer. 23, 14. 27, 18. Ez. 13, 3, לְבִלְתִּי is followed, apparently, by the same tense, though, as it would seem, incompatible with the meaning borne by this conjunction. But in Ezek. we must either render, 'and after (that which) they have not seen' [Ew. Hitz. Smend], or, as בלתי as a *categorical* negation with a finite verb is opposed to usage, read for וּלְבִלְתִּי ראו, לְבִלְתִּי יראו 'that they (the people) should not see,' cf. *v.* 22 [1]; in Jer. 27, the abnormal punctuation בֹּאוּ seems due to a feeling—perhaps to a tradition—that the impf. was really demanded, and we should most probably therefore restore יָבֹאוּ, the first letter of which might readily drop out after the י of לְבִלְתִּי (so Ew. § 337[b], König i. 645, etc.). In Jer. 23 (Graf's explanation being inconsistent with the meaning of לְבִלְתִּי) it is likewise necessary to suppose an error of transcription, and for שָׁבוּ to restore either יֵשְׁבוּ or שׁוּב. Many instances of the accidental transposition of letters occur in the O. T.: 62 noted by the Massorah (some, however, assumed needlessly) are collected in the 'Ochlah we-'ochlah, edited by Frensdorff (Hannover, 1864), No. 91; see e. g. Josh. 6, 13. Jer. 2, 25. 8, 6. 17, 23. 32, 23. In Josh. 4, 24 the perf. after לְמַעַן is still less defensible: but here again the punctuation is already irregular (יְרָאוּם, whereas elsewhere the pf. of יָרֵא exhibits uniformly *sere*), and with Ewald, § 337[b], König i. p. 637, and Dillmann, *ad loc.*, the infinitive יִרְאָתָם must be read.

42. The following passages are left to the reader to examine for himself: to some of them we may, perhaps, have occasion to revert elsewhere. (*a*) Jud. 6, 4. 1 Sa. 27, 9. 1 Ki. 7, 15. Pr. 7, 8. 1 Sa. 13, 17. Neh. 3, 14 f. Jer. 13, 7; לֹא יוּכַל Gen. 48, 10. Josh. 15, 63 Kt. 1 Sa. 3, 2. 2 Sa. 17, 17.

---

[1] Comp. Cornill, *ad loc.*, who, however, strangely retains the perfect.

(β) Gen. 2, 25 ולא יתבששו. Jud. 12, 6 ולא יכין. 1 Sa. 1, 7ᵇ.
2, 25. 27, 4 Kt. 2 Sa. 2, 28. 1 Ki. 1, 1. 8, 8. Jer. 5, 22. 6,
10. 20, 11. 44, 22. Ps. 44, 10. Job 42, 3. Lam. 3, 7. Cant.
3, 4. Dan. 12, 8.

43. At this point it may be worth while, even at the risk
of some repetition, to indicate briefly one or two of the more
important *general* results which I trust will have become
clear in the course of this and the preceding chapter. The
reader who has attentively followed the analysis which has
been there given of the nature and use of the Hebrew tenses
will, it is hoped, find himself able to appreciate and realize,
more fully than was possible at an earlier stage, the truth and
purport of the considerations advanced in the Introduction.
He will recognize, in the first place, the importance and wide
application of the distinction there drawn between *kind* of
time and *order* of time. By means of this distinction it at
once becomes possible to explain both the theory of the
Hebrew tenses and the practice of the Hebrew writers. *Diversity of order is fully compatible with identity of kind;* this
explains the theory: *identity of order in no way excludes
diversity of kind;* this explains the practice.

'Diversity of order is compatible with identity of kind.'
Differences of order (or date), then, are not *necessarily* at-
tended by concomitant differences of tense: the *future*, as
well as the past, may be indicated by the form expressive of
the idea of completion; the *past* (under particular aspects),
no less than the future, may be described by the form which
denotes action as inchoative or incomplete. Each tense,
indeed, but especially the imperfect, exhibits a singular flexibility: at the same time it will be clear that this flexibility
does not overreach the limits prescribed by the most rigorous
logic. The meanings assumed, however divergent, do not in
reality involve any contradiction: a fundamental principle
can be discovered which will embrace them all—a higher
unity exists in which they meet and are reconciled. Although,

however, one paradox which the use of the tenses seems to present is hereby solved, there still remains another difficulty, which these considerations do not touch. If a difference of *tense* is no criterion of difference of *date*, if events occurring at every conceivable moment of time *must* be denoted by two forms, and *may* be denoted by one, how is it possible to avoid ambiguity? The answer has been already incidentally alluded to more than once. The *context,* intelligently apprehended, constitutes the differentiating factor which *fixes* the signification of the tense. Taken by itself the meaning of the tense may be ambiguous and uncertain : a reference to the context—to the whole, of which it is itself an inseparable part—makes clear the relation subsisting between them, and reduces the ambiguity to a minimum.

But, secondly, ' identity of order in no way excludes diversity of kind.' One and the same event may be described either as nascent, or as completed : each tense, therefore, preserves always its own proper force, which must not be lost sight of because difficult of reproduction in another language, or because the genius of our own tongue would have been satisfied with, perhaps, some more obvious mode of expression. The line of demarcation between the two tenses is as clearly and sharply drawn as between the aorist (or perfect) and the imperfect in Greek or Latin. Whichever tense is used, it is used by the writer *with a purpose :* by the choice of the other tense, the action described would have been presented under a more or less modified aspect. הֵן הִכָּה־צוּר וַיָּזוּבוּ מַיִם וּנְחָלִים יִשְׁטֹפוּ Ps. 78, 20 the change of tense is no less marked, the colouring imparted by it to the description no less perceptible, than in the line '*Conticuere* omnes, intentique ora *tenebant*,' where the effect produced by the variation is closely similar. And often there is a manifest beauty and propriety in the tense selected. Ps. 19, 2–4 the *continual* declaration of the heavens, the *reiterated* announcement of day and night, the *established fact* that this proclamation is audible wherever their dominion extends, could not be more concisely and expressively indicated than is here done by a simple variation in tense[1]. And few languages would indicate as much with greater ease and neatness, or by a lighter touch. This single instance will suffice to shew how much may be lost by disregarding a seemingly slight and trivial change: to examine and note the exact force of each tense he meets, until practice enables him to catch it instinctively and without reflection, should be the first duty of the student.

---

[1] Compare Jer. 36, 18 (the process of dictation described with precision—ברוך מפיו יקרא אלי . . . . . ואני כתב על הספר בדיו).

A curious misreading of a paragraph in Gesenius, in consequence of which the writer, without the smallest misgivings, transfers to the perfect a sense belonging to the imperfect, may be seen in the *Speaker's Commentary*, iv. 623[b].

CHAPTER IV.

The Cohortative and Jussive.

44. WE saw above, § 23, how readily the imperfect might lend itself so as to become the vehicle for expressing a volition; and of its use with a permissive force we have already seen examples in § 38. There the imperfect appeared with its form unaltered: and this is often the case, not merely when this permissive force becomes so intensified as to be equivalent to a petition or a command (see, for example, Ps. 17, 8. 43, 1. 51, 9 f. 14. 59, 2. 60, 3. 61, 7 f. etc., where it is parallel to the imperative[1]), but also when it is used in the first person[2] to express an intention or desire on the part of the speaker—the mere future 'I shall' gliding insensibly into the more decided 'I will.' But Hebrew possesses two special forms, commonly known as the *jussive* and *cohortative*[3], which are very frequently used to indicate more explicitly when the imperfect bears these two significations respectively. Both these forms exist in Arabic in a more complete and original condition than they exhibit in Hebrew: developed at an early period in the history of the Semitic languages, in

---

[1] And add Gen. 1, 9. 41, 34. Jud. 6, 39. 1 Ki. 15, 19. Isa. 47, 3. Ps. 109, 7. Job 3, 9. Neh. 2, 3 al. In many of these passages the unshortened form occurs in close proximity to an actual jussive.

[2] Not so often, however, as with the second or third persons, in which the modal force can be less frequently distinguished by the form: cf. 1 Sa. 12, 19. 2 Sa. 10, 12. Jer. 8, 14. Ps. 59, 17 (cf. 18). 2 Sa. 22, 50 (Ps. 18, 50 אֲזַמְּרָה). Jud. 5, 3. Job 21, 3. 33, 31 (13, 13 אֲדַבְּרָה).

[3] I sometimes use the common term *voluntative* to embrace both.

Arabic after having reached a certain point of perfection, they there remained stationary, without experiencing any of the levelling influences which caused them partially to disappear in Hebrew. Although, however, limited in range of application, their distinctive character remained substantially unimpaired; and they continued to constitute an integral and important element in the syntax of the language.

45. The *cohortative* is scarcely ever found except with the first[1] person, either sing. or plur. as the case may be. It is formed by adding to the verb the termination הָ‑[2] (e. g. אֶקְטְלָה; but if preceded by a long vowel it is toneless, like הָ‑ *locale*[3], and in accordance with the rule mentioned p. 18, as אָשׁוּבָה), which has the effect of marking with peculiar emphasis the concentration of the will upon a particular object —נֵלְכָה *let us go, we would fain go*, the idea being expressed with more keenness and energy, and with a deeper personal interest or emotion, than by the mere imperfect נֵלֵךְ.

46. The *jussive*, on the other hand, belongs almost exclusively to the second and third persons[4] (in the second person principally after אַל, which is not used with the imperative). It is obtained by shortening the imperfect in such

---

[1] In the 3rd pers. Dt. 33, 16 תְּבוֹאתָה (where the strange form can be hardly anything but an error for תָּבֹאָה; see König i. p. 646f.; Ges.-K. § 48. 3 *Rem.*); Is. 5, 19 וְתָבוֹאָה ... יָחִישָׁה; Ps. 20, 4 יְזַכְּרֶנָה; Job 11, 17 תָּעֻפָה (see § 152. iii : Hitz. and Bickell, however, with Pesh. Targ. read a subst. תְּעֻפָה). Job 22, 21 תְּבוֹאָתְךָ is supposed by those who defend the MT. (e. g. Del.) to be a case not of the -*ah* of the cohortative, but of a double feminine : far more probably, however, the text is in error (see König i. p. 644, and the suggestions in Delitzsch).

[2] Or once הֶ‑ Ps. 20, 4, cf. 1 Sa. 28, 15 ; and similarly in the imperative once or twice, דְעֶה Pr. 24, 14 for the usual דְּעָה, and רַבֶּה Jud. 9, 29 ; compare Isa. 59, 5. Zech. 5, 4. Ez. 25, 13 (quoted by Delitzsch).

[3] In thus comparing the הָ‑ *locale* with the הָ‑ of the cohortative, I do not wish to assert or assume their original identity.

[4] The exceptions are 1 Sa. 14, 36. 2 Sa. 17, 12. Isa. 41, 23 Kt. 28. 42, 6 ; and cf. Job 23, 9. 11.

a manner as the form of each particular word will allow:
e.g. יָכְרֵת from יַכְרִית, יָגֶל (through the intermediate, but seldom
actually occurring type, יִגְל) from יִגְלֶה (Hif.), תְּגַל from תְּגַלֶּה,
etc.[1] The parallelism of form between the jussive and the
imperative (גַּל, הַךְ, הֵעַל, הַכְרֵת) makes it probable that the
origin of this abbreviation or apocopation is to be traced to
the quickened and hasty pronunciation of a person issuing a
command: the curtness and compactness of the form corresponding to the abrupt and peremptory tone which the
language of one in such a situation would naturally assume[2].

47. So much for the origin and primary meaning of
these two modal forms. It only remains to mention, before
noticing instances of their use, that in Hebrew many classes
of verbs do not admit of the modifications of form by which
they are distinguishable from the ordinary imperfect. Thus
verbs ל"ה hardly ever[3] receive the הָ‑ of the cohortative,
and verbs ל"א only very rarely. The jussive is seldom distinguishable, except in verbs ע"ו, ל"ה, and the Hif'il generally;
while before suffixes both forms are equally incapable of
recognition[4]. From this it follows that they are not indis-

---

[1] The analogy between the abbreviated forms in verbs ל"ה and the
forms of segolate nouns is very complete and worth noticing: thus יָגֶל : יַגְל
(presupposed from יַגְלֶה; cf. יַפְתְּ, יָרֶךְ) :: (יָרֶךְ : דָּרֶךְ (presupposed from
דַּרְכִּי); with יַעַשׂ cf. נַעַר, with יָתַע פֶּתַח, with הֵתַע תֵּתַח, with נֵצַח, with אֶרָא and
אֵפֶן, שֵׁבֶם, with יַבְךְ the rare form נֶרְדְּ: in יְהִי from יִהְיֶה, the yod becomes
vocalized exactly as in פְּרִי (in pause פֶּרִי, יָהִי); and in יִשְׁתַּחוּ (in pause
יֶ‑חוּ) from יִשְׁתַּחֲוֶה the same process is undergone by waw precisely as
in יָהוּ (in pause יִשְׁעָיָהוּ etc.) from יַהְוֶה (cf. also אָחוּ, שָׁחוּ, and with a different
vowel בֹּהוּ, אֹהוּ). It should be stated that some of the forms quoted
occur only after וַ, and not as independent jussives.

[2] Cf. Ewald, Gramm. Arab. § 210: 'cuius [modi iussivi] haec est
summa lex, ut forma a fine rapidius et brevius enuncietur, prout ipse
iubentis animus commotior, sermo rapidior est.'

[3] Twice (according to the punctuation): Isa. 41, 23. Ps. 119, 117.

[4] The only exceptions are Isa. 35, 4. Dt. 32, 7.

pensable elements in Hebrew; and the truth of the remark
made at the beginning of the chapter, that the unmodified
imperfect is sufficient for the expression of any kind of volition, becomes self-evident. So, too, it may be noticed that
they are not always used, even in cases where their presence
might naturally be expected : e. g. Gen. 19, 17. 1 Sa. 25, 25 :
Gen. 9, 25 (יהיה, but יהי, יפת). Jud. 6, 39[b]. 19, 11. Isa. 1, 25.
Jer. 28, 6[a]. Ruth 1, 8 Kt. Job 3, 9[c] etc. Still, upon the
whole, where the modal forms exist, they are employed by
preference.

48. The ordinary usages of the cohortative and jussive
are so readily intelligible that a small selection of instances
will suffice, the variations in meaning presented by different
passages depending entirely upon the tone and manner of
the speaker and the position which he occupies relatively to
the person spoken of or addressed. Both forms are often
rendered more emphatic and expressive by the addition of
the particle נָא; e. g. Gen. 18, 21 אֵרֲדָה־נָּא. 30 אַל־נָא יִחַר לַאדֹנָי;
26, 28 תְּהִי נָא.

49. The cohortative, then, marks the presence of a
strongly-felt inclination or impulse : in cases where this is
accompanied by the ability to carry the wished-for action
into execution, we may, if we please, employ *I, we will* . . .
in translating ; where, however, the possibility of this depends
upon another (as when permission is asked to do something,
or when the cohortative is employed in the plural, in accordance with the etymological meaning of the name, to instigate
or suggest), we must restrict ourselves to some less decided
expression, which shall be better adapted to embody a mere
proposal or petition.

Thus (*a*) Gen. 12, 2 f. 18, 21 *I will* go down, now. 27,
41. 33, 12 etc. Isa. 8, 2. Ps. 7, 18 אֲזַמְּרָה *I will* sing. 9, 2 f.
13, 6. 18, 50 etc.; in 1 pers. plur. Gen. 22, 5 נֵלְכָה *we* (I and
the lad) *will* go. 24, 57. 29, 27.

(*β*) Gen. 33, 14. 50, 5 אֶעֱלֶה־נָּא וְאֶקְבְּרָה *let me* go up, I

pray, and bury my father. Ex. 3, 18 *we would fain* go. Nu.
21, 22 (in the message to Sihon, craving leave to pass
through his territory) *let me* pass through. Jud. 12, 5 *I should
like* to cross. 15, 1 אֶבְאָה. 1 Sa. 28, 22. 1 Ki. 19, 20 etc. Ps.
17, 15 O *may I be* satisfied . . . ! 25, 2. 39, 5. 61, 5. 65, 5.
69, 15 אַל־אֶטְבְּעָה *let me* not (or *may I* not) sink! Jon. 1, 14[1]:
and as a literal 'cohortative,' Gen. 11, 3. 19, 32, and often;
Jer. 18, 18. Ps. 2, 3. 34, 4 etc.; cf. 85, 9. Hab. 2, 1 אעמדה
ואתיצבה.

50. In the same way the jussive assumes different shades
of meaning, varying with the situation or authority of the
speaker: it is thus found—

(*a*) As a 'jussive,' in the strict sense of the term, to convey
an injunction or command, Gen. 1, 3 יְהִי אוֹר etc. 22, 12. 30,
34. 33, 9. 45, 20. Ex. 16, 19. Dt. 15, 3. Isa. 61, 10 תגל נפשי.
Ps. 13, 6. 97, 1 etc. 2 Chr. 36, 23; and the same in a tone
of defiance or irony[2], Ex. 10, 10 יהי כן יי עמכם וגו'. Jud. 6, 31
if he is a god יָרֶב לוֹ *let him* (or *he may*) strive for himself! Isa.
47, 13. Jer. 17, 15.

Obs. In commands אַל (*do not*) and לֹא (*thou shalt not*) are sometimes
found interchanging: see Ex. 23, 1. 34, 3. Lev. 10, 6. Jud. 13, 14. 1 Ki.
20, 8. Ezra 9, 12. But only very seldom indeed is the jussive (or cohortative) form employed after לֹא: Gen. 24, 8. 1 Ki. 2, 6. 1 Sa. 14, 36.
2 Sa. 17, 12. 18, 14.

Sometimes, from the circumstances of the case, the command becomes a permission: so Num. 24, 7 וְיָרֹם and *let* his
king *be higher* than 'Agág, 19 וְיֵרְדְּ and *let* him *rule.* Deut. 20,
5. Isa. 27, 6 (where observe the simple impf. יָצִיץ parallel to
a jussive). 35, 1 f. Hos. 14, 6 f. I will be as the dew to
Israel: *let* him flourish וְיַךְ *and strike forth* his roots like

---

[1] Cf. Job 32, 21[a] אל־נא אשא פני־איש 'I *hope I may not* shew unfair
favour to any one.'
[2] Cf. the imperative 1 Ki. 2, 22. Isa. 47, 12. Job 40, 10; Ez. 20, 39.
Amos 4, 4. 1 Ki. 22, 15. Nah. 3, 15[b].

Lebanon. Zech. 10, 7 יִגֵּל לִבָּם. Ps. 14, 7 *let* Jacob rejoice. 22, 27 *let* your heart revive. 69, 33. 2 Ki. 2, 10.

(β) In a somewhat weaker signification, to impart advice or make a suggestion :—

Gen. 41, 33 f. and now יֵרֶא *let* Phar'oh *look out* a man etc. Ex. 8, 25. Jud. 15, 2. 1 Ki. 1, 2. Ps. 27, 14 (31, 25). 118, 1–4. Pr. 1, 5. 9, 4 etc.

(γ) To express an entreaty or request, a prayer or wish, and in particular blessings or imprecations :—

Gen. 9, 27. 31, 49 Yahweh יִצֶף *watch* between me and thee! 44, 33 יֵשֶׁב־נָא *let* thy servant remain, I pray. 45, 5. Ex. 5, 21. Nu. 12, 12. Dt. 28, 8. 1 Sa. 1, 23. 24, 16. 1 Ki. 10, 9. 20, 32. Ps. 7, 6. 27, 9. 35, 6. 69, 26. 80, 18. 109, 12–15. 19. 2 Chr. 14, 10b (a prayer like Ps. 9, 20).

Obs. In the second person the jussive is very rare, except after אַל, its place being naturally occupied by the imperative ; see, however, 1 Sa. 10, 8. Ez. 3, 3. Ps. 71, 21 הֶּרֶב O multiply my greatness ! Dan. 9, 25; and cf. the phrase יְדוֹעַ תֵּדַע, Gen. 15, 13. 1 Sa. 28, 1. Jer. 26, 15. Pr. 27, 23 al. בִּין תָּבִין, 23, 1 (the special form not being needed, § 44).

51. Thus far all is plain and clear. The use of both the modal forms is so simple and natural as seemingly to preclude even the possibility of any obscurity or difficulty emerging. And yet we are on the verge of what may be termed the *vexatissima quaestio* of Hebrew syntax.

Does the cohortative ever signify '*must?*' Startling as such a question may appear, after what has been said respecting the nature of this mood, and corroborated by the examples cited in proof of it, it is nevertheless a question which has to be asked, and one to which we must endeavour to find, if possible, a satisfactory answer. The fact is, that a small number of passages exist in which the intention or wish which the cohortative properly expresses, appears to be so limited and guided by external conditions imposed upon the speaker that the idea of impulse from within seems to disappear before that of compulsion from without. So much so is this the case that many modern grammarians do not hesitate to affirm that under such circumstances the cohortative has the signification *must*[1]. Such a sense, however, is so completely at variance with the meaning this form bears elsewhere that considerable caution should be taken before adopting it : indeed, stated absolutely and unreservedly, it cannot be adopted at all. Now it is observable that in almost all the passages in question the doubtful expression occurs in the mouth of a person suffering from some great depression or distress : however *involuntary*, therefore, the situation itself may be in which he is placed, the direction taken by his thoughts is *voluntary*, at any rate so long as his circumstances do not wholly overpower him. His thoughts may, for example, either suggest some action tending to relieve his feelings, or they may form themselves into a wish expressive of disconsolate resignation.

52. By keeping these considerations in mind, we shall generally be able to interpret the cohortative without departing so widely from its usual signification as to do violence to reason. How natural, Ps. 42, 5. 10, for the exiled poet to find relief[2] in tearful recollections of the days כִּי אֶעֱבֹר בַּסָּךְ ; or, *v.* 10, to give free course, as Job 10, 1, to his plaint! And similarly 55, 3. 18. 77[3], 4. 7[a, b]. Isa. 38, 10 (in *despair*,

---

[1] Comp. Ewald, § 228[a] ; Böttcher, ii. 186 ; Hupfeld and Delitzsch on Ps. 55, 3 : on the other hand, Müller, *Schulgrammatik*, § 382[a].

[2] This is of course said upon the assumption that Hitzig's objection, that ' pouring out one's soul ' is not a voluntary act, is unfounded. Comp., however, the imperative שִׁפְכוּ לֵב Ps. 62, 9. Lam. 2, 19 ; and for the practical identity of נפשׁ and לֵב in expressions of this sort, comp. Ps. 61, 3 with 107, 5. Jon. 2, 8.

[3] The following appears to be the best articulation, grammatically, of this difficult Psalm. *Ver.* 3 is evidently descriptive of the past, *I sought*, etc.; *v.* 4 pictures, under the form of a quotation, how the Psalmist at the time thus indicated *abandoned* himself to his distress of mind ; *vv.* 5 f. the narrative is resumed ; *v.* 7[a, b] again, as *v.* 4, represents his passionate reflections on the יָמִים מִקֶּדֶם (cf. Job 29, 2); *vv.* 7[c]–10 ' and my spirit inquired, (saying), " Will the Lord cast off for ever ? "' etc.;

'let me go, then; I am ready to die,' the feeling פקדתי יתר שנותי extorts from him the wish to relinquish the life now suddenly become a βίος ἀβίωτος : comp., though the tone is different, Gen. 46, 30). 59, 10 (describing the *efforts* made to find the way[1]). Jer. 3, 25 נשכבה בבשתנו (in despondent resignation, as perhaps Ps. 57, 5 with the same verb).

53. In these passages it will be observed that while the usual signification of the cohortative seems at first sight somewhat obscured, there is no necessity to suppose it absent, still less to imagine it superseded by a contrary signification. And, in fact, Ewald's words, § 228[a], are only to the effect that the cohortative is used to designate voluntary actions, whether they proceed from perfectly free choice, or are '*at the same time* conditioned from without[2].' This language is intelligible and consistent; but commentators sometimes forget the limitation with which it is accompanied, and express themselves as though they thought it possible for the cohortative to denote external compulsion ('must') *alone*, to the exclusion of any internal impulse occasioned or suggested by it[3]. Accordingly they find no difficulty in accounting for the presence of the form under discussion in Jer. 4, 19. 21. Ps. 88, 16, where אָפֿוּנָה, אֶשְׁמְעָה, אָחֹוּלָה seem to be *exclusively* 'determined from without,' in such a manner as to leave the speaker without even the most limited scope for personal choice. But upon what principle the cohortative can then be employed to express such an idea with any propriety, it is impossible to understand; in preference, there-

---

lastly, *v.* 11 *Then I said*, introduces the thought with which he finally put his questionings to silence. (So Cheyne.)

[1] Cf. Delitzsch's note : 'the impulse of self-preservation, which drives them in their ἀπορία to feel for a way of escape.'

[2] Similarly Delitzsch on Ps. 55, 3 : the cohortative not unfrequently denotes '*ich soll* oder *ich muss* von *Selbsterregungen*, die von aussen bedingt sind.'

[3] E. g. even Hupfeld expresses himself incautiously on Ps. 57, 5. 88, 16.

fore, to supposing that the הָ‍ has in these passages assumed
a meaning diametrically opposed to, and incompatible with,
that which it holds elsewhere, it is better to adopt the opinion
of Hitzig that it has *lost its significance*[1]. This is certainly
the case at times with the so-called הָ‍ *locale* (in such words
as עֶזְרָתָה, עוֹלָתָה, which appear as simple nominatives, or
לְשִׁאֵלָה, לְישׁוּעָתָה, where it is at least redundant after the preposition[2]), and is more in accordance with other phenomena
of language than the violent transition which the other explanation involves[3].

54. We saw above, § 27, how the impf. could be used in
poetry to give a vivid representation of the past; and there
are a few passages in which, as it seems, the cohortative is
employed similarly, the context *limiting* the action to the
past, and the mood, apparently, indicating the energy or impulse with which it was performed. So 2 Sa. 22, 38 ארדפה
(for which in Ps. 18 ארדוף). Ps. 73, 17 עד אבוא . . . אבינה
לאחריתם (under the influence of the rhythm of Dt. 32, 29?
Hitz.). Pr. 7, 7 אָבִינָה . . . וָאֵרֶא. Job 19, 18 [4]אָקוּמָה וַיְדַבְּרוּ־בִי
(on 30, 26 comp. § 66 *n*.). Possibly, also, Ps. 55, 18[a]; on 66,
6, however, see Perowne's note : and Hab. 2, 1 the eagerness
of the watchman preparing for his post is graphically depicted

---

[1] Hitzig himself explains the other passages in the same way, or else
by supposing וֹ omitted : but in most of them, at any rate, the more emo-
tional and emphatic form appears appropriate.

[2] See Hupfeld on Ps. 3, 3, and especially Philippi, *Wesen und Ursprung des St. constr. im Hebräischen*, pp. 128, 143 f.

[3] The real difficulty lies not in understanding how the original meaning
of a termination may have been lost or forgotten, but in understanding
how at one and the same time it could have been treated as both significant and non-significant. And yet, even if we accept Hitzig's view as
at least defensible by analogy, this is what must have been done by
Jeremiah. The cases referred to above are scarcely in this respect
parallel.

[4] Or should we supply in thought אמרתי before אקומה? Hitz. 'will
ich aufstehn, so reden sie über mich.'

in the form of a quotation, the narrative proper beginning only with *v.* 2 : Cant. 3, 2ᵃ is similar, the quotation implied by the cohortative being followed in 2ᵇ by the perfect בקשתי. Cf. Ps. 77, 4 (p. 56 *n.*).

55. The appearance of the cohortative after אוּלִי Ex. 32, 20, cf. Jer. 20, 10, or לְמַעַן Ps. 9, 15, will not require further comment.   In Ps. 26, 6. 71, 23. 77, 12 *for I will remember*, it retains its usual force, merely indicating more decidedly than the bare impf. would have done the unconstrained readiness felt by the writer.   It is found also in the phrase עַד אַרְגִּיעָה *while I would wink*, Prov. 12, 19 : cf. Jer. 49, 19= 50, 44.

56. We may now turn to the anomalies presented by the use of the jussive. Not unfrequently in poetry the jussive occurs under circumstances where, from the general context, the simple imperfect would seem the more natural form to employ; and where, owing to the consequent difficulty of marking its special force in translating, its presence is apt to be overlooked. The explanation of this usage will be best introduced and most readily understood, if we first of all notice some instances in which the *imperative* is similarly employed. The difficulty, it will be seen, is this : we seem to require only the statement of a *fact;* we find instead a form preferred which expresses a *command:* are we now at liberty to disregard the mood altogether, and to treat the jussive as equivalent to a simple imperfect? or ought we rather to seek for some explanation which will account for and do justice to the form chosen by the writer? Although a few passages remain unexplained, the analogy of the imperative, the meaning of which can be neither forgotten nor evaded, will lead us to decide in favour of the latter alternative.

57. The appearance of imperative and jussive alike, under the circumstances alluded to, is to be referred simply to a familiar characteristic of the poetical imagination. To the poet, whatever be his language or country, the world is animated by a life, vibrating in harmony with his own, which the prosaic eye is unable to discern : for him, not merely the animal world, but inanimate nature as well, is throbbing with human emotions, and keenly susceptible to every impression from without (e.g. Ps. 65, 14. 104, 19. 114, 3–6. Isa. 35, 1 f.); he addresses boldly persons and objects not actually present (e.g. Isa. 13, 2. 23, 1 f. 4. 40, 9 etc. Ps. 98, 7 f. 114, 7 f.), or peoples a scene with invisible beings, the creations of his own fancy (Isa. 40, 3. 57, 14. 62, 10) ; he feels, and expresses, a vivid sympathy with the characters and transactions with which he has to deal. The result is that instead of describing an occurrence in the language of bare fact, a poet often loves to represent it under the form of a command proceeding from himself. Now in the majority of cases, those viz. which resemble Isa. 23, 1 etc., no difficulty arises : the difficulty first meets us in those passages where the command seems to be out of place, in consequence of the state of things previously described rendering it apparently superfluous and nugatory. But the fact is, these are only extreme instances; and the two considerations just mentioned will really be found sufficient to explain the anomaly.

Perhaps the strongest case is Isa. 54, 14 '*be far* from anxiety, for thou wilt not fear; and from terror, for it will not come nigh thee,' where the imperative occurs in the midst of a series of verbs describing the Zion of the future, and is clearly only the more nervous and energetic expression of what in prose would run ' thou *mayest* be far from anxiety,' or (changing the form) ' thou *needst* not be anxious.' Isa. 33, 20 is similar. The construction is more frequent in negative sentences, i. e. with אַל and the jussive : so Ps. 41, 3. Job 5, 22. Prov. 3, 25. Isa. 2, 9. Jer. 7, 6 (where וְדָם נָקִי אַל־ תִּשְׁפְּכוּ, involving a change of construction, is in fact parenthetical). Cant. 7, 3.

58. These passages, in all of which the verb is in the second person, and so distinctly imperative, establish a pre-

cedent which justifies us in interpreting the instances which
follow in the same way. It will be seen that by adhering to
the strict grammar, instead of deserting it on account of a
superficial difficulty, a more pointed and appropriate sense
will disclose itself. (The verb will now be always in the third
person.) Ps. 34, 6[1]. 50, 3 וְאַל־יֶחֱרַשׁ *and let him not be silent*
(the scene is introduced by the pf. הוֹפִיעַ *v.* 2 : but the poet,
instead of continuing in the same style, and writing simply
'he comes and is not silent,' imagines himself as an eager
and interested spectator, praying the Deity, already visible in
the distance, to come near, Ps. 7, 7 f., and declare his will).
66, 7 (where, however, the jussive is probably to be understood as conveying a *literal* warning). 121, 3 (contrast לֹא 4 :
'אַל adds to לֹא the sympathy of the speaker with the expected
future, and expresses consequently a hope' (Hitz.): in *v.* 4
this hope is raised to a certainty by לֹא). Jer. 46, 6. 51, 3.
Zech. 9, 5. 10, 7 (§ 50 *a*). Job 20, 17 אַל יֵרֶא (the interest
felt by the writer betrays itself by causing him to glide insensibly from the language descriptive of a fact into that
which is expressive of emotion). And without a negative :
Ps. 11, 6. 12, 4. 72. 8. 13. 16. 17. 85, 14 let justice go before him and etc. (as in the passages quoted from Jer. and
Zech., a future fact represented by the poet under the form
of a command). Dt. 28, 8 יְצַו יְהוָֹה אִתְּךָ אֶת־הַבְּרָכָה. 21 יַדְבֵּק.
36 יֹלֵךְ.

Hitherto we have found no occasion to relinquish the
recognized and usual signification of the jussive. Some
other passages, in which the occurrence of this mood seems
abnormal, will be noticed in the chapters which follow : and
a few that remain even then will be examined in Appendix II.

Obs. 1. The true character of the cohortative, although now universally recognized, was for long disregarded or unobserved : it was for the

---

[1] Sept. Pesh. Jerome, however, express here פְנֵיכֶם, with imperatives
in 6ᵃ. This reading is probably correct (so Ewald, Cheyne, Kirkpatrick).

first time clearly and convincingly established by Gesenius, in his *Lehr-gebäude der Hebr. Sprache* (Leipzig 1817), App. ii. p. 870, where a large number of instances are collected and examined, 'since it is not fair or right that a matter which can be despatched at a single stroke, if one will only submit to the labour of exhaustive investigation, should remain any longer an object of uncertainty and dispute.' Previous grammarians had, however(as Gesenius himself remarks), maintained the same opinion : and, indeed, so soon as Arabic began to be studied systematically, with a view to the illustration of Hebrew, the analogies presented there by the use of the 'jussive' and 'energetic' moods could not fail to arrest attention. Accordingly we find Albert Schultens in his *Institutiones ad fundamenta Linguae Hebraeae* (Lugduni Batavorum 1756), p. 432, asserting that by the addition of ה—' simul *accessionem* fieri *significationis* non ambigendum ;' and Schröder, *Institutiones* (Ulmae 1785), p. 198, speaking of it as 'vocum formam et significationem augens.' A few years later, however, Stange in his *Anticritica in locos quosdam Psalmorum* (pars prior, Lipsiae 1791), p. 45, writes as follows on the same subject :— ' Quod supra scripsi, ה quod vulgo, idque male paragogicum vocant, non temere vocabulis apponi, sed futuris et imperativis adiectum . . . . exprimere Latinorum coniunctivum aut si mavis subiunctivum, multis fictum et falsum videri facile possum coniicere ; nam quae imberbes in Grammaticis non didicimus, ea fere contemni ac reiici solent : id tamen ex multis exemplis verissimum reperiri, nemini in posterum dubium esse debet.' It appears, then, that in the Hebrew grammars of his day, *quarum tamen numerus infinitus est, ac quibusque nundinis Lipsiensibus augetur* (ibid.), the view thrown out by Schultens and Schröder had met with as little approval as at the time when Gesenius published his *Lehrgebäude*. Stange himself supports his statement by a considerable list of instances, though not so copious or accurate as the one afterwards given by Gesenius.

Obs. 2. The existence of a special meaning attaching to the shortened forms of the impf., at least in the case of the verbs ה״ל, had been previously noticed, though here likewise it was Gesenius who, in the first edition of his smaller grammar (1813), and more fully in his *Lehrgebäude*, confirmed and demonstrated the correctness of the observation. Thus Schröder, p. 212, writes :—'Secunda ratio retracti ex syllaba ultima ad penultimam accentus posita est in singulari emphasi, qua vox pronunciatur, uti fit in mandato, hortatione, precatione, vel in interdicto, dehortatione, deprecatione, vel in voto, vel ubi gravior quidam subest animi adfectus :' compare also Schultens, p. 443. So far, however, as the *theory* here stated is concerned (which is identical with Ewald's, § 224[a, c], above § 46, *note*), it is singular that, if it be true, the retrocession is not more frequent: except in the few cases cited below, § 70 (where it is to be attributed to the presence of אל), the tone never recedes in the jussive beyond the limits of verbs ל"ה. It is plain that the jussive *shortened* (or, as in Arabic, *cut off*) the last syllable of the verb: there seems to be no evidence that in doing this it likewise produced any retrocession of the tone. On the jussive forms of verbs ל"ה compare Olshausen, § 228ᵃ.

Obs. 3. As regards any ambiguity which may be thought to arise from the use of the unmodified impf. to denote a command or wish, the reader will remember that our own language offers a close parallel. I quote the following from E. A. Abbott's *Shakespearian Grammar*, a book in which the method commended in the extract from Gesenius (see Obs. 1) has been admirably carried out, § 365 :—'The reader of Shakespeare should always be ready to recognize the subjunctive, even where the identity of the subjunctive with the indicative inflexion renders distinction between two moods impossible except from the context. Thus:

" Therefore take with thee my most heavy curse,
Which in the day of battle tire thee more
Than all the complete armour that thou wear'st!
My prayers on the adverse party *fight*,
And there the little souls of Edward's children
Whisper the spirits of thine enemies,
And *promise* them success and victory."
Rich. III. iv. 4. 187 ff.'

Add further :
' But all the charms of love
Salt Cleopatra, *soften* thy waned lip!'
Ant. and Cl. ii. 1, 20-21.

And (from § 364) :
' For his passage,
The soldiers' music and the rites of war
Speak loudly for him.'
Hamlet v. 2. 409–411.

CHAPTER V.

The Voluntative with Waw.

59. In the present chapter we have to examine the use of the imperfect when combined, in its capacity as a voluntative, with the simple or *weak* וְ (with *shwa'* וְיִקְטֹל, וְאֶסְלַח: when the first letter of the verb has *shwa'* likewise, we obtain, of course, the forms וַאֲגַדְּלָה, וּתְהִי, וִידַבֵּר: these must be carefully distinguished from (וְאֲגַדְּלָה, וַתְּהִי, וַיְדַבֵּר, וְאֶסְלַח, וַיִּקְטֹל). Inasmuch as the particular signification it then assumes depends upon its being, not a *mere* imperfect, but a *voluntative*, it is important to recollect what was remarked in § 44, that the voluntative force may be really present even though the corresponding modal form does not meet the eye.

60. This weak וְ is used with the imperfect—as a jussive or cohortative by preference, if these exist as distinct forms, though not exclusively even then—in order to express the design or purpose of a preceding act, which it does in a less formal and circumstantial manner than בעבור, למען etc., but with greater conciseness and elegance. An instance or two will make it clear in what way this is effected. 1 Sa. 15, 16 הֶרֶף וְאַגִּידָה let alone *and I will tell* thee: inasmuch as it is the wish to tell which occasions the utterance of הֶרֶף, this is equivalent to saying 'let alone *that* I may tell thee.' Gen. 19, 20 let me flee thither וּתְחִי *and let* my soul live (=*that* it may live). Jer. 38, 20. Ex. 10, 17 entreat God וְיָסֵר *and may he remove* (=*that* he remove) from me only this death[1]. In

---

[1] As this combination of the voluntative with וְ expresses an *ulterior issue*, advancing beyond, but regulated by, the principal verb, it is called

translating, we may sometimes preserve the force of the jussive or cohortative; sometimes it is better to employ *that*: care ought to be taken, however, never to confuse (say) וִיהִי with either וְהָיָה or וַיְהִי, from both of which it is entirely distinct, but to both of which it may seem superficially similar in meaning—to the former when referring to future time, to the latter when relating to the past.

61. The ambiguity, so far as the future is concerned, arises from the following cause. In English, when we desire to express our opinion that one given event will occur in consequence of another, we commonly employ the *future*, provided that this second event may be viewed by the speaker as more or less probable in itself—not as purely dependent upon the preceding action as its antecedent: in other words, our language *states* only the *post hoc*, leaving the *propter hoc* to be *inferred* from the juxtaposition of the words in the sentence. Thus, if we regard the result as tolerably certain, we say *and it will* . . .; if as uncertain, we say *that it may* . . .: we *can*, of course, employ the latter form in both instances, but our idiom *prefers* the former, if the circumstances will allow its use. Hebrew, on the other hand, employs the latter form regularly: hence it results that the same phrase can be rendered into English by *two* equivalents, one of which at the same time corresponds in addition, so far as the mere words go, to another totally different expression in Hebrew. The fact, however, that *and it will be* corresponds to וְהָיָה as well as to וִיהִי must not mislead us into imagining the latter to be identical with the former; for in meaning and use alike the two are quite distinct. To avoid confusion, therefore, it is safer, as well as more accurate, when we meet with a jussive after וְ, either to preserve the jussive form, or to confine ourselves to the perfectly legitimate equivalent, *that*

---

by Ewald the *consecutive* or 'relatively-progressive' voluntative. (Respecting these terms more will be found, p. 71, *note* 4.)

and the subjunctive. In Ex. 10, 17 we at once feel that we cannot render *and he shall remove :* v. 21 on the contrary, for וִיהִי the sense would *permit* the rendering *and there shall be*, the writer, however, as before, brings the result into more intimate connexion with the previous act נְטֵה, *that there may be :* so 7, 19ᵃ וְיִהְיוּ that they *may* become, but 19ᵇ והיה *and there will be*.

62.. The following examples will sufficiently illustrate the construction :—Lev. 9, 6 this shall ye do וְיֵרָא *that* the glory of Yahweh *may appear.* 26, 43 וְתִרֶץ. Nu. 25, 4. Amos 5, 14 *that he may be.* Ps. 9, 10 וִיהִי *and let Yahweh be* etc., or, in so far as this is a consequence of the characteristics described 8 f., *so may he be,* or *that* he may be a high tower etc. 90, 17 וִיהִי (a deduction from v. 16). Mic. 7, 10 ; 1 Sa. 7, 3. 18, 21. 28, 22 ויהי בך כח *that so* thou mayest have strength. 1 Ki. 22, 20. Job 16, 21. Isa. 5, 19 (parallel לְמַעַן). 35, 4. Ps. 39, 14 *that* I may look bright. 41, 11 etc.; Pr. 20, 22 wait for Yahweh וְיֹשַׁע *and he will save thee* (not as an *absolute* future, but dependent on קַוֵּה being carried into effect)[1]. 2 Ki. 5, 10ᵇ. After מִי, Jer. 9, 11 מִי הָאִישׁ הֶחָכָם וְיָבֵן אֶת זֹאת. Hos. 14, 10. Ps. 107, 43[2]; Esth. 5, 3. 6. 7, 2. 9, 12 וְתֵעָשׂ after *What is thy request ?* comp. 1 Sa. 20, 4.

Instances in which the special forms are not used :—Ex. 14, 1 וַיָּשֻׁבוּ etc. 2 Sa. 9, 1. 3. 16, 11 וַיְקַלֵּל. 24, 21 (cf. 2 Chr. 29, 10). Isa. 43, 9ᵇ. 55, 7 וִירַחֲמֵהוּ. Job 21, 19. 32, 21. 38, 35. Jon. 1, 11 what shall we do וְיִשְׁתֹּק *that* the sea may be calm? Ps. 59, 14 *and let* them (=*that* they *may*) know. 86, 17. Neh. 2, 5 ; Jer. 5, 1ᵇ.

---

[1] Comp. below, §§ 151 *Obs.,* 152.—It is only the *connexion* which sometimes permits the jussive to be rendered *must ;* e. g. 1 Ki. 18, 27 perchance he sleepeth וְיִקָץ *so let him* be awakened, where the general sense is fairly expressed (as A. V.) by *and must be awakened.*

[2] Elsewhere, in answer to . . . . מִי, we find the simple impf., or the imper.: Ex. 24, 14. Isa. 50, 8. 54, 15. Jud. 7, 3 al.; Ex. 32, 24. Ps. 34, 13 f. 1 Sa. 11, 12 (where see the writer's note).

Where clauses of this nature have to be negatived, לֹא not
אַל is almost invariably employed[1]:—Ex. 28, 43. 30, 20. Dt.
17, 17 (וְלֹא יָסוּר (cf. *v.* 20 לְבִלְתִּי סוּר). 2 Sa. 21, 17. 1 Ki. 18, 44.
Jer. 10, 4. 25, 6 etc. Here the connexion between the two
actions is considered to be indicated with sufficient clearness
by the וְ, without the need of specifying it more minutely by
means of אַל. It is very unusual, however, to find the jussive
or cohortative forms after לֹא (see § 50 *a*, *Obs.*).

63. The same construction is also found in relation to
past time : 1 Ki. 13, 33 וִיהִי *that* there *might* be [2] (not וַיְהִי *and*
there *were*) priests of the high places. 2 Ki. 19, 25 וּתְהִי *that*
thou *mightest* (or mayest) be. Isa. 25, 9ᵃ *that* he *might* save
us (not future, as A.V., because (9ᵇ) they are represented as
already saved). Ps. 49, 10 (where וִיהִי is dependent upon *v.* 8,
v. 9 being parenthetical) *so that* he should live. 81, 16 *that so*
their time might be for ever. Lam. 1, 19 that they might
refresh their soul (where וַיָּשִׁיבוּ '*and* they refreshed' could
obviously not have stood). 2 Chr. 23, 19. 24, 11 ?

Obs. It may be wondered how the jussive can find place where, as in
these cases, the allusion is to the *past*. No doubt, as often happens in
language, the literal meaning of the formula in course of time was obscured and forgotten ; and it was thought of solely with reference to its
derived function of expressing succinctly a purpose or intention, quite
irrespectively of time.

64. After a negative [3]:—Nu. 23, 19 God is not a man

---

[1] אַל is in fact not used with a verb unless an imperative or jussive
force is distinctly felt. Its use is therefore far more restricted than that
of the Greek μή, with which it is often compared. Thus in final sentences
(as after למען or אשר Gen. 11, 7) לֹא not אַל is always found : and before
infinitives לבלתי (=τοῦ μή . . .). Similarly in the case before us אַל is
quite exceptional, being only found where it is desired to place the second
clause upon an independent footing, and to make it co-ordinate with the
first : Ps. 69, 15. 85, 9. 2 Chr. 35, 21.

[2] The singular as 5, 6. 29. 8, 26 Kt. 10, 12. 26. 11, 3. 22, 13ᵇ Kt.

[3] In the instances quoted, the subordinate clause is dependent upon
the principal verb *without the negative*. Comp. in Arabic the similar
use of فَ, with however not the jussive, but the *subjunctive: e. g.* Qor'an

וְיִכַּב *so that* he might lie (or, *that* he should lie): the force of
the expression is well illustrated by a parallel passage 1 Sa.
15, 29 לְהִנָּחֵם *for repenting* (or, *so as* to repent: LXX Num.
infin. alone, 1 Sa. infin. with τοῦ). Ps. 51, 18[1] thou desirest not
sacrifice וְאֶתֵּנָה *so that* I should give it. 55, 13[1] it was not an
enemy who reproached me וְאֶשָּׂא *so that* I might bear it: similarly וְאֶסָּתֵר. Isa. 53, 2[b] and he had no beauty *that* we should
desire him. Jer. 5, 28[2].

Or an interrogative:—Isa. 40, 25 to whom will ye compare
me וְאֶשְׁוֶה *that* I may be like him? 41, 26 וְנֵדְעָה. 28 *that* I
might ask them וְיָשִׁיבוּ and that they might return answer.
46, 5[b]. Lam. 2, 13. Jer. 23, 18[a] who hath stood in the council
of Yahweh *so as* to see? etc. (different from 18[b], which resembles rather Job 9, 4; § 19, p. 25). Job 41, 3.

Obs. Occasionally the ו is dispensed with: Ex. 28, 32. 39, 23 (the same,
narrated when done: 'that it *might* not be torn'). Isa. 41, 2 יַרְדְּ =*to
subdue.* 50, 2. Ez. 16, 15 לוֹ יְהִי *that* it (sc. יְפִיךְ) *might* be his[3]. Ps.
61, 8 מַן יִנְצְרֻהוּ. Job 9, 33. Neh. 13, 19[b]. And after a negative Ps. 140,
9 promote not his device יָרוּמוּ *so that* they be exalted[4]. Add also

---

7, 17 and do not come nigh to this tree ·*so as to* become evil-doers (in
Engl. we should rather change the form, and say *lest* ye become evil-
doers). 71 do not touch her *so that* (*lest*) punishment seize you. See
also 6, 108. 154. 8, 48. 10, 95. 11, 115. 12, 5 etc. And after an interrogative, 6, 149. 7, 51 have we any intercessors *that* they *should* intercede
for us?

[1] The rendering '*else* would I give it,' '*then* I could have borne it,'
implies merely a different expression in English of the demonstrative ו
(comp. §§ 62, 122 *Obs.*), which, whether represented by *so that*, or by
so, then, in that case, equally limits the giving, or the bearing, to a case
conceived (in virtue of the preceding negative) to be non-occurrent.

[2] Which differs from 20, 17. Gen. 31, 27, in that the second event is
regarded as *resulting from* the first, while in these it is viewed simply as
succeeding it; cf. § 74 a.

[3] לוֹ is here slightly emphatic; but its position is due rather to the
desire for rhythmical distinctness; comp. לוֹ לְאִשָּׁה Gen. 16, 3 (after
לְאַבְרָם). 29, 28 (after a previous לוֹ), *v.* 29; also Lev. 7, 7. יְהִי לוֹ or
וִיהִי לוֹ would be extremely weak as an ending.

[4] The harshness of the construction in *v.* 10[a] makes it almost certain,

the passages in which the cohortative appears after מִי יִתֵּן *O that* . . . :
Isa. 27, 4. Ps. 55, 7 O that I had the wings of a dove, אָעוּפָה וְאֶשְׁכֹּנָה
that I might fly away and be at rest. Job 23, 3–5. Compare Jud. 9, 29.
Jer. 9, 1, where the cohortative is preceded by וְ ; Job 6, 8 f. (jussive).

65. Sometimes the *imperative* is found instead of the
jussive, to express with rather greater energy the intention
signified by the preceding verb[1].

Gen. 12, 2 and I will make thee into a great nation . . .
וֶהְיֵה *and be* (that thou mayest be) a blessing. 20, 7. Ex. 3, 10.
2 Sa. 21, 3 and wherewith shall I make expiation, וּבָרְכוּ *and
bless* (that ye may bless) etc. 1 Ki. 1, 12 וּמַלְטִי. 2 Ki. 5, 10.
Ruth 1, 9. 4, 11[b]. Amos 5, 4. Ps. 37, 27. 128, 5 may Yahweh
bless thee, וּרְאֵה *and see* (that thou mayest see) the prosperity
of Jerusalem !

---

however, that the text is here corrupt ; and that ירומו (which is in fact
redundant in *v.* 9) belongs in reality, in the form ירימו, to *v.* 10 ; cf.
Perowne, Delitzsch, Cheyne (p. 404).

[1] Compare Ewald, § 347ᵃ.

CHAPTER VI.

The Imperfect with Waw Consecutive.

66. By far the most usual method in which a series of events is narrated in Hebrew consists in connecting each fresh verb with the clause which precedes it by means of *waw consecutive*, or, as it was formerly called, *waw conversivum* (וַ) and the imperfect. This waw consecutive, in both meaning and use, is radically different from the simple waw with *shwa'* (וְ), which is likewise prefixed to the imperfect: but it can always be at once recognized and distinguished from the latter by its peculiar form: before י, נ, and ת the waw consecutive *uniformly* has pathach, with dagesh in the letter following — the dagesh being, however, regularly dropped, from the difficulty of then pronouncing the double letter, before י when accompanied by *shwa'* (וַיְהִי not וַיִּהִי): before א of the first person it has, with all but equal invariability, the compensatory long vowel *qameṣ*[1] (וָאָבֹא)[2].

67. This somewhat singular construction was formerly supposed to be peculiar to the Hebrew of the Old Testa-

---

[1] Comp. with the article הַיְלָדִים, הָאָדָם etc.

[2] The only exceptions are a few occasions in Pi'el, where pathach appears: Jud. 6, 9 וַאֲגָרֵשׁ. 20, 6. 2 Sa. 1, 10. Ez. 16, 10; cf. also Zech. 8, 10. Ps. 73, 16. 119, 163. Job 30, 26: and, according to some, Ps. 26, 6. In Isa. 43, 28 it can hardly be doubted that the punctuators (like the Targum) understood the verbs (incorrectly) of the future, and pointed accordingly: the LXX and the Syriac render by the past, as is done also by most modern commentators (vocalizing, of course, וָאֲחַלֵּל and וָאֶתְּנָה: comp. 42, 25. 47, 6).

ment[1]. It is, however, known now to have been in familiar use in Moab[2], so that it was probably common to both Hebrew and the kindred Semitic dialects spoken by the immediate neighbours of the ancient Israelites[3]. Other Semitic languages (Arabic, Aramaic, Ethiopic, etc.), in cases where Hebrew uses regularly the impf. with ·וֹ, employ what might seem to be the obvious and natural construction of the perfect and וֹ: but this is avoided, almost uniformly, by the purest Hebrew; and it is not till the later period of the language, and even then but partially, that it is able to gain an acknowledged footing (see Chap. IX). The principle upon which the imperfect is here employed will not, after what was said in §§ 21, 26, be far to seek. The imperfect represents action as *nascent:* accordingly, when combined with a conjunction connecting the event introduced by it with a point already reached by the narrative, it represents it as the *continuation* or *development* of the past which came before it[4].

---

[1] Though a few instances occur apparently in the Samaritan Version of the Pentateuch; see Uhlemann, *Inst. Linguae Sam.* § 64. 1 *Anm.* In Hebrew of a later date, it is found only in books written in intentional imitation of the Biblical style, for instance, in the Hebrew version of the Book of Tobit, or in Josephus Gorionides. But it is not the idiom of the Mishnah, or of the Rabbinical Commentators.

[2] On the Inscription of Mesha‘ (the 'Moabite Stone') we find not only וַיֵּשֶׁב, וָאֶהֱרֹג etc., but even the same apocopated forms as in Hebrew, וָאֵרֶא, וָאִבֶן, וָאַעַשׂ. The language of this inscription does not in fact differ from Hebrew except dialectically, the resemblances in idiom and general style being especially striking. See a transcription of the inscription (in square characters) with grammatical explanations, in the writer's *Notes on Samuel*, p. lxxxv ff. (The impf. with ·וֹ occurs also, as might naturally be expected, on the ancient Hebrew Inscription found on the wall of the Pool of Siloam, *ib.* p. xv.)

[3] It is not, however, found in Phoenician (which has many points of contact with Hebrew, though not so numerous as Moabitish). See Schröder, *Die Phönizische Sprache* (1869), and especially, on the relation of Phoenician to Hebrew, B. Stade in *Morgenländische Forschungen* (1875), pp. 169–232.

[4] As the date of the new event expressed by the impf. is determined by

וַיֹּאמֶר is thus properly not *and he said*, but *and he proceeded-to-say*. The pathach of the *waw* is probably to be explained as the fuller, more original form of the conjunction (in Arab. *wă*), which, for the sake of distinction, was preserved in this case, and prevented from being weakened to וְ, by the dagesh in the following letter[1].

Obs. 1. The title *waw conversive* is a translation of the name וָו הִפּוּךְ, which originated with the old Jewish grammarians, who conceived the waw under these circumstances to possess the power of changing the signification of the tense, and turning a future into a past, just as in a parallel case (to be examined hereafter), they imagined it capable of turning a past into a future[2]. Now that the theory of the Hebrew tenses has been entirely remodelled, and it is seen that they involve no intrinsic relation to actions as past or future, but only as completed or incomplete, irrespectively of date, the old term has been very generally discarded as unsuitable. The title *waw consecutive*, adopted by Ewald and most modern grammarians, was originally suggested by Böttcher in 1827. Hitzig used always the term *vav relativum*, the meaning of which will be apparent from what has been stated above.

Obs. 2. The explanation here given of the nature of this construction (which is, in effect, merely Ewald's thrown with a little expansion into

---

the conjunction connecting it with a particular point in the past, to which therefore it is *relative*, the construction is termed by Ewald the *relatively-progressive* imperfect (das *bezüglich-fortschreitende* imperfectum).

[1] Comp. Olshausen, § 229[b]; and for the preservation of a vowel by the duplication of the following consonant, cf. בַּמֶּה ,כַּמֶּה ,לָמֶה (*ib.* § 83[d]). Ewald (§ 231[a]) thought that the pathach and the dagesh were the only surviving traces of some adverbial root concealed between the conjunction and the verb: but this is hardly probable.

[2] Compare Reuchlin, *Rudimenta Hebraica* (Phorcae [Pforzheim] 1506), p. 619, 'Quamquam ne hoc quidem omiserim quod mihi de vau praepositiva particula humanissimus praeceptor meus ille Iacobus iehiel Loans doctor excellens (misericordia dei veniat super eum) apud Cecios discenti monstravit, Cum enim vau per seva notatum praeponitur verbo praeteriti temporis quod transfert accentum suum in ultimam, tunc idem verbum mutatur in tempus futurum .... Similiter cum praeponitur vau cum patha verbo futuri temporis, tunc futurum convertit in praeteritum.' Cf. L. Geiger, *Johann Reuchlin*, pp. 105 ff.

an English dress) was written before I had seen the following passage of Schröder's *Institutiones ad fundamenta linguae Hebraeae* (Ulmae 1785), pp. 261 f., in which, in all essential points, the same view is not only anticipated, but stated also with singular lucidity :—' Praeter varios hosce usus, Futurum habet adhuc alium plane singularem, et Hebraeis peculiarem, quod illud vim accipit nostri Praeteriti, et rem revera praeteritam designat, non tamen per se, et absolute, sed in relatione ad praecedens aliquod Praeteritum, spectatam. Quando enim diversae res factae, quae continua quadam serie aliae alias exceperunt, narrandae sunt, Hebraei primam quidem per Praeteritum, alias autem subsequentes, quas, ratione praecedentis, tamquam futuras considerant, per Futurum exprimunt. Hoc itaque, quia id, quod in relatione ad aliam rem praeteritam posterius et futurum fuit, notat, *Futurum relativum* dici potest.'

68. It is evident that this use of the imperfect is closely parallel to some of the constructions noticed in § 27. In instances such as אָז יָשִׁיר, וְהָאֲנָשִׁים יְנַחֲשׁוּ, וַאֲבְשָׁלֹם יָבֹא, the imperfect depicts action as incipient, in strict accordance with what appears to have been the primitive signification of the tense : it is just in virtue of this, its original meaning, that, in coalition with וַ, it grew up into a fixed formula, capable of being generally employed in historical narrative. That a series of past facts should ever have been regularly viewed in this light (a supposition without which the construction before us remains unaccountable), that in each term of such a series the salient feature seized upon by language should be not its character as past, but its character as nascent or progressive, may indeed appear singular : but the ultimate explanation of it must lie in the mode of thought peculiar to the people, and here reflected in their language. Only, inasmuch as the formula became one of the commonest and most constant occurrence, it is probable that a distinct recollection of the exact sense of its component parts was lost, or, at any rate, receded greatly into the background, and that the construction was used as a whole, without any thought of its original meaning, simply as a form to connect together a series of past events into a consecutive narrative.

69. The form which the imperfect takes after the ·וֹ is, however, very generally modified. It frequently, at any rate externally, resembles the voluntative—in the second and third person appearing as a *jussive*, in the first person as a *cohortative*. Without going here with any minuteness into the details (which must be sought in the larger grammars, which treat the accidence at length), we meet, for example, regularly with such forms as these, וַיָּבֹא, וַיֵּבְךְּ, וַיֵּעַשׂ¹, וַיְצַו, וְאֲדַבְּרָה, וַיִּבְדֵּל etc. A second noticeable characteristic is this, that after waw consecutive *the tone frequently*, though not universally², *recedes*. Accordingly we obtain וַיִּנְרָשׁ, וַיֵּאָסֶף, וַתִּתְפְּעֶם Dan. 2, 1, וַיֵּשֶׁת וַיֵּשֶׁב, וַיֵּלֶךְ, וַתֵּלֶךְ etc.

Obs. The cohortative form is so much less common than the jussive, that a few particulars respecting its usage (derived chiefly from Böttcher, ii. 199, and the list given by Stickel, *Das Buch Hiob*, pp. 151–4) will not be out of place. It occurs only at rare intervals except in two or three of the later writers, some ninety instances of its use being cited altogether. Thus, in the historical books (to 2 Sa.), it occurs Gen. 32, 6. 41, 11. 43, 21. Nu. 8, 19. Josh. 24, 8 Kt. Jud. 6, 9. 10. 10, 12. 12, 3. 1 Sa. 2, 28. 28, 15. 2 Sa. 4, 10. 7, 9. 12, 8. 22, 24: but never in the books of Kings, or in Isaiah (in Deutero-Isaiah, 43, 28: cf. § 66 *note*); and in the other prophets, only Jer. 11, 18. 32, 9. Ez. 9, 8. 16, 11. Zech. 11, 13. In the Psalms, 3, 6. 7, 5. (not 18, 24). 69, 12. 73, 16. 90, 10; and several times in Ps. 119. In Job, 1, 15 ff. 19, 20. 29, 17. 30, 26. It is principally found in those portions of Daniel, Ezra, and Nehemiah, where the narrative is told in the first person. In Ezra 7, 27–9, 6 there are seven-

---

¹ In so far as verbs ל״ה are concerned, Böttcher, ii. 196 f., collects of the first pers. sing. forty-nine instances of the shortened form, against fifty-three in which it remains unabbreviated. In the other persons, however, the full form is very exceptional; e. g. ויהיה never, ויראה four times (against some 130 instances of וירא).

² The conditions under which the retrocession may take place are (1) the syllable of the ultima, which is to become toneless, must be one originally *short ;* (2) the syllable which is to receive the tone, must be an *open* one, with a *long* vowel. It does not, however, always take place, even when these conditions are present ; and never in the 1st pers. sing. (in 1 Ki. 21, 6. Ez. 16, 6 the retrocession is occasioned by position): in pause, also, the tone reappears on the ultima, as וַיֵּלַךְ׃. Comp. Olsh., § 229ᵇ.

teen instances of the first pers. with -*ah*, against only two without it
(there is a third case, however, in 10, 2): it is here that its predominance
is most marked. In Dan. 8–12 there occur ten cases with -*ah*, against
eight without it (verbs ל״ה of course not reckoned): and in Neh. 1. 2.
4–7. 12, 31. 13 the numbers are about thirty-two to thirty-seven. But
it is not used by the writer of the Chronicles: a comparison of 1 Chr.
17, 8 with 2 Sa. 7, 9 would seem to shew that he even intentionally
rejected it: nor is it found in Zech. 1–8 although ויאמר occurs fifteen
times and ואשוב twice. In Esther, neither form is met with at all.

70. We have here to ask two questions: firstly, what is
the meaning of the apparently modal forms? secondly, what
is the cause of the retrogression of the tone?

It is maintained by Ewald, § 231ᵃ, that the imperfect after
וֹ possesses really a modal force: and he remarks in a note
that such an assumption is especially necessary on account
of the הָ in the first person, which cannot otherwise be
explained. Certainly the coincidence is a remarkable one,
and constitutes a *prima facie* argument in favour of this view,
which it is unquestionably difficult to meet. The same distinction of usage between the first person on the one hand,
and the second and third on the other, is observable here,
precisely as when the usual voluntative force is indisputably
present: the former appears as a cohortative, the two latter
as jussives. But the impossibility of giving a satisfactory or
even an intelligible account of the presence of a *real* cohortative or jussive in forms descriptive of simple historical fact,
constrains us to seek for some better explanation. Let us
begin by considering the case of the second and third persons. It is, in the first place, obviously impracticable to do
anything with the jussive, taken in its literal sense: a command, a permission, or a wish are all equally out of place in
a form descriptive of the simple straightforward past. Ewald
(§ 231ᵃ) seeks to overcome this difficulty by weakening and
generalizing the force of the jussive mood in a manner
which it is impossible to regard as legitimate. Another objection against supposing the form to be that of a real jussive

is the fact that the alterations arising from abbreviation or apocopation *extend over a much wider area* than in the case of the actually existent jussive. Thus the jussive proper in the first person is extremely rare: but not only do we meet with וָאֵשֵׁב, וָאֹלֵךְ etc., but some fifty instances are cited of verbs ל״ה, which appear thus in the shortened form, some of them, as וָאֵרָא, וָאֱהִי, being of repeated occurrence. On the other hand, there are phenomena which appear to reveal the direction in which the true explanation must be sought. The question was asked just now, What is the cause of the retrocession of tone observable e. g. in וַיֹּאסֶף? It cannot be accounted for by the supposition that the verb after וְ is a jussive, because יֵאָסֵף, יְשָׁרֵת etc. are unheard of as independent jussive forms: where they do appear, their occurrence is in no way connected with the modal form as such, but is an accidental consequence of *position* (e. g. Ps. 102, 19 תִּכָּתֶב־זֹאת, 104, 20 תָּשֶׁת־חֹשֶׁךְ). In verbs ל״ה, as יֶגֶל, the vowel in the ultima (as in the segolate nouns) is an auxiliary vowel; and the place of the tone is thus a secondary phenomenon: here, therefore, the apparent retrocession is due to the weak letter which constitutes the third radical of the verb. In no case is the jussive mood by itself sufficient to produce retrocession; nor, in fact, does it shew the smallest tendency to produce it. Even supposing, therefore, that the verb after וְ were jussive, this would fail to account for the retrocession of the tone. It can hardly be doubted that the true cause lies in the *heavy prefix* וְ, which was once probably, as the dagesh seems to shew, even heavier than it is now. The effect of this being added to the impf. would be to create a tendency to *lighten* the latter part of the word, which would operate sometimes by simply causing the tone to recede, sometimes by giving rise to an accompanying apocopation. It must be remembered that we have not much opportunity of watching in Hebrew the changes produced by an alteration at the *beginning* of a word: most of the variations in the vowels or the tone are the results of alterations at the *end* of a word, or of some modification in its relation to what follows it in the sentence rather than to what precedes. Thus the *st. constr.*, the addition of a suffix, the presence of a heavy termination (קְטַלְתֶּם, in contradistinction to a light one קְטַלְתְּ), the proximity of a tone-syllable, all operate from below : examples of an influence working in the opposite direction are more difficult to find. Nevertheless, we are not left entirely destitute of indications as to the effect which a heavy prefix, in constant coalition with a flexible verb-form, might be expected to produce. Instances occur in which אַל [1], when closely united to a jussive by *maqqeph*, gives rise to an alteration in the form of the verb similar to that observable after waw consecutive : thus Ex. 23, 1 אַל־תָּשֵׁת. 2 Sa. 17, 16 אַל־תָּלֶן : see further Dt. 2, 9. 3, 26. 1 Sa. 9, 20. 1 Ki. 2, 20. Pr. 30, 6, cf. Ex. 10, 28. Compare also אַל־תֵּשְׁתְּ, exactly like וַתֵּשְׁתְּ, whereas without אל the full form יִשְׁתֶּה is used with a jussive force Job 21, 20. And probably Ps. 21, 2 Qri מַה־יָּגֶל and the *sere* in שֶׁיּוֹלֵךְ Qoh. 5, 14 [2] are to be explained in the same way [3]. The case then, as a whole, may be stated thus. On the one hand, the forms under discussion cannot be explained as jussives (for the jussive as such never assumes them), nor can they be explained as arising from position (for they are found where no tone-syllable follows) : they can only be explained as arising from the influence of the ·וֹ (for the presence of this is the one property they possess in common), and this opinion is confirmed by the parallel instances which have been just quoted [4].

---

[1] See Ewald, § 224[b]; Böttcher, i. 166. ii. 172 ; Olshausen, § 229[c].

[2] Compare the shorter form after אז 1 Ki. 8, 1 אָז יְקַהֵל.

[3] In the Psalm, however, the retrocession might be caused by the following tone-syllable מֵאָר (the *shwa'* not reckoning, precisely as Gen. 1, 11 ; see Gesenius, Lg. § 51. 1[d] Anm. 1, or Ewald, § 100[a]).

[4] Ewald himself accounts in the same way for an analogous phenomenon in Arabic (*Gramm. Arab.* i. p. 124). *Lam,* 'not,' always takes

Obs. There is one remaining ground upon which it might be thought possible still to defend the assumption of a jussive. Granted the power of the ·וַ to alter the place of the tone, it will be urged that such forms as וַיָּ֫שָׁב, וַיֵּ֫שֶׁב would be most naturally treated as derived immediately from the *jussives* יֵשֶׁב, יָשֹׁב, rather than from the simple imperfects יָשׁוּב, יֵשִׁית. This certainly sounds plausible: but it must be remembered that no basis exists for the assumption that יֵשֶׁב in וַיֵּ֫שֶׁב must necessarily and exclusively be *jussive:* the ·וַ, which is able to produce וַיִּשְׁבַּ, וַיִּשָּׁאֵר etc., is a sufficient cause to account for the presence of *sere* in וַיֵּשֶׁב; and when it had gone thus far, when it had produced וַיָּ֫שֶׁת[1] out of יֵשִׁית, the tendency visible elsewhere could not have failed to operate here likewise, so as from וַיָּ֫שֶׁת to give rise to וַיָּ֫שֶׁת[2]. Such instances only require us to suppose *two* stages in the action of the ·וַ: the possibility of the first stage is established by the effects observable in other cases, and when once this is admitted, the second will follow as a matter of course.

71. The form before us, then, is only apparently, not really, jussive: it exhibits, in fact, one of those *accidental coincidences* not unknown to language. Why the shortened form was selected for the jussive may be uncertain, though we know the fact that it was so selected: we seem, at least partially, to detect some reasons why it appears after ·וַ, but there is no indication that the identity of form in the two

---

an impf. after it, just as טרם generally does in Hebrew: but the impf. is universally in the *jussive* mood. Thus the unmodified impf. of *nazzala*, ʻto bring down,' is *yunazzilu* (he *will, used* etc. to bring down), whereas the jussive is *yunazzil;* and so we find Qor. 3, 144 *lam yunazzil* in the sense of ʻhe has not brought down,' 185 *lam yafʻalû* (not *yafʻalûna*) ʻthey have not done.' The conjunction is always closely followed by the verb, no intervening words being permitted: accordingly Ewald writes, ʻQuare ob nexum hunc praepositi لِ vique certâ pronunciandi necessarium et perpetuum forma verbi in fine *brevius* pronunciatur.' And if a double origin for the shortened form is postulated for Arabic (ʻex duplici quae formam decurtatam postulet causa,' ibid.), it may be conceded, without any greater hesitation, for Hebrew.

[1] Through an intermediate *yāshĭth*, Ewald, §§ 33[b], 224[n]; Olshausen, §§ 57[b], 228[a].

[2] This indeed is the form which almost everywhere occurs: see, however, Gen. 47, 11, and Böttcher, § 497. 9.

cases, such as it is (for we have seen that it is not perfect throughout), originated in an intentional adoption of the jussive as such.

72. The explanation of the ה◌ָ in the first person is more difficult. It should, however, be borne in mind that even in the cohortative proper, the *-ah* does not *add* to the simple imperfect the 'intentional' signification expressed by that mood: the signification is already there, and the new termination merely renders it more prominent. This seems clear from the fact that the imperfect may—and in verbs ל״ה, if such an idea is to be expressed at all, *must*[1]—in its unmodified form signify an intention or desire. The termination, therefore, is not specially cohortative or intentional, it is merely *intensive:* and we are at least relieved of the logical contradiction involved in the supposition that a real cohortative form was used in the *mere* description of a past fact. The time and mode of occurrence are here, of course, limited by the prefixed וַ; and if (as appears probable) the *-ah* was felt to indicate the direction in which the will exerted itself, or to add emphasis to the idea of movement conveyed by the tense, its use with the first person would be nothing surprising or inappropriate.

Obs. Compare Stickel, *Das Buch Hiob*, p. 151, who supposes that in the cohortative the influence of the *-ah* is exerted in giving prominence to the feelings *internally* actuating the speaker, while with the first person after וַ it lays stress upon the results *externally* produced. He is thus often able to imitate the effect of it in German by the use of *hin*, as וְנַחְלְמָה 'und wir träumten *hin:*' so in English שָׁכַבְתִּי וָאִישָׁנָה might be very fairly represented by 'I lay down, and slept *away*,'—*hin* is, however, capable of a wider application than our *away*. Delitzsch (on Ps. 3, 6 and Gen. 32, 6) speaks of the *-ah* as a termination *welches . . . die Lebendigkeit des Verbalbegriffs steigert.*

Another suggestion is due to Prof. Aug. Müller (in the *Luth. Zeit- schrift*, 1877, p. 206). The form of the impf. after ·וַ became, through the influence of this prefix (as explained, § 70), identical externally with

---

[1] With the rare exceptions noted, p. 52, *note* 3.

that of the jussive : and hence, in process of time, the difference in origin
of the two was forgotten.   But, as the other parts of both moods fell
into disuse, the cohortative came to be practically regarded as the first
person of the jussive, and consequently was used in cases analogous
to those in which the form outwardly identical with the jussive made its
appearance, i. e. after waw consecutive.   In other words, וישב *resembled*
the real jussive ישׁב: and then, through the influence of a false analogy,
ואשׁובה came gradually into use by the side of it.

73.   We may now proceed to examine the manner in
which this construction is employed : and, in the first place,
let us enquire more closely into the nature of the relation in
which an action thus introduced may stand towards the preceding portion of the narrative.   The most obvious and
frequent relation is naturally that of simple chronological
succession, Gen. 4, 8 and Cain rose up וַיַּהַרְגֵהוּ *and slew* him :
but of this there is no need to give further examples, as
they abound throughout the historical portions of the Old
Testament.

74.   At times, however, when of the two ideas thus connected, one is really a *consequence* of the other, it is convenient and desirable to make this fact more explicit in
English by translating *and so :* similarly, where the two ideas
are in reality *contrasted* we may with advantage make the
contrast more perspicuous by rendering *and yet.*

Thus (*a*) Gen. 20, 12 *and so* she became my wife. 23, 20
וַיָּקָם *and so* the field was ensured to Abraham. Ps. 92, 11.
Jer. 20, 17 because thou didst not kill me from the womb
so[1] *that* my mother might have become my tomb (the two
verbs are strictly co-ordinated under אשׁר, but the relation
between them in English can hardly be exhibited except as
above). Gen. 12, 19 ואקח. 31, 27 why didst thou not tell me
וָאֲשַׁלֵּחֲךָ *and so*[2] I could have sent thee away (='that so I

---

[1] וַתְּהִי is, however, not the same as וּתְהִי: could we use the *same*
person in translating, we should escape all danger of confusing them :
'*because thou didst* not kill me *and let* my mother become my tomb.'

[2] Above, 'so' pointed to the actual consequences of a real occurrence,

might have sent thee away,' or more freely, but avoiding the
change of mood, 'and so allow me to send thee away') with
mirth? Isa. 36, 9 *and so* or *so then* thou trustest.

(β) Gen. 32, 31 I have seen God face to face, וַתִּנָּצֵל *and
yet* my soul is delivered. Dt. 4, 33 did ever people hear the
voice of God . . . וָיֶחִי׃ *and* live (=*and yet* live)? 5, 23. Jud.
1, 35 וַתִּכְבַּד. 2 Sa. 19, 29 ותשת *and yet* thou didst set, etc. Mal.
1, 2ᵇ. Ps. 73, 14. For some additional instances, see § 79.

Sometimes the consequence is also the climax; in other
words a sentence summarizing the result of the events just
before described is introduced by ·ו: the apparent tautology
may then be avoided in English by rendering *so* or *thus*, as
is often done in our Version, Ex. 14, 30. Jud. 4, 23. 9, 56.
20, 46. 1 Sa. 17, 50. 31, 6.

75. But chronological sequence, though the most usual,
is not the sole principle by which the use of ·ו is regulated.
Where, for example, a transaction consists of two parts
closely connected, a Hebrew narrator will often state the
principal fact first, appending the concomitant occurrence by
help of ·ו; or again, in describing a series of transactions,
he will hasten at once to state briefly the issue of the whole,
and afterwards, as though forgetting that he had anticipated,
proceed to annex the particulars by the same means: in
neither of these cases is it implied that the event introduced
by ·ו is subsequent to that denoted by the previous verb; in
reality the two ·ו are *parallel*, the longer and the shorter
account alike being attached by ·ו to the narrative preceding
them both. Instances: (a) Ex. 2, 10 she called his name
Moses; *and she said*[1]. Jud. 16, 23. 1 Sa. 7, 12. 18, 11. 25,
5. 2 Ki. 1, 2; (β) Gen. 27, 24[2] ויאמר (not subsequent to

---

here it points to the imaginary consequences of a hypothetical occurrence
(*killing, telling*).

[1] Elsewhere we find כי as Gen. 4, 25. 16, 13. Ex. 2, 22 etc., or לאמר
as 1 Sa. 4, 21; or ותאמר precedes ותקרא as Gen. 29, 33 etc.

[2] For some of these references, compare Hitzig, *Jeremia*, p. 288,

ויברכם, *v.* 23 : the words of the blessing do not, as might have been expected, follow immediately, but only after the particulars accompanying it have been described, *vv.* 24–27ᵃ)[1]. 37, 6 (describing how Joseph told his dream ; 5ᵇ is *anticipatory*). 42, 21 ff. (the details of the compendious ויעשו כן, *v.* 20). 45, 21–24. 48, 17 (notice ישית, § 39 β). Ex. 40, 18 (see 17ᵇ). Josh. 18, 8 (ויצו after וילכו). Jud. 5, 1 (see 4, 24). 6, 27. 1 Sa. 10, 9ᵇ–11.

76. In the instances just mentioned, the disregard of chronological sequence is only apparent : but others occur in which no temporal relation is implied at all, and association in *thought* is the principle guiding the writer rather than association in *time*. Thus ·1 may be used to introduce a statement immediately suggested by a preceding word or phrase ; it is even, occasionally, joined to a *substantive standing alone*, in order to expand its meaning or to express some circumstance or attribute attaching to it. Or, secondly, a fresh circumstance is mentioned, in the order in which it naturally presents itself for mention at the stage which the narrative has reached ; or a new account commences, amplifying the preceding narrative regarded as a *whole*, and not meant merely to be the continuation, chronologically, of its concluding stage : in both these cases, also, ·1 is employed.

Examples : (*a*) Gen. 36, 14 וַתֵּלֶד. 32 (epexegetical of 31ᵃ). 45, 7 וישלחני (connected in thought only with *v.* 6). 46, 18. 25. Nu. 4, 40. 44. 10, 28 ויסעו. 20, 15 (expansion of the תלאה *v.* 14). 33, 3. Josh. 22, 17 is the iniquity of Peor too little for us … ויהי *when* there was (lit. ‘ *and* there was ’) the plague in

Böttcher, ii. p. 214, and especially Ewald, *Komposition der Genesis* (1823), pp. 151–156. On such occasions (in Ewald's words) the narrator ‘ überspringt Mittelglieder um das Ziel zu erreichen : ’ he is then compelled ‘ durch Nebenumstände zu erläutern und zu ergänzen, was sein Eile eben übersprungen hatte.’

[1] Some scholars, however, suppose here *v.* 28 to connect immediately with *v.* 23, *vv.* 24–27 being derived by the compiler from a different source. A similar supposition is made in ch. 48, for *vv.* 15–16.

the congregation? Jud. 11, 1ᵇ; 1 Sa. 15, 17 yet art thou head etc., *and* Yahweh *hath anointed* thee etc. 2 Sa. 14, 5 וימת אישי. 1 Ki. 11, 15 (developes a particular episode in Hadad's life, in continuation of 14ᵇ: cf. 1 Sa. 25, 2ᵇ). Isa. 49, 7 for the sake of Yahweh who is faithful, (and) the Holy One of Israel *who* hath chosen thee (lit. ' *and* he hath chosen thee,'—a fresh idea loosely appended by the help of ·ו). Job 10, 22ᵇ. It is also sometimes used in order to explain and define עשה, as Gen. 31, 26. 1 Sa. 8, 8. 1 Ki. 2, 5. 18, 13 (וָאַחְבִּא = *how* I hid): cf. Neh. 13, 17.

(β) Gen. 2, 25. 5, 5 ויהי. 41, 56 ויחזק (synchronizing with וישבר). Ruth 2, 23. Nu. 10, 35. 15, 32. 1 Sa. 14, 25ᵇ. 49. 1 Ki. 5, 2. 12. 26ᵇ. 2 Ki. 17, 7 ff.; Ex. 4, 31[1]. Isa. 39, 1 he sent messengers וַיִּשְׁמַע *and* he heard[2] (parallel, 2 Ki. 20, 12 כי שמע). 64, 4 ונחטא (this is, however, uncertain: comp. Del. and Dillm.); Pr. 12, 13ᵇ. Job 14, 10ᵇ (new statements parallel to those in the first clauses).

(γ) Jud. 17, 1. 1 Sa. 9, 1. 18, 6. 1 Ki. 7, 13 (the entire buildings having been described, the part taken in their erection by Hiram is mentioned separately[3]). 2 Ki. 18, 1 (comp. the date in 17, 6); cf. Ex. 12, 1.

---

[1] Where LXX, however, read וישמחו.

[2] This instance is such an extreme one that Delitzsch and others are doubtless right in supposing the reading וישמע to have arisen out of that in Kings by the corruption of כ into ו. LXX has γάρ, the Peshiṭṭo ܡܛܠ. We find the two letters confused elsewhere: 1 Sa. 2, 21 (where in the *Speaker's Commentary*, 'that' must be a slip of the pen for 'when:' the *that* which follows ויהי would, of course, be represented by ו, § 78, and, moreover, requires always some intervening clause) כי פקר yields no sense, and we must from LXX restore ויפקר; similarly Jer. 37, 16. Compáre also, in the Heb. text itself, וכסאו 1 Chr. 17, 14 for כסאך 2 Sa. 7, 17; and in LXX ו for כ 1 Sa. 2, 33. 4, 7. 24, 20. 2 Sa. 3, 21. 5, 6 (apparently הסירו). 7, 16. 14, 10. 19, 7 (LXX 6), and כ for ו 1 Sa. 1, 23 (so too Pesh., and, probably, rightly). 2 Sa. 20, 1.

[3] LXX, it may be noticed, place the section 7, 13-51 more naturally after 6, 36: but even in that case, the force of the ·ו remains the same.

Obs. It is a moot and delicate question how far the imperfect with ־ַו denotes a *pluperfect*. There is, of course, no doubt that it may express the *continuation* of a plupf.: e. g. Gen. 31, 34 had taken *and placed* them; but can the impf. with ־ַו *introduce* it? can it instead of conducting us as usual to a *succeeding* act, *lead us back* to one which is chronologically anterior? The impf. with ־ַו is, in the first place, certainly not the usual idiom chosen by Hebrew writers for the purpose of expressing a plupf.: their usual habit, when they wish to do this, is to *interpose* the subject between the conjunction and the verb, which then lapses into the *perfect*, a form which we know, § 16, *allows scope* for a plupf. signification, if the context requires it [1]. This will be evident from the following examples:—Gen. 24, 62 ויצחק בא and Isaac *had come:* the writer wishes to combine two streams, so to speak, in his narrative: he has (1) brought Rebekah to the termination of her journey, but (2) desires to account for Isaac's presence at the same spot. In order thus to prepare the way for their meeting, he is obliged to *go back*, and detail what had taken place *anterior* to the stage at which his narrative has arrived: he therefore *starts afresh* with the words ויצחק בא, the whole of *vv.* 62 f. bears reference to Isaac, and the two streams, terminated respectively by וילך *v.* 61 and וירא *v.* 63, *converge* in ותשא *v.* 64. So 31, 19 ולבן הלך and Laban *had gone* away (before Jacob left Paddan-arám, 18 f.: וַתִּגְנֹב, because the possibility of Rachel's stealing the Teraphim is a consequence of Laban's absence). 34. Nu. 13, 22 *had been built.* Josh. 6, 22. 18, 1 (וַתִּכָּבֵשׁ would have suggested that the subjugation was *subsequent* to the meeting at Shiloh). 1 Sa. 9, 15 (notice the *crucial* significance of יום אחד). 25, 21 (David's thoughts *before* meeting Abigail). 28, 3. 2 Sa. 18, 18. 1 Ki. 14, 5. 22, 31. 2 Ki. 7, 17. 9, 16[b] (obviously prior to Jehu's arrival): in each of these passages, by avoiding ־ַו, the writer *cuts the connexion* with the immediately preceding narrative, and so suggests a plupf.[2] Observe also how Ezekiel abandons

---

[1] It will be understood that the pf. in this position does not *always* bear a plupf. signification: it is often so placed simply for the purpose of giving emphasis to the subject (see further App. I).

[2] In Gen. 20, 4. 1 Sa. 14, 27 ־ַו could not have been used on account of the negative: but even here it may be noticed that the same *order* of the words is observed. Compare Pusey, *Lectures on Daniel*, p. xix, who speaks similarly of this idiom as one ' which expresses a past time, anterior to what follows, but in no connexion of time with what precedes;' the reader who refers further to p. lxxxvi (ed. 2) will find a considerable list of instances (all cases in which the verb is היה) to add to the one given in the text.

his customary formula (3, 22. 8, 1ᵇ. 14, 2. 20, 2) as soon as he has occasion to carry his narrative back, 33, 22, over the space of twelve hours. And in the second place, the mode of connexion which, as usage shews us, was suggested by וַ, and which is recognized by all grammarians, is with difficulty reconcilable with the idea of a pluperfect: for the consecution inherent in the one seems to be just what is excluded by the other. Under these circumstances we shall scarcely be wrong in hesitating to admit it without strong and clear exegetical necessity.

Let us examine, therefore, the passages in which the pluperfect signification of וַ has been assumed, whether by the native Jewish grammarians, or (through their influence) by the translators of the Authorized Version, or, within narrower limits, by modern scholars: many, it will be observed, break down almost immediately. Kalisch, § 95. 3, cites Gen. 2, 2. 26, 18. Ex. 11, 1. But Gen. 2, 2 is not an instance: see Delitzsch's note, and below § 149 *n.:* while in 26, 18 ויסתמום (which the note in Kalisch's *Commentary* shews to be the verb intended) is simply the continuation of the plupf. חפרו. In Ex. 11, 1 the narrative is obscure, owing to its not being so circumstantial as in the preceding chapters: but it is important to notice that, apart from the grammatical question, the interpretation is not relieved, even though ויאמר be rendered by a plupf.: if this verb be supposed to relate to any period anterior to the ninth plague—Ibn Ezra suggests 4, 23, Keil 3, 19–22—the sense of עוד נגע אחד is sacrificed: if, on the other hand, it be interposed between 10, 23 and 10, 24, then, since the terms of the declaration are in no way *conditional*, it will be evidently premature. All difficulty ceases, and the tense ויאמר retains its usual force, if the interview 11, 4–8 be regarded as a different one from that of 10, 24–29[1]; nor is the language of 10, 28 f. conclusive against this view, for it would be quite in keeping with Pharaoh's character, when his passion cooled, to relent from the threat which is there expressed by him, and which is at any rate broken, subsequently (12, 31), on both sides[2]. (Dillmann,

---

[1] Comp. 1 Ki. 1, 28 from which it is plain that, though the narrative does not mention it, Bathsheba must have withdrawn after the interview, *vv.* 15–22.

[2] It is indeed stated in the *Speaker's Commentary*, ad loc., that Smith, *Pentateuch*, pp. 557–560, 'completely disposes of the objections of German and English critics' to the rendering *had said;* but this is one of those adventurous statements, in which Canon Cook was too often apt to indulge. The reader who consults the volume referred to will find (p. 113) merely four of the least conclusive passages cited, viz. Jud. 1, 8. Ex. 12, 1. 18, 2. 2 Sa. 5, 8. 1 Chr. 21, 6.

however, supposes that 11, 1–3 has been accidentally misplaced, and that it stood originally after 11, 4–8.) From Hitzig we obtain Isa. 8, 3. 39, 1. Jer. 39, 11. Jon. 2, 4. But in the first of these passages the supposition is not required : the second is a more than doubtful instance to appeal to (p. 83 *n.*) : the third may be explained by § 75 β (or 76 γ) : and on the fourth, Dr. Pusey (*Minor Prophets,* ad loc.) corrects the A.V. thus :— ' *For Thou hadst* [*didst*] *cast me into the deep.* Jonah continues to describe the extremity of peril' etc. Keil adopts the plupf. for Gen. 2, 19, comparing Jud. 2, 6. 1 Ki. 7, 13 ff. 9, 14. But Jud. 2, 6 is an uncertain passage to rely upon : the verse itself (together with *vv.* 7–9) is repeated from Josh. 24, 28–31 (where it harmonizes perfectly with the context) ; it is moreover the beginning of a new section (§ 76 γ), and was perhaps written originally without reference to the date in 1, 1ᵃ : cf. the *Speaker's Comm.* ii. 424 (8), the writer's *Introduction,* pp. 153, 155, and Budde, *Richter und Samuel,* 1890, p. 161. 1 Ki. 7 has been dealt with already, § 76 γ : 9, 14 is obscure : but the verse *seems* to be in continuation of 11ᵃ. Gen. 2, 19 even Delitzsch rejects, though allowing that the plupf. rendering is possible, and citing for it Isa. 37, 5. Jon. 2, 4. Isa. 37, 5, however, belongs to § 75 β : and in Gen. the plupf. sense is inadmissible, for the reason stated below on Jud. 1, 8.

Further : Gen. 12, 1 A.V. (see § 76 γ). Ex. 4, 19, where Ibn Ezra explains וכבר אמר; but the *v.,* as Keil supposes, may well refer to a distinct occasion ; 27 (cf. *v.* 14 : still ויאמר is not necessarily anterior to *vv.* 20–26) ; 18, 2 (where, however, ויקח, as Gen. 12, 5 etc., refers naturally to Jethro's action in *taking* Zipporah for the purpose mentioned *v.* 5 : to *take in* in the sense of *receive, entertain* is אסף not לקח). 32, 1 (§ 76 γ) ; 32, 29 and 33, 5 A.V. (as also Ibn Ezra), but comp. Keil : Lev. 9, 22 וירד (Kimchi; also Abulwalid, *Sefer hāriqmah,* p. 22, ed. Goldberg, 1856). Jud. 1, 8 A.V. (see the note in the *Speaker's Comm.,* where the Bishop of Bath and Wells remarks with truth, that ' there is nothing in the original to suggest or justify such a change of tense' as *had fought* for וילחמו[1]). 1 Sa. 14, 24 A.V. (so Kimchi, וכבר השביע; but see Keil) ; 17, 13 (§ 76 β). 23, 6 (compared with 22, 20; the *v.,* however, though the latter part is obscurely worded and probably in some disorder (cf. p. 90, and the writer's note *ad loc.*), relates apparently to a subsequent stage in the flight of Abiathar, and is meant to describe how, when in company with David in Keilah, he had the ephod with

---

[1] This verse is thought by some (Budde, *Richter u. Samuel,* p. 4) to be an incorrect gloss, due to a misunderstanding of *v.* 7 (as though the pronoun ' they' denoted the Israelites rather than the people of Adoni-bezek), and intended to explain how the Israelites were able to take Adonibezek to Jerusalem.

him). 2 Sa. 5, 8 (= 1 Chr. 21, 6 : a *detail* connected with the capture of Zion described in *v.* 7, § 75 β). 1 Ki. 13, 12ᵇ וַיִּרְאוּ A.V., Kimchi, but in this passage, which is perhaps the strongest that can be urged in favour of the plupf. sense of ·וַ, it is remarkable that LXX Pesh. Vulg. agree in rendering the verb, as though it were *hifil,* And his sons *shewed* him,' etc., i. e. וַיַּרְאָהוּ[1]. 2 Ki. 20, 8 (ויחי, *v.* 7, anticipatory, § 75 β). Isa. 38, 21. 22 : but it is plain that these two verses are accidentally misplaced : they should (as was long ago remarked by Kimchi, in his Commentary ; similarly Bp. Lowth, cited in Prof. Cheyne's note) occupy the same position as in 2 Ki. 20, 7 f., and follow *v.* 6. Isa. 64, 4 (Kimchi וכבר חטאנו : see § 76 β). Zech. 7, 2 A.V., Kimchi (see Wright, *The Prophecies of Zechariah,* 1879, p. 162). Job 2, 11ᵇ and Dan. 1, 9 A. V. (not necessary). Neh. 2, 9ᵇ (§ 75 β). In Ps. 78, 23 (Ibn Ezra, Kimchi ; comp. A. V.) the narrative is doubtless not intended to be strictly chronological (cf. 105, 28 f.[2]) ; and it would be very artificial to render Nu. 7, 1 And it *had* come to pass etc. on account of the date being a month earlier than that of 1, 1 (see Ex. 40, 17) ; a distinct section here commences, and the case is rather similar to Ex. 12, 1 (§ 76 γ)[3].

Such are the passages from which our conclusion has to be drawn.

---

[1] Klostermann, ingeniously, וַיּוֹרֵהוּ ; but it is doubtful, in spite of Ex. 15, 25, whether הוֹרָה would be used of ordinary ' shewing.'

[2] The case must be similar, as the text stands, in Josh. 24, 12 : but here the LXX read δώδεκα, which is accepted by many modern scholars, and is in all probability correct ; the allusion being not to the well-known defeat of Sihon and Og (which, besides being out of place *after* the passage of Jordan in *v.* 11, has been noticed already in *v.* 8), but to the successes of the Israelites *west* of Jordan. See Hollenberg, *Der Charakter der Alex. Uebers. des B. Josua* (Moers, 1876), p. 16, or in *Stud. und Krit.,* 1874, p. 488 ; and the author's *Introduction,* p. 106 f. So also Wellh., Kuen., and Dillm. (*ad loc.*).

[3] A few additional passages, referred to chiefly by Jewish authorities, will be felt at once to be inconclusive : Gen. 2, 8 Ibn Ezra (see also his note on 1, 9). 26, 18 וישב ויחפר (Rashi : וקודם שנסע יצחק חזר וחפרן). 20, 16 (וכבר נבקעו המים ואחר כך שם הים לחרבה). Ex. 14, 21 (Kimchi : אחר שבאש). Nu. 1, 48 A.V. 1 Sa. 17, 21 A.V. Jon. 1, 17 A.V. (see 4, 6. 7). Job 14, 10 ויחלש. Kimchi's view may be seen also in his *Michlol,* p. 50ª, ed. Fürth (1793), or p. 44ᵃ⁻ᵇ, ed. Lyck (1862): ויש ו"ו. שמורה הזמן שכבר עבר קודם הפעל אשר לפניו. Other instances may probably be found in A.V. In the Revised Version, all except 1 Ki. 13, 12 (the reading of the Versions being cited on the margin). Isa. 38, 21. 22. Zech. 7, 2. Neh. 2, 9 have been corrected.

In those occurring at the beginning of a narrative, or paragraph, there are, we have seen, reasons for presuming that the chronological principle is in abeyance, and that it is not the intention of the author, or compiler, to express the precise temporal relation with the occurrence last described. Some of these apparent instances have arisen, doubtless, from the manner in which the Hebrew historical books are evidently constructed, distinct sections, often written by different hands, being joined together without regard to *formal* unity.   Others of the alleged instances are cases in which a circumstantial detail belonging to a preceding general statement is annexed by means of וְ: that here, however, it is not equivalent to a true pluperfect, is manifest as soon as the attempt is made to render into English accordingly; a translation such as ' And David took the stronghold of Zion : the same is the city of David. *And David had said* in that day,' etc. stands self-condemned. I find it difficult to believe that in the midst of a *continuous* piece of narrative, such as Gen. 2, 19, or even Ex. 11, 1, it is legitimate to abandon the normal and natural sense of וְ in favour of one which, at best, rests upon precarious and unsatisfactory instances, and which, *had it been designed by the author*, could have been easily and unambiguously expressed by a slight change of order. For when a Hebrew writer wishes to explain or prepare the way for what is to follow by the mention of some fact which *lies outside* the main course of his narrative, the passages quoted at the beginning of this note shew conclusively that he *purposely disconnects* it with what precedes, by the choice of a construction not suggestive of chronological sequence, which, in these two cases, would have given us respectively ויהוה אמר and ויהוה אלהים יצר.   The authority of the Jewish grammarians, strange as it may seem to say so, must not be pressed ; for although they have left works which mark an era in the development of Hebrew grammar, and are of inestimable value for purposes of exegesis, still their syntactical, no less than their phonetic principles, have constantly to be adopted with caution or even rejected altogether.   Their grammar is not the systematization of a living tradition, it is a reconstruction as much as that of Gesenius, or Ewald, or Philippi, but often, unfortunately, without a sound basis in logic or philology. And a question such as that now before us is just one upon which their judgment would be peculiarly liable to be at fault. All that a careful scholar, like Mr. Wright (*l.c.*), can bring himself to admit, with reference to the plupf. sense of וְ, is that while ' no clear instances can be cited in which it is distinctly so used,' there are cases in which ' something like an approximation to that signification can be detected.' And it is rejected unreservedly by Böttcher, ii. p. 215 f. (see in particular, § 980. 4); by Quarry, *Genesis*, pp. 99, 418; by Dr. Pusey, who on Jonah 4, 5

writes, 'Some render, *contrary to grammar,* " And Jonah had gone,"
etc.,' and by Dillmann (on Ex. 4, 19 etc.).

77. So much for the logical relation subsisting between
the two ideas connected by וֹ: we must now consider the
nature of the fresh action which is thus introduced.

Most commonly, and especially in the historical books, as
in the passage Gen. 4, 8 cited above, the fresh action both
developes and finishes in the past. But it may likewise so
happen that the action is of such a character that while itself
starting or developing in the past, its results continue into
the present—terminating there or not, as the case may be :
or, thirdly, the action may originate wholly in the present.
Future time is *never* expressed by וֹ, except where the prophetic perfect has preceded, or where the principle involved
in it is really present. Nor does it express modality : Ps. 8, 6
וַתְּחַסְּרֵהוּ does not follow תִּפְקְדֶנּוּ, in dependence upon כִּי, but
introduces a fresh fact : cf. Ez. 13, 19.

78. It will hardly be necessary to cite instances in which
the new action lies wholly in the past. Notice must, however,
here be taken of a construction which is of constant occurrence in the historical books of the Old Testament. When
the Hebrew writers have occasion in the course of their
narrative to insert a clause specifying the circumstances under
which an action takes place, instead of introducing it abruptly,
they are in the habit of (so to speak) preparing the way for
it by the use of the formula וַיְהִי *and it was* or *came to pass.*
Thus in place of וּבָעֵת הַהוּא אָמַר אֲבִימֶלֶךְ, particularly in the
earlier books [1], preference is generally given to the form וַיְהִי
בָּעֵת הַהוּא וַיֹּאמֶר א' *and it came to pass,* at that time, *and* or
that Abimelech said etc., Gen. 21, 22. And the same construction is usual with every kind of temporal or adverbial
clause, whatever be the particle by which it is introduced, e. g.

---

[1] Contrast, for instance, Ezra 9, 1. 3. 5. 10, 1; 2 Chr. 7, 1 and often
וככלות (1 Ki. 8, 54 ויהי ככלות). 12, 7. 15, 8. But Nehemiah commonly
makes use of ויהי. Comp. the writer's note on 1 Sa. 17, 55.

Gen. 4, 3 מקץ ימים. 8 בהיותם בשדה. 19, 17 כהוציאם. 34 ממחרת.
20, 13 כאשר. 26, 8 [1]. The sentence is not, however, always
resumed by וְ as in the example quoted, though this is the
most frequent form : the וְ may be omitted, or be separated
from the verb, and then the perfect will reappear. Thus the
main sentence may be resumed (1) by the perfect alone, as
Gen. 14, 1 f. 40, 1. Ex. 12, 41[b]. 51. 16, 22. 27. Dt. 1, 3. 9, 11.
1 Sa. 18, 30. Isa. 7, 1. Jer. 36, 1. 16. Ez. 1, 1 etc., or, though
more rarely, by the impf.[2] if the sense be suitable, Jud. 11, 40,
1 Ki. 9, 10 f. (with אָז). 14, 28. 2 Ki. 4, 8[b]. Jer. 36, 23. Or
(2) by וְהִנֵּה as Gen. 15, 17. 29, 25. 42, 35 (הם מריקים). 2 Ki.
2, 11. 13, 21 al. Or (3) by וְ with the subject *before* the verb,
as Gen. 7, 10. 22, 1. 41, 1. Ex. 12, 29. 34, 29. Josh. 6, 8.
1 Sa. 18, 1. 2 Sa. 13, 30 al.[3]

But (1) with וְ and (3) without וְ are alike exceedingly rare :
2 Chr. 24, 11 (where, however, וּבָא is frequentative : see Chap.
VIII); 1 Sa. 23, 6 (corrupt). perhaps 1 Ki. 21, 1[4].

79. We may now pass to those cases in which the action,
or its results, continues into the writer's present : here, as with
the perfect in the parallel instances, it is often best to translate
by a present. Thus Gen. 32, 5[b] וָאֵחַר. Ex. 4, 23 וָאֹמַר *and I
say* (*have said*, in the immediate past), Let my son go, וַתְּמָאֵן
and thou refusest (or hast refused) to let him go[5]. Num. 22, 11

---

[1] Of an exceptional type are 1 Sa. 10, 11. 11, 11 ויהי הנשארים ויפוצו.
2 Sa. 2, 23 (comp. § 121 *Obs.* 1).

[2] This, if a frequentative, is more usually preceded by וְהָיָה (§ 121).

[3] It may, perhaps, be thought that in these cases the clause beginning
by the perfect or וְ is rather a subordinate circumstantial clause (see
Appendix I), and that the real continuation of ויהי is afforded by the וַ
following. This is possible : but in some of the instances quoted this
sequence does not occur, and in others the clause itself has not the
appearance of being subordinate.

[4] Ez. 9, 8 the monstrous ונאשאר is doubtless (see Hitz.) a confusion
of two readings, וְנִשְׁאָר (to be explained by § 159), which is accepted as
the original text by Hitz. and Keil, and וָאֶשָּׁאֵר (cf. 1 Ki. 19, 10 for the
position of אני), which is preferred by Ew. and Smend.

[5] With this sentence as a whole, cf. Jer. 23, 2. 34, 17.

וַיְכֵם‎. Josh. 4, 9 ויהיו שם‎ and *they are* there unto this day.
1 Ki. 8, 8ᵇ. 19, 10 *and* I alone *am left, and they seek* (have
sought and continue seeking) my life to take it away. Isa. 3,
16. 30, 12. 41, 5 קרבו ויאתיון‎. 50, 7 ואדע‎. 59, 15 *is* or *has
become* missing. Hos. 8, 10. 13. Hab. 1, 3 ויהי‎. 14. 3, 19. Ps.
35, 21. 38, 13 (*have laid* and continue to lay *snares*). 52, 9.
55, 6. 119, 90 *and it abideth.* Job 11, 3 f. 7, 15 *and* (so) my
soul *preferreth* suffocation. 14, 17. 30, 11 f. Gen. 19, 9 this
one entered to sojourn (here), וַיִּשְׁפֹּט שָׁפוֹט‎ *and goes on to* play
the judge amidst us! 31, 15. 49, 24 *and yet* his bow dwelleth
etc. 2 Sa. 3, 8 וַתִּפְקֹד‎ *and yet* thou visitest upon me. Job 10, 8
וַתְּבַלְּעֵנִי‎ *and* (yet) thou goest on to swallow me up (cf. Ps. 144, 3
what is man וַתֵּדָעֵהוּ‎ *and* (yet) thou *knowest* him[1]?). 21, 14.
Isa. 51, 12 who art thou, *and* (yet) thou *fearest* etc. Pr. 30,
25–27.

Even where the event spoken of has not actually been
accomplished, Jer. 38, 9 *and he is going on to die* (we might
have expected וָמֵת‎, cf. Gen. 20, 11: but ʿEbed-melekh sees
Jeremiah on the very road to death). Job 2, 3 *and thou art
enticing* me. Ps. 29, 10 Yahweh sat at the deluge וַיֵּשֶׁב‎ *and*
Yahweh *sitteth on* (from that moment *went on* and *continues*
sitting) a king for ever (not *shall* or *will* sit, which would
break the continuity existing in the writer's mind between the
two actions described: moreover, the future would, according
to uniform usage, have been expressed by וְיֵשֵׁב‎, or at least
וְיֵשֶׁב‎. The addition of לעולם‎ does not necessitate our rendering by the future any more than in the cases where it
occurs with a *perfect*, Ps. 10, 11. 74, 1). 41, 13 וַתַּצִּיבֵנִי לְפָנֶיךָ
לְעוֹלָם‎. Amos 1, 11 (similarly with לָעַד‎). 1 Chr. 23, 25 *and
dwelleth* in Jerusalem for ever.

80. In continuation of the *present*, as expressive of a
general truth, whether this be denoted in the original by a
perfect, § 12, an imperfect, §§ 32, 33, or a participle, we meet

---

[1] The construction in Ps. 8, 5 כי תזכרנו‎ is different (§ 39 δ).

with ·וַ and the impf.: 1 Sa. 2, 6 Yahweh bringeth down into the Underworld, *and bringeth up*, 29. Isa. 31, 2. 40, 24 he bloweth upon them *and they wither*. 44, 12–15. 57, 20 for it cannot rest *and* its waters *are troubled*. Jer. 10, 13. Amos 5, 8 וַיִּשְׁפְּכֵם. Mic. 6, 16. Nah. 1, 4 f. Ps. 34, 8 the angel of Yahweh encampeth (ptcp.) . . . *and delivereth them*. 49, 15 like sheep are they set (pf.) for She'ōl, while death is their shepherd ; וַיִּרְדּוּ *and* the righteous *rule* over them in the morning[1]. 65, 9 *and* (so) *they are afraid*. 90, 3. 10[b]. 92, 8. 94, 7. Pr. 11, 2 pride cometh וַיָּבֹא *and* humiliation *cometh* (i. e. follows quickly after it : cf. § 153). Job 5, 15. 6, 20. 7, 9 a cloud cometh to an end *and vanisheth*. 12, 22–25 (cf. Ps. 107, 40). 14, 2 ; Ps. 7, 13 he hath drawn his bow (p. 21, towards the bottom) וַיְכוֹנְנֶהָ : *and made it ready*. Job 20, 15 he hath (in a given case, pictured by the poet) swallowed down riches וַיְקִאֶנּוּ *and vomiteth them up* again (not as R.V.).

After a pure present, Job 4, 5 now it cometh to thee *and* thou *art* overcome. 6, 21. 2 Sa. 19, 2 בֹּכֶה וַיִּתְאַבֵּל is weeping *and mourning*. Jer. 6, 14.

81. In the description of future events, the impf. with ·וַ is used upon exactly the same principle as the perfect, i. e. it represents them as simple matters of history. There are two cases to be distinguished : (1) where the impf. is preceded by the prophetic perfect itself, (2) where it is not so preceded.

(1) Little need be said in explanation of the first. Just as elsewhere the impf. with ·וַ marks a continuation of the preceding tense, so here, too, it is employed if a writer desires to pourtray a future scene or series of events, as though they were unfolding themselves before his eyes, in the manner of ordinary historical occurrences. For one or two reasons, however, the impf. is not by any means so frequent in this

---

[1] I. e. Death, as at the Exodus, or Isa. 37, 36. Job 27, 20, performs his mission in the night. ויררו can only be referred to the future on the assumption of a change of standpoint, § 82, which, *in this connexion*, cannot be regarded as probable.

sense as the perfect : the prophets generally either 'prefer, after beginning with an emphatic perfect, to break off into the proper future form, or else they omit ו altogether, or separate it from the verb in such a manner as to make it impossible for the impf. in this form to appear. Isa. 5, 25. 9, 5 unto us a son is given וַתְּהִי *and* the government *is* upon his shoulder, וַיִּקְרָא *and* his name *has been* (or *is*—past extending into present, § 79) called etc.[1] 9, 18–20 (perhaps ; see § 82). 24, 6. 48, 20 f. he hath redeemed Jacob . . . ויבקע *and hath cleft* the rock (here A.V. retains the pf.). 53, 2. 9 (in accordance with the *perfects* in the intermediate verses : יפתח, *v.* 7, § 36. The prophet only begins to use the future in *v.* 10). Joel 2, 23. Mic. 2, 13. Ps. 22, 30 all the fat of the earth *have eaten and worshipped* (A.V. '*shall* eat and worship,' which would be יאכלו והשתחוו, or in the slightly more energetic poetical form יאכלו וישתחוו, as *v.* 27). 109, 28.

82. (2) This case is entirely parallel to the use of the prophetic perfect noted in § 14 γ, the only difference being that, the conjunction being followed *immediately* by the verb, the tense employed (as the *perf.* with ו would by Hebrew usage throw the event to be described into the future) is naturally the imperfect with ·ו. The ·ו in such cases also represents the event, often very aptly, not merely with the certainty of the prophetic perfect, but as *flowing* naturally *out of*, being an *immediate consequence* of, the situation described in the preceding sentence. It is under circumstances like these, when the transition to the new standpoint in the future is made for the first time, not by a pf. but by the impf. with ·ו, that we are

---

[1] The change of tense made in the course of this verse by the A.V. '*and* the government *shall be*' etc. is only defensible as a concession, for the sake of clearness, to English idiom ; it should not be forgotten that it presupposes a different point of view from the one adopted by the prophet. Isaiah retains the ideal standpoint, which is recognized also in the renderings *have seen, is born, is given*, till 6ᵇ תעשה : the change in question substitutes the *real* standpoint prematurely, and breaks the continuity of the description.

most apt to find this tense translated by a *future:* but unless
this be done solely for the sake of the English reader, who
might be slow to realize the, to him, unwonted transition, it
is a gross error, and implies an entire misapprehension of the
Hebrew point of view.　The use of וֹ in the historical books,
times without number, renders it inconceivable that it should
have suggested anything except the idea of a *fact done*, which
is clearly not that conveyed by our future ; the question
whether a future occurrence may be *meant*, resolving itself
into this other question, whether, viz. upon a given occasion,
the change of standpoint is probable, and consistent or not
with analogy.

Isa. 2, 9 *and* (so) the mean man *is bowed down, and* the
great man *humbled* (the consequences of *v.* 8, though actually
appertaining to the future, described as though they had
already ensued)[1]. 5, 15ᵃ (15ᵇ, § 36).　16ᵃ ויגבה (notice in 16ᵇ
the *perfect* נקדש).　9, 10–15 (perhaps, but not certainly : see
the Commentators). 59, 15ᵇ–17[2] (notice 16ᵇ the perf. סמכתהו :
the *actual* future only begins with *v.* 18). Ez. 28, 16 וָאַחֶלֶּלְךָ
(in the קִינָה upon the king of Tyre : *v.* 17, where there is no וֹ,
we have the pf. השלכתיך).　31, 12. Jer. 4, 16 they are coming,
וַיִּתְּנוּ *and they have* uttered etc. (observe in *v.* 17 the pf. היו).
15, 6ᵇ–7 (perhaps). 51, 29. Ps. 64, 8–10 וַיֹּרֵם וג׳ *and* (so) God
hath shot at them etc. (where observe that even if, in the teeth
of grammatical analogy, we render וַיֹּרֵם *and he shall shoot*
them, the difficulty is only deferred, not surmounted : the next
verb היו is an unmistakeable perfect, for which the sense
of the past, whether ideal or actual, must be uncon-

---

[1] 'Vortrefflich fügt Jesaja, beim zweiten Modus [p. 3 *n.*] mit *Vav relat.*
[p. 72] verharrend, *v.* 10 unmittelbar die Strafe solches Beginnens hinzu,
die noch zukünftig ist, aber so gewiss eintritt, als die Sünde, ihre Be-
dingung, schon da ist' (Hitzig, *ad loc.*).

[2] The sudden transition in Rev. 11, 11. 20, 9 is worth comparing : see
the rendering in Delitzsch's Hebrew translation of the N. T. (published
by the British and Foreign Bible Society).

ditionally accepted. The perfect stands similarly in *v.* 10ᵇ)[1]. 94, 23.

Obs. Some passages in which ·וַ has the *appearance* of being future, although not so in reality:—Ps. 50, 6 (וַ is the legitimate continuation of the pff. 1, 2, 3ᶜ, describing the *scene*, pictured by the poet)[2]. 55, 18ᵇ (either a conviction as to the future like Ps. 64, 8, or an allusion to the past, comp. § 54 : in either case ·וַ is in strict conformity with the pff. *v.* 19, and must stand or fall with them). 92, 11 f. On 77, 7ᶜ, see § 54 *note :* Hab. 1, 9ᵇ. 10ᵇ belong most probably to § 80. Can Dt. 33, 27ᵇ–28 וַיֹּאמֶר . . . וַיִּגְרֶשׁ be fairly explained by this § ? The reader has before him, if I mistake not, the passages by which his decision must be guided.

This use of ·וַ, rare even with the prophets, is evidently unadapted to the language of ordinary life ; and Mr. Espin's recommendation on Josh. 9, 21 וַיִּהְיוּ to render 'they shall be' is an unfortunate one. The verb must be taken in its usual sense, viz. *and they became :* and the verse, which in *form* resembles Gen. 11, 3, is to be explained by § 75 β. 'They shall be,' as may be learnt from the first chapter of Genesis, would have been וְהָיוּ.

The verbs in Joel 2, 18 f. are to be understood as descriptive of what ensued after the delivery of the prophecy 1, 2—2, 17, the past time, of which they are the continuation, being that which is *implied* in 1, 1. Mic. 3, 1 וָאֹמַר (which historically can only be attached to 1, 1). Jer. 11, 5ᵇ וָאַעַן וָאֹמַר (following similarly *v.* 1). 14, 11. 34, 6 are closely parallel, and meet the grammatical objection raised by Dr. Pusey (*Min. Proph.* pp. 96, 122), which derives its force from the supposition that the verbs in question must be in continuation of the tenses *immediately* preceding. The past sense is adopted, not only by Ewald and Hitz., but also by Delitzsch (in his article on Joel in the *Luth. Zeitsch.* 1851, p. 306), Keil (*ad loc.*), and modern scholars generally (cf. R.V.).

---

[1] 'Natürlich steht wie *v.* 11, so auch *vv.* 8–10, Zukunft in Rede ; und gleichwohl ist kraft des ersten Mod. 8ᵇ. 10ᵇ mit Recht überall וֹ vor dem 2 Mod. als relatives punktirt. Es handelt sich *vv.* 8–10 um eine Sache, die mit Gewissheit erhofft wird, gegenüber von einer gleichgültigen Folge *v.* 11,' Hitzig, excellently. Comp. Prof. Cheyne's note. The English Versions, rendering as futures, *change* the point of view of the original author, just as in Isa. 9, 5.

[2] It is noticeable that in Ps. 97, the opening verses of which are clearly imitated from Ps. 50, we have, *v.* 6, the *perfect* הִגִּידוּ in exact correspondence with וַיַּגִּידוּ here.

83. We know from § 27 (*a*) that the impf. can be employed by itself to describe single events occurring in past
time. The instances there quoted were restricted to those in
which the copulative *and* could have found no place, the verb
being disconnected in sense with the preceding words: but
cases also occur, especially in an elevated or poetical style, in
which the writer, instead of adopting the usual prosaic construction of the impf. with ·ן, makes use of the impf. alone,
or merely attaches it to what precedes by the simple *waw* ן.
The ordinary mode of smooth progression being thus abandoned, the action introduced in the manner described is, on
the one hand, cut off from the previous portions of the sentence, and rendered independent, while, on the other hand, it
is depicted with the vividness and force which are characteristic of the tense, but which are disguised, or destroyed,
when it is in combination with ·ן. Our own language hardly
affords us the means of reproducing the effect thus created:
sometimes, however, the use of the *present*, or even the addition of a note of exclamation, may enable us partially to
do so.

In some of these cases the impf. appears in the *jussive*
form, which seems to shew that we are right in regarding
them as instances of ·ן being actually omitted, rather than as
instances of the bare imperfect (according to § 27). Otherwise, indeed, the appearance of the jussive in pure narrative
would be inexplicable.

Obs. The omission of ·ן has been compared by Ewald to the omission
of the augment in Sanskrit and Greek. The illustration is very complete:
in the first place, the shorter or 'secondary' person-endings which
appear after the augment were in all probability (see G. Curtius, *Das
Griechische Verbum seinem Baue nach dargestellt*, i. p. 45) originally
produced through the influence of this prefix: ἐ-δίδω-ν (Sk. *á-dadā-m*),
ἔ-φερε (*á-bhara-t*) differ in no essential element from δίδω-μι (*dadā-mi*),
φέρει (*bhára-ti*), except in the presence of the accented demonstrative
prefix which was employed in order to throw the action into the past,
and the weight of which caused a compensatory change to take place in

the termination. And in the same way וַתָּ֫שֶׁת etc. seem clearly to have
arisen. But, in the second place, when this change had become fixed in
language, the altered termination became as characteristic of past times,
as the augment itself: it thus *acquired* a significance which primarily,
as we just saw, belonged exclusively to the latter; and so the augment,
at one time essential and indispensable, could be dropped (in poetry)
without detriment to the sense. And upon the same principle, it would
seem, we meet with יָקֶם, יָ֫שֶׁת etc., the altered ultima suggesting past
time as unmistakeably as if the ·וַ itself had been also present. But it
does not appear legitimate to have recourse to this explanation in those
passages where (as Ps. 11, 6) the context does not *immediately suggest*
to the reader that the conjunction has been omitted. To do so would
be to presuppose that a Hebrew author used a form which (whatever
the cause) has a *double* meaning, under circumstances where, so far from
there being anything either to intimate the sense in which it is to be
taken, or to justify his putting such a sense upon it, the reader's natural
impulse would be to impose upon it the meaning which was not intended.

84. We find accordingly—

(*a*) with וַ: Isa. 10, 13^{b1}. 43, 28² (but see p. 70, *note*). 48, 3.
51. 2^b as a single man did I call him, *and* I blest him, *and*
I multiplied him! 57, 17. 63, 3–6. Hab. 3, 5. Ps. 18, 38
(2 Sa. 22 וַ). 43. 46. 104, 32^b (or *that*, § 63). 107, 27. Job
29, 21. 25 (freq.); and apparently also the following :—Isa.
63, 3³ וַיֵּז. Pr. 15, 25³. Job 13, 27³. 15, 33³. 27, 22³. 36, 15³.
Hos. 11, 4³. It is, however, singular that, though the tense
is in the abbreviated form, the conjunction should still be
pointed וַ rather than ·וַ: either וַיַּצֵּב or וַיַּצִּיב, for example,
would have been at once intelligible, and would not have occasioned the surprise we undoubtedly experience at meeting

---

¹ 'וְאָסִיר ,וְאוֹרִיד zum Ausdruck des wiederholt Geschehenden: wahr-
scheinlich ist aber (vgl. וַתִּמְצָא *v.* 14) das Impf. consec. beabsichtigt'
(Dillm.). In some of the other passages also it is doubtful whether the
present punctuation represents the intention of the original author : see
Appendix II.

² Cohortative form.

³ Jussive forms. For a further consideration of some of these pas-
sages, see Appendix II.

וַיִּצֶב. But when an impf. follows, not a perfect, but another impf., even if וֹ be still admissible (§ 80), a preference is frequently shewn in favour of וֹ; and the shorter form, its *origin* being disregarded, appears to have been treated in accordance with the same analogy.

(β) without וֹ: Isa. 12, 1 [1] יֵשֹׁב אַפְּךָ וּתְנַחֲמֵנִי. Hos. 6, 1 [1] יָךְ. Hab. 3, 16 יָבוֹא. Ps. 8, 7ᵃ hast made him rule (cf. 7ᵇ, and 6 וַיְּתִי). 11, 6[1]? 18, 7 (2 Sa. 22 וֹ). 12 [1] (2 Sa. וֹ). 14 (2 Sa.). 16 (2 Sa.). 17. 18. 20. 21ᵃ. 37. 38 (2 Sa.[2] אַרְדְּפֵה followed by וֹ). 39 (2 Sa. וֹ). 40ᵇ. 42. 44 (2 Sa. וֹ). 25, 9[1]. 44, 3. 11–15. 47, 4[1]. 78, 15 etc. 26[1]. 81, 8. 90, 3[1]. 107, 14. 20. 26. 27. 29[1]. 33[1]. 35[1]. 139, 13. Pr. 7, 7[2] אֲבִינָה. Job 18, 9[1]. 12[1]. 33, 27[1]. 37, 5. 38, 24[1].

85. In prose where, for variety or emphasis, a verb which would naturally be connected with the foregoing narrative by וֹ, is preceded by its subject or object, or in any other way separated from the conjunction, the tense which then appears is almost always the perfect. Thus Gen. 1, 5 we first have וַיִּקְרָא, but so soon as for the sake of contrast the order is changed, we find the perfect וְלַחֹשֶׁךְ קָרָא: this is constantly the case, *v.* 10. 3, 3. 17. 4, 1. 2. 4. 18. 22. 6, 8. 7, 19 etc.; or without וֹ, 1, 27. 3, 16.

Poetry, however, in cases like these usually prefers the imperfect as the means of presenting the livelier image: not, of course, that the imperfect ever ' stands for ' the perfect, or assumes its meaning (!), but the poet takes the opportunity thus offered of imparting brilliancy and variety to his description, the legitimate signification of the tense chosen, whether as an inceptive or as a frequentative, being always distinctly traceable. E.g. Isa. 2, 6. Hab. 3, 16. 19; often in the historical Psalms, as 18, 8 וֹ . . . . ירגזו. 9 וֹ . . . . תאכל. 14 etc.

---

[1] Jussive forms. For a further consideration of some of these passages, see Appendix II. On Isa. 50, 2 וְתָמֹת . . . . תבאש, see § 64 *Obs.*

[2] Cohortative forms; cf. above, §§ 54, 72.

24, 2. 50, 19. 78, 20 *and* torrents *overflowed.* 29 etc. 81, 7. 13. 104, 6–9. 105, 44. 107, 6 etc. Pr. 7, 21[b]. Job 4, 12. 15. 10, 10. 11.

On the occasional use of ·וֹ in introducing the predicate, or apodosis, see § 127.

Obs. It is maintained apparently by some scholars (see Hitzig on Jer. 44, 22. Ps. 27, 10. 44, 10, and compare Ewald, § 346[b]) that these and certain similar passages present examples of what may be termed a dissolution or disintegration of the construction with waw consecutive— the verb, after its separation from וֹ, being permitted to remain in the imperfect without any special significance being attached to it[1]. But this opinion cannot be deemed probable. No fact about the Hebrew language is more evident than the *practical equivalence* of ויקרא and קרא ... וֹ: these are the two alternative formulae which in countless passages inter- change with one another: the peculiar point of view which determined the selection of the construction with ·וֹ (even if then always consciously preserved) was entirely dropped when the verb parted company with its conjunction. In the *comparatively* few[2] cases, therefore, where instead of קרא ... וֹ we find the formula יקרא ... וֹ, it is fair to conclude that the writers had some special object in selecting the unusual tense: even in poetry, if we find *x* used where a prose writer would have employed *y*, we cannot assume the two to be identical, but must suppose that the choice of the one in preference to the other rested upon some particular ground, such as that suggested in the text.

The theory offered by Hitzig to account for the presence of the imper- fect in passages such as Ps. 32, 5 seems too artificial to be probable.

---

[1] Hitzig quotes Dt. 2, 12. Josh. 15, 63. 1 Sa. 27, 4. 2 Sa. 15, 37. 1 Ki. 20, 33. Isa. 40, 14. 41, 6. Jer. 52, 7. Job 3, 25. Cant. 3, 4. But in all these places the impf. possesses a marked significance according to §§ 27, 30, where, indeed, several of the passages have been already cited.

[2] Even after a little word like לא it is quite rare to find the impf.; against nearly fifty cases of ולא שמע and ולא שמעו, there is but one (in past time) of ולא ישמעו, viz. 1 Sa. 2, 25.

CHAPTER VII.

Accents.

86. It was remarked incidentally § 69 that when the imperfect was preceded by ·֖ a retrocession of tone frequently
took place : beyond endeavouring, however, to assign a cause
for this phenomenon, we did not pause to examine the laws
by which it is governed, or to lay down rules by which the
place of the tone might be ascertained.   In the construction
which will have to be explained in the next chapter, that,
namely, of the *perfect* with waw consecutive, a change takes
place (if circumstances permit it) in the *opposite* direction,
the tone, if ordinarily upon the penultima, being *thrown
forward* on to the ultima : this alteration forms such a
noticeable and striking feature, and is, moreover, of such
extreme importance as an index to the meaning conveyed
by the tense, that the rules by which it is determined must
be carefully stated and ought to be thoroughly understood
and mastered by the reader.   For this purpose it will be
necessary to refer briefly to the nature of the *accents* in
Hebrew, and to the principles upon which the use made of
them depends[1].

---

[1] The English reader is advised, with reference to what follows, to
consult Gesenius, §§ 15, 16, 29.   The standard work on the subject
consists, however, of the two companion treatises of Dr. W. Wickes,
*On the Accentuation of the Three so-called Poetical Books of the Old
Testament* (Oxford, 1881), and *On the Accentuation of the Twenty-one
so-called Prose Books of the Old Testament* (Oxford, 1887), which contain

87. The student will be aware that in Hebrew the accents serve two purposes : by their disposition in a given verse, they indicate the subdivisions, whatever their number, into which it naturally falls when recited by an intelligent reader ; these subdivisions, determined as they obviously are by the sense of the passage, will on the one hand correspond with our *stops*—so far, at least, as the latter go (for they are by no means so numerous as the Hebrew accents) : on the other hand, inasmuch as in every sentence when spoken, unless it is intentionally delivered in a monotone, the voice rises or falls in accordance with the meaning, they will clearly be equally well adapted to mark the changes in the modulation of the voice during chanting or solemn recitation. It is in their first character, as grammatical or syntactical symbols, that we have here to regard them.

88. The principles regulating accentuation—of which, as is well known, there are two different systems, one applied in the prose books of the Old Testament, the other in the three (specially) poetical books, Psalms, Proverbs, Job (the dialogue parts, from 3, 2 to 42, 6)—are complicated and abstruse. For practical purposes, however, a few simple rules will be found sufficient ; and those who will take the trouble to acquaint themselves with no more than what is stated in Gesenius' Grammar, or even with the briefer and, of course, only provisional exposition which will be given here, will, it is believed, derive no small advantage from the study[1].

---

a lucid and admirable exposition of the principles of Hebrew accentuation, together with abundant illustrations of the use of the accents as logical or syntactical symbols. For those who desire to master the subject of Hebrew accents these two treatises are indispensable.

[1] The purport of this chapter will not, it is hoped, be misunderstood. Some acquaintance with accents is indispensable to the Hebrew student : not only for the single object, with a view to which this account of them has been inserted here, but upon more general grounds as well : they frequently offer material assistance in unravelling the sense of a difficult

89. The presence of waw consecutive is often marked by a change of the tone-syllable : our first question, then, will be, How can the tone-syllable be ascertained ?

The answer is very simple : with one or two exceptions it will be found that in every word provided with an accent, *the accent marks the tone-syllable.*

Without, therefore, as yet even knowing the *name* of the accents employed, we at once see that in וְכָפַרְתָּ Gen. 6, 14. וְהִקַמֹתִי 9, 11. וְכָרַתִּי 15[1], וְאָסַפְתָּ 21. the waw is consecutive : contrast 9, 17 הֲקִמֹּתִי. Qoh. 2, 15 וְאָמַרְתִּי *and I said* (for which the older language would have written וָאֹמַר). 8, 15 וְשִׁבַּחְתִּי.

90. Some of the accents, however, have the peculiarity of being always affixed to the *first* or the *last* letter of a word, whether it begin a tone-syllable or not : these are called respectively *prepositives* and *postpositives.* When these occur, the reader can only determine where the tone really lies from his knowledge of the language : but he will not be unnecessarily misled by them, because the other accents (which *do* mark the tone) are always placed above or below

---

passage; and the best authorities continually appeal to them, on account of their bearing upon exegesis. Experience tells me how liable they are to be overlooked; and the object of the present chapter is merely to smooth the way for those who may desire to pursue the subject more thoroughly afterwards, or, for such as have not the time or inclination to do this, to lay down a few broad rules which may be of practical service.

[1] The *metheg* (i. e. *bridle*) in these words is added in order to support or *hold back* the voice from hurrying onwards and so shortening the ante-penultima unduly (as in זְכַרְתֶּם). In any word the second syllable before that on which the principal tone rests will be felt to have a secondary accent or *counter-tone* (e.g. con′demna′tion, cor′respond′) : in Hebrew, when this is an *open* syllable, the counter-tone is marked by *metheg* (Gen. 20, 5 אָמַר־לִי, וְהִיא־גַם־הִיא, but בְּתָם־לְבָבִי without it), or, in certain cases, by some other accent which fills its place (8, 19 לְמִשְׁפְּחֹתֵיהֶם).

the *first consonant* of the syllable to which they refer, and *immediately to the left* of the vowel-point (if the consonant in question have one in such a position that the accent might clash with it), whereas the *pre-* and *postpositives* always stand on the *extreme right* or *left* respectively of the word to which they belong.

Thus no one can doubt that in עֵ֫שֶׂב Gen. 1, 11. דֶּ֫שֶׁא 12. בִּלְבַבְכֶם Ps. 4, 5 we have instances of prepositives (contrast בֵּ֣ין Gen. 1, 7. וְהָיָ֣י 1, 15); or that in אֱלֹהִ֖ים 1, 7. הָֽאָדָ֖ם 2, 23. בְּעֵ֖ץ Ps. 1, 3 we have before us post-positives (contrast שִׁרְצ֣וּ Gen. 1, 21: though similar in form, the difference of position is enough to discriminate the accent here from that upon לָאוֹ֖ר 1, 5: compare, too, אֲשֶׁ֖ר 2, 19 with אֲשֶׁ֖ר 1, 7).

Whenever, then, an accent appears on the *extreme* right or left of a word, it cannot be regarded as an index of the tone-syllable: of course it *may* mark it (though even then it will not be in its proper position, as regards the *whole* syllable, for so doing), but it will do it only accidentally.

91. There are only eight pre- and postpositives: some of the latter, however, when they are attached to words accented on the penultima (*mil'el*) are written twice—on the ultima as being postpositive, on the penultima to mark the actual tone of the word. This is always the case with *pashṭa*, an accent which from this circumstance catches the eye very frequently: as Gen. 1, 1 תֹ֫הוּ. 7 הַמַּ֫יִם. 9. 11. 12 etc.: and in Baer and Delitzsch's editions (of Genesis and of other books) the same duplication is adopted with the other post-positives[1] as well, 'ut omnis dubitatio, utrum hoc illudve vocabulum milel sit an milra, praecaveretur' (praef. p. vii); see 1, 7 אֶת־הָרָקִ֫יעַ. 2, 23 וַיֹּ֫אמֶר. 13, 1 וַיַּ֫עַל etc. Thus where

---

[1] And likewise with *telisha magnum* among the prepositives, e. g. 7, 2 אֲשֶׁ֫ר. 27, 46; Isa. 36, 11 אֱלִיקִ֫ים etc.

we find the *same* accent repeated upon one word we may
know that *the tone is on the penultima*[1].

92. On the other hand where (for reasons which need
not be here discussed) two *different* accents appear attached
to one word, *the tone is indicated by the second*[2]. Thus Gen.
17, 24 וָאֲבְרָהָם. 25. 19, 27 אֶל־הַמָּקוֹם; Ps. 1, 1 רְשָׁעִים. 2 חָפְצוּ.
3. 4 אִם־כַּמֹּץ (tone indicated by the point over מ *above* the
cholem). 2, 2 עַל־יְהוָה. 3, 8 קוּמָה. 4, 9 לְבֶטַח.

93. These short and simple rules will be found sufficient
for the purpose of ascertaining on what syllable in a given
case the tone lies : we must next consider some of the
general principles of accentuation, from which it results as
particular instances that the tone after *waw consecutive* in the
perfect, in certain cases, is not thrown forward on to the
ultima. The regular form for *and I will kill* is וְקָטַלְתִּי
wĕqâṭaltí, the double beat being as distinctly marked as in the
English words *per'severe'*, *cor'respond'*: but under certain conditions we find וְקָטַלְתִּי *wĕqaṭálti* with the same meaning : and
the nature of these conditions must be here examined[3].

94. Hebrew accents are of two kinds. The first kind,
called *distinctive* accents, correspond roughly to modern
stops, and, like the latter, indicate the breaks or divisions
in a sentence required by the meaning : they are, however,
more numerous than our stops, because they measure with

---

[1] This rule is valid for all ordinary editions of the Hebrew text (in
which, indeed, its application is limited to the single case of *pashṭa*):
the reader who uses Baer and Delitzsch may easily modify it as follows :—
Where a *postpositive* accent is repeated, the tone is marked by the *first*
accent; where a *prepositive* is repeated, the tone is marked by the *second*
accent.

[2] Except in the rare case of 'incomplete retrocession,' Kalisch, ii.
§ xi. 5; Ges.-Kautzsch, § 29. 3[b].

[3] The tone likewise remains upon the penultima in particular forms
of the *weak* verb: but as the rules for the cases in which this occurs are
independent of accentual considerations, they will not be stated till the
next chapter.

greater minuteness the precise length of each break, and because they mark further those slighter and sometimes hardly perceptible pauses which in most languages are regulated by the voice alone. The other kind, termed *conjunctive* accents, are peculiar to Hebrew: they shew, generally, that the word to which one of them is attached is closely connected in sense with that which immediately follows it: in English this would only be denoted by a smooth and unbroken pronunciation.

95. For our present purpose it is the distinctive accents which possess the greatest interest: it will be accordingly worth while to specify the more important among them, i.e. those which mark some considerable break in the sense, and which, therefore, in translation will commonly be represented by a stop.

96. Firstly, in the prose books:—

The end of a verse is always indicated by the perpendicular line called *sillūq*, followed by *sôph-pāsūq* (: 'end of the verse'): thus Gen. 1, 4 : הַחֹשֶׁךְ (the *sillūq* on the tone-syllable according to rule, חשך being a segolate noun, and consequently *mil'el*).

Every verse (except a few, and these generally short ones, as Gen. 2, 1, though not always, as Dt. 5, 23. 6, 22) is divided into two parts—but by no means necessarily *equal* parts, see e.g. Gen. 1, 11. 2, 19. 7, 21. Lev. 8, 19—by *athnach:* this marks the principal pause in the whole verse. Thus Gen. 1, 1 אֱלֹהִים. 2, 17 מִמֶּנּוּ.

The two perpendicular dots ⸪, so frequently meeting the eye, mark a break of shorter duration: this accent is called *zaqef,*—or *zaqef-qaṭon*, if it be desired to distinguish it from ⸢, which is termed *zaqef-gadol:* see Gen. 2, 9 הַגָּן and עֵץ. 10 מֵעֵדֶן, and 3, 10 וָאֹמַר.

Zaqef may stand in either the first or the second half of a verse, i.e. it may precede either *athnach* or *sôph-pāsūq:* in the former case (but in that only) its place is, under certain circumstances[1], taken by *segolta* ⸳͟. as Gen. 1, 7. 28. 2, 23 הָאָדָ֑ם.

A still slighter pause is indicated by *revîa‘*, as Gen. 1, 2 וְהָאָ֗רֶץ. 2, 21 וַיִּקַּ֗ח. 23 הַפַּ֗עַם. 3, 16 אָמַ֗ר.

The last prose accent which need be considered for our present purpose is *tifcha*[2]*:* this strictly marks a greater break than *revîa‘*, although from the position which it occupies in the verse, it often cannot be so readily represented in English. Examples: Gen. 2, 7 הָֽאָדָ֖ם. 18 עֵ֖זֶר.

97. Two or three verses translated with the stops or pauses indicated, will make this perfectly clear: it ought, however, to be observed that in Hebrew the various parts of a verse are proportioned out and correlated to each other somewhat differently from what might appear natural in English.

Gen. 3, 1 now the serpent was subtil, (*zaqef*, comma,) beyond any beast of the field (*zaqef*[3], slight pause, in German a comma before the following relative) which the Lord God had made: (*athnach*, colon, or even full stop, as A. V.:) and he said unto the woman, (*zaqef*, comma,) Yea, hath God said, (*zaqef*,) Ye shall not eat (*zaqef*, slight pause) of every tree of the garden? 3 but of the fruit of the tree which is in the midst of the garden, (*segolta*,) God hath said,

---

[1] See Wickes, *Prose Accents*, p. 71 ff.

[2] Otherwise called *tarcha:* and this is the name it bears (in most editions) in the Massoretic notes, e.g. on Jud. 17, 1, where the marginal comment upon אֶפְרָיִם is בטרחא קמץ i.e. *qames* with *tarcha*. The Massorah here calls attention to the *pausal* form of the word being generated by a *smaller* distinctive: this it does continually; see, for instance, Josh. 5, 14. 8, 1. 17, 14. 19, 50. Jud. 1, 15. 5, 27. 7, 5. 8, 26 (all cases of the pausal form with *zaqef*, which is considerably more common than with *tarcha*).

[3] Where the same disjunctive accent is *repeated* (without one of greater value intervening), the first marks a greater break than the second. This is often evident from the sense and rhythm, e.g. Gen. 18, 25. 19, 21. 22. 29. 20, 7. 13.

(*revía'*, comma,) Ye shall not eat of it, (*zaqef,*) neither shall ye touch it : (*athnach*, followed, after a pause, by the reason, added emphatically and by itself :) lest ye die.

In *v.* 6ᵃ מִפְּרִי (comma, A. V.) we have an instance of *ṭifcha* exhibiting a disjunctive force, which can be felt even by the English reader : similarly 6ᵇ עָמָה. 9 לוֹ. 10 אָנֹכִי. 12 מִן־הָעֵץ etc.; elsewhere its value is not equal to more than that of a slight pause in the voice, as *v.* 8 בַּגָּן. 11 אֲכָל־מִמֶּנּוּ.

98. Secondly, in the poetical books :—

Here, as before, *sillūq* with *sôph-pāsūq* marks the end of the verse, Ps. 2, 2 וְעַל־מְשִׁיחוֹ: 3 עֲבֹתֵימוֹ:. The other principal divisions are indicated by *athnach* (as Ps. 1, 6 צַדִּיקִים), and a compound accent called *merkha with mahpakh*, or *merkha mahpakhatum*[1], as Ps. 1, 2 חֶפְצוֹ. 3, 6 וְאִישְׁנָה: this accent is always placed *before athnach*, corresponding, in this respect, to *segolta* in prose. In the poetical books *athnach* does not mark such a decided break[2] as *merkha mahp.;* the latter, accordingly, in verses consisting of only two members, is not unfrequently employed by preference, to the exclusion of *athnach*[3]. The only other distinctive accents which need be noticed here are—

ṣinnor, a postpositive (to be distinguished from *ṣinnorith*, which is a *conjunctive* accent and *not* postpositive), as Ps. 3, 3 רַבִּים. 13, 6 בָּטַחְתִּי;

revía', as Ps. 4, 2 צִדְקִי. 2, 8 מִמֶּנִּי; often preceded by *geresh* on the same word, and then called accordingly *revía' mugrāsh*, as Ps. 1, 1 לֵצִים. 2, 8 וְאֹחַזְתָּךְ. 4, 2 חָנֵּנִי; and

dechi (prepositive), as 2, 9 תְּרֹעֵם. 10 וְעַתָּה.

Examples :—

Ps. 1, 1 happy is the man (*revía'*, slight pause) who hath

---

[1] Sometimes also (e. g. by Delitzsch) termed, from its situation *above* and *below* the word, עולה ויורד *'oleh wᵉyored.*

[2] See Ps. 3, 6. 4, 7. 9. 14, 2. 30, 10. 45, 15 etc.

[3] E. g. Ps. 1, 2. 3, 3. 4, 5. 5, 7. 11, 6 etc.

not walked in the counsel of the wicked; (*merkha ;*) and in
the way of sinners (*dechi,* slight pause) hath not stood, (*athnach,*) and in the seat of the scornful (*revîa'*) hath not sat.

27, 4 one thing have I asked of the Lord, (*şinnor,*) *it* will
I seek for : (*merkha,* chief pause :) that I should dwell in the
house of the Lord (*dechi*) all the days of my life; (*athnach ;*)
to gaze on the pleasantness of the Lord, (*revîa',*) and to
meditate in his temple[1].

40, 13 for evils have compassed me about (*pazer,* slighter
than *dechi,*) till they are beyond numbering; (*revîa' ;*) my
iniquities have taken hold upon me, (*dechi,*) and I cannot
look up : (*athnach :*) they are more than the hairs of my
head; (*revîa' mugrāsh ;*) and my heart hath forsaken me.

99. Now there are one or two peculiarities of Hebrew
usage dependent upon the position assumed by a word in a
sentence, and consequently of such a nature as to be relative
to, and ascertainable by, the accents with which it is provided, which materially modify the general rule that when
the perfect is used with the waw consecutive the tone is
thrown forward on to the ultima.

100. The first of these is the dislike felt to *two accented
syllables succeeding one another, unless separated by a decided
pause in pronunciation,* i.e. unless the first has a distinctive
accent : where this is the case, however short the pause may
be, the voice has time to take rest and recover strength, so
as to give proper utterance to what follows. But where
such a pause cannot be made, the collision is very commonly
avoided by one of the following two expedients: either,
namely, the tone of the first word is *forced back* (the vowel
in the now toneless ultima being, if necessary, shortened),

---

[1] Observe here how accurately the accentuation reflects the sense; the
two infinitives introduced by ל, *to gaze* and *to meditate,* stand by themselves as the two co-ordinate objects of שבתי : they are accordingly
marked off from the latter by means of *athnach.*

or recourse is had to *maqqef*, which, throwing the two words
into one, causes the *proper* tone of the first to disappear [1].
Instances may readily be found: Gen. 4, 2 רֹעֵה צֹאן. 6 חָרָה לָךְ.
שֹׁפְטֵי אֶרֶץ 23 נֶשְׁבָּה בּוֹ. Isa. 40, 7 הִפָּרֶד נָא. 13, 9 תֵּבֵל קָיִן 22
will exemplify the first expedient: Gen. 6, 14 עֲצֵי־גֹפֶר. 9, 7
וּרְבוּ־בָהּ: will exemplify the second.

Now when either of these expedients is adopted with a
perfect preceded by וְ consecutive, it is plain that the characteristic position of the tone will cease to exist.

Thus Dt. 14, 26 וְאָכַלְתָּ שָּׁם, although in the same verse we
have both וּנְתַתָּה and וְשָׂמַחְתָּ; Amos 1, 4. 7 וְשִׁלַּחְתִּי אֵשׁ, but
v. 5 וְשָׁבַרְתִּי. 8 וְהִכְרַתִּי. Lev. 26, 25 וְשִׁלַּחְתִּי דֶבֶר and even Dt.
4, 25 וַעֲשִׂיתֶם פֶּסֶל. Ez. 39, 17: in all these cases the tone
has been *driven back* on to the penultima [2]. Instances of the
second expedient are rarer: see Zech. 9, 10 וְהִכְרַתִּי־רֶכֶב.
Ez. 14, 13[b]. Isa. 8, 17 וְקִוֵּיתִי־לוֹ: (Baer).

101. The second of the peculiarities alluded to is that owing
to the manner in which the voice is naturally inclined to rest on
the last accented syllable before a pause, the vowel belonging
to that syllable is, if possible, *lengthened* (as הַמָּיִם Gen. 1, 6),
or, if it be a verbal form such as שִׁמְעוּ (*milra'*), the *shwa'* is
replaced by the original vowel, *to which the tone then recedes* [3],
as שְׁמָעוּ (*mil'el*). Thus, for example, Gen. 2, 25 יִתְבֹּשָׁשׁוּ:.
9, 4 תֹּאכֵלוּ:. 24, 46 הִשְׁקִתָה:. Isa. 53, 7 נֶאֱלָמָה (pf., not the
participle, which is *milra'*; see 1, 21. 26 [4]). 54, 11 לֹא נֻחָמָה.

---

[1] Comp. Ges.-Kautzsch, § 29. 3[b, c], etc.

[2] The rule, however, is not carried out with perfect uniformity: for
instances occur in which the tone is permitted to remain on the ultima:
e.g. Ex. 29, 5. 43. 30, 26. Dt. 23, 14 al. But in this respect the practice
with regard to the perfect and וְ only presents us with similar exceptions
to those which meet us elsewhere: cf. Dt. 7, 25. 20, 6 al.

[3] But this recession does not take place when the old heavy termination וּן- is retained in the impf., as Ps. 12, 9.

[4] Cf. above, p. 18 *n.:* and contrast further Nu. 21, 20 with Cant. 6, 10;
1 Ki. 2, 46 נָכוֹנָה with Ps. 5, 10 נְכוֹנָה; Esth. 8, 15 שָׂמֵחָה *she rejoiced*

This is almost always the case with the two principal distinctive accents *sillūq* and *athnach* (except in a very few words[1] such as מֶלֶךְ, which never change), and not unfrequently with those of smaller value, particularly *zaqef*[2], although with these the usage fluctuates.

Similarly, when a perfect with waw consecutive stands in pause, in order, apparently, to afford the voice a more suitable resting-place than it would find if the accent were violently thrown forward to the ultima, the tone is allowed to *revert to the penultima*, e.g. Dt. 8, 10 וְשָׂבַעְתָּ וְאָכַלְתָּ. 28, 39. Jud. 4, 8 וְהָלַכְתִּי.

102. We thus obtain *two* cases in which a *regular* verb, that would under other circumstances have the tone thrown forward, *retains it on the penultima*, (1) where the verb is *immediately followed* by a tone-syllable, (2) where the verb is *in pause*. The position thus assumed by the tone, it will be seen, follows naturally from the general principles regulating the changes that take place in all other words similarly placed.

103. It will not be necessary to comment further upon the first of these cases: nor does the second call for any additional remark so far as *sillūq* and *athnach* are concerned, as the usage is there clear and uniform. But in reference to the smaller distinctive accents, the practice of the language must be more attentively examined, as it will be found to explain a difficulty which arises from a certain small number

---

(wrongly cited in Fürst's *Concordance* as an *adjective*) with Ps. 113, 9 שְׂמֵחָה *rejoicing*.

[1] A list of the exceptions in Genesis may be found in Baer and Delitzsch's convenient edition of the text of that book, pp. 79 f.: see, further, their *Isaiah*, p. 82; *Job*, p. 64; *Liber xii Prophetarum*, p. 96; *Psalms* (1880), p. 151; and Kalisch, ii. § xiii. 7.

[2] In these cases attention is often (though not always) called to the change by a Massoretic note at the bottom of the page: see p. 106 *n.*; also Baer and Delitzsch, *Genesis*, p. 96; *Isaiah*, p. 95 etc.

of seemingly anomalous instances in which the tone is *not* thrown forward after ׀ consecutive, although, at first sight, no reason seems to exist for the neglect of the usual rule. The fact is, that in these cases a *smaller distinctive* is really present, which the eye is apt to overlook: *sillūq, athnach,* and *zaqef* are better known and more readily distinguished. In order to exhibit the influence of these smaller distinctives in as clear a light as possible, it will be well, in the first place, to shew that instances occur in which they produce the same lengthening of a vowel as those accents which note a more decided pause: when this has been done, it will no longer surprise us to find that they likewise resemble the latter in hindering the tone after waw consecutive from passing forward to the ultima. It will be observed, that the lengthened vowel marks usually a word upon which some peculiar emphasis rests.

Thus with *ṭifcha,* Gen. 15, 14 עֲבָדוֹ. Lev. 27, 10. Nu. 21, 20 וְנִשְׁקָפָה. Dt. 13, 5 תֵּלֵכוּ. 1 Ki. 20, 18. 40ᵇ. Isa. 3, 26 וְנִקָּתָה. 9, 9. 27, 10[1]. Jer. 1, 8. Hos. 7, 11. 8, 7 יִזְרָעוּ. Amos 3, 8 שָׁאָג al.

revia‘, Lev. 5, 23 גָּזֵל. Dt. 5, 14 בְהֶמְתֶּ֫ךָ. 13, 7. Ez. 23, 37 כִּי נָאֵפוּ. Hos. 7, 12 יֵלֵכוּ. Hag. 1, 6. Neh. 12, 43 etc.

pashṭa, Isa. 33, 20 בַּל־יִצְעָן. 2 Ki. 3, 25 יַסְתֹּ֫מוֹ. Dan. 9, 19 שְׁמָעָה. Neh. 3, 34 al.

And in the poetical books :—

sinnor, Ps. 31, 11 חַיָּי. 93, 1 מְלָה.

great revia‘, Ps. 19, 14 עַבְדֶּ֫ךָ, 37, 20 יֹאבֵדוּ. 47, 10 al. Job 21, 17. 24, 12 יִנְאָקוּ; and when preceded by *geresh,* Ps. 37, 6. 23 כּוֹנָ֫נוּ. Job 9, 20ᵇ אָנִי. 17, 1 נִזְעָ֫קוּ.

dechi, Ps. 5, 12 יְרַנֵּ֫נוּ. 45, 2 אָ֫נִי. 97, 1. Job 9, 20 f. 17, 1 חֻבָּ֫לָה[2].

---

[1] Cf. Isa. 64, 3 יַעֲשֶׂה, with Delitzsch's note; cf. also Ges.-K. § 75. 17; König i. p. 531.

[2] And with still smaller accents Lev. 5, 18. Ez. 40, 4. 1 Ki. 1, 26.

104. These instances (which might readily be multiplied) afford ample proof that a smaller distinctive is competent to give rise to the pausal change of vowel—a power only regularly exercised by *athnach* and *sillūq* : it will not, therefore, now seem anomalous when we see that, like the latter, they also prevent the tone after waw consecutive from being thrown forward, even though the pause in the sense indicated by their presence may not be sufficiently decided to produce at the same time the accompanying lengthening of the vowel which usually ensues in the case of the other two accents named. Accordingly we find—

In prose books :—

With *zaqef*, Dt. 2, 28 וְאָכַ֫לְתִּי. 1 Sa. 29, 8 ונלחמתי. Ez. 3, 26 וְנֶאֱלַ֫מְתָּ ; and *zaqef-gadol*, Dt. 32, 40 ואמרתי.

tifcha, Joel 4, 21 וְנִקֵּ֫יתִי. Obadiah 10 וְנִכְרָ֑תָּ. Isa. 66, 9 וְעָצַ֫רְתִּי (where the וְ is consecutive, and introduces a question, as 1 Sa. 25, 11 וְלָקַ֫חְתִּי).

revia, 2 Sa. 9, 10 וְהֵבֵ֫אתָ[1].

pashṭa, Jer. 4, 2 וְנִשְׁבַּ֫עְתָּ.

In poetical books :—

With *great revia*, Ps. 50, 21 וְהֶחֱרַ֫שְׁתִּי Hitz. Pr. 30, 9ª פֶּן אשבע וכחשתי וְאָמַ֫רְתִּי[2]. Job 7, 4ª וְאָמַ֫רְתִּי.

And *revia* with *geresh*, Ps. 19, 14 וְנִקֵּ֫יתִי. 28, 1 פֶּן תחשה וְנִמְשַׁ֫לְתִּי. Pr. 23, 8 וְשִׁחַ֫תָּ. 30, 9ᵇ וְתָפַ֫שְׂתִּי. Job 31, 29 ... אם

3, 25. Dt. 13, 7 : Ps. 5, 12 בָּךְ. Prov. 30, 4. For several of the passages referred to I am indebted to Ewald, § 100ᶜ.

[1] Disallowed by Böttcher, ii. 204, who appeals to 2 Ki. 9, 7. Jer. 21, 6. But הביא, in both the first and the second person, is everywhere else *milra* (Lev. 26, 36 is, of course, to be explained by § 102. 1), and as regards the two passages cited, it is the exception for the tone in Hif'il not to be thrown on, and no one contends that the usage, with the smaller distinctives, is so uniform that they *always* keep it back. Probably also in Gen. 24, 8. 1 Sa. 23, 2ª. Isa. 8, 17ª וחביתי the *mil'el* tone is to be attributed, at least partially, in the two former to the presence of *zaqef*, in the latter to that of *pashṭa*.

[2] So in ordinary texts : Baer, however, has ואמרתי.

אֶשְׂמַח . . . וְהִתְעֹרָרְתִּי *if I used to rejoice . . . and elate myself.*

dechi, Job 5, 24 f. וְיָדַעְתָּ (the absence of *metheg* under יְ, unlike the otherwise similar passage 11, 18. 19, is an indication that the tone must be *mil'el*[1]). 22, 13 וְאָמַרְתָּ. 32, 16 וְהוֹחַלְתִּי[2].

The reader will now be prepared to proceed to the closer examination of the remarkable idiom which, without some elucidation of the nature of accents and the laws which regulate their use, it would be impossible properly to understand.

---

[1] Baer, however, reads וְיָדַעַת, in which case the passage will offer no irregularity.

[2] So in ordinary texts: Baer, however, reads in these two passages וְאָמַרְתָּ and וְהוֹחַלְתִּי, with 'heavy' metheg, or *Ga'ya*, attached to the *Shwa'*. The position of the tone is in this case ambiguous: on the one hand, it may be *milra'*, the *Ga'ya* standing in accordance with the rule in Baer's 'Methegsetzung' (in Merx, *Archiv für wissenschaftliche Erforschung des AT.s,* i. 1869), p. 202, § 35 (where Job 32, 16 is quoted); on the other hand, it may be *mil'el*, the *Ga'ya* being explained by the rule, *ib.* § 37. According to the note in Baer's *Job,* p. 62, Ben Asher (whom Baer follows) reads in 32, 16 וְהוֹחַלְתִּי (which Baer now, in opposition to his view in 1869, refers to § 37, and treats as *mil'el*), Ben Naphtali וְהוֹחַלְתִּי (*milra'*). If the tone be *milra'*, there will, of course, be no irregularity.

I believe these are all the occasions upon which the accents named prevent the tone being thrown forward after waw consecutive. It must be understood, however, that the influence of the smaller distinctives, as exhibited in both these sections, is exceptional: in the majority of instances they effect no change in the form of a word: see, for example, Ex. 18, 16. Dt. 8, 6. 2 Sa. 11, 21. On the other hand, we occasionally find the non-pausal form retained even with *athnach* and *sôph-pāsūq:* see instances in Kalisch, ii. § xiii. 3, and add Prov. 30, 9ª.

CHAPTER VIII.

The Perfect with Waw Consecutive.

105. A construction which is the direct antithesis of that which was last examined (in Chap. VI) will now engage our attention. Both are peculiar to Hebrew: and both, where possible, declare their presence to the ear by a change in the position of the tone; but while in the one the tone recedes, in the other it advances. The one is the form adapted to represent actions conceived as *real*, or as appertaining to a definite date, the other—and we shall perceive this distinction most plainly when we come to compare the cases in which the infinitive and participle break off into one or other of these constructions respectively—is the form adapted to represent such as can be only *contingently* realized, or are indeterminate in their character or time of occurrence. If the one can be applied to the future only when it is contemplated as fixed and definite, the other can be applied to events in the past or present only so long as the time of their taking place is conceived as unfixed and indefinite. The one, accordingly, is the companion and complement of the *perfect*, the other is the companion and complement of the *imperfect*. יָרַד וַיַּעֲמֹד denote two concrete events: יָרַד וְעָמַד denote two abstract possibilities, the context fixing the particular conditions upon which their being realized depends. And exactly as before, when the verb became separated from the וְ, it lapsed into the *perfect*, so here, when its connexion with וְ is broken, it lapses regularly into the *imperfect*:

in both cases, then, it is essentially the *union* of the verb with the conjunction which produces, and conditions, the special signification assumed by the formula as a whole.

Obs. The present idiom is peculiar to the Hebrew of the Old Testament, and to such Hebrew of a later date as is written in imitation of the Biblical style: it is not found in the 'New Hebrew' of the Mishnah, etc., nor is it used in Aramaic. Though no example occurs on the Inscription of Mesha', it may however be inferred that, like the corresponding construction of the impf. with ·ן, it was in use in Moabitish (see p. 71, *note* ²), and probably also in the kindred dialects spoken by other neighbours of the ancient Hebrews. On some passages in the Qor'an, where the perfect, both with and without the conjunction ﻭ, is used of *future* time, see App. III.

106. However difficult it may appear to find a satisfactory explanation of this waw consecutive with the perfect, one thing is perfectly clear, and ought most carefully to be borne in mind : a *real difference* of some kind or other exists between the use of the perfect with simple *waw*, and the use of the perfect with waw consecutive, and the external indication of this difference is to be found in the *alteration of the tone* which constantly attends and accompanies it. This alteration of tone must unquestionably have constituted a recognized element in the traditions now embodied in the Massoretic system of punctuation ; and the authorities who added the points must have felt that in indicating this change of tone they were only adhering to a practice current in their day, and doubtless handed down from a period when Hebrew was a living and growing language. For, it must be distinctly remembered, the cases in which ן consecutive is employed are, in a syntactical point of view, *totally dissimilar* to those in which the simple ן is used. The difference in form is thus essentially relative to a difference in grammatical value ; and, slight though the change may appear, וְקָטַלְתָּ can never be substituted for וְקָטַלְתָּ without introducing a material modification of the sense. Exactly, therefore, as in English and German, we do not stultify ourselves by reading *con'vict*, *inva'lid*, *pre'sent*, *geb'et* (give !), where the context demands *convict'*, *in'valid'*, *present'*, *gebet'* (prayer), so in Hebrew we must beware of saying *wᵉqaṭálta* when grammar and logic call for *wᵉqáṭaltá*.

107. But upon what principle does the change of tone correspond to or represent a change of meaning? Or, putting for the moment the change of tone out of the question, what principle will explain the use of the perfect in the present connexion at all? What is the mysterious power which enables the Hebrew to say פֶּן־יָבוֹא וְהִכַּנִי *lest he come and smite me*, but peremptorily and inexorably forbids him to say פֶּן־יָבוֹא וְאֹתִי הִכָּה, which, if he desires to throw the verb later on in the sentence, forces him to write פֶּן־יָבוֹא וְאֹתִי יַכֶּה, while it vetoes absolutely פֶּן־יָבוֹא וַיַּכֵּנִי?

Although one of the most prominent uses of the perfect with *waw* is after an imperative, or in the description of the future, and it might therefore be thought capable of explanation on the principle of the prophetic perfect, or the perfect of certitude, it must not be forgotten that there are many other occasions of a widely different character, upon which, nevertheless, the same construction is employed[1]: we thus require some more *general* principle than that of the prophetic perfect, which will at the same time account for its appearance in the latter cases as well. We also require some explanation of the fact that, while the form וְכָפַרְתָּ אֹתָה Gen. 6, 14 occurs often enough, we never meet with וְאָתָה כָּפַרְתָּ, or even וְאָתָה כָּפַרְתָּ, but only with וְאָתָה תִכְבֹּר (or the imperative, if necessary).

---

[1] This is important, though it is apt to be imperfectly apprehended: Mr. Turner, for example (*Studies*, etc., pp. 398–402), draws no distinction between the 'prophetic perfect' (§§ 13, 14 above) and the perfect with ו consecutive, and omits altogether to notice the use of the latter after לְמַעַן, פֶּן etc. (§ 115).

108. According to Ewald, § 234[a, b], the construction of the perfect with ו consecutive (the 'relatively-progressive' perfect: cf. above, p. 71, *n.* 4) was originally evoked by the opposite idiom of the imperfect with ו consecutive : there are many well-known aspects under which the two tenses stand contrasted, and the use of the one naturally suggests the other as its antithesis, and so in the present case a specific application of the latter generated as its counterpart a corresponding application of the former.   Just as before we saw how sequence in time or association in thought caused an already completed action to be viewed as passing into a new phase, assuming a fresh development in the next act taken up by the narrative, so here it has the contrary result of occasioning a *nascent* action to be viewed as *advancing to completion*, as no longer remaining in suspension, but as being (so to say) precipitated.   Olshausen, § 229[a], and Böttcher, § 975 D, express themselves similarly—the former remarking further that the use of the perfect rests originally upon a 'play of the imagination,' in virtue of which an action when brought into relation with a preceding occurrence as its *consequence*, from the character of inevitability which it then assumes, is contemplated as actually completed. To this we must add, however, that the consciousness of this relation is to be conceived as essentially dependent upon *union* with *waw*, of which union the change of tone (where not hindered from taking place by external or accidental causes) is the inseparable criterion and accompaniment : dissolve this union, and the sense of any special relationship immediately vanishes.   In fact, the *waw* possesses really in this connexion a demonstrative significance, being equivalent to *then* or *so*[1]: in this capacity, by a pointed reference to

---

[1] This is no imaginary meaning, invented for the purpose of overcoming a difficulty, but one which actually, and constantly, occurs; cf. 'in the day that ye eat thereof ונפקחו *then* (Germ. *so*) are your eyes opened;' and see also the numerous passages cited, §§ 123–129.

some preceding verb, it *limits* the possible realization of the action introduced by it to those instances in which it can be treated as a direct consequence of the event thus referred to. And we may conjecture that the emphatic alteration of tone is designed to mark this limitation: the changed pronunciation *wᵉqátaltí, wᵉqátaltá* seems to cry *There!* to attract the hearer's attention, and warn him against construing what is said in an absolute and unqualified sense, to direct him rather to some particular locality, some previously marked spot, where, and where alone, the assertion may be found verified. An action described by this construction is regarded, it is true, as completed, but *only with reference to the preceding verb*, only so far as the preceding action necessitates or permits. נָפַ֫לְתָּ means unreservedly and unconditionally *thou hast fallen:* וְנָפַלְתָּ֫ means 'so hast thou fallen,' 'so,' namely, confining the possible occurrence of the event to a particular area previously implied or defined [1]. Whatever, therefore, be the shade of meaning borne by the first or '*dominant*' verb, the perfect following, inasmuch as the action it denotes is conceived to take place under the *same* conditions, assumes it too: be the dominant verb a jussive, frequentative, or subjunctive, the perfect is virtually the same. To all intents and purposes the perfect, when attached to a preceding verb by means of this waw consecutive, *loses its individuality:* no longer maintaining an independent position, it passes under the sway of the verb to which it is connected [2].

---

[1] Steinthal (*Characteristik*, p. 262) speaks of this alteration of tone as *eine höchst sinnige Verwendung des Accents:* he himself, observing that it throws a new emphasis on the person-ending, considers that its effect is to render prominent the personal aspect of the action, to limit it, in other words, by representing it as subjective or conditioned. It seems a fatal objection to Mr. Turner's view (p. 402), that the change of tone never takes place with the prophetic perf., though its 'position and significance' may even be more emphatic than that of the pf. with ו.

[2] This peculiarity may sometimes be imitated in English by linking

109. But upon what ground, it will be asked, can the marked avoidance of ·ֽ in all such cases be accounted for? What is there to deter the Hebrew from saying, 'lest he come *and go on* to smite me?' The fact is, ·ֽ was so appropriated by the universal custom of the language to the description of actual fact, that a sense of incongruity and anomaly would have arisen had it been adopted also on occasions where the events spoken of were merely *contingent.* Moreover, it must have been felt that with an action in itself only *incipient* or nascent, any idea of *continuation* or development was out of place : where the series is begun by a form which, like the imperfect, denotes essentially an act that is inchoate or incomplete, all possibility of free and unconditional progress (such as is expressed by ·ֽ) is at once obviously checked : the only kind of *ulterior advance* imaginable under the circumstances is that which may ensue when the now indeterminate and incomplete act is *determined and completed.* After בָּא, וַיַּכֵּנִי denotes a subsequent act without any kind of reserve or limitation, בא ויכני *he came and smote me :* after יְבֹא, nothing thus *unconditionally* subsequent can find place because יבא itself is inchoate and incomplete ; nothing therefore definite can be annexed to יבא, *until it has matured into* בָּא. Still, upon the hypothesis that it has matured, further eventualities may be conceived : and so we find יבא followed by וְהִכַּנִי, where the *perfect* tense implies that the eventuality has occurred, while the *waw* limits its occurrence to such occasions as fall within the scope of the preceding dominant verb. Accordingly we get אִיךְ, פן יבא והכני למען, למען, אם, אולי, למה 'lest, that, if, he come— *then* or *so* (i. e. upon the supposition that the first statement is realized)—*has* or (as our idiom would prefer on account

---

together as infinitives under the same auxiliary (instead of repeating the latter with each different verb) the perfects connected in the original by means of *waw.*

of the *condition* implied) *had he smitten me'* = 'lest he come *and smite me:'* 'perhaps he may come—*and then has he* or *had he smitten me'* = 'perhaps he may come *and smite me:'* 'why, how should he come—τότε ἐπάταξεν ἄν ἐμέ [1], so hätte er mich geschlagen, *then had he smitten me'* = 'why, how should he come *and smite me?'* יבא והכני 'he was liable or likely to come, would or used to come—*and then* (whenever this actually happened) *he has* or *had* smitten me' = 'he would come *and smite me.'* Should it be objected to such an explanation that it presupposes a crude and constrained mode of expression, incompatible with the ease and freedom with which the construction in question is actually employed, it may be replied that the primitive form of many of the Aryan moods and tenses was even rougher in structure; and although the adaptation of such forms as instruments of thought is doubtless facilitated by phonetic decay obliterating the separate traces of their ultimate elements, it is not dependent upon it altogether. When a compound phrase or formula is analysed, we are often surprised to discover the circuitous path by which expression has been given to an apparently simple idea; the mind, however, treats the phrase as a whole, and does not, on every occasion of its use, pass consciously through the individual steps by which its meaning has been acquired.

And now we may be able to discern a reason why the Hebrew could say פן יבא והכני, but never פן יבא ואתי הכה : in the former case, the relative nature of הכני and its dependency upon יבא is patent from the intimate union with ו; but in the latter case, on account of the isolated position taken by it, הכה seems to be stated absolutely, to have no *special* reference to any other fact. It is in order to preserve a keen sense of the subordination thus essential to the meaning of the construction that the connexion with what precedes

---

[1] Cf. with the stronger או, 2 Ki. 13, 19.

is so jealously guarded : the moment this connexion is broken, the verb lapses into the imperfect, which is, of course, under the same government as the dominant verb, and indeed co-ordinate with it.

Obs. The preceding remarks will make it plain in what manner the *waw* in this construction can be spoken of as the '*waw* relativum,' and the idiom as a whole as the 'relatively-progressive perfect.' A question, however, here arises, analogous to the one discussed § 85 *Obs.*, whether, namely, the perfect may not be occasionally preserved after its separation from *waw*, or even when the waw has been entirely dropped. The vast number of instances, occurring under every conceivable variety of circumstance, in which the verb, after separation, appears as an *imperfect*, furnishes a strong argument against supposing this to be possible: though an opposite view is expressed by Ewald, § 346[b], by Böttcher, ii. p. 205, and by Hitzig (on Job 5, 9), who cite passages in support of their opinion. These alleged instances, when examined, resolve themselves either into cases of the proph. perfect, or into cases where an obvious change of construction has supervened: in fact, with two or three exceptions, they have been already explained above, § 14 γ. The perfect, standing by itself, or preceded by כי, § 14 α, β, is used of the future precisely as in the passages alleged ; now it is impossible to explain the two former cases by supposing waw to have been dropped, for the simple reason that *it could never have been present:* if, therefore, the perfects in § 14 α, β, can be accounted for without having recourse to an imaginary waw consecutive, no necessity can exist for having recourse to it in order to account for the perfect in § 14 γ. The question is to a certain extent one of *degree:* the force of the tense is undoubtedly *limited* both in the proph. perf. and after waw consecutive; but in the one case it is the intelligence of the reader, aided only by the context, that *determines* the limitation, and *localizes* the action in the future; in the other case this function is performed by the connecting particle alone. It is thus the context that fixes the meaning of חשך Isa. 5, 30, or הדה 11, 8, no less than that of גלה 5, 13, or מלאה 11, 9. It would take too long to examine the other instances in detail; it is at least suspicious that more numerous and clearer cases do not occur of the bare perfect after למען, אם, כי, etc. Naturally, it cannot be seriously maintained that הסיר התז ' stands for ' יסיר והתז; while, as to Prov. 9, *vv.* 4 and 16 are different; *v.* 4 is to be explained by § 12 (cf. the pff. *vv.* 1–3), *v.* 16 by § 123 α.

110. But before analysing the construction in its syntactical aspect, we must first of all state the laws which regulate the *change of tone* previously alluded to. Many forms of the perfect, as קָטְלוּ, אֲמַרְתֶּם, רָעוּ (from רָעָה,), שָׁתָה (*he drank*, not שָׁתָה 3 *fem.* from שִׁית) etc., are already *milra'*, and with such, of course, no change is possible: in other cases the general rule is that where the perfect is preceded by waw consecutive, *the tone is thrown forward on to the ultima.* But to this law there is a considerable list of exceptions: it will be seen, however, that for the most part they fall into three or four broad groups which can be recollected without difficulty.

Including, for the sake of completeness, the two rules established in the last chapter, we get the following:—

The tone is *not* thrown forward

(1) Generally, though not quite uniformly (see Dt. 21, 11. 23, 14. 24, 19), when the perfect is immediately followed, without any break in the sense (i.e. without a *distinctive* accent), by a tone-syllable in the succeeding word.

(2) When the perfect is *in pause*—almost invariably with the greater distinctives, and sometimes also with those of smaller value. Of these two rules no further illustrations will be needed.

Obs. So far as the *regular* verb is concerned, the tone is *uniformly* thrown on in the 1st and 2nd sing., except in the cases covered by these two rules. In 1 Sa. 17, 35. Job 7, 4^b (assuming the verbs to be frequentative) the accentuation וְהִצַּלְתִּי, וְשָׁבַעְתִּי appears to have arisen from a misconception: the preceding verbs וְיָצָאתִי, וּמָדַד were really frequentative, but, there being no change of tone (see rule 4) to mark this fact, it was forgotten, and then the perfects following were subjoined by means of simple *waw* according to § 132.

(3) In 1 *plur.* of all the modifications, and in 3 *fem. sing.* and 3 *plur.* of Hif'il. Thus Gen. 34, 17 וְלָקַחְנוּ. Ex. 8, 23 וְזָבַחְנוּ: Lev. 26, 22 וְהִכְרִיתָה. Amos 9, 13 וְהִטִּיפוּ. Ezek. 11, 18 וְהֵסִירוּ. It is also naturally not thrown on in 2 *fem. sing.* of verbs with a guttural as their third radical, as וְיָדַעַתְּ Hos. 2, 22.

Obs. Twice in Hif'il the general rule is observed: Ex. 26, 33 וְהִבְדִּילָה. Lev. 15, 29 וְהֵבִיאָה.

(4) In the *Qal* of verbs ל״א and ל״ה, as Gen. 7, 4 וּמָחִיתִי.
וְנִשְׂאתִי 18, 26. וְקָרָאתָ 19. וְהָיִיתָ 17, 4.

Obs. If the list in Böttcher, ii. 204, is complete, besides וּבָא (and this only before a guttural) there are but two instances of Qal *milra'* after ו, viz. Lev. 24, 25. 2 Sa. 15, 33[1] (both gutt.). But in the other modifications the tone is, in the majority of instances, thrown on according to rule, as Ex. 25, 11. Lev. 26, 9 etc.; although a few exceptions are found, cf. Dt. 4, 19. 11, 10. 28, 12. Job 15, 13 al.

(5) Often in those forms of the *Qal* and *Nif'al* in verbs ע״ע and ע״ו which end in ו- or ה-, as Ex. 7, 28 וּבָאוּ. Isa. 6, 13 וְשָׁבָה. וְסָרָה 11, 13. וְנָמַסּוּ 34, 3. וְנָסוּ 35, 10: but the usage here is very fluctuating, as many of these verbs also occur *milra'*; see Ex. 8, 7 וְסָרוּ. וְרַבָּה 23, 29. וְעָפוּ Isa. 11, 14. וְשָׁבָה 23, 17 etc.

Obs. In the other forms the general rule is adhered to, as Gen. 28, 21 וְשַׁבְתִּי. וְשָׁבְתָּ Dt. 4, 30. וְכַתּוֹתִי Ps. 89, 24. והסרתי Ex. 23, 25. והנחתי Ezek. 16, 42. וְהֵמַתָּה Nu. 14, 15 etc. Exceptions (unless when occasioned in accordance with rules 1 or 2, as Gen. 19, 19[b]. Ex. 33, 14) are extremely rare: 1 Ki. 2, 31. Jer. 10, 18[2]. Amos 1, 8[2] being probably all that exist.

111. It has been already remarked that the peculiar position occupied by the perfect, when thus annexed by ו, as regards the dominant or principal verb, causes it virtually to assume the particular modal phase belonging to the latter. If, for instance, the principal verb involve *will, would,* or *let . . .,* the subordinate verbs connected with it by ו consecu-

---

[1] He cites indeed 1 Sa. 10, 2. Jer. 2, 2. 3, 12 as well: but there is no reason for supposing that in these verses the perfects are *milra'*. There is no metheg in the antepenultima, and Böttcher seems to have been inadvertently misled by the *postpositive* accent *small telisha;* see Isa. 62, 4. 66, 20.

[2] In these two passages the *mil'el* tone is attested by the Massorah: but Zeph. 1, 17 (cited in my first edition), the correct reading (as noted also by Kimchi, ad loc.) has the tone *milra':* see Baer's *Liber xii Prophetarum* (1878), pp. iv, 79.

tive must be understood in the same tense or mood; in
other words, as governed by the same auxiliary: 2 Ki. 5, 11
I said וְקָרָא וְעָמַד יֵצֵא he *will* (or *would*, if in oratio obliqua)
come out and stand and call: the writer might, had he
chosen, have repeated the impf. וְיִקְרָא וְיַעֲמֹד יֵצֵא he would
come out, and would stand, and would call: this would
have been somewhat more emphatic, and greater stress would
have been laid on the precise manner in which each individual action was conceived: but, writing in prose, he adopts
the shorter and more flowing mode of expression. Now
where—as is continually the case in Hebrew—there is a
change of person between the first and any of the following
verbs, we shall find it in English awkward, if not impossible,
to adopt such a succinct method of translation: either the
auxiliary will have to be repeated each time the person
changes, or, since the perfect in the original really indicates
a result or consequence (but not the *design*, § 61) of the
action denoted by the principal verb, we may even employ
that with the subjunctive. Gen. 24, 7 may HE send his angel
before thee וְלָקַחְתָּ *and mayest* thou take (or, *that* thou mayest
take) a wife for my son from there. 18, 25 far be it from
thee ... לְהָמִית to slay the righteous with the wicked וְהָיָה *and*
for the righteous *to be* (see § 118) as the wicked (or, *that so*
the righteous *should* be as the wicked: more neatly in Latin,
Absit a te *ut occidas* justum cum iniquo, *fiatque* justus sicut
impius). Jer. 48, 26 make him drunk ... וְסָפַק *and let* Moab
vomit (or, *that* Moab may vomit).

112. We may now proceed to analyse the mode in which
this idiom is employed.

The perfect with וֹ consec. appears as the continuation of
(i) the imperative.

Gen. 6, 14 make thee an ark וְכָפַרְתָּ *and pitch* it. 21 וְאָסַפְתָּ.
8, 17 bring them out with thee וְשָׁרְצוּ *and let* them swarm in
the earth.

Here notice 1. the *grammar* alone shews that the *waw* is consecutive: the tone in שׁרצוּ is already *milra'*, so that no alteration can take place from the accession of וּ: we must, however, judge of such cases by the analogy of those in which, under similar syntactical conditions, i. e. in the present case, after an imperative, the change of tone can be observed: this analogy leaves us no doubt that the waw is consecutive here as well. Notice 2. that the dependency of וּשׁרצוּ upon the imperative is *obscured* in English by the singular weakness of our language, which all but forbids our using a genuine third pers. imperative, except in exalted or poetical style: the interpolation of *let* makes it seem as though *let them swarm* were independent of *bring them out:* whereas in the Hebrew the sense to be given to וּשׁרצוּ is *wholly determined* by the meaning of the dominant verb, which is here an imperative. In a point like this, either German, Latin, or Greek has the advantage of English.

Ex. 3, 16 go וְאָמַרְתָּ . . . וְאָסַפְתָּ. 7, 15 f. 26 etc. 19, 23. Lev. 24, 14 bring forth him that cursed, וְסָמְכוּ *and let* all those that heard *lay* their hands upon his head (*educ et ponant,* Vulg.). Nu. 4, 19 this do to them וְחָיוּ *and let* them live וְלֹא יָמֻתוּ (note the *impf.*) *and not die* etc. 1 Sa. 6, 7 f. 15, 3. 2 Sa. 11, 15 set Uriah etc. וְשַׁבְתֶּם מֵאַחֲרָיו וְנִכָּה וָמֵת *and retire* from behind him, *and let him be* smitten and die. 24, 2 go now through all the tribes וְיָדַעְתִּי *and let* me know. Ezek. 20, 20 et sabbata mea sanctificate וְהָיוּ *et sint* signum inter me et vos.

This is by far the most common construction after an imperative: sometimes, however, a succession of imperatives is preferred, and sometimes the perfect and imperative alternate: Gen. 27, 43 f. וְיָשַׁבְתָּ . . . קוּם בְּרַח. 45, 9. 1 Sa. 6, 7 f. 2 Ki. 9, 2–3. Pr. 23, 1 f. etc.

113. (ii) After an *imperfect,* in any of its senses: thus—
(1) After the impf. as a pure future:—
Gen. 12, 3[b]. 18, 18 and Abraham will be a great nation וְנִבְרְכוּ־בוֹ *and* all nations of the earth *will be* blessed in him. 40, 13 he will lift up thy head וַהֲשִׁיבְךָ *and restore* thee to thy place, וְנָתַתָּ *and thou wilt give* etc. Jud. 6, 16 I shall be with thee וְהִכִּיתָ *and* thou *wilt* smite Midian (or, *will* and *shalt*).

1 Sa. 2, 35 f. 8, 11. 18. 17, 32 thy servant will go וְנִלְחַם *and fight.* 46. Isa. 1, 30 f. 2, 2 f. 13, 11. 14, 1. 2. 4. 60, 5. Jer. 16, 4 etc.; or as expressing a purpose or a command (*I will, thou shalt*), Gen. 17, 16 וּבֵרַכְתִּי. 24, 4. 32, 21. Ex. 8, 23. 20, 9 etc.

Constantly, also, after other words pointing to the future, as a *participle*, Gen. 6, 17 f. and behold, I am bringing the deluge upon the earth וַהֲקִמֹתִי *and will* establish etc. 48, 4 behold, I am making thee fruitful וְהִרְבִּיתִךָ *and will* multiply thee . . . וְנָתַתִּי[1] *and give* this land etc. Isa. 7, 14 *and will call* his name 'Immanu'el. 8, 7 f. 13, 19. 19, 1 ff. Jer. 30, 22. 37, 7 f. וְשָׁבוּ. Hosea 2, 8. 16 f. Amos 2, 14 וְאָבַד. 6, 14 etc.; or an *infin. absolute*, as Gen. 17, 11. Isa. 5, 5. 31, 5. Ezek. 23, 47.

And after the *prophetic perfect*, the announcement *opening* generally with the proph. perf., which is then followed by the perfect with *waw consec.*: thus Gen. 17, 20 I have blessed him וְהִפְרֵיתִי and I *will* make him fruitful. Nu. 24, 17 a star *hath proceeded* out of Jacob, וקם *and* a sceptre *shall* arise out of Israel. Isa. 2, 11 ונשגב (cf. *vv.* 12–17). 5, 14[b]. 43, 14 שׁלחתי I send to Babel וְהוֹרַדְתִּי *and will bring down* etc. 48, 15. 52, 10 Yahweh hath laid bare his holy arm, וראו and all the ends of the earth *shall see* etc. Jer. 13, 26. 48, 41.

(2) After the impf. as a jussive or cohortative :—

(*a*) Gen. 1, 14 יְהִי let there be lights וְהָיוּ *and let them be* . . . 28, 3. 43, 14 ושלח. 47, 29 f. bury me not in Egypt וְשָׁכַבְתִּי *but let* me lie with my fathers. Ex. 5, 7 הם ילכו *let* THEM go וקששו *and gather* themselves straw. 34, 9. Dt. 28, 8. 1 Sa. 12, 20. 24, 13 *let* Yahweh judge וּנְקָמַנִי *and* avenge me! 1 Ki.

---

[1] The two accents on this word must not be confused with the double *pashṭa* on words *mil'el*, § 91: the first accent is a conjunctive termed *Qadma*, which is here used in place of metheg to mark the counter-tone (p. 102, *n.* 1). Cf. Ewald, § 97[g].

1, 2. 8, 28 (after 26). 22, 12 (ironical) *and* Yahweh give it into thy hands! Ps. 64, 11. 109, 10. 143, 12 וְהַאֲבַדְתָּ.

(β) Gen. 31, 44 come let us make a covenant וְהָיָה *and let* it be etc. Jud. 19, 13 לְךָ וְנִקְרְבָה *come and let* us draw near to one of the places וְלַנּוּ *and* pass the night in Gibeah. Mic. 4, 6 f. Ruth 2, 7 let me glean, I pray, וְאָסַפְתִּי *and gather* etc.

(3) After an impf. denoting *would* or *should* :—Amos 9, 3 f. from there *would* I command the sword וְהָרַגְתַּם *and* it *should* slay them וְשָׂמְתִּי *and I would* etc. Job 8, 6. 9, 17 with a tempest *would* he overwhelm me וְהִרְבָּה *and multiply* my bruises without cause. 31. Jud. 16, 5 (*may*).

(4) Or after the impf. as a frequentative, whether of present or past time, indifferently :—

(*a*) Gen. 2, 24 therefore doth a man leave his father and mother ודבק *and cleave* to his wife והיו *and they are* one flesh. Ex. 18, 16 when they have a matter coming to me [1], וְשָׁפַטְתִּי then (§ 123) *I decide* between them וְהוֹדַעְתִּי *and declare* etc. Dt. 5, 21 כי ידבר אלהים that God speaketh (or may speak) with man וְחָי: *and he liveth.* Isa. 5, 12 והיו (observe *v.* 12[b] יביטו . . . ו). 27, 10. 44, 15 יַשִּׂיק וְאָפָה kindleth fire *and baketh* bread. Jer. 12, 3 [2] thou seest me וּבְחַנְתָּ *and triest* my heart. 20, 9 [2] וְאָמַרְתִּי and *I keep saying* 'I will not speak of him' . . . והיה *and then* there comes in my heart as it were a burning fire וְנִלְאֵיתִי *and I am weary* of forbearing etc. [3] Ezek. 29, 7

---

[1] So the *text* must be rendered (cf. 22, 8): for the apodosis after כי, in the sense of *whenever*, to be introduced by the bare perfect, would be without parallel. If we desire to render *they come to me*, we must read וּבָא.

[2] These two passages (cf. 6, 17. Ex. 18, 16. Amos 4, 7) are important as shewing that the *waw* after a *frequentative* impf. is really consecutive: as it happens, the verb under such circumstances is generally in the *third* person, in which the distinctive change of tone can rarely occur.

[3] A. V. here seems to describe a *single* occurrence, which would have been denoted by וַיֹּאמֶר etc., and conveys no idea of the *repetition* so plainly discernible in the original: R.V. rightly *if* etc.: see § 148.

תרוץ ובקעת (a description of Egypt's *general* character). Hos.
4, 3. 7, 7 יחמו וַאֲכְלוּ (their *reiterated* ebullitions described).
Mic. 2, 2 (after יעשׂוה *v.* 1). Ps. 10, 10 יָשֹׁח ונפל. 17, 14 יִשְׂבְּעוּ
בָנִים they have their fill of children וְהִנִּיחוּ *and leave* etc. 46,
10 ימצו after ואמרו 73, 11 יאבדו ועזבו. 49, 11 יִשֹׁבֵר וקצץ
v. 10. 78, 38 but he is merciful, forgiveth iniquity, and doth
not destroy (impff.), וְהִרְבָּה *and is bounteous* to turn his anger
away. 90, 6. Pr. 16, 29. 18, 10. 20, 28. 24, 16. 29, 6. Job
5, 5. 14, 11 and a river will (freq.) decay וְיָבֵשׁ *and dry up.*
33, 18 f. 34, 7 f. So after the exclamatory, impassioned *inf.
abs.* (Ew. § 328ᵇ), Jer. 7, 10.

(β) Gen. 2, 6 a mist *used to* go up וְהִשְׁקָה *and water* the
ground. 10. 6, 4. 29, 2 f. an instructive passage : ' three
flocks *were lying* there (partcp.), for ישקו they *used* to water
flocks from that well,' this is then followed by four pff. freqq.
The course of the narrative is resumed only at ויאמר 4 : it is
clear that *v.* 3 cannot belong to it, for *v.* 8 shews that the
stone *had not been* rolled away, so that וגללו describes what
used to be done. The sudden change of tense—from impf.
with ·וַ to pf. with וְ—is most noticeable, and immediately
arrests the attention. Ex. 33, 7–11 יקח ונטה-לו *would* (or
used to) *take and pitch it* (contrast this with a passage like
35, 21–29, ·וַ describing what took place upon only *one*
occasion). 34, 34 f. Dt. 11, 10 where תִזְרַע אֶת־זַרְעֲךָ וְהִשְׁקִיתָ
thou *usedst to* sow thy seed, *and water it* with thy foot. 1 Ki.
14, 28 *used to* bear them והשיבום *and bring them* back. 2 Ki.
3, 25 ישליכו ומלאוה . . . ו יהרסו (a graphic picture of the way
in which the people occupied themselves during their sojourn
in Moab). 12, 15–17. Job 31, 29 if I *used to* rejoice . . .
וְהִתְעֹרַרְתִּי (tone as Ps. 28, 1, § 104) *and elate* myself. Ez. 44, 12¹.

After a partcp.:—Isa. 6, 2 f. were standing וקרא *and each
kept* crying. Pr. 9, 14 וישבה *and keeps* sitting (after הומיה, *v.* 13).

And an inf. abs.:—2 Sa. 12, 16 וַיָּצָם צֹם ובָא וְלָן וְשָׁכַב and
he fasted on, *repeatedly* (during the seven days, *v.* 18) going

---

¹ The correction in Stade, *ZATW.* 1885, p. 293, is gratuitous.

in, and passing the night (there), and lying on the earth.
13, 19. Jos. 6, 13 הלכים הלוך ותקעו (contrast 1 Sa. 19, 23.
2 Sa. 16, 13 ·וֹ). Jer. 23, 14.

114. Sometimes after a fact has been stated summarily
by a perfect, we find this tense succeeded by perfects with
וֹ *consecutive*, as though to remind the reader of the real
character of what is described : that in such cases the *waw*
is consecutive, and not merely conjunctive (Chap. IX), is
often shewn by the proximity of an *imperfect*, the frequentative sense of which is unmistakeable. At other times, on
the other hand, when the frequentative nature of the events
described has been sufficiently indicated, the writer, feeling
that this circumstance does not call for *continual* prominence,
reverts to the ordinary form of prose narrative, as carried
on by ·וֹ.

Thus (*a*) Nu. 11, 8 שטו ולקטו (observe the impf. יֵרֵד *v.* 9).
Amos 4, 7 וְהִמְטַרְתִּי . . . מָנַעְתִּי (a noticeable passage on
account of the clear change of tone : observe, too, the
following impff.). 2 Ki. 6, 10. 2 Chr. 12, 11 באו . . . ונשאום.

(*β*) Jud. 12, 5 והיה כי יאמרו and it used to be whenever
they said . . . וַיֹּאמְרוּ that they replied etc. 1 Sa. 2, 16ᵃ. 13,
22ᵇ (cf. the impf. *v.* 19). 14, 52. 2 Sa. 15, 2. Jer. 6, 17
והקמֹתי . . . וַיֹּאמרו (§ 120). 18, 4. Ps. 78, 40 f. Job 1, 4 f.

The same transition occurs also after the imperfect
itself :—Isa. 44, 12. Ps. 106, 43 וַיִּמֹּכּוּ . . . ימרו. Job 3, 24.
5, 15 f. 7, 18 yea, thou *visitest* him (even with לבקרים). 11,
3. 12, 25. 14, 10. 21, 14 (Ps. 73, 11 ואמרו). 31, 27 (contrast
v. 29 quoted § 113) etc.

Obs. In some of these cases the ·וֹ introduces the definite act which
terminates a scene previously described, or the settled state which
succeeds or accompanies the reiterated actions : so Jud. 6, 5. Ps. 78, 35:
cf. 99, 7. Pr. 7, 13ᵇ (in 13ᵃ the pff. are frequentative). Nu. 9, 23ᵇ. 2 Chr.
33, 6ᵇ. Comp. Böttcher, ii. 216.

115. The perfect with *waw consecutive* is further found
where the imperfect is preceded by various particles : as

אוּלַי *perhaps :* Gen. 27, 12 *perhaps* my father will feel me וְהָיִיתִי and I shall be . . . וְהֵבֵאתִי *and* I *shall* bring upon myself a curse. Nu. 22, 11 after אוכל (in *v.* 6 the *impf.*). 23, 27. 2 Sa. 16, 12. 2 Ki. 19. 4.

אוֹ *or if :* 1 Sa. 26, 10 *or if* his day should come וָמֵת *and* he *die.* Ez. 14, 17. 19.

אָז *then :* 1 Sa. 6, 3 *then* will ye be healed וְנוֹדַע לָכֶם *and* it *will be known* to you etc. Ps. 19, 14 (tone, § 104).

אֵיךְ *how ?* Gen. 39, 9 *how* can I do this great evil וְחָטָאתִי *and sin* against God? 2 Sa. 12, 18 *how* shall we say to him, The child is dead, ועשה (translating freely to shew the connexion) *and so* make him vex himself? So אֵיכָכָה Esth. 8, 6 (with אוכל).

אַל : Jer. 17, 21 *do not* bear any burden on the sabbath-day וַהֲבֵאתֶם *and bring* it etc. Ps. 143, 7 *do not* hide thy face from me וְנִמְשַׁלְתִּי *and let me be* like them that go down into the pit (tone as in the parallel Ps. 28, 1, after פֶּן)[1].

אִם *if :* Gen. 28, 20 f. 32, 9 *if* 'Esau comes to one camp וְהִכָּהוּ *and smites* it. Dt. 8, 19. 11, 28 וַסַרְתֶּם. 20, 11 וּפָתְחָה. Jud. 4, 20 וְשָׁאַל וְאָמַר. 14, 12 וּמְצָאתֶם. 1 Sa. 12, 14. 15. 17, 9 ; and so constantly : see §§ 136, 138.

Similarly after אם in an oath : Gen. 24, 38. Ez. 20, 33 f. as I live, if I will not . . . reign over you וְהוֹצֵאתִי *and bring* you forth from the peoples, וְקִבַּצְתִּי *and gather you !*

אֲשֶׁר = *so that :* Dt. 2, 25. 4, 6 *so that* they will hear ואמרו *and say* (cf. *v.* 10 . . . . וְ ... ילמדון).

= *when :* Lev. 4, 22 when a ruler יחטא ועשה sinneth *and doth* etc. (not *hath sinned,* A.V.). Nu. 5, 29 ונטמאה.

= *who so* (the person indicated being essentially indefinite ὅστις or ὃς ἐάν with subj. : this construction of אשר is quite distinct from another which will be immediately noticed):

---

[1] The second verb separated from וְ, and accordingly in the impf. Ps. 38, 2 ; ἀσυνδέτως, 35, 19. 75, 6. 1 Sa. 2, 3.

Gen. 24, 14 the girl *to whom* אֹמַר I may say, Let down thy pitcher, וְאָמְרָה *and she reply*, Drink (puella cui ego dixero ... et illa responderit—the girl, whoever she may be, in whom these two conditions are fulfilled). 43 (where the tone of וְאָמַרְתִּי proves, if proof were needed, that וְאָמְרָה in 14 has וְ *consecutive*). Lev. 21, 10. Jud. 1, 12 LXX rightly ὃς ἂν πατάξῃ καὶ προκαταλάβηται. 1 Sa. 17, 26. Isa. 56, 4 אֲשֶׁר יִשְׁמְרוּ וּבָחֲרוּ, LXX ὅσοι ἂν φυλάξωνται καὶ ἐκλέξωνται. Jer. 17, 5. 7. 27, 11 τὸ ἔθνος ὃ ἐὰν εἰσαγάγῃ ... καὶ ἐργάσηται αὐτῷ. Ps. 137, 9 (שֶׁ).

Lev. 18, 5 which a man *may* do וָחַי *and live* in them, or since, in the double statement enunciated, the occurrence of the second is so linked to that of the first as to be dependent upon it (cf. § 147), 'which *if* a man do, he *may* (or *shall*) live in them.' Ez. 20, 11. 13. Neh. 9, 29. Dt. 19, 4. Isa. 29, 11 f. 36, 6.

Obs. There is, however, another construction of אשר followed by the *perfect*, or by the impf. and then ·וְ, which must not be confused with that just explained. There the writer had an indefinite contingency in view: here he contemplates a distinct occurrence [1]: compare, with the perfect alone, Lev. 7, 8 the skin of the burnt sacrifice which הִקְרִיב he *hath* offered (in the case assumed). Thus we find Dt. 17, 2–4 a man who יַעֲשֶׂה doeth evil וַיֵּלֶךְ *and goeth* and serveth other gods, וְהֻגַּד *and it be* told thee etc.; or the two constructions united, as Lev. 15, 11 every one whom the זב touches (יִגַּע), and who לֹא שָׁטַף *has* not (or shall not have, in the assumed case) drenched his hands with water. 17, 3 f. whoso slays an ox ... and לֹא הֱבִיאוֹ *hath* not brought it etc. (*v.* 9 we find the impf. and *doth* not bring it: Onqelos אַיְתֵיהּ, יְיתִינֵהּ, and the Peshito ܐܝܬܝܗ, ܡܝܬܐ retain the difference of tense, which the other versions fail to reproduce). 9, 13 (וחדל and לא היה). Ez. 18, 6 (*hath not* eaten, *never* draws near).

הֲ *interrogativum*: Ex. 2, 7 *shall I* go וְקָרָאתִי *and call?* Nu. 11, 22 *shall* flocks be slain for them וּמָצָא *and it be*

---

[1] Cf. the similar case of אם Nu. 5, 27 etc. if she *have* made herself unclean, וְתִמְעֹל *and played* false: see below, § 138 *Obs.*

enough for them? (with change of subject: LXX μὴ σφαγή-
σονται . . . καὶ ἀρκέσει;) Jud. 15, 18 *shall I* die of thirst וְנָפַלְתִּי
and fall into the hand of the uncircumcised? 1 Sa. 23, 2.
Ruth 1, 11 *have I* still sons in my womb וְהָיוּ *and will* they
be (=for them to be) to you for husbands? 1 Chr. 14, 10.

Obs. After the 'modal' perfect (§ 19. 2), Jud. 9, 9. 11. 13 am I to have
ended my fatness וְהָלַכְתִּי *and go?* So 1 Sa. 26, 9 כִּי מִי שָׁלַח יָדוֹ בִּמְשִׁיחַ
י״ וְנִקָּה *for who is to have* put forth (=*can* put forth) his hand against
Yahweh's anointed *and be guiltless?* (entirely different from Dt. 5, 23
מִי . . . אֲשֶׁר שָׁמַע . . . וַיֶּחִי: =who *ever* heard . . . *and lived?* cf. the remark
in § 19. 2.)

הֲלֹא: 2 Sa. 4, 10 *shall I not* seek his blood from your
hand וּבִעַרְתִּי *and sweep* you from the earth? 2 Ki. 5, 12 *shall
I not* wash in them וְטָהָרְתִּי *and be clean?* Ez. 38, 14 f. Amos
8, 8. Pr. 24, 12.

הֵן =*if:* Jer. 3, 1 if a man divorces his wife וְהָלְכָה *and she
goes* etc. Hag. 2, 12 [1].

טֶרֶם or בְּטֶרֶם *ere that:* Jer. 13, 16.

כַּאֲשֶׁר *as when:* Dt. 22, 26 as when a man יָקוּם rises up
against his neighbour וּרְצָחוֹ *and smites* him mortally. Isa. 29,
8. 65, 8. Amos 5, 19 as when a man flees before the lion
וּפְגָעוֹ *and* the bear *meets* him.

כִּי =*that:* Gen. 37, 26 what gain כִּי נַהֲרֹג that we should
slay our brother וְכִסִּינוּ *and conceal* his blood? 1 Sa. 29, 8
what have I done . . . that I am not to go וְנִלְחַמְתִּי *and fight?*
(tone as § 104.) Job 15, 13 why doth thy heart carry thee
away . . . that thou shouldst turn thine anger against God
וְהֹצֵאתָ *and so utter* words out of thy mouth? (tone, § 110.
4 *Obs.*) Cf. Neh. 6, 11.

=*when:* Ex. 21, 20 when a man smites his servant וּמֵת
and he dies. Dt. 4, 25. 6, 10 f. when Yahweh bringeth thee

---

[1] For the position of הַ before the apodosis, cf. Gen. 18, 24. 28. 24,
5 after אוּלַי; Job 14, 14 after אִם; 2 Ki. 7, 2. Ez. 17, 10 after הִנֵּה.

into the land . . . : וְאָכַלְתָּ וְשָׂבָעְתָּ *and thou eatest and art satisfied*, take care etc. 12, 20. 29. 17, 14: and so constantly.

כִּי אִם = *surely:* 1 Ki. 20, 6 surely I will send my servants וְחִפְּשׂוּ. (2 Sa. 15, 21 Kt. followed by a single verb only.)

Obs. After a perfect (according to § 14*a*), 2 Ki. 5, 20 כי אם־רצתי ולקחתי surely I will run *and get* something from him! Jer. 51, 14 (Ges. Hitz. Graf, RV.): cf. Jud. 15, 7, where after a perfect similarly placed we have ואחר אחדל: had not אחר intervened, this would have been וחדלתי.

לֹא or בַּל *not* (the negative not being repeated, but its influence extending *over two clauses:* Ges.-Kautzsch, § 152. 3): Ex. 28, 43 that they may *not* bear (incur) iniquity וָמֵתוּ *and die*. 33, 20 man *cannot* see me : וָחָי *and live*. Lev. 11, 43[b]. 19, 12 *not shall you* swear falsely וְחִלַּלְתָּ *and thou* profane the name of God. 29. 22, 9. Nu. 4, 15 they shall not touch what is holy ומתו *and so* die. 20. Dt. 7, 25 ולקחת. 26 *and so* become accursed. 19, 10. 22, 1. 4 והתעלמתָּ. 23, 15. Isa. 14, 21 בל. 28, 28 *not* for ever does he thresh it והמם *and drive* the wheel of his cart over it. 2 Chr. 19, 10 והיה. And with the verb separated from וְ and so in the impf., Lev. 10, 6.

כִּמְעַט *almost:* Gen. 26, 10 (with pf. as first verb) almost had one of the people lain with her וְהֵבֵאתָ *and so thou hadst* brought guilt upon us.

לוּ *if:* Ez. 14, 15 if I were to cause noisome beasts to pass through the land וְשִׁכְּלָתָּה *and they were to* make it bereaved, והיתה *and it were to* become desolate.

למה *why?* 2 Ki. 14, 10 (= 2 Chr. 25, 19) why wouldst (or *shouldst, wilt*) thou challenge misfortune ונפלתה *and fall?* Jer 40, 15 why *should* he smite thee *and all Israel be scattered?* Qoh. 5, 5. Dan. 1, 10 אֲשֶׁר לָמָּה יִרְאֶה...וְחִיַּבְתֶּם for why should he see (= lest[1] he see) your faces sad . . ., *and ye inculpate* my head to the king.

---

[1] See the writer's note on 1 Sa. 19, 17.

Obs. The impf. after למה *may* be frequentative, as 1 Sa. 2, 29, in which case it can be followed by בְ·, § 114 (β).

לְמַעַן *in order that:* Gen. 12, 13 *that* it may be well with me וְחָיְתָה *and* my soul may live because of thee. 18, 19. Ex. 10, 2. Dt. 5, 30 וְטוֹב. 6, 18 that it may be well with thee וּבָאתָ וְיָרַשְׁתָּ *and that thou mayest* go and inherit the good land. 13, 18. 16, 20. 22, 7. Isa. 28, 13 למען ילכו וכשלו אחור ונשברו ונוקשו ונלכדו. 66, 11 and often.

מִי with impf. expressing a *wish:* 2 Sa. 15, 4 O that some one would make me judge, ועלי יבא that to me might come every one who . . . (where if עלי were not intended to be emphatic, we should have had וְהִצְדַּקְתִּיו (וּבָא עלי) *and I would* give him justice! Dt. 5, 26 O that this their heart might be theirs always! (lit. 'who will grant והיה *and so* this their heart had been[1].')

מִי יוֹדֵעַ =*perhaps:* 2 Sa. 12, 22 Qri (Kt. יחנני, impf. as Joel 2, 14. Jon. 3, 9).

מָתַי *when?* Ps. 41, 6 when will he die וְאָבַד *and* his name *perish?*

עַד or עַד אֲשֶׁר *until:* Ex. 23, 30 until thou multiply וְנָחַלְתָּ *and inherit* the land. Nu. 11, 20 והיה. Isa. 32, 15 עַד יֵעָרֶה וְהָיָה יֵחָשֵׁב . . . וְ Hos. 5, 15. Mic. 7, 9. Qoh. 12, 1. 2. Neh. 4, 5: עַד שֶׁ· Ct. 2, 17. 4, 6.

Obs. So when the verb after עד is a perfect (§ 17), Isa. 6, 11 f.

Similarly in the other construction of עד with an infinitive, Gen. 27, 45. Jud. 6, 18 עַד בֹּאִי וְהֹוצֵאתִי; or a substantive, 1 Sa. 14, 24 until (it be) evening וְנִקַּמְתִּי *and I avenge* myself: this passage shews how Lev. 11, 32. 17, 15 should be understood ('till the evening (come) and it be clean'). 2 Ki. 18,

---

[1] Elsewhere מִי יִתֵּן is construed with the bare impf. Job 6, 8 תָּבוֹא. 13, 5. 14, 13; with the impf. and וְ 19, 23 וְיִכָּתְבוּן; with the pf. 23, 3 יָדַעְתִּי; usually with the inf. 11, 5. Ex. 16, 3 al.

32. Isa. 5, 8 until there is no more room וְהוּשַׁבְתֶּם *and ye are made to* dwell by yourselves in the midst of the land.

Obs. In a few passages a rather singular usage is found after עַד, Jud. 16, 2 saying עַד אוֹר הבקר והרגנוהו till the morning dawns and *we kill* him. Jos. 1, 15. 6, 10 till the day when I say to you, Shout, והריעותם *and ye shout* (cf. Esth. 4, 11 וחיה). Gen. 29, 8. 1 Sa. 1, 22 for she said, Till the lad be weaned *and I bring him* etc. 2 Sa. 10, 5 (= 1 Chr. 19, 5) tarry in Jericho till your beards grow ושבתם *and ye return.* Dan. 8, 14. Is the perfect in these cases to be considered as under the government of the infinitive or imperfect after עַד (as I have translated), or as under that of a preceding verb implied or expressed, thus '*(wait)* till the day when I say, Shout, *and then* shout,' '*tarry* till etc. *and then* return?' The general structure of the sentence seems to favour the former supposition, and, if the latter were true, we might expect אחר added, as Jos. 2, 16. Compare Hdt. iii. 181. 5 ἀποκλινομένης δὲ τῆς ἡμέρης ὑπίεται τοῦ ψυχροῦ, ἐς οὗ δύεταί τε ὁ ἥλιος, καὶ τὸ ὕδωρ γίνεται χλιαρόν· where the determining moment and the determined event are similarly made coordinate, but where in English (disregarding the τε) we should probably exhibit their relation to each other somewhat more explicitly by rendering 'till the sun sets, *and then* the water becomes warm.'

עֵקֶב *in return for:* Dt. 7, 12 as a return for (Onqelos חֲלַף דְּ) your hearkening[1] to these statutes וּשְׁמַרְתֶּם *and observing* them[1].

פֶּן *lest:* Gen. 3, 22. 19, 19 lest some evil cleave to me וָמַתִּי: *and I die* (tone as § 110. 2). Ex. 1, 10. 23, 29. 34, 15 f. פֶּן־תִּכְרֹת וְזָנוּ . . . וְאָכַלְתָ וְלָקַחְתָ. Dt. 4, 16. 19. 8, 12–17. 15, 9 וְקָרָא . . . וְהָיָה . . . וְלֹא תִתֶּן לוֹ . . . וְרָעָה . . . פֶּן־יִהְיֶה. 2 Sa. 12, 28. Hos. 2, 5. Amos 5, 6. Ps. 28, 1 פֶּן־תֶּחֱשֶׁה וְנִמְשַׁלְתִּי lest thou be silent *and I become like* etc. Pr. 30, 9 (for the tone in these two passages, see § 104). 5, 10 ff. וְנָהַמְתָּ . . . וְאָמַרְתָּ etc.[2]

---

[1] תשמעון in a frequentative sense: cf. 8, 20.

[2] So Baer: in some texts וְאָמַרְתָּ, the *metheg* being thrown back from the syllable which has the counter-tone on to a preceding *shwa'*: it is then sometimes called *Ga'ya'* גַּעְיָא i.e. *crying*, from its causing the *shwa'* to be *sounded* rather more audibly than usual. Compare Kalisch, pt. ii. § 10. 3 (*b*); Ewald, § 96ᶜ; Böttcher, i. p. 122; or (exhaustively) Baer, in his papers on metheg in Merx's *Archiv*, 1870, pp. 56, 194.

Obs. After a perfect (§ 41 *Obs.*), 2 Sa. 20, 6 lest he *have gotten* him fenced cities והציל עיננו and *pluck out* our eye. Or should we read ימצא for מצא?

שֶׁ Qoh. 2, 24 שֶׁיּאכַל וְשָׁתָה *that he should* eat and drink. 3, 13. 12, 3. Cf. p. 131 (Ps. 137, 9).

116. After all these particles to find the *imperfect repeated* (as Ps. 2, 12 פֶּן יֶאֱנַף וְתֹאבְדוּ) is very unusual; the following are, I believe, nearly all the instances of such repetition :—

אולי Nu. 22, 6. 1 Ki. 18, 5. Jer. 20, 10. 21, 2. אִיךְ 3, 19. אִם 31, 36. Job 11, 10. 20, 12 f. 36, 11. 2 Chr. 7, 14. הֲלֹא Hab. 2, 6. כִּי (= *though*) Ps. 49, 19. Lam. 3, 8. לֹא Job 7, 21. לָמָה Isa. 40, 27. Pr. 5, 20. Job 13, 24. לְמַעַן Ex. 23, 12. Isa. 41, 20. 43, 10. Ps. 78, 6. מָתַי Ps. 42, 3. עַד Hos. 10, 12. Qoh. 12, 6. Lam. 3, 50 וְיֵרֶא. פֶּן Jer. 51, 46. Ps. 2, 12. Pr. 31, 5.

Obs. 1. In several of these examples, a reason may be found for the repetition of the same tense in the fact that the second verb indicates not a progress of thought, as compared with the first, but a parallelism; where a distinct idea follows afterwards, the pf. and ו *consec.* may then be used, Jer. 26, 3. Ez. 6, 6. Hab. 2, 7. The opposite transition occurs Qoh. 12, 4ᵇ–5ᵃ, perhaps, the sentence being a long one, to give it fresh strength.

Obs. 2. Whenever the impf. with ־ו appears after any of these particles, it is because some *definite* act is alluded to: see, for instance, Gen. 3, 17 (כִּי *because*). 12, 19 why didst thou say, She is my sister וָאֶקַּח *and lead* me to take her? (so we may render to avoid the awkward change of person). 31, 27. 1 Sa. 19, 17ᵃ (different from 17ᵇ למה אמיתך *why should I slay thee?* which would be succeeded by a pf. and ו). 1 Ki. 10, 7 after עַד.

Obs. 3. The usage with regard to פֶּן is not stated with the precision of which it would admit in the note of Dean (now Bishop) Perowne on Ps. 28, 1. The two *regular* types (which are also the same for כִּי, עַד לְמַעַן, etc.), alternating merely in accordance with the order of words, are פֶּן יבוא ויאמר : פֶּן יבוא... יאמר and פֶּן יבוא ואמר is *exceptional*. The only supposed instance of פֶּן יבוא... אמר is Ps. 38, 17ᵇ; this, however, is clearly an independent statement, in no way under the government of the preceding פֶּן. Comp. § 14 *end.*

117. The reader will be aware (see Ges.-Kautzsch,

§§ 114. 3 Rem. 1; 116. 5 Rem. 7) that it is a common custom with Hebrew writers, after employing a participle or infinitive, to *change the construction*, and, if they wish to subjoin other verbs which logically should be in the partcp. or infin. as well, to pass to the use of the finite verb. Thus Gen. 27, 33 הַצָּד צַיִד וַיָּבֵא ὁ θηρεύσας θήραν καὶ εἰσενέγκας (lit. ὁ θηρεύσας θήραν καὶ εἰσήνεγκε). 39, 18 כַּהֲרִימִי קוֹלִי וָאֶקְרָא LXX ὅτι ὕψωσα τὴν φωνήν μου καὶ ἐβόησα (where, by the alteration of form undergone by the first verb through the use of ὅτι, the change of construction is disguised: elsewhere, by rendering literally, LXX have distorted the real sense of the original, e.g. Ps. 92, 8. 105, 12 f. ἐν τῷ εἶναι αὐτοὺς ... καὶ διῆλθον). Now, under what circumstances do the partcp. and infin. break off into the *perfect* with וְ, and into the *imperfect* with וַ respectively? The answer to this question will be found to be in strict accordance with what we know already concerning the nature of the two constructions. Wherever the partcp. or infin. asserts something indefinite or undetermined —wherever, therefore, it may be resolved into *whoever, whenever, if ever* etc. (ὃς ἄν not ὃς, ἐπειδὰν not ἐπειδὴ etc.)—we find the *perfect* with וְ *consecutive* employed: where, on the contrary, the partcp. or infin. asserts an actual concrete event, we find the following verbs connected with it by the *imperfect* and וַ. Even when the partcp. is used in characterizing a person, or class of persons, the choice of the form which is to follow it is evidently regulated by the same distinction; the one *localizes* the action specified, perhaps embodies an allusion to a definite case, the other leaves it more vague, though at the same time suggesting forcibly its potential, or actual, repetition[1].

Thus, Ex. 21, 12 מַכֵּה אִישׁ וָמֵת the smiter of a man

---

[1] The difference may be compared to that in Greek between ὁ οὐ ... and ὁ μὴ ... with the participle.

(= whoever smites a man), *and he dies.* 16. Nu. 19, 13 [1].
Jer. 21, 9 he that goeth out וְנָפַל *and falleth;* and as a
frequentative, 22, 14 הָאוֹמֵר... וְקָרַע לוֹ חַלּוֹנָי סְפוּן² בָּאֶרֶז וּמָשׁוֹחַ
בַּשָּׁשַׁר. Ex. 34, 7 [1]. Isa. 5, 23 [1]. 44, 25 [1]. 26 [1] that confirmeth
the word of his servant, *and accomplisheth* the counsel of his
messengers. Ez. 22, 3. 33, 30. Hab. 2, 12. Ps. 18, 34 [1]. 35.

But ·וְ of a *fact:*—Gen. 35, 3 who answered me וַיְהִי *and
was* with me. 49, 17 [b]. Nu. 22, 11. Isa. 14, 17 [3]. 30, 2 [3]. 43,
7 [3]. Jer. 23, 31 f. Amos 5, 7 [3]. 12 [3]. 9, 6. Pr. 2, 17 [3].

Occasionally, we have וְ with the impf.: 2 Sa. 5, 8 (rendering doubtful). Dan. 12, 12.

Obs. Sometimes the two forms interchange (comp. above, § 35),
though each has still its proper force: thus Am. 6, 1 [b] ובאו *and* the
house of Israel *come* (freq.) to them (so 8, 14 ואמרו), but 3 ye that put
far the evil day ותגישון, *and have brought near* the seat of violence;
6, 6 which drink with bowls of wine ו... ימשחו *and anoint themselves* (freq.) etc. ולא נחלו but *are not* grieved etc.; comp. similarly 5,
8 (§ 12) and 9 (§ 33); 9, 5 and 6; Isa. 29, 15. 21. Contrast also
(though these are somewhat different) Jer. 48, 19 וְנִמְלָטָה *and her that
escapeth* (whoever she may be), and Isa. 57, 3 וַתִּזְנֶה *and of her that
hath* (in a definite case) played the whore.

118. The distinction will be more conspicuous in the
case of the infinitive: Gen. 18, 25 וְהָיָה ... לְהָמִית. Ex. 1, 16.
33, 16 בְּלֶכְתְּךָ וְנִפְלִינוּ *in* thy going (= if thou goest) with us
and we are separated from etc. Dt. 4, 42 ... לָנֻס שָׁמָּה
וָחָי ...⁴ וְנָס. 30, 16 וְחָיִיתָ ... לָלֶכֶת. Gen. 27, 45 until thy
brother's anger turn וְשָׁכַח *and he forget* etc. 1 Sa. 10, 8. 2 Sa.
13. 28 וְאָמַרְתִּי ... כְּטוֹב at the moment when Amnon's heart
is merry *and I say.* 1 Ki. 2, 37. 42. 8, 33 בְּהִנָּגֶף עַמְּךָ *when*

---

[1] The verb separated from וְ, and consequently in the impf.

[2] Read so for חלוני וספון: see the *Variorum Bible,* ad loc.

[3] Perfect, for the same reason.

[4] ונס here is merely *resumptive,* reinforcing the idea conveyed by לנס
after the long intermediate clause: cf. 18, 6 ובא. Lev. 17, 5. Jer. 34,
18–20 ונתתי. Zech. 8, 23; והיה Nu. 10, 32. Dt. 20, 11.

thy people are smitten וְשָׁ֫בוּ *and turn* (a hypothetical case).
35, 60 f. (לְמַ֫עַן דַּ֫עַת . . . וְהָיָה). Ez. 3, 20 *when* he turns וְעָשָׂה
and does evil. 5, 16 f. 12, 15ᵇ. 18, 23. Job 37, 15. Amos 1,
11 because he pursued . . . וְשִׁחֵת and (repeatedly) ruined
mercy וַיִּטְרֹף *and so* his anger *goes on* to tear for ever (where
the change of tense is noticeable).

Of course, as before, when separated from ו, as often
happens, especially in poetry, for the sake of variety, the verb
falls into the imperfect tense :—after לְ *that*, Ex. 28, 28. Jos.
20, 9. Isa. 10, 2 יָבֹ֫וּ . . . וְ לִהְיוֹת. 13, 9. 14, 25. 32, 6. 45, 1.
49, 5. Ps. 105, 22. Pr. 2, 8. 5, 2. 8, 21. Job 33, 17 etc.;
after כְּ Isa. 5, 24; בְּ Isa. 30, 26. Pr. 1, 27 : and without *waw*,
Isa. 64, 1 (ירגזו virtually governed by לְ in לְהוֹדִיע). Pr. 2, 2[1].

With these contrast Gen. 39, 18. Lev. 16, 1. Jos. 8, 24
וַיִּפְּלוּ . . . כְּכַלּוֹת 1 Sa. 24, 12 הֲרַגְתִּ֫יךָ וְלֹא . . . בְּכָרֵ֫תִי. 1 Ki. 18,
18 in thy forsaking וַתֵּ֫לֶךְ *and going* (definite acts extending
into the present). Isa. 47, 10 (ותבטחי after ברב *v.* 9). Ez.
16, 31. 36. 25, 6 al. Ps. 50, 16 what is it to thee לְסַפֵּר *to tell*
my statutes וַתִּשָּׂא *and take* my covenant upon thy mouth ?
(two facts which have actually occurred : not 'that thou
shouldst take,' וְנָשָׂ֫אתָ). 92, 8. 105, 12 f. etc. Cf. Ez. 36,
18 טִמְּא֫וּהָ וְ . . . עַל הַדָּם because of the blood *and that* they
have defiled her ; and Jer. 30, 14 (ἀσυνδέτως).

Obs. As before, contrast Ez. 18, 27 ויעש *and has done*, with *v.* 26 :
comp. § 138. ii. (*a*).

119. But the perfect with *waw consecutive* is also found
without being attached to any preceding verb from which to
derive its special signification : from constant association
with a preceding imperfect it became so completely invested
with the properties of the latter that, though not originally
belonging to it but only *acquired*, it still continued to retain
and exhibit them, even when that in which they had their

---

[1] Cf., in inferior prose, Ezra 10, 7 f. Neh. 10, 36–9. 2 Chr. 15, 12 f.
Dan. 1, 5. Esth. 9, 27 f.

proper seat was no longer itself present. We have already spoken of it as the *companion construction* of the imperfect: it has, in fact, grown so like its partner as to be able to assume its functions and act as its substitute. It may thus occur at the beginning of a sentence or after a verb which, unlike the 'dominant' verb, has no influence in determining the range of its meaning; the force it is then intended to convey must, as in the case of the imperfect, be gathered from the context: for although most commonly, perhaps, possessing the signification of a future, it must often be understood in one of the numerous other senses borne by the many-sided imperfect.

Thus (*a*) Gen. 17, 4. 26, 22 now hath Yahweh made room for us וּפָרִינוּ *and* we *shall* be fruitful in the land. Ex. 6, 6 I am Yahweh; וְהוֹצֵאתִי *and I will bring you out* etc. Nu. 21, 8. Jos. 2, 14 והיה *and it shall* be, when etc. Jud. 13, 3 behold thou art barren and hast not borne; וְהָרִית *but thou shalt* conceive, and bear a son. 1 Sa. 15, 28 and *will* give it. 17, 36. 20, 18. 2 Sa. 7, 9ᵇ–10. 1 Ki. 2, 44 *and* Yahweh *will* requite. 9, 3 והיו *and* my eyes and heart *shall* be there. Isa. 2, 2 והיה. 6, 7 see, this hath touched thy lips, וְסָר *and so* thy iniquity *shall pass away*. 30, 3. Ez. 17, 24ᵇ אני יי דברתי ועשיתי have spoken, *and I will* perform. 22, 14 al. 23, 31. 30, 6. 10. 34, 11 (cf. Jer. 23, 39). 35, 11. Isa. 56, 5. Hos. 8, 14 ושלחתי. 10, 14. 11, 6. Amos 5, 26 [1] (or, at any rate, *v.* 27).

---

[1] The sense of this much-disputed verse can scarcely be settled by grammatical, apart from exegetical, considerations: the *presumption* afforded by the general usage of the prophets favours the future meaning for ונשאתם, which was already adopted by Rashi: on the other hand, the pf. with simple *waw*, giving a past sense, meets us occasionally unexpectedly, e.g. 7, 2. Ez. 20, 22. Job 16, 12. Still, in these passages, the context precludes misunderstanding, in a way in which it would not do, had the prophet used ונשאתם while intending that sense here. Cf. the note in Smith's *Dict. of the Bible* (ed. 2), s.v. AMOS, *ad fin.*

Or to express what is not certain to happen, but is only probable, and so, perhaps, feared :—2 Sa. 14, 7 *and* they *will* quench. Gen. 20, 11 there is no fear of God in this place, וַהֲרָגֻ֫נִי *and* they *will* kill me. 34, 30 : cf. 1 Ki. 18, 14ᵇ.

(β) With the force of a positive command, usually in the second person :—Nu. 4, 4 f. this is the service of the sons of Qŏhāth וּבָא Aaron *shall* come and take down etc. Dt. 18, 3ᵇ ; 10, 16 וּמַלְתֶּם. 19 ואהבתם *and* or *so* ye *shall* love the stranger. 29, 8 ושמרתם *and ye shall* observe. Jos. 22, 3ᵇ (cf. the imper., *v.* 5). 23, 11. 2 Ki. 5, 6 (the following verses shew that the king of Israel understood וַאֲסַפְתּ֖וֹ as practically a *command* which could not very conveniently be declined : not, therefore, as 1 Sa. 20, 5). Jer. 7, 27. 29, 26ᵇ. Ez. 22, 2 wouldst thou judge, judge the bloody city ? וְהוֹדַעְתָּהּ *then declare* unto her all her abominations (cf. the imper. 20, 4. 23, 36). Zech. 1, 3. Mal. 2, 15ᵇ. 16ᵇ.

(γ) Sometimes it is interrogative :—Ex. 5, 5 וְהִשְׁבַּתֶּם *and*[1] *will* ye stop them[2] ? Nu. 16, 10 (ה 9). 1 Sa. 25, 11 וְלָקַחְתִּי *and shall I* take ? 2 Ki. 14, 10 (2 Chr. 25, 19). Isa. 66, 9 am I he that causeth to bring forth וְעָצַ֫רְתִּי *and shall* I shut up ? (cf. the *impf.* ולא אוליד in 9ᵃ : the break in the sense before אמר אלהיך co-operates with the *ṭifcha* to keep the tone back, § 104). Ez. 18, 13 וָחָ֑י. Mal. 1, 2. 2, 14. 17. 3, 7. 8. 13. Ps. 50, 21 ('and shall I keep silence ?' Hitz. : tone as

---

[1] This use of וְ is completely parallel to the way in which *et* appears in Latin ' to subjoin an emphatic question or exclamation :' the force of וְ Ex. 5, 5. 1 Sa. 25, 11 is just that of *et* Verg. Georg. ii. 433 (*and yet*, after and in spite of 429–432, *do men hesitate?* etc.). Aen. i. 48. vi. 806 etc. Compare further how וְ is employed to introduce an empassioned speech, without anything expressed previously to which it can be attached. Nu. 20, 3 ולו *And* if we had only perished with our brethren ! 2 Sa. 18, 11 והנה. 12. 24, 3. 2 Ki. 1, 10 (but 12 אם alone). 7, 19 (sarcastic : yet cf. 2). So before מי, 1 Sa. 10, 12. 15, 14 (מה). Jud. 9, 29. Nu. 11, 29 ; and very often before למה or מדוע.

[2] Comp. in separation from וְ, the impf., Ez. 33, 25. 26 והארץ תירשו. Jer. 25, 29 ואתם הנקה תנקו. 49, 12.

28, 1 after פֶּן). Job 32, 16 [1] ('and shall I wait?' Hitz. Del. Dillm. RV.). 1 Chr. 17, 17 and wilt thou regard me?

(δ) In entreaty or suggestion, as a precative or mild imperative:—Gen. 24, 14 וְהָיָה *may* it be that . . . (possibly under the influence of the imperatives, *v.* 12). 47, 23 *sow then.* Dt. 2, 4[b] וּנְשַׁמַרְתֶּם. 4, 15. 7, 9 and often וִידַעְתָּ *know then.* 30, 19 behold I set before thee life and death, וּבָחַרְתָּ *so choose* life. Jud. 11, 8 וְהָלַכְתָּ. 1 Sa. 6, 5. 20, 5. 24, 16. 25, 27 וְנָתְנָה (see § 123). 1 Ki. 2, 6 וְעָשִׂיתָ *do therefore* according to thy wisdom. 3, 9. 8, 28. Ruth 3, 3. 9 I am Ruth וּפָרַשְׂתָּ *so pray spread* etc.

And with נָא added:—Gen. 40, 14 only [2] if thou rememberest me with thyself, when it is well with thee, וְעָשִׂיתָ־נָּא *then shew,* I pray, mercy etc.; and with the נא thrown back into a preceding protasis (to indicate as early as possible the 'petitionary' character of the speech) in the formula אִם־נָא מָצָאתִי חֵן בְּעֵינֶיךָ, Gen. 33, 10 וְלָקַחְתָּ. Jud. 6, 17 (cf. the jussive or imperative alone, Gen. 18, 3. 47, 29. 50, 4. Ex. 33, 13: Gen. 30, 27 the perfect obviously does nothing more than assert a fact).

120.   But the most noticeable use of the perfect and *waw*

---

[1] וְהוֹחַלְתִּי *must,* of course, be so taken, if read *milra'*, and *may*, if it be read *mil'el:* see § 104 (p. 113).

[2] A most difficult verse. I know of no justification for the usual rendering of the *bare* pf. זְכַרְתַּנִי as either an imperative, or a 'modal' future (*mögest du* . . .): Ewald, § 356[b], appears to regard it as the pf. of certitude, ' but thou shalt remember me ' etc. though it is scarcely a case where that use of the pf. would be expected. The natural rendering of אם זכרתני is *if thou rememberest me* (§ 138): this agrees with what follows, but seems to allow no room for the preceding כי. Might we, on the strength of 23, 13, substitute אַךְ for כי? (so Wellhausen, *Jahrb. f. Deutsche Theol.* 1876, p. 445 = *Composition des Hexateuchs,* 1889, p. 57.) Delitzsch, in his note on the passage, *Genesis* (1887), fails to remove the difficulty of the verse: it is true, when a future tense has preceded, the pf. introduced by כִּי אִם may relate likewise to the future (see 2 Sa. 5, 6): but this will only justify Ewald's rendering 'shalt remember me,' not ' *mayest* thou remember me.'

consecutive, though the one least likely to attract attention, is *as a frequentative.* After the list of instances in § 113. 4 the reader will find no difficulty in recognizing this force in the perfect and *waw* after a preceding dominant imperfect: but where no such imperfect precedes, it will irresistibly occur to him to ask why the *waw* may not be simply copulative instead of consecutive; the more so, inasmuch as owing to the verbs being almost always in the third person, the crucial change of tone cannot take place? Why, he will not unreasonably ask, why should it be asserted that וְשָׁפְטוּ Ex. 18, 26 means *and used to judge*, when the obvious and natural rendering seems to be simply *and judged?* why seek to import a far-fetched and improbable sense into such a plain combination of verb and conjunction?

The answer to such objections will be found in the manner in which the perfect and waw thus appears. In the first place, it does not occur *promiscuously:* it is not intermingled with the construction with ·וַ in equal proportions, but is commonly found thickly sprinkled *over detached areas* (e. g. 1 Sa. 7, 16). Now when a writer abandons a construction which he employs in nine cases out of ten in favour of another, and that, too, under the peculiar circumstances just described, it is, at least, reasonable to infer that he means *something* by the change. In the second place, our knowledge that the perfect with *waw consecutive* follows the imperfect as a frequentative, coupled with the analogy presented by its use in the last §, raises the suspicion that it may possibly have the same value even when no imperfect precedes. This suspicion is strengthened by the fact that it is constantly found *in company with a bare imperfect*, even though not actually preceded by it. In the passage from Exodus, for example, ושפטו is immediately followed by יביאון and ישפוטו: if, then, these verbs are frequentative (as they clearly are), it is reasonable to infer that ושפטו is so too. It is inconceivable that a coincidence of this sort should be accidental: it is inconceivable that in a

multitude of passages the change from ·וֹ to the perfect and
waw (in itself a striking variation) should take place *con-
currently with* another change, that, viz. from the perfect
(which, as we know, § 85, is the regular alternative for ·וֹ) to
the imperfect, without the existence of some common cause
accounting for both : but the reason why the imperfect is
chosen is patent, it must, therefore, have been the same
reason which determined the choice of the perfect and waw.
Having once vindicated for this idiom a frequentative force,
we shall not hesitate to adopt it in cases where no imperfect
follows to precipitate our decision.   And the change of tone
in Jer. 6, 17 וַהֲקִימֹתִי is a final confirmation of the justice of
our reasoning.

Thus Gen. 30, 41 f. (cf. the impf. יָשִׂים 42). Ex. 17, 11
וְהָיָה and it was, *whenever* יָרִים he raised up his hand, וְגָבַר
Israel prevailed. 18, 26 (cf. the impf. יָבִיאוּן). 40, 31 f. (cf.
יִרְחָצוּ). Jud. 2, 18 f. וְהָיָה, וְהוֹשִׁיעָם (cf. יִנָּחֵם). 1 Sa. 1, 4 וְנָתַן
(cf. יִתֵּן 5). 6ᵃ (the account of the particular occasion which is
the subject of the narrative begins וַתִּבְכֶּה 7ᵇ). 2 Sa. 12, 31.
14, 26. 17, 17 J. and A. remained at ʿEn-rogel, וְהָלְכָה *and* a
girl *used to go and tell* them, וְהֵם יֵלְכוּ וְהִגִּידוּ and they *would go
and tell* (notice the impf.) the king: (the *narrative* recom-
mences וַיַּרְא 18, with ·וֹ just as Gen. 29, 4 [§ 113, 4 β]. 1 Sa.
1, 7). 1 Ki. 4, 7. 5, 7 וְכִלְכְּלוּ (cf. 7ᵇ לֹא יַעְדְרוּ).

Gen. 47, 22 וְאָכְלוּ. 1 Sa. 1, 3 וְעָלָה (followed by מִיָּמִים
יָמִימָה). 7, 16 וְהָלַךְ מִדֵּי שָׁנָה בְּשָׁנָה *and he would go* year by
year, וְסָבַב *and come round* to Beth-el etc., וְשָׁפַט *and judge*
Israel at all these places. 13, 21 f. 16, 23. 2 Sa. 15, 2. 5
(the *succession* of pff. in most of these passages is very
striking). 1 Ki. 9, 25 וְהֶעֱלָה *used* to offer (notice the words
three times a year). 18, 4ᵇ וְכִלְכְּלָם (plainly a *repeated* act,
exactly as 5, 7). 2 Ki. 3, 4 וְהֵשִׁיב *used* to render. 12, 12–17.
Jer. 6, 17 *and I kept raising up* over you watchmen. Am. 7, 4[1].

---

[1] וְאָכְלָה, in contradistinction to וַתֹּאכַל, seems to imply that the act of

Job 1, 4. See also the passages cited in the foot-note, § 133, p. 162.

Obs. 1. There is one place in the Old Testament where the appearance of this idiom is so curious and interesting as to merit special notice. Throughout the whole of the first fourteen chapters of the book of Joshua, although occupied by historical narrative, the nature of the events described is such as not to give opportunity for the use of the perfect and *waw* except on *three* occasions :—Josh. 6, 8 and 13 in the account of the blowing of the trumpets during the day's march round Jericho (an act which would obviously involve *repetition*), and 9, 12, where the waw is not consecutive but simply copulative, according to § 132 : except in these three passages, the narrative is *exclusively* carried on by means of ·וֹ, alternating, at times, with the bare perfect. Suddenly, upon arriving at chap. 15 (in which the history proceeds to delineate the course taken by the boundaries of the various tribes), the reader is startled by finding *vv.* 3–11 a succession of *perfects* connected by *waw* (וְיָצָא, וְעָבַר, וְעָלָה etc.). What can be the object of the change? In the teeth of the constant usage in the preceding portion of the book, it is highly improbable that the perfect and waw should be a *mere* alternative for ·וֹ: and its known meaning elsewhere affords a strong presumption that here, too, it has a frequentative force, descriptive of the course which the boundary *used to take—used to take*, namely (not, as though a participle, *continuously took*), whenever any one passed along it or examined it. Let us see whether there is anything to confirm this presumption. After the historical episode 15, 13–19, and the enumeration of cities of Judah, 15, 20 ff., 16, 1 states how the lot fell for the children of Joseph, *v.* 2 proceeds to describe their boundaries, and the *perfect* with *waw* reappears, continuing as far as the end of *v.* 3. Here follows another break; but *v.* 6 the perfect is again resumed till we reach *v.* 8, where the presumption we had formed is triumphantly corroborated. *In v.* 8 *the imperfect*, the constant companion of the perfect with waw consecutive, *makes its appearance:* יֵלֵךְ, the force of which cannot be mistaken, vindicates and establishes for all the neigh-bouring and preceding perfects with *waw*, the frequentative sense assigned to them above. Nor is this all. In 17, 9 we have the perfect again : *v.* 10 we have the attendant impf. יִפְגְּעוּן. By the side of the long series of perfects and *waw* 18, 12–21, we find *v.* 20 and the Jordan

---

devouring was in process, but not complete (so Hitz.). Hence R.V. ' would have eaten.'

יגבול *used to bound* it on the east: with *v.* 21 והיו of *cities,* cf. 21, 40 תהיינה similarly used. On the contrary, 19, 11–14. 22. 26–29. 34 present no case of an imperfect: but we shall not on that account feel any hesitation in supposing that, as before, a frequentative signification is still intended to be conveyed[1]. (In 19, 29 Kt. 33ᵇ, we have ·ו֗, according to § 114: cf. the perfect, *vv.* 13. 34ᵇ.)

Obs. 2. It is worthy of note that the frequentative force of the perf. with ו consecutive (even when unaccompanied by an impf.) was often fully felt by the translators of the ancient Versions. Notice, for example, the *impf.* in the LXX, and the *participle* in the Targ. and Pesh., in the following passages: Gen. 38, 9 (§ 121), 47, 22 (καὶ ἤσθιον, ואכלין, ܘܣ ܐܟܠܝܢ). Ex. 18, 26. 33, 8–10. 34, 34. Nu. 11, 9 (§ 121). 1 Sa. 1, 3. 7, 16. 16, 23. 2 Ki. 3, 4 (καὶ ἐπέστρεφε, ומתיב, ܘܣ ܡܗܦܟ), etc.[2] (The same tenses are used often to express the frequentative force of the Hebrew impf.; e. g. Gen. 6, 4 LXX; Ex. 17, 11 LXX, Pesh. Targ.; 19, 19 Pesh. Targ.; etc.)

121. In the same way that we saw ויהי employed, § 78, in reference to the past, we find its counterpart וְהָיָה used in a *future* or *frequentative* sense: the discourse, or narrative, after the termination of the adverbial clause, being resumed either by another perfect with *waw consecutive,* or by the imperfect alone. The power of this idiom to produce a balanced rhythm, and to ease any sentence which involves a series of conditions or premises (as Gen. 44, 30 f. 1 Ki. 18, 11 f.; Ex. 1, 10. Dt. 29, 18 after פֶּן), by affording a rest for voice and thought alike, will be manifest.

---

[1] יהיה 15, 4ᵇ is not cited, because in our text the second person לכם follows, which necessitates the rendering *shall be.* Elsewhere, however, in these topographical descriptions, the third person is regularly employed: it seems, therefore, either that להם (LXX αὐτῶν) must be read for לכם; or, as the sentence thus produced is not quite in the style of the rest of the description, that the words זה יהיה לכם גבול נגב, as Dillmann suggests, have been transposed here from Nu. 34, 5 (where a comparison of *vv.* 6ᵇ, 9ᵇ, 12ᵇ shews that such a clause is now missing).

[2] On ὅταν, ἡνίκα ἄν, ὡς ἄν, with the impf. indic., found in some of these passages with a frequentative force, see Winer, *Gramm. of N. T. Greek,* § xlii. 5ᵇ *end* (see Mark 3, 11), and cf. the writer's *Notes on Samuel,* p. 112.

Examples of its use in the former signification :—Gen. 9, 14. 12, 12. 27, 40 etc. Isa. 2, 2. 7, 18. 21. 23. 14, 3 f. וְהָיָה בַיּוֹם . . . וְנָשָׂאתָ *and it shall be*, in the day when etc. *and* (=*that*) *thou shalt take up* this proverb: so often, especially in the prophets. And in giving expression to a wish, entreaty, or injunction (§ 119 δ), Jud. 4, 20. 7, 4. 17. 9, 33. 11, 31 etc.[1]

As a frequentative :—Gen. 38, 9. Nu. 21, 9. Jud. 6, 3 וְהָיָה אִם זָרַע יִשְׂרָאֵל וְעָלָה מִדְיָן *and it used to happen*, when Israel had sown, *that* the Midianites *used to* (or *would*) come up ; and breaking off into an impf., 2, 19. Ex. 33, 7. 8. 9 וְהָיָה כְּבֹא מֹשֶׁה הָאֹהֱלָה יֵרֵד *and it used to be*, when Moses entered into the Tent, the pillar of cloud *would* come down.

Obs. 1. והיה is met with also, more frequently than ויהי in the corresponding case § 78 *Obs.*, before a clause which, whether constituted by a ptcp. or otherwise, is resolvable into *who-, which-, what-ever*, and implies, therefore, virtually, a hypothetical occurrence: Gen. 4, 14 והיה כל מצאי יהרגני *and it shall be, whosoever finds me* [2], *he will slay me* (where, for יהרגני, וַהֲרָגְנִי : would have been equally idiomatic). Nu. 10, 32[b]. 17, 20 *and it shall be*, the man whom I shall choose, his rod shall blossom. 21, 8. Dt. 12, 11. 18, 19. 21, 3 and it shall be, the city that is nearest to the slain man, ולקחו the elders of that city shall take etc. Jud. 7, 4. 11, 31. 19, 30 והיה כל־הראה ואמר and it was (freq.), as regards every one that saw them, that he said etc. 1 Sa. 2, 36. 17, 25. 1 Ki. 18, 24. 19, 17 *and it shall be:* him that escapeth (=*whoso* or *if any* escapeth) from the sword of Hazael shall Jehu slay. 20, 6. Isa. 4, 3 והיה כל הנשאר בציון . . . קדוש יֵאָמֶר לו and it shall be, (as regards) every one left in Zion, holy shall be said unto him (i. e. he shall be called holy). 24, 18. Joel 3, 5. Nah. 3, 7. Occasionally, indeed, it serves as a *mere* intro-

---

[1] It is very unusual for the sentence to be resumed by the imperative, Dt. 6, 10–12[a]. 1 Sa. 10, 7 ; cf. 29, 10.

[2] Observe how the sing. ptcp., especially with כָּל־ prefixed, is used idiomatically, as a *casus pendens*, with a distributive force, so as to denote succinctly a *hypothetical* occurrence : see (besides Gen. 4, 14. Nu. 21, 8. Jud. 19, 30. 1 Sa. 2, 36) 1 Sa. 2, 13. 3, 11. 10, 11 (p. 90 *n.*). 2 Sa. 2, 23 (*ib.*). 20, 12: also Gen. 9, 6. Pr. 17, 13. 18, 13. 20, 20. 27, 14. 28, 9. 29, 12; 9, 7[b]. 13, 3. 17, 21. 28, 27[a]. 29, 9. Job 41, 18; and cf. Ges.-K. § 116. 5 Rem. 5, and below, § 126.

ductory formula, no such clause whatever following, Ex. 4, 16. 1 Ki.
17, 4 *and it shall be :* of the torrent shalt thou drink ; and even immediately before the verb, Ez. 47, 10. 22.

Obs. 2. Nu. 5, 27 והיתה is very irregular. Jer. 42, 16 והיתה. 17
ויהיו resemble Gen. 31, 40 הייתי ביום אכלני חרב. The accents also,
by connecting והיה with the subst. following, express apparently the
same broken construction for several of the passages cited in *Obs.* 1,
e. g. *And the place* which Yahweh shall choose etc. *shall be*—thither
shall ye bring that which I command you : comp. § 165 *Obs.*[1]

Obs. 3. On four occasions, 1 Sa. 10, 5. 2 Sa. 5, 24 (1 Chr. 14, 15).
Ruth 3, 4. 1 Ki. 14, 5ᵇ, where we might have expected והיה, we find ויהי.
It is impossible to dismiss this so unconcernedly as is done by Ewald,
§ 345ᵇ : either ויהי must be a mere copyist's error, or some definite
explanation must be found for the adoption of so unusual a form :
observe how in 1 Sa. ויהי is followed within a few verses by two instances
of the customary והיה.   In the first three passages, at any rate, the verb
has the force of a legitimate jussive : יהי is simply prefixed to the adverbial clause in the same manner as וְיְהִי and והיה.   Thus, 1 Sa. *and let
it be* (a permissive edict, issued through the medium of the prophet :
cf. 2 Ki. 2, 10), when thou goest into the city and meetest (after כבא,
§ 118 : for the *co-ordination* of the two clauses, cf. p. 135 *Obs.*) a band
of prophets . . . וצלחה *that* the spirit of Yahweh *fall* upon thee etc.;
2 Sa. the sentence is resumed by a second jussive : Ruth 3 *and let it be*,
when he lieth down, *and observe* (or *that thou* observe) the place where
he lieth.   In 1 Ki. *and it shall be* (A. V.), for ויהי, is quite out of the
question : for how could a mere piece of information have been ever
expressed by a *jussive ?* We must then either correct והיה, or suppose
that some words have dropped out : the sentence reads as though it were
incomplete, and והיא מתנכרה suggests irresistibly the idea that it must
be a ' circumstantial clause ' (see App. I).   If we assume that some such
words as ואמרת אליה למה זה את מתנכרה (cf. *v.* 6) have fallen out, the

---

[1] See, however, Wickes, *Prose Accents*, p. 37.   At the same time, it
may be noticed that והיה when followed by a clause introduced by
כי etc. has commonly a distinctive accent (e. g. Gen. 27, 40. 44, 31.
Ex. 12, 25. 26. 13, 11. 14) ; so that the view expressed in the text appears
to be a tenable one.   But the usage, even in the cases referred to, fluctuates (contrast e. g. Gen. 4, 14. Nu. 10, 32ᵇ with Nu. 16, 7. 17, 20. Josh.
2, 19) ; and of course the accentuation, though it may indicate the sense
in which a sentence was understood in 7–8 cent. A. D., does not determine the construction attached to it by the original author.

jussive ויהי is at once explained, an appropriate sense is obtained (*and let it be,* when she enters in disguised, *that thou say* etc.), and the cause of the omission becomes plain in the ὁμοιοτέλευτον מתנכרה.

122. We have already had occasion to call attention to the *demonstrative* force of the conjunction *waw;* and in several of the passages cited in § 119 this meaning displayed itself undisguisedly. Certainly the וֹ did not there indicate a *formal* consequence, as when followed by the voluntative (Chap. V): but a *material* consequence conceived as arising out of, or suggested by, the situation described in the preceding words was none the less clearly intimated. E. g. Ruth 3, 9 the petition וּפָרַשְׂתָּ is plainly based upon the relation borne by the speaker towards Bo'az, as expressed in the words *I am Ruth:* and the *waw* may fairly be rendered by 'so,' 'then,' '*itaque*[1].' It is but a stronger instance of the same demonstrative usage when, as will have now to be explained, וֹ is employed in certain cases in order to introduce the *predicate*, or, more often, the *apodosis*.

Obs. The relation subsisting between the copulative conjunction and demonstrative roots can be illustrated from Greek and Latin. Of καί Curtius *Grundzüge der Griech. Etymol.* No. 27, p. 128 ed. 2 writes, 'The form appears to be the Locative of a pronominal stem κα, κο (cf. Lith. *kai,* how?), which has here preserved its demonstrative signification. From the same stem springs τε with τ for κ' (on this change see *ibid.* pp. 426 ff., and cf. τίς with *quis,* τέσσαρες with *quatuor,* Sk. *chat-vâras* etc.): in -*que,* on the contrary, as in Sk. *cha,* the guttural is retained. On this stem *cha* (from which ποῦ; πότε; Ion. κοῦ; κότε; etc. *who, where, whether* etc. are derived), Curtius remarks further, p. 410, ' The earliest use of the stem *ka* was probably, like that of all the

---

[1] Compare further, in connexion with this use of וֹ, Gen. 27, 8 and often ועתה νῦν οὖν. 34, 21 וישבו. Ex. 2, 20 ואיו *and* where is he? (or, where is he, *then?*) 1 Sa. 26, 22 וְיַעֲבָר *so* let one of the young men come over. 2 Sa. 18, 22 וְיְהִי מֶה *well,* come what may. 2 Ki. 4, 41 וקחו fetch meal then! 7, 13. 2 Chr. 18, 12 וְיְהִי *so* let thy word, I pray, be like one of theirs (1 Ki. 22, 13 יהי only). Isa. 47, 9 וְתָבֹאנָה (*v.* 11 ובא). Ps. 4, 4 ודעו *know, then.* Cf. Il. xxiii. 75 καί μοι δὸς τὴν χεῖρα.

pronominal stems, as a demonstrative. It is preserved in the Locative ἐ-κεῖ, with which -*ce* [as in *illi-c.* etc.], Lat. *cis, ci-tra* must be compared.' In a similar way δὲ (cf. δή, ὅ-δε), if not *et* (cf. ἔτι), is probably to be explained: see pp. 560 f., 188. Upon this view ἄνδρες τε θεοί τε literally means '*there* men, *there* gods,' i. e. both together = '*both* men *and* gods.' And the theory derives a striking confirmation from Latin, where we are in fact able to watch the transition from the demonstrative to the copulative signification taking place beneath our eyes. *Tum* unquestionably means *then :* but in such a sentence as '*tum* homines, *tum* equi aderant' (the structure of which exactly resembles that of ἄνδρες τε θεοί τε) we see it possessing virtually a copulative force,—literally '*then* men, *then* horses were there,' i. e. they were both there together = '*both* horses *and* men were there.'

Without assuming that the Hebrew ו֫ had once a distinctly demonstrative force, it does not appear possible to explain or account for the phenomena which its use actually presents. Starting from a meaning not stronger than that of our modern *and*, we do not readily perceive how such a weak word as ו must then have been, could ever stand in the emphatic positions it really occupies: starting on the other hand with a *demonstrative* signification, we at once comprehend, even without the aid of the Aryan analogies, and especially, because best attested, the Latin *tum*, by what steps this might become merely copulative. If the latter view be correct, *three* different modes present themselves in which it is employed; the first, comprising those cases in which the stronger and more decided sense is still evidently retained; the second (the *waw consec.* generally, but more particularly with the *perfect*), comprising those in which the earlier meaning has to be assumed (see p. 117) in order to explain the usage, but where the conscious recollection of it was probably as much forgotten in practice by the ancient Hebrew as it is disregarded by the modern reader in translation; the third, comprising the instances in which its force is equivalent to that of the copulative conjunction—'the heavens, *then* the earth,' being identical with 'the heavens *and* the earth.' The Arabic language possesses two forms of the copulative, ـفَ *fa* as well as ﻭ *wa:* the latter being the *mere* copulative, the former carrying the stronger meaning *then, so,* οὖν etc., and being employed generally in all those cases which correspond to the *first* class just mentioned. It lies near to conjecture that both *wa* and *fa* (cf. the Heb. אַף) are but modifications of the same original labial stem, that in Arabic the two words once existed side by side as by-forms, but that, in process of time, a differentiation was effected, in consequence of which *fa* was reserved for emphatic occasions, while in Hebrew *fa* as such fell out of use, and the single form *wa* had to do double duty. And that a demonstrative signification is not foreign to the syllable *fa*, may be inferred from the adverbs פֹּה *here*, אֵיפֹה *where?* (formed from פֹה, like אֵי־זֶה from זֶה), אֵפוֹ or אֵפוֹא *then, so, δή*. Upon the whole, then, we seem sufficiently justified in assigning a *demonstrative* origin to the Semitic ו: the conclusion suggested, if not necessitated, by the usages of Hebrew syntax receiving independent confirmation from the analogies offered by the Aryan family of speech.

123. Accordingly, וְ is met with before the verb (*a*) when the sentence has commenced with the *casus pendens*, i. e. where, the logical subject or object being prefixed, the place which they would ordinarily occupy is filled grammatically by either a suffix or a fresh substantive.

Thus Ex. 4, 21 כָּל־הַמּוֹפְתִים אֲשֶׁר ... וַעֲשִׂיתָם all the signs which etc., *thou shalt do them* (§ 119 β: so 12, 44 וּמָלְתָה אֹתוֹ 2 Sa. 14, 10 the man that speaketh unto thee וַהֲבֵאתוֹ אֵלִי *bring him* unto me. 2 Chr. 19, 10). 9, 19 all the men who are found in the field וְיָרַד עֲלֵיהֶם the hail *shall come down* upon them. 21, 13 וְשַׂמְתִּי after אשר *whoso* (so Jud. 1, 12). Lev. 20, 6. 26, 36. Nu. 10, 32ᵇ. 14, 31 וְהֵבֵאתִי אתם ... וטפכם. 17, 3. Isa. 56, 6 f. 65, 7. Jer. 27, 11. Ez. 17, 19. Mi. 3, 5. Pr. 9, 16 (*freq.* cf. וישבה *v.* 14: *v.* 4 the construction is different, § 12).

Gen. 17, 14. Ex. 12, 15 every one eating leavened bread וְנִכְרְתָה הַנֶּפֶשׁ הַהוּא that soul *shall be cut off:* so 31, 14ᵇ. Lev. 7, 20. 25, and often; similarly Dt. 17, 12. 18, 20. Jer. 23, 34.

Even the direct predicate may be thus introduced, though usually only when it is separated from its subject by several intervening words: Ex. 30, 33. 38. Nu. 19, 11 ... הַנֹּגֵעַ בְּמֵת הַבְּרָכָה ... וְנָתְנָה. 24, 24. 1 Sa. 25, 27 2 Ki. וְטָמֵא שִׁבְעַת יָמִים. 11, 7. Isa. 9, 4 for every boot of him that trampeth etc. .... וְהָיְתָה *it shall be* for burning; and in a freq. sense, 44, 12 וּפָעַל¹

---

¹ The construction of the present text is, however, here so harsh as to leave it scarcely doubtful that a verb has fallen out either before or after חרש ברזל. LXX has ὤξυνεν, Pesh. ܚܰܕܶܕ, whence Delitzsch would prefix חִדֵּד, Cheyne (*Notes and Criticisms on the Hebrew Text of Isaiah,* 1868) still better הֵחַד, which might easily drop out from similarity with

(observe the following יְצַרְהוּ). Jer. 51, 58[b] (see Hab. 2, 13).
2 Chr. 13, 9 : 1 Sa. 17, 20 וְהֵרֵעוּ ... וְהֶחֱיִל, if the text be correct,
will also belong here.

(β) Very frequently after various time-determinations :—
Gen. 3, 5 in the day of your eating from it, וְנִפְקְחוּ your eyes
will be opened. Ex. 16, 6 עֶרֶב וִידַעְתֶּם at even—*then* ye will
know. 7. 32, 34[b]. Nu. 10, 10. 18, 30[b]. Dt. 4, 30 (וְשַׁבְתָּ). 2 Sa.
7, 14. 15, 10. 1 Ki. 13, 31 when I die, וּקְבַרְתֶּם *ye shall bury*
me by the man of God. 14, 12. Ez. 24, 24[b]. 33, 18 ומת (19
the impf.). Ob. 8 : after the phrase הִנֵּה יָמִים בָּאִים, 1 Sa. 2, 31
behold days are coming וְגָדַעְתִּי *and I will hew off* thy arm.
2 Ki. 20, 17 (Isa. 39, 6). Amos 4, 2. 8, 11. 9, 13; and often
in Jeremiah (the expression does not occur elsewhere): after
עוֹד מְעַט, as Ex. 17, 4 a little while וּסְקָלֻנִי *and they will* stone
me. Isa. 10, 25. 29, 17. Jer. 51, 33 (וּבָאָה, § 112. 5) etc.; cf.
Isa. 16, 14. 18, 5 וכרת. 21, 16. Pr. 6, 10 f.[1] And involving
a question (cf. § 119 γ), 1 Sa. 24, 20[a]. Ez. 15, 5[b] וְנֶעֱשָׂה *shall
it* be yet made into any work ? Compare also Pr. 24, 27
אַחַר וּבָנִיתָ afterwards, *and* (or *then*) thou shalt build thy house
(cf. the impf., Gen. 18, 5. 24, 55 al.): Ps. 141, 5 is probably
only an extreme instance of the same construction.

And without any verb following :—Isa. 17, 14. Ps. 37, 10.

In a frequentative signification :—Gen. 31, 8 וילדו *then they
used* to bear. Ex. 1, 19[b] before the midwife comes to them,
וילדו *they bear*. Nu. 9, 19. 1 Sa. 2, 13 כָּל־אִישׁ זֹבֵחַ זֶבַח וּבָא
when any one sacrificed (cf. p. 147, *n.*), the young man *used
to come* (cf. יקח, יעשו 14). 15 LXX excellently πρὶν θυμιαθῆναι
τὸ στέαρ ἤρχετο τὸ παιδάριον καὶ ἔλεγε.

---

the preceding יחד. Another suggestion would be יַחַד, as in Pr. 27, 17,
or, if the jussive form be objected to, יַחַד or יֶחַד: in this case the *tense*
would accord better with the two verbs following; we should obtain
for 12[a] three frequentatives, which naturally go together (וַ 12[b], § 114 β).

[1] 2 Chr. 10, 5 we have the imperative ושובו after עוד : but in 1 Ki.
12, 5 לכו is added before עֹד, which LXX read likewise in 2 Chr.

(γ) After other words, as טֶרֶם Isa. 66, 7[b] (7[a], without וְ, the instantaneous perfect, § 136 γ); יַ֫עַן, 1 Ki. 20, 28 because they have said ... וְנָתַ֫תִּי *I will give* etc. 42. Isa. 3, 16 f. 37, 29 וְנָתַתִּי. Jer. 7, 13 f.; כִּי *since* or *because*, Gen. 29, 15; עֵ֫קֶב, Nu. 14, 24; תַּ֫חַת, Isa. 60, 15. 2 Ki. 22, 17 וְנִצְּתָה; Dan. 8, 25. Ps. 25, 11 for thy name's sake וְסָלַחְתָּ *so pardon* or *pardon then* (§ 119 δ) mine iniquity! and constantly in introducing the apodosis after כִּי and אִם, Dt. 6, 21. 13, 15. 22, 2. 21 etc.: see Chap. XI, §§ 136–138.

Obs. In all these cases the impf. alone might have been used, the only advantage of the pf. with וְ being that it marks the apodosis more distinctly, and by separating the initial words (the subject or protasis) from those which follow renders them more emphatic. Frequently, indeed, we meet with the two forms in close proximity to each other: see Gen. 44, 9 and 10. Jud. 8, 7 and 9; cf. also Gen. 4, 15 with Ex. 12, 15. Nu. 19, 11; Gen. 40, 13 with Isa. 21, 16.

Where a more special emphasis is desired, a different method is commonly employed: the subject is *reinforced* by the personal pronoun. A few examples will suffice: Gen. 3, 12. 15, 4 but one that shall come forth out of thine own bowels הוא יירשך *he* shall be thine heir. 24, 7 Yahweh, the God of heaven, who took me etc. הוא ישלח *he* shall send his angel etc. 42, 6. 44, 17 (cf. 9, just cited). Ex. 12, 16[b] only what is eaten etc. הוא יעשה *that* may be done of you. Isa. 34, 16[b]. 38, 19. 47, 10 היא. 59, 16[b]. 63, 5[b]. (The same *principle* in oblique cases: Lev. 25, 44 מן; Dt. 13, 1. Jud. 11, 24. Isa. 8, 13 את; Ez. 18, 24. 27, 21. 33, 13[b] ב; Lev. 7, 8. 9. 14. 21, 3 ל; 2 Sa. 6, 22 עם. Cf. Dt. 14, 6. 20, 20. 1 Sa. 15, 9[b].)

124. If the וְ becomes separated from the verb, the latter naturally appears in the impf.: this, however, is comparatively a rare occurrence [1].

After הן or הנה Ex. 8, 22 וְלֹא will they not stone us? (where הֲלֹא might have been expected). 1 Sa. 9, 7 וּמַה; Gen. 2, 4[b]– 5[a]. Ex. 25, 9 וְכֵן ... בְּכֹל, cf. Nu. 9, 17 (freq.); Lev. 7, 16 וּמִמָּחֳרָת וְהַנּוֹתָר יֵאָכֵל. Josh. 3, 3 (but no וְ appears in the similar injunction 8[b]). 1 Ki. 8, 32 ואתה. 34. 36. 39 (omitted 43).

---

[1] Nearly all the instances are cited.

Isa. 8, 7 ולכן (after יען כי). 57, 12 ולא (after ואת, Ew. § 277ᵈ²: cf. Nu. 35, 6. 3, 46 f.). 65, 24 ואני (after טרם, and also a partcp. with עוד). Jer. 7, 32 ולא. Ez. 5, 11 וגם אני. 16, 43 (cf. 23, 35); Zech. 3, 7 וגם אתה (Hitz.). Ps. 115, 7 (different from *v.* 5 f.). Job 20, 18ᵇ ולא. 23, 12 ולא אמיש. 25, 5. 31, 14 ומה. 35, 15ᵇ (Ew. Dillm. Del.). See also § 136 *a Obs.*

The ‎ו is followed by a *perfect*, Ruth 4, 5 thou *wilt have* purchased (but for וּמָאֵת we should here certainly read גַּם אֶת, as in *v.* 10); and by a *participle*, Jon. 3, 4. Hag. 2, 6—both after עוד.

125. Sometimes further, though still more rarely, we have ‎ו closely joined to the *imperfect:*—Ex. 12, 3 in the tenth day of the month וְיִקְחוּ. Nu. 16, 5 in the morning וְיֹדַע Yahweh will shew. 1 Sa. 30, 22ᵇ. 2 Chr. 34, 25 וַתִּתַּךְ[1] (altered—or corrupted—from 2 Ki. 22, 17, § 123 γ). Isa. 19, 20 וישלח. 43, 4 ואתן. Jer. 8, 1 Kt. 13, 10 וִיהִי *let it be*, then, as this girdle (the jussive implying the *abandonment* of the nation, that it may follow freely its course of ruin). Ez. 12, 12 בעלטה וְיֵצֵא. 31, 11. 33, 31. Hos. 4, 6 (Baer) because thou hast rejected knowledge, וָאֶמְאָסְאָ. 10, 10 בְּאַוָּתִי וְאֶסֳּרֵם. Ps. 69, 33 וִיהִי. 91, 14 (unless כי=*for*). Job 15, 17 that which I have seen, וַאֲסַפֵּרָה *let me tell it.*

Obs. Compare the cases in which the predicate or apodosis *without a verb* is introduced in the same way:—Gen. 40, 9. 16 בחלומי והנה. 2 Sa. 15, 34 thy father's slave, ואני מאז I was *that* before; but now, ואני עבדך *now* I will be thine! 23, 3 f. *when one ruleth* over men, as a just one, when one *ruleth* in the fear of God, וכאור *then* is it like the shining of the morn at sunrise. Isa. 34, 12 (an extreme case) her nobles ... שם ואין *there is none* there that etc. Ez. 1, 18 וגבה. Job 4, 6ᵇ (see Del.). 36, 26ᵇ. Pr. 10, 25ᵃ when a tempest passes by רשע ואין *then* the wicked is not. 1 Chr. 28, 21. Gen. 20, 16ᵇ. Cf. too 2 Sa. 22, 41 (which differs from Ps. 18, 41 exactly as Pr. 23, 24ᵇ Kt. does from Qrê): the misplacement of ‎ו in *one* of the two texts would be parallel to that which we are almost obliged to assume Ps. 16, 3. But 2 Ki. 11, 5 ושמרי is very harsh: read rather ושמרו (*v.* 7) or ישמרו; and comp. on the graphical confusion of ‎י and ‎ו *Notes on Samuel*, p. lxvi. f.

---

[1] In some edd. וַתַּתֵּךְ (§§ 81, 127).

126. A special case of this use of the perfect with *waw* consecutive is when it is preceded by a *participle*, which is then often introduced by הִנֵּה.

Thus with הנה:—1 Ki. 20, 36 וְהִכְּךָ ... הִנְּךָ הוֹלֵךְ behold thou art going from me, and a lion will smite thee (=*as* thou goest from me, a lion *will* etc.). Jud. 7, 17. 9, 33 (*as* he comes out, thou shalt etc.: Vulg. excellently *illo autem egrediente . . .* fac ei quod potueris). Gen. 24, 13 f. (a *wish* or *hope*, § 119 δ).

Without הנה:—1 Ki. 18, 11 f. 14. 2 Ki. 7, 9 וַאֲנַחְנוּ מַחְשִׁים *and if* we are silent and wait (pf. as § 117) וּמְצָאָנוּ iniquity will find us out (*si tacuerimus*, Vulg.). Pr. 29, 9 (p. 147 *n.*), cf. *v.* 21 and 20, 21 (וְ separated from the verb); of past time, 1 Sa. 2, 13 (frequentative: p. 152).

The same use of the partcp. appears likewise with the impf. alone in the apodosis :—

Josh. 2, 18 behold *as* (or *when*) *we come* אֶת־תִּקְוַת חוּט תִּקְשְׁרִי thou shalt bind this thread on to the window (ingredientibus nobis). Gen. 50, 5. Ex. 3, 13 behold אָנֹכִי בָא וְאָמַרְתִּי *if I go* and say (§ 117) . . . , and they say, What is his name? (here comes the apodosis) *what* shall I say to them? cf. Nu. 24, 14. 1 Sa. 16, 15 f.; and with an imperative or participle in the apodosis, Gen. 49, 29. Ex. 9, 17 f. Cf. § 165.

127. Similarly, when the reference is to what is past or certain rather than to what is future or indefinite we find the predicate or the apodosis introduced by וְ, though not with nearly the same frequency as by the perf. and *waw* consecutive[1].

(*a*) With subject prefixed :—Gen. 22, 24. 30, 30 for the little that thou hadst before I came, וַיִּפְרֹץ *it* hath increased etc. Ex. 9, 21. 38, 24. Nu. 14, 36 f. וימתו (with repetition of the subject האנשים). 1 Sa. 14, 19 וילך. 17, 24. 2 Sa. 19, 41 Kt. 1 Ki. 11, 26. 2 Ki. 2, 14ᵇ (accents). Jer. 44, 25. Ps. 107, 13 (the subject of ויזעקו being ישבי חשך 10). 2 Chr. 25, 13.

---

[1] Nearly all the instances are cited.

With object prefixed :—2 Sa. 4, 10 for he that told me saying, Saul is dead, וָאֹחֲזָה בּוֹ I took hold of him etc. 1 Ki. 9, 20 f. וִיעָלָם (cf. 2 Chr. 8, 7 f.). 12, 17. 15, 13 וְנַם אֶת־מַעֲכָה וַיְסִרֶהָ מִגְּבִירָה. 2 Ki. 16, 14 (אֵת). 25, 22. Jer. 6, 19 וְתוֹרָתִי וַיְמָאֲסוּ בָהּ. 28, 8. 33, 24 וַיִּמְאָסֵם.

(β) After time-determinations :—as בְּ Gen. 22, 4 on the third day וַיִּשָּׂא Abraham lifted up his eyes (=*it was* on the third day *that* Abraham lifted up his eyes : cf. 1 Chr. 16, 7, where אָז is similarly introduced). Dt. 9, 23. Nu. 7, 89. 12, 12. Jud. 11, 16. 1 Sa. 21, 6 בְּצֵאתִי וִיהִיוּ¹. 2 Ki. 25, 3=Jer. 52, 6. Isa. 6, 1. Jer. 7, 25. Ez. 20, 5. Ps. 138, 3. 1 Chr. 21, 28. 2 Chr. 13, 1 (2 Ki. 15, 1 מֶלֶךְ only). 28, 22 ; בְּטֶרֶם, Gen. 37, 18 ; כְּ, Gen. 27, 34. 1 Sa. 4, 20. 17, 57. Hos. 13, 6. Esth. 5, 9ᵇ; כַּאֲשֶׁר, 1 Sa. 6, 6. 12, 8 ; כְּמוֹ, Gen. 19, 15; כִּי *when*, Josh. 22, 7. Hos. 11, 1. Ps. 50, 18. Jer. 37, 16 f.²; מֵעֵת, 2 Chr. 25, 27 ; Dan. 1, 18.

(γ) After other words :—כַּאֲשֶׁר *as*, Ex. 16, 34. Nu. 1, 19 ; יַעַן, 1 Sa. 15, 23 *because* thou hast rejected Yahweh וַיְמָאָסְךָ *he* has rejected thee ; כִּי, Hos. 4, 6 (edd. : not Baer ; see § 125). 2 Chr. 24, 20ᵇ; 1 Ki. 10, 9. Isa. 45, 4 (after לְמַעַן). 48, 5 (after מִדַּעְתִּי, *v.* 4 ; cf. Nu. 14, 16 after . . . מִבִּלְתִּי). Ez. 16, 47. Ps. 59, 16 (after אִם). Job 36, 7 ³. 9 (Hitz. Del. Dillm.). 1 Chr. 28, 5 ; Dan. 1, 20 (cf. 1 Sa. 20, 23. 2 Ki. 22, 18ᵇ–19).

---

¹ As usually rendered : see, however, W. R. Smith, *The Religion of the Semites*, 1889, p. 436 (quoted in the writer's *Notes on Samuel*, p. 293).

² But here וַיָּבֹא (LXX) should no doubt be restored in *v.* 16 for כִּי בָא : cf. p. 83 *note*.

³ But Job 19, 18 will be most safely and naturally explained by § 54 or 84, and for 30, 26 see p. 70 *note :* it is too precarious to suppose that the ·וַ in וידברו and ויבאו should mark, as it marks nowhere else, the apodosis to a hypothetical voluntative, §§ 150–152.

In the Hebrew translation of the New Testament, published by the Society for Promoting Christianity among the Jews (London, 1867), the construction with ·וַ is employed in answer to כאשר etc. with a frequency and freedom quite without precedent in any of the Old Testament historians ; in the more recent editions, however (the latest, 1890), revised by Professor Delitzsch for the British and Foreign Bible Society, this

128. When the verb no longer stands at the beginning of the clause, the pf. tense reappears, but usually, as in the parallel case § 124, the וֹ is then altogether dispensed with :— Gen. 19, 4, so 2 Ki. 6, 32 (וְהוּא אָמַר); Jud. 11, 26 while Israel dwelt in Heshbon etc. three hundred years, וּמַדּוּעַ לֹא הִצַּלְתֶּם *pray* why did you not deliver them during that time? Isa. 48, 7 before to-day, וְלֹא שְׁמַעְתָּם thou hast not heard them. Ps. 142, 4. Dan. 10, 4. 9[b]. 2 Chr. 5, 13. 7, 1. 26, 19.

129. In the few isolated cases where the *perfect* with וֹ occurs thus in relation to the past or present, it is either frequentative (§ 123 β), or else altogether exceptional :—Ex. 36, 38. 2 Ki. 11, 1 Kt. Isa. 37, 26 מִימֵי קֶדֶם וִיצַרְתִּיהָ (cf. 48, 7). Jer. 40, 3[b]. Ez. 16, 19.

---

and many other faults of style have been corrected. (Comp. on this version an article by the present writer in the *Expositor*, April, 1886, p. 260 ff.; also a *brochure* by Delitzsch himself, entitled *The Hebrew New Testament of the British and Foreign Bible Society*, Leipzig, 1883, and papers by him in the *Expositor*, Feb., Apr., Oct. 1889, and in *Saat auf Hoffnung*, Feb. 1890, p. 67 ff.) For παραγενόμενοι δὲ (or ἐπεὶ δὲ παρεγένοντο) εἶπον, classical Hebrew says, either ויבואו ויאמרו (§ 149 n.), or if the subordinate clause calls for greater prominence ויהי כבאם ויאמרו. It does not say וכבואם ויאמרו, though this type, of course, is met with *occasionally*, but in the best authors the introductory ו is usually avoided. And even וכבואם אמרו is only common as a later idiom (see 1 Chr. 21, 15. 2 Chr. 12, 7. 12. 15, 8. 20, 20. 22. 23. 22, 7. 24, 14. 22[b]. 25. 26, 16. 29, 27. 29. 31, 1. 5. 33, 12. 34, 14. Ezra 9, 1. 3. 5. 10, 1. Esth. 9, 1 f. Dan. 8, 8[b]. 18. 10, 11[b]. 15. 19[b]. 11, 2. 4. 12, 7[b]: cf. with ו 2 Chr. 5, 13. 7, 1. 26, 19. Dan. 10, 9[b], § 128); the earlier writers, as a rule (comp. p. 89 n., and the writer's note on 1 Sa. 17, 55), prefer ויאמרו כבואם, or prefix ויהי.

CHAPTER IX.

The Perfect and Imperfect with Weak Waw.

130. IT will appear to the reader almost ludicrous to devote a separate chapter to the consideration of what will seem to be such an elementary phenomenon of language as the union of either the perfect or the imperfect with the simple conjunction ן. Yet, common and constant as this union is in the case of most other Semitic languages, in Hebrew, especially so far as the *perfect* is concerned, it is such a rare and isolated occurrence as both to invite and demand a somewhat minute investigation.

131. Although in Hebrew the continuation of a historical narrative is most usually expressed by the impf. with ·ן, we find, occasionally in the earlier books of the Old Testament, and with increasing frequency in the later ones, that this idiom, which is so peculiarly and distinctively a creation of the Hebrew language, has been replaced by the *perfect* with the simple or weak *waw*, ן. Generally, indeed, as we saw in the last chapter, and invariably when the verb to which the perfect is annexed is a bare imperfect, §§ 113. 4, 120, the *waw* prefixed to the perfect is consecutive, and the sense consequently frequentative: but a certain number of passages exist in which this signification is out of place; in these, therefore, we are compelled to suppose that the *waw* is the *mere* copulative, and that it no longer exerts over the following verb that strong and peculiar modifying influence which we term conversive. There are two principal cases in which the perfect with weak *waw* is thus met with. The feature common to them both is this—that the idiom employed, instead of representing a given event as *arising out of*, or *being a continuation of*, some previous occurrence (in the manner of the idiom with ·ן), represents it as standing on an independent ground of its own, as connected indeed with what precedes, but only externally and superficially, without any inner bond of union existing between them: in a word, it causes the narrative to advance not by development but by *accretion*. Accordingly we find it used (1) upon occasions when a writer wishes to place two facts in *co-ordination* with one another, to exhibit the second as simultaneous with the first rather than as succeeding it; for instance, in the conjunction of two synonymous or similar ideas: and (2), chiefly in the later books, when the language was allowing itself gradually to acquiesce in and adopt the mode of speech customary in the Aramaic dialects current at the time around Palestine[1], in which the rival construction with ·ן, at least in historical times, was never employed.

132. Thus (1) Gen. 31, 7 [2] הֵתֶל בִּי וְהֶחֱלִף. Nu. 23, 19 [3]

---

[1] On the different Aramaic dialects see Nöldeke's art., 'Semitic Languages,' in the *Encyclopaedia Britannica*, ed. 9 (reprinted separately in German under the title, *Die Semitischen Sprachen*, Leipzig, 1887); Dr. Wright's *Comparative Grammar of the Semitic Languages*, Chap. ii; Kautzsch, *Grammatik des Biblisch-Aramäischen*, p. 12 ff.; or, more briefly, the writer's *Introduction to the Literature of the O.T.*, p. 471 f. The dialects spoken in and about Palestine are represented at present (1891) in their oldest known forms by the Palmyrene and Nabataean Inscriptions (the former principally in De Vogüé, *Syrie Centrale*, 1868, the latter in Euting, *Nabatäische Inschriften*, 1885), dating mostly from third cent. B.C. to first cent. A.D., and the Aramaic sections of Ezra and Daniel; also (though these are marked by the singular difference of זי, זנה, for the relative and demonstrative pronouns די and דנה) by the Têma Inscriptions (Part ii, Tom. i, Nos. 113 ff. of the *Corpus Inscriptionum Semiticarum*), and the Egyptian Aramaic Inscriptions (*ibid.*, Nos. 122 ff.), the earliest dating from the fifth cent. B.C. The Aramaic of the Targums is in certain features of a somewhat later type than any of these dialects.

[2] This may possibly be freq.: for the pf. הֵתֵל, cf. § 114 a.

[3] On *v.* 20 וּבָרֵךְ, see § 148 *end*: on 24, 17 וְקָם (future), § 113. 1.

(coupling a parallel term to אָמַר under הֵ). Dt. 2, 30. 33, 2. 20. Josh. 9, 12 (cf. *v.* 5, where ו is omitted). Jud. 5, 26[1]. 1 Sa. 12, 2 זקנתי ושׂבתי *am old and grey-headed.* 1 Ki. 8, 47[b]. 20, 27. Isa. 1, 2 גדלתי ורוממתי. 8. 2, 11 וּשׁח. 5, 14[a]. 8, 8 (ועבר שׁטף § 14 γ). 19, 6 וחרבו. 13. 14. 24, 6[b] (cf. the ἀσύνδετα, *vv.* 5. 7 f.). 29, 20. 34, 14[b]. 15. 37, 25. 27 וְיָבֹשׁי (2 Ki. 19, 26 וַיֵּבֹשׁוּ). 38, 12. 40, 12. 41, 4. 43, 12 (as in 1, 2, observe there is no change of tone). 44, 8. 55, 10 (*might* be consecutive: see 6, 11 f.). 11. 63, 10. Joel 1, 7.

Omitting instances in Jeremiah and Ezekiel, we have several from the Psalms: 20, 9[a] (9[b] ·ו, more euphonious than the pf., and in sharper contrast to 9[a]). 27, 2. 34, 11. 37, 14. 38, 9. 20[2]. 66, 14. 76, 9. 86, 13. 17. 131, 2. Add further, Pr. 22, 3. Job 16, 15. 18, 11. 29, 21[a]. Lam. 2, 22. 3, 42. And after an impf. with ·ו, Gen. 49, 23. Isa. 9, 19. Hab. 1, 11.

Obs. Sometimes, however, in cases of this sort, the second verb is annexed by means of ·ו: cf. Ex. 31, 17. Isa. 57, 11. Ps. 7, 16. 16, 8. 119, 73 (cf. Job 10, 8).

133. (2) Such are the only instances which seem capable of being reduced to a definite rule. Of the instances which remain, those which occur in the later books may be fairly regarded as attributable to the influence of Aramaic usage: but for the few which are met with in the earlier books (Genesis—2 Samuel, Amos, Isaiah), it is more than doubtful whether such an explanation is admissible. For, independently of the question of date, it is hardly credible that had the Aramaic influence existed it should only have made itself felt on such *exceedingly rare* occasions in all the historical

---

[1] In this Song (except once, *v.* 28), as in Ex. 15, ·ו appears to be intentionally avoided: אז, or the bare impf. (§ 27 *a*), suit better the empassioned style of both.

[2] Here, though the tone is on the ultima, the waw is not necessarily consecutive: in verbs ע″ע, even where no waw consecutive is prefixed, the tone is sometimes *milra*, as Ps. 69, 5 רַבּוּ. See Kalisch, ii. § lxii. 1 (*b*).

books from Genesis to Samuel: in the later portions of the Old Testament, it will be remembered, it shews itself much more frequently. Why, upon these rare occasions, the construction observed uniformly elsewhere (ויאמר דוד, or the alternating ודוד אמר) was abandoned must, I think, remain an insoluble enigma : all that can be said is that in some few of the instances the novel construction introduces the mention of a fact not perhaps meant to be *immediately* connected with the previous narrative, while in others, by no longer representing the idea conveyed by the verb as part of a continuous series, it may allow it greater prominence and emphasis than it would otherwise have received. Even so, however, most would yet remain unexplained : and though the latter supposition would be suitable enough in the case of ונפל, ונעל, for example, still, if such were felt to be the force of the idiom, it is remarkable that advantage should not have been taken of it more frequently. The instances which occur must simply be recorded as *isolated irregularities*, of which no entirely adequate explanation can be offered [1].

Gen. 15, 6 והאמן. 21, 25 והוכח. 28, 6. 38, 5 והיה (a uniquely-worded sentence, which can scarcely be before us in its original form : LXX αὕτη points to וְהוּא : cf. 1 Sa. 23, 15. 24. 2 Chr. 10, 2). Ex. 5, 16. 36, 38. 38, 28. 39, 3. Jud. 3, 23 ונעל. 7, 13 ונפל. 16, 18 (*might* be freq.: cf. 6, 3). 1 Sa. 1, 12 והיה. 3, 13 והגדתי. 4, 19. 10, 9 והיה. 17, 38 ונתן. 48 והיה. 25, 20 והיה. 2 Sa. 6, 16. 7, 11[b] והגיד. 13, 18 ונעל again. 16, 5. 23, 20. 1 Ki. 3, 11[b]. 6, 32. 35. 11, 10. 12, 32. 13, 3 ונתן. 14, 27. 20, 21. 21, 12. Isa. 9, 7. 22, 14. 28, 26 [2]? 38,

---

[1] This use of the pf. with ן is undeniably anomalous, as it is also an inelegancy : but in view of the number of instances it can scarcely be maintained with Stade (*ZATW.* 1885, pp. 291–3) that all examples found in pre-exilic passages are due to corruption of the text.

[2] ויסרו ' mit der einfachen Copula, weil die Unterweisung dem Thun des Landmanns vorangeht, also in der Zeit zurückgeschritten wird,' Hitz. Still, a *general* course of dealing is described : in the context fre-

15 ('both'). Amos 7, 2. Ps. 22, 6. 15. 28, 7. 34, 5. 6 [but see § 58 *note*]. 35, 15. 135, 10. 12. 148, 5 [1].

In 2 Kings, Jeremiah, Ezekiel [2], Chronicles, this usage becomes somewhat more frequent, but the reader may there collect examples for himself. The impf. and ·וֹ, however, continues still to be distinctly the predominant construction : in Ezra, for example, the pf. with וֹ occurs only 3, 10. 6, 22. 8, 30. 36. 9, 2 (9, 6. 13, § 132), in Nehemiah only 9, 7 f. 10, 33. 12, 39. 13, 1. 30, and in Esther 2, 14. 3, 12. 8, 15. 9, 23. 24. 25 ? 27 ; though, in the last-named book, it is possible that the preference for the other form may be a feature due not to the natural usage of the author, but to a studied imitation of the earlier historical style. Similarly in Daniel (excluding of course the Aramaic portion, from 2, 4[b] to 7, 28), ·וֹ is constantly employed, though in chs. 8–12 a few instances of the perfect are met with [3]. There is only

---

quentative forms abound (the parallel clause has יוֹרְנוּ) ; and as Isaiah evidently desires his hearers to be led by the contemplation of certain facts (*v.* 24 f.) to reflect upon their cause, it is natural that these should have been mentioned first.

[1] In the Psalm-passages, due probably to lateness.

In some passages where, at first sight, the use of the perfect seems anomalous, it must be explained in a frequentative sense, § 120 ; this is certainly the case in Ex. 36, 29 f. (notice יִהְיוּ). Nu. 10, 17 f. 21 f. 25 (notice the *participles* in Onqelos : cf. above, p. 146, *note*). 1 Sa. 2, 22 (notice יַעֲשׂוּן). 16, 14[b] (observe the partcp. *v.* 15). 27, 9 (cf. יִחְיֶה). 2 Sa. 16, 13 וְעִפַּר בֶּעָפָר (notice the partcp. הֹלֵךְ : Targ. וּמְשַׁדֵּי). 19, 19 (but it is doubtful if the text here is correct : see the writer's note *ad loc.*). 20, 12 (continuation of הַבָּא, § 117) ; probably also in the following, Gen. 34, 5. 37, 3 (cf. 1 Sa. 2, 19). Nu. 21, 15 וְנָשַׁ֫עַן. 20 וְנִשְׁקְפָה (pf. § 103 : *used to look* or *looketh*, cf. § 120 *Obs.*: Onq. וּמְסָֽתְּמֵיךְ and וּמְסַֽתַּכְיָא). 1 Sa. 5, 7. 17, 34 f. (cf. p. 122). 24, 11 (text probably corrupt : read either וַיֹּאמֶר, or, with LXX, וָאֹמְאַן). Isa. 40, 6 וְאָמַר, cf. 57, 14 : but LXX, Vulg. וָאֹמַר). Ps. 26, 3[b] (cf. 4[b]. 5[b]). 80, 13 (cf. the impff. *v.* 14). But Ex. 36, 1 וְעָשָׂה is no doubt future (continuation of 35, 30 ff. .

[2] The list given by Smend, on 40, 36, is far from exhaustive.

[3] Viz. 8, 7. 10, 7. 12, 5 (but cf. 8, 2. 3. 10, 5. 8) ; 10, 1. 14. In 8,

one book in the Old Testament in which this state of things is reversed, and the perfect with simple *waw* obtains a marked and indeed almost exclusive preponderance. In the whole of Qohéleth ·וֹ occurs not more than *three* times, 1, 17. 4, 1. 7, whereas the other construction is of repeated occurrence [1]. This circumstance, estimated in the light of what is *uniformly* observable in other parts of the Old Testament, is of itself, though naturally it does not stand alone, a strong indication of the date at which that book must have been composed. In the Song of Songs ·וֹ occurs but twice, 6, 1 : in this book, however, there is very little occasion for *either* form being used, and in fact the perfect with *waw* occurs only twice likewise (2, 3. 10), a circumstance too slight to base an argument upon.

134. Exactly as the perfect with simple *waw* is in Hebrew superseded, and in fact almost banished from the language, by the imperfect with *waw* consecutive, so the impf. with

---

4[b] we have evidently two frequentatives, cf. יעמדו; *v.* 12 the perfects follow תשלך (§ 113. 2, 3); and *vv.* 11. 27. 9, 5 (cf. 1 Ki. 8, 47). 10, 15 are to be explained by § 132.

[1] Chiefly in chs. 2. 3, 22. 4, 1. 7. 8, 17. 9, 16—just in the narrative of successive experiences and resolutions, where ·וֹ might have been expected (see Dt. 1–3. Neh. 2. 13. Ps. 55, 7. 77, 11 : cf. 78, 59. 65. 106, 23. Ez. 20), and where the connexion was so strongly felt by our translators that in 13 out of 21 cases in 1st pers. they render by *so, then* etc., which elsewhere, § 74, is used for ·וֹ. The anonymous author of a *Treatise on the Authorship of Ecclesiastes* (London, 1880) deserves credit for his industry and independence ; but, though able to shew that several of its linguistic peculiarities may be paralleled by *isolated* passages in earlier writings, he fails to account for their co-existence and repetition : a method which would prove that the style of Esther did not differ from that of Genesis cannot be a sound one. His contention that the *bare* pf. may have a freq. sense (pp. 192–4, 220) cannot certainly be sustained : the fact that it may be used to *narrate* recurrent events (grouping them as one) is no more a proof that it *expresses* their recurrency than the use of the aorist in, e. g. Hdt. 5, 92, 21 (τοιοῦτος δή τις ἀνὴρ ἐγένετο· πολλοὺς μὲν Κορινθίων ἐδίωξε, πολλοὺς δὲ χρημάτων ἐστέρησε), can shew that it bears there the sense of the impf.

simple *waw*, although not quite to the same extent, is yet in the great majority of cases superseded by the pf. with *waw* consecutive. Allusion has been already made (§ 116) to the rarity with which two imperfects are found united by וֹ, after conjunctions like פֶּן or אִם : although it is not so uncommon to find them coupled in this way when they bear a frequentative, future, or jussive sense, yet the other construction is still decidedly preferred, and the occurrence of *two* imperfects must even then, comparatively speaking, be termed exceptional. In general the imperfect is only repeated when it is desired to lay some particular stress on the verb, or, as before, in order to combine synonyms : the repetition is also more frequent in the poetical than in the historical books. Examples in a future or jussive sense :—Gen. 1, 9. 26. 9, 27. 17, 2. 22, 17. 27, 29. 31. Ex. 24, 7. 26, 24. Nu. 14, 12. 21, 27. Dt. 17, 13 (= 19, 20. 21, 21). 30, 12 f. Josh. 7, 3, cf. 9. Jud. 7, 3. 13, 8 al.; Isa. 41, 11. 15. 22. 42, 6. 14. 21. 23. 44, 7. 45, 24. 25. 46, 4. 5. 47, 11. 49, 8 etc. As a frequentative, however, this repetition of an imperfect is considerably rarer : —Ex. 23, 8 (= Dt. 16, 19). Isa. 40, 30. 44, 16 f. 46, 6 f. 59, 7. Ps. 25, 9. 37, 40. 49, 9. 59, 5. 7. 73, 8. 83, 4. 97, 3. See also § 84.

CHAPTER X.

The Participle [1].

135. THE participle is in form a noun, but one partaking at the same time of the nature of the verb, inasmuch as it declares not the fixed and settled embodiment of an attribute in an individual object, but the *continuous manifestation*, actively or passively, as the case may be, of the idea expressed by the root. It predicates, therefore, a *state*, either (actively) constituted directly and essentially by the action or actions necessary to produce it, or (passively) conceived as the enduring result of a particular act. עָשׁוֹק designates simply the possessor of the attribute of oppressiveness, whether shewing it at the moment of speaking or not: עוֹשֵׁק describes one who is actually exhibiting it; עָשׁוּק one in whom a condition resulting from one or more definite acts is being experienced. So שָׁכֵן is *a dweller* or *resident*, שֹׁכֵן *dwelling ;* אַסִּיר *a prisoner* (the condition conceived generally), אָסוּר *emprisoned* (the condition conceived with reference to the action producing it). Possessing thus a distinct verbal force, the participle admits of being used where neither of the two special 'tenses' would be suitable, in the frequently recurring cases, namely, where stress is to be laid on the *continuance* of the action described. In itself it expresses no difference of time, the nature of the 'tenses' not favouring, as in Greek, the growth of a separate form corresponding to

---

[1] The aim of the present chapter is not to treat the syntax of the participle under all its aspects, but only in so far as it occupies a place, in its function as *predicate*, by the side of the two tenses.

each; and the period to which an action denoted by it is to be referred, is implied, not in the participle, but in the connexion in which it occurs. The Hebrew authors avail themselves of it very freely, but at the same time with such limitations and reserve that (as compared, e. g. with Syriac) it rarely fails of effect : its descriptive power is great; and if the narrative, strictly so called, of the O. T. owes much of its life and variety to the use of the bare imperfect (§§ 30, 31), many of the instances immediately following will shew to what an extent the truthful and animated representation of particular scenes is due to the appropriate use of the participle.

It is used accordingly—

(1) Of past time, whether independently to emphasize the duration of a given state—for instance, of a particular behaviour or frame of mind—or, with more immediate reference to the main narrative, to shew (if the expression may be allowed) the figures moving in the background: it is thus the form adopted commonly in ' circumstantial ' clauses for the purpose of bringing before the eye the scene in which some fresh transaction is to be laid. Thus Gen. 13, 7 the Canaanite and the Perizzite אָז יֹשֵׁב was then *dwelling* in the land. 37, 7 and behold, אֲנַחְנוּ מְאַלְּמִים we were *binding* sheaves in the field. 41, 1–3 (the progressive stages of a dream). 42, 23 that Joseph was *hearkening* (i. e. understood). Dt. 4, 12. Jud. 7, 13. 9, 43. 14, 4 for he was *seeking* an occasion etc. 1 Sa. 1, 13. 9, 11 הֵם עֹלִים *they* were *going up*, when they found. 13, 16. 2 Sa. 1, 6 and lo Saul נִשְׁעָן עַל חֲנִיתוֹ ἐρηρεδμένος. 12, 19 that his servants מִתְלַחֲשִׁים were *whispering*. 17, 17 (§ 120). 1 Ki. 1, 40. 22, 10. 12. 20 (*was saying* on this wise : cf. 3, 22. 26). Instances of *tableaux* : 2 Sa. 6, 14. 15. 13, 34. 15, 18. 23. 30. 16, 5. Of the use of the participle in circumstantial clauses, sufficient examples will be found in §§ 159, 160, 169.

(2) Of present time similarly: Gen. 4, 10. 16, 8b from

Sarai my mistress אָנֹכִי בֹּרַחַת am I *fleeing*. 37, 16 tell me
אֵיפֹה הֵם רֹעִים where they are *shepherding*. Nu. 11, 27 Eldad
and Medad מִתְנַבְּאִים are *prophesying* in the camp. Jud. 17, 9
אָנֹכִי הֹלֵךְ. 18, 18ᵇ. 1 Sa. 14, 11. Isa. 1, 7 your land, זָרִים
אֹכְלִים אֹתָהּ strangers are *devouring* it. 41, 17 מְבַקְשִׁים. Jer.
7, 17 f. 25, 31 נִשְׁפָּט הוּא¹. 37, 13. Ps. 3, 3. 4, 7. 42, 8. 45,
2. 56, 3.   And in Dt., in accordance with the situation presupposed by that book, 4, 5. 7, 1 whither *ye are going* to
possess it: also 4, 1 אֲשֶׁר אָנֹכִי מְלַמֵּד אֶתְכֶם which *I am teaching* you. 4, 40 which I מְצַוְּךָ am commanding thee this day.
5, 1. 8, 5 etc.

When there is nothing to imply that the state denoted by
the ptcp. extends beyond the moment of speaking, the force
of the phrase is as nearly as possible that of the true English
present²:—Jud. 9, 36 the shadow of the mountains *thou seest*
as men. 2 Sa. 18, 27. 1 Ki. 2, 16. 20 אָנֹכִי שֹׁאֶלֶת. 22. Jer.
1, 11. 13 al.

Obs. Less frequently, particularly in the earlier books, to denote not a
continuous state, but a fact liable to *recur* (which, in past and present
alike, is more properly expressed by the *impf.*, §§ 30–33): Gen. 39, 3. 6.
22 (contrast 1 Sa. 14, 47. 18, 5). Ex. 13, 15. 1 Ki. 3, 2 (8, 5 is different).
22, 44 and often מְנַבְּחִים. Esth. 2, 11. 13 בָּאָה. 14. 3, 2.

It is used, however, in the pregnant delineation of a *fixed character*,
for which, with such words as אֹהֵב, שׂוֹנֵא, יֹדֵעַ, בֹּטֵחַ, it is even better
adapted than the impf.: Pr. 10, 5. 17 מַתְעֶה. 11, 13. 15. 17. 12, 1. 10.
13, 3. 4. 24 etc. Jer. 17, 10 חֹקֵר לֵב = καρδιογνώστης. Nah. 1, 2.

The ptcp., it should be remembered, may be represented by the English 'present' in three separate cases, which need to be distinguished:

---

¹ Lit. is *in a state of controversy*: cf. 2 Sa. 19, 10 נָדוֹן, Job 23, 7 נוֹכָח,
Ex. 2, 13 נִצִּים, and the common נִלְחָם; also נַעֲנֶה Ez. 14, 7.

² It is worth noticing that a similar principle appears to have determined the form by which present time is expressed in Greek: in the
present tense, the stem is variously expanded and strengthened for the
purpose, most probably, of implying duration, as opposed to what is
merely momentary (λαμβάνω, λείπω by the side of ἔ-λαβ-ον, ἔ-λιπ-ον).
See Curtius, *The Greek Verb*, p. 10 (Engl. Tr.).

1. when it expresses real duration (Ps. 7, 12. 19, 2. 29, 5. 7) ; 2. when it is in apposition to a preceding subst. (18, 34 f. (that) *maketh.* 65, 7 f.) ; 3. when it denotes a general truth (37, 12. 21. 26). This last usage is a mark of the later period of the language : even Ps. 34, 8. 21. 23. 69, 34. 145, 15 f. 146, 7–9. 147, 6. 9. 11 will be felt to differ from Pr. 10, 5 etc. cited above ; and the earlier Psalmists cast their descriptions of the Divine dealings into a different form.

(3) The ptcp. is used, lastly, of future time (the *fut. instans*), which it represents as already beginning : hence, if the event designated can only in fact occur after some interval, it asserts forcibly and suggestively the certainty of its approach. In the latter case, however, its use is (naturally) pretty much restricted to announcements of the Divine purpose ; but even then, whether an imminent or still distant realization be what is intended, is not contained in the form employed, but remains for the event to disclose. When applied to the future, the ptcp. is very frequently strengthened by an introductory הִנֵּה.

Gen. 6, 17 and I, הִנְנִי מֵבִיא behold *I am bringing* etc. ; the same formula often : 15, 14 the nation which they shall serve דָּן אָנֹכִי *I am judging.* 17, 19 Sarah thy wife יֹלֶדֶת *will bear* thee a son. 18, 17. 19, 13 for we *are destroying* (are about to destroy) this place. 41, 25ᵇ עֹשֶׂה. 28ᵇ. Ex. 9, 3 behold the hand of Yahweh הוֹיָה. 18. 10, 4. Dt. 1, 20. 25 which Yahweh thy God נֹתֵן is *giving* us ; so constantly in this book : 4, 14 and often אַתֶּם עוֹבְרִים. 1 Sa. 3, 11. 12, 16 which Yahweh *is doing* before your eyes. 19, 11 מָחָר אַתָּה מוּמָת. 20, 36 which I *am about* to shoot. 2 Sa. 12, 23ᵇ. 20, 21 מֻשְׁלָךְ (after הנה). 1 Ki. 13, 2 הנה־בן נוֹלָד. 3 נקרע. 2 Ki. 2, 3. 7, 2ᶜ. 22, 20 ; in the prophets continually : Isa. 3, 1. 5, 5. 7, 14 הרה וְיוֹלֶדֶת בן. 10, 23. 33. 13, 17. 26, 21 (Mic. 1, 3). 37, 7. 43, 19 הִנְנִי עֹשֶׂה etc. See also § 137.

Obs. 1. But the participle, after הנה, does not necessarily refer to the future : whether it does so or not in a particular case must be determined by a regard to the context, and to the signification borne by that particle. הנה introduces something specially arresting the attention ; accordingly

the ptcp. following it may, when linked to a preceding narrative by
וְ, describe a scene in the past, as Jud. 9, 43. 11, 34. 1 Ki. 19, 5. Ez.
47, 1; or it may describe an occurrence in the present, Jud. 9, 36. 1 Sa.
14, 33; in a passage such as Isa. 24, 1, however, there would be no
motive for the combination, if the past were referred to.

Obs. 2. The copula must sometimes be conceived in a jussive or conditional sense: Isa. 12, 5 Kt. מְיֻדַּעַת זֹאת *be this* made known in all the
earth, and (often) with בָּרוּךְ and אָרוּר; in a real, or virtual, apodosis
Jer. 2, 22 נִכְתָּם. Ps. 27, 3[b] (§ 143). Job 23, 7 there an upright man
would be disputing with him (§ 142), and after לֹו, § 145.

(4) As a rule the subject *precedes* the ptcp., the opposite
order being exceptional, and only adopted when a certain
stress falls naturally on the idea conveyed by the verbal form
(for instance, in assigning a reason after כִּי): Gen. 18, 17
9, הֲרֹאֶה אַתָּה Ez. 8, 6. הַמְקַנֵּא אַתָּה לִי Nu. 11, 29. הַמְכַסֶּה אֲנִי
8; Gen. 3, 5 כִּי יֹדֵעַ אֱלֹהִים. 19, 13. 27, 46 אִם (see also § 137).
30, 1. 41, 32. Jud. 2, 22. 8, 4. 19, 18. 1 Sa. 3, 9. 13 כִּי
שֹׁפֵט אֲנִי. 19, 2. 23, 10. 2 Sa. 15, 27 (as Ez. 8, 6,—if the text
be correct). Isa. 36, 11 כִּי שֹׁמְעִים אֲנַחְנוּ. 48, 13 קֹרֵא אֲנִי. 52, 12.
Jer. 1, 12. 3, 6. 38, 14 שֹׁאֵל אֲנִי. 26 (of past time). 44, 29.

Obs. In many of these cases the subject is a pronoun: and in Aramaic,
as in the idiom of the Mishnah, this usage is extended much further, a
regular *present tense* being formed by the union of the pronouns of the
first and second persons with the participle into a single word. But in
Biblical Hebrew the parts are quite distinct; and the predicate is able
accordingly to receive a separate emphasis of its own, for which in this
compound idiom there is no scope. On the usage of the Mishnah, see
Geiger, *Lehrbuch zur Sprache der Mischnah*, p. 40; Strack and Siegfried,
Lehrbuch der Neuhebräischen Sprache und Litteratur, 1884, p. 82.

It is in order to reproduce as closely as possible the Aramaic form
אֲמֵינָא—אָמֵן אֲמֵינָא being contracted from אָמַר אֲנָא (Dan. 4, 4)—most
probably used by Christ, that in Delitzsch's N. T. λέγω ὑμῖν (after ἀμὴν)
is rendered by אֹמֵר אֲנִי (which does not so occur in O. T.): see the
Luth. Zeitschrift, 1856, p. 423, or the *Academy*, Nov. 1879, p. 395 (where
S. John's ἀμὴν ἀμὴν is explained as due to the attempt to represent the
phrase in Greek letters).

(5) Occasionally the idea of duration conveyed by the
ptcp. is brought into fuller prominence, and defined more

precisely, by the addition of the *substantive verb*. Two cases may be distinguished, according, namely, as the state thus described is conceived implicitly in its relation to some other event, or stands upon an independent footing. Of the former, some four or five instances will be found in most of the earlier books : the latter is rarer. But altogether the more *frequent* use of the combination is characteristic of the later writers—in the decadence of a language, the older forms are felt to be insufficient, and a craving for greater distinctness manifests itself : the rarer, however, its occurrence in the earlier books, the more carefully it deserves notice.

Gen. 4, 17. 37, 2 הָיָה רֹעֶה *was shepherding* (at the time when the events about to be described took place). 39, 22. 1 Sa. 2, 11 הָיָה מְשָׁרֵת. 7, 10. 18, 14. 29. 23, 26 נֶחְפָּז ... וַיְהִי 2 Sa. 3, 6. 8, 15. 19, 10. 1 Ki. 5, 1. 24. 12, 6. 20, 40 (let the student note instances in 2 Ki. for himself !). Jer. 26, 18. 20. Job 1, 14.

Some clear examples of the second usage are Gen. 1, 6 וִיהִי מַבְדִּיל *and let it be* (permanently) *dividing*. Ruth 2, 19. Nu. 14, 33. Dt. 9, 7 from the day etc. until this place מַמְרִים הֱיִיתֶם *ye have* been rebelling ; so *vv.* 22. 24. 31, 27[1]; 28, 29 וְהָיִיתָ מְמַשֵּׁשׁ and thou *shalt be groping* etc. Isa. 2, 2. 9, 15? 14, 2[b]. 30, 20 and thine eyes *shall be beholding* thy teachers. 59, 2. Ps. 10, 14. 122, 2. With a *passive* ptcp., 1 Ki. 13, 24 Nah. 3, 11. Jer. 14, 16. 18, 23. Ps. 73, 14 ואהי נגוע. Josh. 10, 26 ויהיו תלוים.

Contrast examples from Nehemiah[2], 1, 4[b]. 2, 13. 15. 3, 26.

---

[1] The idiom in these four passages may be attributed fairly to the desire for emphasis, which is evident : 2 Sa. 3, 17 הייתם מבקשים is an early parallel, cf. also 7, 6. (Contr. Ryssel, *De Elohistae Pentateuchi Sermone*, pp. 27, 58.)

[2] But it does not appear to be correct to say here it 'nihil differre a verbo finito' (Ryssel, p. 59): it is used clearly with the intention of giving prominence to the idea of duration, though an earlier writer would not have done this so persistently, or confined himself so much to the same idiom. Comp. Mark 13, 25 ἔσονται ἐκπίπτοντες : Winer, § 45. 5.

4, 10. 5, 18 הָיָה נַעֲשֶׂה. 6, 14[b]. 19. 13, 5. 22. 26 : Esth. 1, 22.
9, 21 with לִהְיוֹת.

(6) As a rule, the subject to the ptcp. is in Hebrew expressed separately : but scattered instances are met with in
which (as in 3rd pers. of the verb, p. 7) this is not the case.
The subject to be supplied may be either indefinite, or definite—most commonly the former, except when the ptcp. is
introduced by הנה, the subject itself having been named immediately before. (1) Gen. 39, 22[a] עשׂים[1]. Ex. 5, 16 and
bricks, אמרים לנו עשׂו *say they* to us, Make ye. Isa. 21, 11
קֹרֵא *one is calling.* 24, 2 the lender כַּאֲשֶׁר נֹשֶׁא בוֹ as he to
whom *any one* lendeth[2]. 26, 3[b]. 30, 24 which זֹרֶה *one is sifting*
etc. 32, 12 סוֹפְדִים. 33, 4[b] שֹׁקֵק. Jer. 33, 5 בָּאִים. 38, 23
מוֹצִיאִים. Ez. 8, 12 כִּי אמרים. 13, 7. Job 41, 18[3]. Neh. 6, 10[b]
כִּי בָאִים. (2) with הנה Gen. 24, 30. 37, 15[4] and a man found
him וְהִנֵּה תֹעֶה בַשָּׂדֶה. 41, 1. 1 Sa. 10, 11. 15, 12. 16, 11.
30, 3. 16. Isa. 29, 8. Ez. 7, 10 al. הנה בָאָה (cf. Ex. 7, 15. 8,
16 הנה יֹצֵא). 19, 13. Amos 7, 1 ; without הנה, Gen. 32, 7.
Dt. 33, 3. 1 Sa. 6, 3[5]. 17, 25. 20, 1. Isa. 33, 5[a] שֹׁכֵן. 40,
19[b]. Ps. 22, 29[b] וּמֹשֵׁל *and he ruleth.* 33, 5. 37, 26. 97, 10.
Neh. 9, 3[b]. 37[b][6].

Obs. 1. It is sometimes uncertain whether the ptcp. may have been
conceived by the writer as an independent predicate, or in apposition to

---

[1] Expressed as vaguely as possible, in intentional contrast to 22[b],
where (as Roorda, § 379, remarks) the use of היה allows an emphasis to
the *pronoun.*

[2] A comparison of Dt. 24, 11 will make the construction clear.

[3] (When) *one approacheth him* (cf. § 126) with the sword, it continueth
(holdeth) not : cf. 2 Sa. 23, 3 (§ 125). Pr. 28, 27. חרב is the 'accusative
of nearer limitation,' defining the *manner* in which the approach is
made : cf. Mic. 7, 2 חרם. Ps. 64, 8 חץ (Ew. §§ 279[c], 283[a]).

[4] In accordance with the use of הנה in other cases, e. g. 16, 14. 18, 9.
1 Ki. 21, 18.

[5] But here אַתֶּם has prob. dropped out after משׁלחים ; cf. LXX, Pesh.

[6] Comp. Pusey on Hab. 1, 5 ; Delitzsch on Job 25, 2 (which passage
itself, however, it seems better to construe, with Hitzig, as explained,
§ 161, *Obs.* 2) ; Ew. § 200. Some additional instances might be given
from the books not named : but they would not be numerous.

a subject previously named, or in his mind : Isa. 40, 29 (prob. the latter). Job 12, 17. 19-24. Ps. 107, 40 ; and of course Am. 5, 8ª (notice the *cstr. st.*).

Obs. 2. A strange extension (as it would seem) of this usage is met with occasionally : Jer. 2, 17 בְּעֵת מוֹלִיכֵךְ in the time *of (him) leading thee* in the wilderness. Ez. 27, 34 עֵת נִשְׁבֶּרֶת in the time *of (thee) broken* (=what time thou art broken : but here, in all probability, עַתָּ נִשְׁבַּרְתְּ should be read, with LXX, Targ. Vulg. and most moderns. Cf. 36, 13 יַעַן אֹמְרִים because of (men) saying to you ; but here also it is doubtful whether the true reading is not אָמְרָם, in accordance with Ez.'s usual construction of יַעַן, the *plena scriptio* having been introduced by error : cf. *Notes on Samuel*, pp. xxxiii f., 16, 22). Gen. 38, 29 כְּמֵשִׁיב is so destitute of Biblical analogy to support it[1] that it is difficult not to think that כְּהָשִׁיב should be restored (the suffix omitted, as 19, 29. 24, 30 and elsewhere)[2]. At the same time, the construction of the text is one tolerably common in the Mishnah; and it is *possible* that it may be an isolated anticipation of the later usage. See Weiss, *Studien über die Sprache der Mischna* [in Hebrew], Wien, 1867 (referred to by Ryssel, p. 29), who cites (p. 89) *Terumoth* 4, 8 בְּיָדוּעַ (=ידוע) בהיותו : the negative in the next line is (וכשאינו ידוע); 10, 1 and elsewhere בִּנוֹתֵן טַּעַם = when it gives a flavour ; *Shabbath* 2, 5 כְּהָס עַל הַנֵּר (= כהיות חס) when he attends to the lamp, etc.

Obs. 3. Instances even occur of an *impersonal* use of the passive ptcp. : at least the passages following are most probably to be so explained : Ps. 87, 3 מְדֻבָּר בָּךְ *it is spoken* (=one speaketh) of thee glorious things[3]. Mal. 1, 11 מֻקְטָר מֻגָּשׁ *lit.* it is incensed, it is offered to my name. Ez. 40, 17. 41, 18. 19. 46, 23 עָשׂוּי.

(7) When the *article* is joined to the ptcp., it ceases to be a mere predicate, and acquires altogether a new emphasis and force : indeed, inasmuch as the article marks that which is *known* and of which something hitherto unknown is pre-

---

[1] Ps. 74, 5 (even though, as is less probable, יודע be neuter). Isa. 17, 5ᵇ are not parallel.

[2] Hitz., followed by Dillm., adds 40, 10 (כהיות פ'=כפורחת), in which case the verse must be rendered 'and it (cas. pend.), *as it was budding*, its blossoms shot forth :' but the comparative sense of כ (Rashi, A. V.) seems simpler and more natural.

[3] The *accus.*, as frequently with a passive *verb*, e. g. Job 22, 9 וזרועות יתומים ידכא and *it is bruised* (=one bruiseth) the arms of the orphans. See Ewald, § 295ᵇ ; Ges.-Kautzsch, § 121. 1.

dicated[1], it is rather to be regarded as the *subject*[2]. Dt. 3, 21
עֵינֶיךָ הָרֹאֹת thine eyes—not *were seeing* רֹאֹת, but—were *those
which saw:* so 4, 3. 11, 7; 8, 18 ὅτι οὗτός ἐστιν ὁ διδοὺς σοί.
Isa. 14, 27 יָדוֹ הַנְּטוּיָה his hand is *that which is stretched out*
(which was spoken of, *v.* 26). 66, 9 אֲנִי הַמַּשְׁבִּיר. Zech. 7, 6[b] ye
are *the eaters* (alluded to, *v.* 6[a]). Gen. 2, 11. 45, 12[b]. Nu. 7, 2.
1 Sa. 4, 16. Ez. 20, 29. Once or twice, peculiarly, after אֲשֶׁר:
1 Ki. 12, 8 who were *those which stood* before him. 21, 11.

It need scarcely be remarked that in passages such as
Ps. 18, 33 the article is resumptive,—32[b] and who a rock
except our God? *the God who* girdeth me etc. 48. 19, 11
הַנֶּחֱמָדִים *which* (10[b]) *are more desirable* than gold [A. V. is the
rendering of נחמדים הם]. 33, 15. 49, 7 *who trust* . . . (taking
עֹקְבִי 6[b] in a personal sense). 94, 10[b]. Job 6, 16. 28, 4 הַנִּשְׁכָּחִים
men who are forgotten etc. (in appos. with the subj. of the preceding פָּרַץ, conceived collectively). 30, 3 *men who* gnaw the
dry ground. 4. Gen. 49, 21 *he that giveth* etc. (in apposition
with נפתלי). Cf. Isa. 40, 22 (in appos. with a subj. implicit in
the prophet's thought). 26. 44, 26[b]–28. Amos 5, 8[b]–9.

Obs. A unique form of expression occurs Isa. 11, 9 כַּמַּיִם לַיָּם מְכַסִּים
lit. as the waters, coverers to the sea. Construed thus as a noun, but
with the לְ of reference, not a following genit., the ptcp. retains still the
freshness of the verb, and has an independence which is commoner in
Arabic than in Hebrew. The nearest parallel in O. T. is Nu. 10, 25
(cited by Ewald, § 292[e])מְאַסֵּף לְכָל־הַמַּחֲנֹת: cf. also 25, 18 צוררים הם לכם.
Dt. 4, 42 והוא לא שֹׂנֵא לוֹ and he being *a not-hater to him* aforetime.
Isa. 14, 2. But the peculiar compactness and force of Isaiah's phrase is
due to the position which he has boldly given it at the end: Habakkuk
in his imitation (2, 14) is satisfied to use an ordinary Hebrew idiom.
In Arabic comp. وَهِيَ مُجَانِبَةٌ لَهُ *eâ illum vitante*, and (where the *order*
is the same) Qor. 15, 9 إِنَّا لَهُ لَحَافِظُونَ lo, of that we (will be) keepers.
12, 81. (Ewald, *Gr. Arab.* § 652; Wright, *Arab. Gr.* ii. § 31 rem.)

---

[1] Hence its name with the Jewish grammarians, הֵא הַיְדִיעָה.
[2] Comp. Mark 13, 11; and Moulton's note on Winer, § 18. 7. See
also below, § 199.

CHAPTER XI.

Hypotheticals.

136. WE arrive at the last part of our subject—the forms assumed in Hebrew by *hypothetical* or conditional sentences. In general, it will be seen, these involve no fresh principles; so that, as the nature of the tenses, and the constructions of which they are capable, have been already fully explained, it will be sufficient in most cases simply to enunciate their different types, without further elucidation beyond such as is afforded by illustrative examples.

I. *If I see him* (the time at which this is imagined as possibly taking place not being further indicated, but belonging either to the real, or to the potential, future), *I will let him know.*

With an *imperfect* in the protasis. The apodosis may then be expressed:

(*a*) By ן consecutive and the perfect; so very frequently:
—Gen. 18, 26 . . . . וְנָשָׂ֫אתִי . . . . אִם אֶמְצָא *if I shall find* (or simply *if I find*) fifty righteous in Sodom, *I will pardon* the whole place for their sakes. 24, 8. 28, 20 f. (cf. Nu. 21, 2. Jud. 11, 30 f.). 32, 9 אִם־יָב֫וֹא עֵשָׂו אֶל־הַמַּחֲנֶה הָאַחַת וְהִכָּ֫הוּ וְהָיָה וג' *if* Esau *come* to one camp and smite[1] it, the remaining camp *will* escape. 18 f. (כִּי). Ex. 19, 5. 23, 22 . . . אִם־שָׁמ֫וֹעַ תִּשְׁמַע בְּקֹלוֹ

---

[1] § 115, p. 130. Observe that it is only the sense which shews that the apodosis begins with והיה, and not with והכהו. The same ambiguity of form occurs constantly in this type of hypothetical sentence in Hebrew.

כִּי־יִשְׁאָלְךָ . . . וְאָמַרְתָּ וג' .Nu. 30, 7 f. Dt. 6, 20 f.

כִּי יִמָּכֵר לְךָ אָחִיךָ וַעֲבָדְךָ שֵׁשׁ שָׁנִים 15, 12 (see Ex. 21, 2). 19, 8 f.

וְאִם־רָעָה תִמָּצֵא (כִּי). Jud. 6, 37. 1 Sa. 14, 9 f. 1 Ki. 1, 52ᵇ

כִּי יֶחֶטְאוּ . . . וְאָנַפְתָּ בָם וּנְתַתָּם 46–49 . . . (כִּי). 8, 44 f. בּוֹ וָמֵת

וְשָׁבוּם . . . וְהֵשִׁיבוּ אֶל־לִבָּם . . . וְשָׁבוּ וְהִתְחַנְּנוּ . . . וְשָׁבוּ . . . וְהִתְפַּלְלוּ . . .

וְשָׁמַעְתָּ וג' *when* they sin, and thou art angry with them, and thou givest them up etc. . . . and they return . . . and pray . . . , *then* hear thou etc. Ps. 89, 31–33 אִם יַעַזְבוּ . . . וּפָקַדְתִּי. Job 8, 18. Qoh. 4, 11 etc.

Obs. 1. The verb is sometimes separated from the וֹ, and so lapses into the imperfect :—Ex. 8, 22 (§ 124). Josh. 20, 5. 2 Chr. 7, 13 f. וַאֲנִי (after a long protasis); Pr. 19, 19. Job 14, 7—both וְעוּר.

Obs. 2. Note that in A.V. *then* of the apodosis represents nearly always וֹ, not אָז: the latter introduces the apodosis only very rarely, where a special emphasis is desired, Isa. 58, 14. Pr. 2, 5; Job 9, 31 (§ 138, i. β), or in a different case, § 139.

(β) By the impf. (without וֹ); this likewise is very frequent, and not distinguishable in meaning from a¹ :—Gen. 18, 28. 30. לֹא אֶעֱשֶׂה אִם־אֶמְצָא שָׁם שְׁלֹשִׁים 42, 37. Ex. 21, 2 (כִּי). Dt. 12, 20. 13, 2–4. 7–9. 20, 19 (all כִּי). Jud. 13, 16. 1 Ki. 1. אִם יִהְיֶה לְבֶן־חַיִל לֹא יִפֹּל מִשַּׂעֲרָתוֹ אָרְצָה 52ᵃ. Isa. 1, 19. 3, 6 f. (כִּי). Ob. 5, cf. Jer. 49, 9ᵃ (9ᵇ, pf. as γ). Jer. 38, 15 (כִּי). Ps. 75, 3 (כִּי). 132, 12. Pr. 4, 16 unless they do evil לֹא יִשְׁנוּ they *do not* (freq., or *cannot*) sleep.

(β*) The simple imperfect may of course be replaced if necessary by a voluntative or imperative :—Dt. 12, 29 f. (כִּי). 17, 14 f. 1 Sa. 20, 21. 21, 10 if thou wilt take *that*², take it. 2 Ki. 2, 10 etc.

---

¹ The type (a) is, however, used by preference, where there is scope for it : (β) is used chiefly (1) when the apodosis precedes the protasis ; (2) when the apodosis begins with לֹא—both cases in which the perf. with וֹ could manifestly not be employed (see 1 Ki. 52ᵃ and ᵇ, cited above).

² אוֹתָהּ is here emphatic : cf. 18, 17. 20, 9. Isa. 43, 22. Jud. 14, 3 : also Ex. 21, 8 Qrê לוֹ (in contrast to לְבְנוֹ, *v.* 9 ; comp. the position of אֶל עִיר, 2 Sa. 17, 13).

With וְ prefixed, very rare:—Gen. 13, 9. 2 Sa. 12, 8.

(γ) By the perfect alone [1] (expressing the certainty and suddenness with which the result immediately accompanies the occurrence of the protasis):—Nu. 32, 23 וְאִם־לֹא תַעֲשׂוּן כֵּן הִנֵּה חֲטָאתֶם and if you do not so, see you *have sinned!* 1 Sa. 2, 16 and if not, לָקַחְתִּי *I take* it by force! cf. Ez. 33, 6 נִלְקָח. Hos. 12, 12 (היו in apod., 'of the certain future'). Job 20, 12–14: comp. 9, 27 f.[2] Cf. after the indefinite אֲשֶׁר Gen. 24, 14 הֹכַחְתָּ.

Obs. Compare the manner in which the perfect is found, not indeed in a formal apodosis, but still with a reference to some preceding conditional clause—implicitly if not explicitly stated. Lev. 13, 25 פרחה. 17, 3 f. the apodosis proper ends at ההוא: then follow the words דם שפך i.e. *he has* (in the case assumed) *shed* blood (cf. § 17). Nu. 19, 13 טמא. 20. 15, 25 והם הביאו (when the directions *v.* 24 have been observed, they *will have* brought their offering). Ez. 33, 5.

(δ) By a participle:—Gen. 4, 7. Lev. 21, 9.

Without any verb in the apodosis:—Gen. 4, 24 וְ. Ps. 8, 4 f. 120, 7. Qoh. 10, 11 וְ.

Slightly different are 1 Sa. 6, 9 if it goeth up by Bethshe-

---

[1] With this use of the perfect compare in Greek Plat. Krat. 432 A ὥσπερ καὶ αὐτὰ τὰ δέκα ἢ ὅστις βούλει ἄλλος ἀριθμός, ἐὰν ἀφέλῃς τι ἢ προσθῇς, ἕτερος εὐθὺς γέγονε. Soph. Phil. 1280 εἰ δὲ μή τι πρὸς καιρὸν λέγων Κυρῶ πέπαυμαι. The *aorist* is also similarly met with, as Il. xvii. 99. Phileb. 17 D ὅταν γὰρ ταῦτα λάβῃς οὕτω, τότε ἐγένου σοφός. Gorg. 484 etc., on which the remark of Riddell, *Apology of Plato*, p. 154, is worth quoting : 'The subjunctive construction with ἄν, not admissible with a past Tense, constrains us to see in the Aorist the expression of an action *instantaneously complete, rather than necessarily past.*' Compare Winer, § 40. 4[b], also 5[b], who quotes Livy xxi. 43 si eundem animum habuerimus, *vicimus.*

In English, the *present* is sometimes used with the same object: Shakespeare, *Ant. and Cl.* ii. 5. 26 If thou say so, villain, thou *kill'st* thy mistress. Milton, *P. L.* 5, 613.

[2] Where, for אמרתי, אם אמרתי, אם אמרי might have been expected, and ought perhaps to be restored; comp., however, the use of the inf. Jud. 19, 9. 2 Sa. 15, 20. Jer. 9, 5. Zeph. 3, 20. Zech. 9, 10[b]. Ps. 23, 6 (וְשַׁבְתִּי).

mesh, עָשָׂה הוּא HE *hath done* us this great evil. 1 Ki. 22, 28 if thou returnest לֹא דִבֶּר י״י בִּי Yahweh *hath not spoken* by me. Nu. 16, 29. Ez. 14, 9[a]: cf. Luke 11, 20.

Obs. Occasionally the imperfect is thus found in the protasis in reference to *past* time :—Gen. 31, 8 אִם יֹאמַר *if ever* he said . . . , וְיָלְדוּ then all the flock *would* bear etc. Ex. 40, 37 (apod. וְלֹא יִסְעוּ); cf. Jud. 12, 5, and the impff. in Job 31, alternating with perff. These differ from Gen. 38, 9. Nu. 21, 9. Jud. 2, 18[a] (כִּי). Ps. 78, 34, where the *perfect* is used : 'and it came to pass, *if* or *when* the serpents *had* bitten a man, that he looked, and lived,'—the idea of repetition is dropped from the protasis, and retained only in the pff. with ו, which introduce the apodosis.

137. Sometimes the participle is found in the protasis— accompanied or not by יֵשׁ or אֵין : the apodosis may then be introduced by—

(*a*) The perfect and ו:—Gen. 24, 42 f. אִם־יֶשְׁךָ־נָּא מַצְלִיחַ דַּרְכִּי הִנֵּה אָנֹכִי נִצָּב . . . וְהָיָה וג׳ . . . *if* thou art prospering my way . . . , behold, (as) I stand by the spring of water, *let it be* (§ 119 δ), etc.[1] Lev. 3, 7. Jud. 6, 36 f. (וְיָדַעְתִּי=*may* I know, § 119 δ, cf. 39 יְהִי־נָא). 11, 9 אִם מְשִׁיבִים אַתֶּם אוֹתִי . . . וְנָתַן י״י אוֹתָם לְפָנַי if you are *going to* bring me back . . . , Yahweh will deliver them up before me.

(β) The imperfect :—Lev. 3, 1. 2 Ki. 7, 2. 19 (after הנה).

(β*) A voluntative or imperative :—Gen. 20, 7. 24, 49. 43, 4, Ex. 33, 15. Jud. 9, 15. Jer. 42, 13 (apod. 15 ועתה).

(δ) Another participle :—Ex. 8, 17. 9, 2 f. 1 Sa. 19, 11. Jer. 26, 15.

138. II. *If I have seen him* (i. till any time in the indefinite or more or less remote future : ii. during a period extending up to the moment of speaking, or to a moment otherwise fixed by the context), *I will let him know.* In the first of these cases the sense conveyed by the perfect is hardly distinguishable from that borne by the imperfect, § 136 (though

---

[1] Notice here the double, and in Jud. 6, 36 f. the *treble*, protasis (one expressed by הנה).

it does not occur so frequently); but it rather contemplates the case assumed *after* its occurrence (*si videro*, § 17, not *si videbo*). Observe that in i. the principal verb is succeeded in the protasis by perfects with *waw* consec. (Gen. 43, 9. Job 11, 13 f.), while in ii. it is succeeded by the impf. and ·וֹ.

i. (*a*) With the pf. and *waw* consecutive in the apodosis :—— as Gen. 43, 9 וְהָטָ֫אתִי ... אִם לֹא הֲבִיאֹתִיו si non *reduxero*, per omnem vitam reus *ero* (cf. 42, 37). 47, 6. Jud. 16, 17 אִם גֻּלַּ֫חְתִּי וְסָר מִמֶּ֫נִּי כֹחִי if I am shaven, my strength *will* depart from me. 2 Sa. 15, 33 LXX ἐὰν μὲν διαβῇς μετ᾽ ἐμοῦ, καὶ ἔσῃ ἐπ᾽ ἐμὲ εἰς βάσταγμα (where καὶ is really superfluous). 2 Ki. 7, 4 אִם אָמַ֫רְנוּ נָבוֹא הָעִיר וָמַ֫תְנוּ שָׁם Vulg. sive ingredi *voluerimus* civitatem, fame *moriemur:* sive *manserimus* hic, moriendum nobis est. Mic. 5, 7ᵇ. Job 7, 4 if (at any time) I lie down, וְאָמַ֫רְתִּי¹ *I say*, When shall I get up? (waiting wearily for the morning). 13 f. when (כִּי) I say etc., וְחִתַּתַּ֫נִי *then thou terrifiest me* with dreams. 10, 14 if I sin, thou watchest me. 21, 6.

(β) With the impf. alone in the apodosis :——Dt. 32, 41 אִם שַׁנּוֹתִי if (at any time) *I have whet* (or simply *I whet*) my glittering sword וְתֹאחֵז so that² my hand takes hold on judgment, אָשִׁיב *I will requite* vengeance etc. Ps. 41, 7. 63, 7. 94, 18 if (at any time) אמרתי *I say*, My foot hath slipped, thy mercy *will hold* (or *holdeth*, freq.) me up. Pr. 9, 12ᵇ (אם understood from 12ᵃ, exactly as in Job 10, 15ᵇ from 15ᵃ; cf. 16, 6. 22, 23ᵇ). Job 9, 30 f. (וְהַזִּכּוֹתִי, §§ 104, 115; אז, p. 175). With וֹ (anomalous) Qoh. 10, 10.

(β*) With an imperative :——Pr. 25, 21. Job 11, 13 f.

(γ) With the perfect alone :——Isa. 40, 7. Jer. 49, 9ᵇ.

And without any verb in the apodosis :——Jer. 14, 18 (וְהִנֵּה). Pr. 24, 14 (וְיֵשׁ).

---

¹ Tone as Ps. 28, 1, § 104.

² According to §§ 61, 62 : were it meant as a *mere* continuation of שנותי, the pf. ואחזה, as the other examples shew, would have been the form employed. (On the *tone* of שנותי, comp. Delitzsch on Job 19, 17.)

ii. As already stated, this class of instances differs from those cited under i. in the nature of the *protasis:* a few examples will make it ·plain in what the difference consists. The apodosis may commence :—

(*a*) With the perfect and וְ:—Gen. 33, 10. Nu. 5, 27 אִם נִטְמְאָה וַתִּמְעֹל וּבָ֫אוּ וג' if she *have* defiled herself *and been faith-less, then shall* they come etc. 15, 24 if it *have been* done (the other case follows *v.* 27 in the imperfect), וְעָשׂוּ etc. 35, 22–24 וְאִם . . . הֲדָפוֹ and if (in the assumed case) *he have hit* him unexpectedly וַיָּמֹת *and he have died,* וְשָׁפְטוּ the congregation *shall* judge.

(β) With the imperfect :—Nu. 30, 6. Jer. 33, 25 f. if I have not made a covenant with the day (as I have done), אֶמְאַס I will also reject the seed of Jacob etc. Ez. 33, 9, cf. 8.

(β*) With a voluntative or imperative :—Jud. 9, 16–19 if ye *have* done honestly (foll. by וְ), rejoice in Abimélekh ! 1 Sa. 26, 19. Ps. 7, 4 f. Job 31, 5 f. 9. 20 f. 39 f.

(γ) With the perfect alone :—Ez. 3, 19 הִצַּ֫לְתָּ (*wilt have* delivered) : cf. Job 33, 23–5.

Obs. The perfect with אם or או is thus met with in *subordinate* hypothetical clauses; so Ex. 21, 36 נוֹדַע או but *if it be known* (a case supposed to have occurred under the conditions stated 35ᵃ). 22, 2 if the sun *have risen.* Lev. 4, 23 si confessus fuerit. 28. 5, 1 או רָאָה או יָדָע. 3–5 or when it touches etc. and it be hidden from him, *but he have* (afterwards) *ascertained it* and be guilty, or when etc. (4 pro-pounding a similar possibility) וְהָיָה *then it shall be,* when etc. 21–23 או מָצָא. 13, 2 f. when there is . . . and the priest sees it . . . and the hair הָפַךְ *have turned* white ; so repeatedly in this chapter after הִנֵּה. Num. 35, 16–18. 20 f. if יֶהְדָּפֶ֫נּוּ he hit him in hatred—או הִשְׁלִיךְ whether he *have thrown* something at him insidiously, או הִכָּ֫הוּ or *have smitten* him with his hand (two alternatives possible under the assumed case of hatred) וְיָמֹת *and he die,* מוֹת יוּמָת he shall be put to death.

139. III. *If I had seen him, I would have told him* (εἰ εἶδον ἀνήγγειλα ἄν· the protasis is supposed not to have been realized, and consequently the apodosis does not take place). For this case Hebrew uses the *perfect* in both clauses, mostly after לוּ Jud. 8, 19 if you had kept them alive (which you did not do) לֹא הָרַנְתִי I should not have killed you οὐκ ἂν ἀπέκτεινα ὑμᾶς (as I am just going to do : not *I should not kill you* οὐκ ἂν ἀπέκτεινον, which would be אהרג, because Gideon has in his mind the time when the action will have been completed). 13, 23 ; or (with a negative) (לוּלֵא) לוּלֵי *if not* 14, 18. 1 Sa. 25, 34 as Yahweh liveth ..., כִּי לוּלֵי מִהַרְתְּ וַתָּבֹאתִי כִּי אִם־נוֹתַר (I say) that, unless thou *hadst hastened and come,* that[1] there *had* not *been left* to Nabal etc. (as now there will be left). 2 Sa. 2, 27 as God liveth כִּי לוּלֵא דְּבַּרְתָּ כִּי אָז מֵהַבֹּקֶר נַעֲלָה וּג׳ (I say) that, *unless* thou hadst spoken, that then (only) after the morning *would* the people *have gotten themselves up,* etc. 19, 7 (likewise with אז in the apod.). Isa. 1, 9. Ps. 94, 17. 106, 23 (apod. put first, as אמרתי Dt. 32, 26, but being connected with what precedes it appears in the form וַיֹּאמֶר, otherwise it would be אָמַר as in Dt.). 119, 92 (without a verb : apod. introduced by אָז). 124, 1–3[2] (apod. introduced by אֲזַי) ; rarely after אִם Ps. 73, 15, or (in the later language) after אִלּוּ Esth. 7, 4.

140. Where no apodosis follows, the perfect with לוּ may denote a *wish*—one, however, which has not been realized.

Num. 14, 2 לוּ מַתְנוּ. 20, 3. Josh. 7, 7 וְלוּ הוֹאַלְנוּ וַנֵּשֶׁב. Isa. 48, 18 f. לוּא הִקְשַׁבְתָּ *O that thou hadst* hearkened to my commandments ! וַיְהִי and so (= then) thy peace had been like a

---

[1] The first כי introduces, as often (e.g. 26, 16. 29, 6. 2 Sa. 3, 35), the assertion following the oath : the second כי is merely *resumptive* of the first, after the clause with לולי ; so 2 Sa. 2, 27. 19, 7, and similarly Gen. 22, 16 f. 2 Sa. 3, 9. Jer. 22, 24, and frequently. Elsewhere the אם belongs to, and slightly strengthens, the כי, as 2 Sa. 15, 21 Kt. (but Qrê omits אם, prob. rightly). 2 Ki. 5, 20 ; also Jud. 15, 7. 1 Sa. 21, 6.

[2] With the pleon. שׁ here (לולי יהוה שהיה לנו) comp. the Aram. ܐܠܟ ܠܐ ܡܕܡ ܚܣܝܢ *except that* 2 Sa. 2, 27. Ps. 106, 23 (ܐܠܟ ܠܐ ܦ), אִילוּלֵי דִי id. Targ. Ps. 27, 13 and here (ܦܡ), אִילמָלֵי דִי id. Cant. 4, 12. Ps. 106, 23 (בסערנא), and אִלְמָלֵא דִי id. Cant. 4, 12. Ps. 106, 23 (אילמלי משה בחיריה) : also לְוֵי דְּ *would that !* (רקם ואתקף בצלו קדמיה)

river. 63, 19 קָרַעְתָּ לוּא *O that thou hadst* rent etc. (viz. now, already; the more empassioned expression for, O that thou *wouldst . . .*, § 142).

141. Again, instead of going on regularly to the apodosis, the sentence sometimes breaks off with an aposiopesis, and the result which would have occurred if the protasis had been realized is introduced more emphatically by כִּי עַתָּה *for then, in that case.* Thus Gen. 31, 42 if the God of my father had not been for me—כִּי עַתָּה שִׁלַּחְתָּנִי *for then* (or, uniting this second clause to the first, and so making it into a formal apodosis, *indeed then*[1]) thou *wouldst have* sent me away empty! 43, 10. Nu. 22, 33 (if for אוּלַי we read לוּלֵי, as seems necessary). 1 Sa. 14, 30 (if with LXX לֹא be omitted).

It is evidently only one step further than this for the clause with כי עתה to be found by itself, the actual protasis being suppressed altogether, and only a *virtual* one being pointed to by עתה:—Ex. 9, 15 for *then* (or *else* i.e. if the intention expressed in 14[b], and further expanded in 16, had not existed) שָׁלַחְתִּי אֶת־יָדִי וָאַךְ *I should have* put forth my hand and smitten thee etc. (i.e. instantaneously instead of slowly: for the idea, cf. Ps. 59, 12). 1 Sa. 13, 13 thou hast not kept the commandment of Yahweh; *for then* (if thou hadst done so) הֵכִין he *would have* established thy kingdom. Job 3, 13[a] (16, 7 is different: עתה there resembles עתה in 1 Sa. 14, 30 if we adhere to the Massoretic text, *as the case actually is*). 31, 28 כי alone. Comp. אָז 2 Ki. 13, 19.

142. If under these circumstances the *imperfect* occurs in the protasis, it naturally denotes a condition realizable in the present or the future: where no apodosis follows, we shall then have, in accordance with the context, and the tone in which the words are uttered, the expression of either hope or

---

[1] Perhaps, to be sure, this idiom is to be explained simply from the asseverative force of כי (cf. its use after an oath, p. 180, *n.* 1) without the assumption of an aposiopesis.

alarm—either a *wish* or a *fear*[1]—thus Gen. 17, 18 לוּ יִחְיֶה *if* Ishma'el might live before thee! (cf. the imperative 23, 13 לוּ שְׁמָעֵנִי[2], the jussive 30, 34 (לוּ יְהִי כִדְבָרֶךָ); and with אִם, Ex. 32, 32 אִם תִּשָּׂא *if* thou wouldst only forgive their sin! Ps. 81, 9. 95, 7[b] (in both these cases the following verses contain the words to be listened to). 139, 19. Pr. 2, 1. 24, 11.

On the other hand we hear the language of alarm :—Gen. 50, 15 לוּ יִשְׂטְמוּנוּ if he were to hate us! Ex. 4, 1 וְהֵן and if they do not believe me!

As before, the protasis may be succeeded by כי עתה :—Job 8, 4–6 (after a triple protasis[3], expressed by אם : כי עתה = *surely then*); and after לוּ, expressing a wish, Job 6, 2 f. *O that* my vexation might be *weighed* . . . כי עתה יכבד *for then* it *would be* heavier than the sand! comp. אָז, after a wish, expressed by אַחֲלֵי, אַחֲלַי, 2 Ki. 5, 3. Ps. 119, 6.

Or the clause with כי עתה may occur without any actual protasis :—Job 13, 19 *for then* (if there were any one able to contend with me and prove me in the wrong) I *would* be silent and die. Cf. with אָז 3, 13 I should have slept, אָז יָנוּחַ לִי *then* were I at rest; שָׁם 23, 7 *there* (= in that case) an upright man (would be) disputing with him; 32, 22 quickly (if I flattered) *would* my Maker take me away.

143. IV. In some of the instances last cited we may notice that the protasis states a case which might indeed conceivably occur (as Gen. 50, 15), but which may also (as Job 6, 2) be purely imaginary. We are thus conducted to another class of conditional propositions, consisting of an *imperfect*[4] *in both*

---

[1] Compare Ps. 41, 9 LXX μὴ ὁ κοιμώμενος οὐχὶ προσθήσει τοῦ ἀναστῆναι ; where the affirmative answer, always expected when μὴ οὐ is employed, is contemplated not with *hope*, but with *alarm* : 'Won't he that is now sick—won't he recover?'

[2] If the text be sound. LXX (πρὸς ἐμοῦ = *on my side* : see 29, 34. 31, 5), Sam. read אם אתה לי שמעני.

[3] So R.V. Most moderns, however, explain 8, 4 by § 127 γ.

[4] It will be remembered that two imperfects have met us before, in the formula *If I see him I will tell him*, ἐὰν ἴδω ἀναγγελῶ, and it

clauses, and corresponding to the double optative in Greek, *If I were to see him* (on the mere supposition, be it ever so unlikely or hyperbolical, that I were to see him) *I would tell him.*

Where the ideas contained in the protasis and apodosis respectively are parallel and similar we must render the conditional particle by *if:* where they are contrasted we may, if we please, employ *though*.

With אִם:—Gen. 13, 16 so that אִם־יוּכַל *if* a man *could* number the stars, thy seed also יִמָּנֶה *might be numbered*. Nu. 22, 18 (cf. 1 Ki. 13, 8). Isa. 1, 18 *though* they were as scarlet, they should become white as snow. 10, 22. Amos 5, 22. 9, 2–4 (notice the apod. continued by וְ and pf. 3, 'from there would I search וּלְקַחְתִּים and take them:' so *v.* 4). Ps. 27, 3. 50, 12. 139, 8ᵃ. 9ᵃ (8ᵇ. 9ᵇ cohort.; cf. Job 16, 6). Job 9, 3. 20. Ct. 8, 7. Jer. 2, 22 though thou wert to wash with potash, thy iniquity נִכְתָּם (would be) ingrained before me. 37, 10 (with a *pf.* after אִם, apparently for the purpose of expressing an extreme case). And with גַּם אִם Qoh. 8, 17.

With כִּי:—Jer. 51, 53 כִּי־תַעֲלֶה בָבֶל הַשָּׁמַיִם . . . . מֵאִתִּי יָבֹאוּ שֹׁדְדִים לָהּ. Hos. 13, 15. Ps. 37, 24ᵃ. 49, 19 f. (apod. תָבוֹא)[1]: with גַּם כִּי Ps. 23, 4. Isa. 1, 15 (with partcp. in apod.)

----

may appear strange that two significations should be assigned to the same combination. But the fact is that in *both* cases, in ἐὰν ἴδω as well as in εἰ ἴδοιμι, it is a mere possibility that is enunciated : now, when from the circumstances of the case the chances of this possible event taking place are but small, we mark in English our sense of the increased improbability by throwing the verbs into a form more expressive of contingency. In employing the optative in place of the subjunctive mood, the Greeks did precisely the same : Hebrew, on the other hand, was satisfied with a single mode of expression. Nor is the ambiguity greater than that which exists in a parallel case in our own language, where *if I had anything, I would give it*, has often to do duty for both εἰ εἶχον, ἐδίδουν ἄν and εἰ ἔχοιμι, διδοίην ἄν.

[1] In none of the examples is the apod. introduced by וְ: Isa. 54, 10 כִּי is, accordingly, best understood as *for*, וַחַסְדִּי being adversative : see 49, 15 (yea, these *may* forget, *but* I will not forget) ; 51, 6.

though ye multiply prayer, אֵינֶנִּי שׁוֹמֵעַ I am not hearing.   Cf. after כִּי alone Jer. 14, 12.

With לוּ:—Job 16, 4 I too like you אֲדַבְּרָה *would gladly* speak: לוּ יֵשׁ נַפְשְׁכֶם if your soul were in my soul's stead, אַחְבִּירָה *I would* heap up words against you, וְאָנִיעָה and *would* shake my head at you. Ez. 14, 15[1].

The above are the most common types of hypothetical constructions in Hebrew: **V** and **VI** are, accidentally, of much rarer occurrence.

144. V. *If I had seen him, I would* (now) *tell him.*

Dt. 32, 29 לוּ חָכְמוּ if they *had been* wise יַשְׂכִּילוּ they would understand this (at the present time—which they do not do). 30 (אִם לֹא כִי). 2 Sa. 18, 13 (אוֹ *or if*, with וְאַתָּה in the apod.). 2 Ki. 5, 13. Ps. 44, 21 f. if we *had* forgotten the name of our God וַנִּפְרֹשׂ and stretched out our hands to a strange god, *would* not God find this out? (he does *not* find it out, because it has not been done: on the contrary, *upon thy account* etc. *v.* 23). 66, 18. Job 9, 15. 16. Jer. 23, 22 (with וְ in the apod.). Mic. 2, 11 (וְהָיָה in the apod.)[2].

Conversely Dt. 32, 26 I *had* (should have) said I would scatter them, לוּלֵי אָגוּר did I not dread the vexation of the enemy (the vexation which his triumph would cause me).

145. VI. *If I saw him* (*now*, which I do not do) *I would tell him* (εἰ ἑώρων, ἀνήγγελλον ἄν): with לוּ and a participle in the protasis.

2 Sa. 18, 12. 2 Ki. 3, 14 לוּלֵי אֲנִי נֹשֵׂא except I *were favourable* to Yehoshaphat, אִם אַבִּיט I would surely not look at thee! Ps. 81, 14-17 לוּ עַמִּי שֹׁמֵעַ *if* my people *were hearkening* to me . . . , quickly אַכְנִיעַ *would I bow* down their enemies etc. (the verses relate, not to what might have happened in

---

[1] Where, however, אוֹ *or if* should perhaps be read for וּ לֹ: cf. *vv.* 17. 19.

[2] The pf. with וֹ is in many relations the syntactical equivalent of the bare impf.: comp. *e.g.* §§ 136 *a* and *β*, 138 *a* and *β*.

the past, but to the possibilities of restoration and prosperity in the *present*).

146. Hebrew, however, is capable of expressing hypothetical propositions without the aid of any hypothetical particle to introduce them[1]. There are three principal forms which such *implicit hypotheticals* may assume : these may be distinguished as the double perfect with ן consecutive, the double jussive, and the hypothetical imperative. In addition to these there are a few isolated forms which resemble the types already discussed, the only difference being that the conditional particle is not present.

147. (i) The double perfect with ן consecutive.

This use of the perfect with ן is nothing more than an extension, in a particular case, of its employment as a frequentative : sometimes, indeed, it is hardly so much as that ; for often the contingent nature of the events spoken of will be sufficiently clear in a translation from the sense of the passage without the addition of any hypothetical particle[2]. A single perfect with ן indicates, as we know, an action the actual date of which is indeterminate, but which is capable of being realized at any or every moment : *two* perfects with ן will indicate therefore *two* actions, which may similarly be realized at any or every moment. Now put the two verbs by each other in a single sentence, and the juxtaposition at once causes them *mutually to determine one another :* the

---

[1] The reader will be tempted to compare this absence of a conditional particle in Hebrew with the omission which not unfrequently takes place in English and German. In these languages, however, the omission is accompanied by an *inversion* of the usual order of words, which, by placing the verb before the subject, suggests to the reader the idea of a question, and so apprises him that the proposition involved is only an *assumption*, and not a fact. But, as will be seen, the relation between protasis and apodosis must be explained in Hebrew upon a different principle.

[2] Hence, some of the passages quoted here will likewise be found cited above, § 113. 4; cf. § 120, p. 162 *note*.

reader feels that the idea intended to be conveyed is just this, that the occurrence of one of the events was always, so to speak, the signal for the occurrence of the other. And thus we see how a *compound frequentative* may be equivalent to a *simple hypothetical.*

148.   (1) In past or present time :—

Ex. 33, 10 וְקָם . . . . וְרָאוּ *and* all the people *used to see and stand up* (or, *would* see and stand up): but the moments of standing up are obviously fixed and determined by the moments of seeing, which are plainly conceived as preceding them : this relation between the two acts may be more explicitly stated in English thus—'*if, when, whenever,* the people saw, they stood (or, used to stand) up.' And our language, it may be noticed, prefers the undisguised conditional construction when the first verb (or that in the protasis) is *subordinate* in importance to the second, when e.g. it is such a word as ראה or שמע, although in Hebrew the two are strictly co-ordinate—an additional instance to the many we have already had of the way in which we bring into relief what the older language· left as a plain surface.

Ex. 16, 21 LXX rightly ἡνίκα δὲ διεθέρμαινεν ὁ ἥλιος, ἐτήκετο. 34, 35. Nu. 10, 17 f. 21 f. (the writer passes *v.* 17 from the description of a *particular* case, with which he began 11–16, to that of the *general* custom : hence the series of perfects with וֹ 17–27; p. 162, *n.* 1). 1 Sa. 17, 34 f. (cf. p. 122). 1 Ki. 18, 10. Jer. 18, 4. 8 וְשָׁב וְנִחַמְתִּי *and if* it turns, *then I repent.* 10. 20, 9 וְאָמַרְתִּי *if I say* (or *said*), I will not make mention of him, וְהָיָה then *there is* (or *was*) in my heart as it were a burning fire (so R.V. rightly: in the rendering of A.V. there is no indication of the *prolonged* agitation, so clearly implied in the idiom used by the prophet).

149.   (2) In the future :—

Gen. 33, 13 and they will overdrive them one day, and all the flock will die (every one feels that it is a contingent, not

a certain result, that is anticipated, cf. the single verb, 20, 11).
42, 38. 44, 22 וְעָזַב אָבִיו וָמֵת *and if* he leaves his father, he
will die. 29. Ex. 4, 14*[1] וראך ושמח and *when* he sees thee,
he will rejoice. 12, 13*. 23*. Lev. 22, 7 (cf. Ex. 16, 21 in
the past). Nu. 10, 3. 5 f. 14, 15 וְהֵמַתָּה and *if* thou killest.
15, 39* (cf. Gen. 9, 16). 23, 20 וברך ולא אשיבנה and *if* he
blesseth, I cannot reverse it (impf., because separated from ו).
Dt. 4, 29ᵃ (cf. Jer. 29, 12 f.). 1 Sa. 16, 2. 19, 3 (cf. Nu. 23, 3).
1 Ki. 8, 30 וְשָׁמַעְתָּ וְסָלַחְתָּ׃ and *when* thou hearest, forgive[2].
Isa. 6, 13 and *if* there be still in it a tenth part, it shall turn
and be consumed (=shall again be consumed). Ez. 3, 17.
17, 15ᵇ. 18, 10 and *if* he begets a son, who etc. . . . (*v.* 13)
וָחָי *shall he live?* 33, 3* (cf. Isa. 21, 7 והקשיב . . . וראה=and
should he see . . . , let him give heed . . .). 39, 15*. Pr. 3, 24
וְשָׁכַבְתָּ (not under the government of אִם: cf. Job 5, 24ᵇ).

Compare further Jud. 6, 13 וְיֵשׁ *and is* Yahweh with us, וְלָמָּה
why then has all this come upon us? 2 Sa. 13, 26 וָלֹא *and not*
(=and if not), let Amnon go with us. 2 Ki. 5, 17. 10, 15 וְיֵשׁ
תנה את ידך *if* it be, then, give (me) thine hand.

---

[1] In the passages marked thus *, the first verb is ראה, which, as is not
unfrequently the case in Hebrew, though against the idiom of our own
language, is treated as though it represented an independent, substantive
idea, equal in importance to that expressed by the succeeding verb.
Thus Gen. 45, 27 'and he saw the wagons, and his spirit revived;'
where *saw* expresses such a subordinate and transitory idea that in
English we feel disposed to render 'and *when* he saw;' this, however,
would strictly have been ויהי כראתו. If we make use of a more
emphatic word, we can retain the Hebrew form of sentence without its
sounding unnatural, thus:—'and he *looked at* the wagons and his spirit
revived.' So 46, 29. 1 Sa. 10, 14. 17, 51ᵇ. Ez. 20, 28. The case is
similar with verbs of *hearing*, Josh. 2, 11. 22, 12; or *finishing*, Ex. 34,
33. 39, 32. Lev. 16, 20. 2 Sa. 11, 27. Ez. 4, 6. 5, 13. Passages such as
those just quoted explain ויכל Gen. 2, 2: the act of *completion* is regarded
as sufficiently distinct and independent to have a special day assigned
to it.

[2] For the *repetition* of the verb שמע after what precedes cf. Lev. 13, 3.
1 Sa. 29, 10: cf. p. 138, *n.* 4.

150. (ii and iii) The hypothetical imperative and double jussive.

The use of the imperative or jussive to indicate hypothetical propositions is to be explained upon the same principle as that of the double perfect, although the use of a different verbal form modifies to a certain extent the nature of the condition expressed. In the present case the first verb enunciates a command or permission: the general sense of the passage, however, or the tone in which the words are uttered may indicate that the speaker does not intend the language to be understood *literally*, or to be carried into actual execution under *all and any circumstances*, but only in so far as is requisite for the purpose of realizing and comprehending the manner in which the action denoted by the second verb is involved in, and results from, that denoted by the first. This may, of course, be done *mentally:* and thus a concise and emphatic mode of expressing a hypothetical sentence is obtained[1].

151. English as well as classical idiom (Aesch. P. V. 728 (709); Verg. Ecl. iii. 104) requires the future[2] in place of the second imperative or jussive: and it is at first sight difficult to discover a justification or satisfactory explanation of the Hebrew construction. The most plausible supposition seems to be this, that the two correlative clauses were originally pronounced in such a manner as to shew that the intention of the speaker was to mark his opinion that the two were equivalent, that you might as well assume the one as the other, that if you imagined the first realized you must conceive the second realized as well, and that continual juxtaposition with this object generated in time a *fixed formula*.

---

[1] Cf. Winer, § 43. 2 'when two imperatives are connected by καί, the first sometimes contains the condition (supposition) upon which the action indicated by the second will take place.'

[2] Or, at any rate, the indicative mood: cf., for example, Pope, *Essay on Man*, i. 251 f. 253-256. iv. 89-92.

Thus Ps. 147, 18 יַשֵּׁב ... יִזְּלוּ is strictly *'let him blow* with his
wind! *let* the waters *flow!'* i.e. assume the one, and you
must assume the other: but by long usage the stiffness
which originally attached to the formula disappeared, and the
collocation of the two verbs ceased to do more than suggest
simply the idea of a hypothetical relation: in the present
case, '*if* or *when* he blows with his wind, the waters flow[1].'

It will be objected that, inasmuch as the second verb in
the example is the simple imperfect[2], if it were understood
and treated accordingly, the meaning would be identical and
the need for a circuitous explanation such as the one here
proposed superseded. To this it must be replied that such
a course would leave unexplained the similar cases in which
(as will appear directly) the second verb is shewn to be a
jussive by its form: the existence of these instances, supported as they are by the parallel construction of the imperative, as well as by the analogy of the corresponding idiom
in Arabic, authorizes us in the inference that the verb is still
jussive, although no visible indication of the fact may exist.

Obs. In Arabic the jussive is the mood which appears regularly after
an imperative (whether the latter is intended to be understood in a hypothetical or a literal sense) for the purpose of indicating the *consequence*

---

[1] We can understand without much difficulty the use of the jussive
when the verb is in the third person : but so arduous is it to pass outside
the magic circle prescribed by the language with which we are most
familiar, that the inability of English to express the *idea* of a jussive in
the first and second persons (except through the medium of a circumlocution by which its presence is disguised) constitutes a serious obstacle
in the way of our realizing its application under the last-named circumstances.

[2] A double impf. in a frequentative sense would be as intelligible as
the double pf., §§ 147, 148, and ought, perhaps, to be adopted for such
cases as Prov. 26, 26 al., where the jussive form, although it exists, has not
been employed, and for Ps. 104, 28-30. 109, 25. 139, 18, where the verbs
have the old termination ן- annexed to them, which in Arabic is dropped
in the jussive, and in Hebrew is at least found with it very rarely (see
Job 31, 10). Cf. also Ps. 91, 7.

that will supervene, if the injunction conveyed by the imperative takes effect. A compound formula thus arises, of which קַח ... יְהִי Ex. 7, 9 may be taken as the type. Inasmuch now as it is never the office of the jussive in Arabic to express a purpose or result (for which other idioms are employed) except when thus preceded by an imperative, it is natural to suppose that its appearance in such a capacity is in some way connected with the presence of this mood. A consequence which only results from the execution of a command is not like the absolute consequence of a certified fact; it is essentially limited by, dependent on, the occurrence of the action denoted by the imperative; virtually, therefore, it stands upon the same footing, and may be enunciated in the same terms—the collocation of the two verbs indicating with sufficient clearness the relation which they are conceived by the speaker or writer to occupy with regard to each other. And this *dependency* may be exhibited in English in more ways than one: sometimes a double imperative will be sufficient, at other times it will be better to adopt the form of an explicit hypothetical, or to employ the final conjunction *that* before the second verb.

Examples are not far to find: Qor'an 27, 12 put thy hand into thy bosom, *let it come forth* white, or, as we should say, *and it shall* come forth white. 2, 38 be true to my covenant, اُوفِ (juss.) *let me be true* to yours! i.e. '*if* you are true to me, I will be true to you.' 129 become Jews or Christians, *be guided aright* (juss.), or, *that* you may be guided aright (contrast 7, 158). 3, 29 if you love God, follow me; *let* God *love* you, and *forgive* you your sins, or, *then* he will love you etc. (by inserting *then*, we assume that the 'following' has actually occurred, and so are enabled to employ the language of assurance—*will;* Arabic and Hebrew do *not* make this assumption, and are therefore obliged to adhere to an expression of contingency, in strict co-ordination with the imperative). 7, 71 (cf. 11, 67. 40, 27) let her alone, تَأْكُلْ *let her eat* = that she may eat. 139. 142. 161. 40, 62 = *if* you call upon me, I will answer you. 46, 30. 57, 28 fear God, and believe in his prophet, *let him give* (= '*that* he may give;' or, '*and* he will give,' viz. provided that you fear and believe) you a double portion of his mercy. 67, 4 etc.

The instances here cited (all of which are in exact conformity with the type קַח ... יְהִי) form a welcome illustration of the Hebrew idiom. It ought, however, to be mentioned that as a general rule in Arabic this mood, when used literally as a 'jussive,' does not stand alone, but is preceded by the particle لِ *li:* in the class of instances under discussion the need of this seems to be superseded by the presence of the *imperative*, which sufficiently indicates the sense to be assigned to the jussive following[1].

152. But however this may be, the formulae in question are of frequent occurrence. We have—

(1) *The hypothetical imperative:*—as Isa. 55, 2 *hearken unto me, and eat ye that which is good:* this might, of course, be a special counsel issued on a particular occasion, but it may have equally a more general purport, and affirm that *granting* or *supposing* the first imperative to take effect at any time, the second will be found to take effect also. Gen. 42, 18 do this וֶחְיוּ *and live:* as the *living* is dependent upon the *doing*, if the double imperative in English be not free from ambiguity one of these equivalent forms may be substituted, ' do this *that* ye may live,' or ' if ye do this, ye shall live.' Amos 5, 4. 6 (וחיו, for which *v.* 14 לְמַעַן תחיו)[2]. Pr. 3, 3 f. ('*and so* find,' or '*that* thou mayest find'). 4, 4 וחיה etc.; or in irony or defiance, Isa. 8, 9 vex yourselves *and be broken!* cf. § 50 *n.*

And without וְ:—Pr. 20, 13[b]. Job 40, 32 lay thine hand upon him, זְכֹר *think of* the battle, אַל־תּוֹסַף׃ *don't* do it again! (i. e. thou wilt not do it again.)

(2) The same with a jussive* (or cohortative†)[3] in the apodosis[4]:—Isa. 8, 10 (ironically) take your counsel וְתֻפָר *and let it come* to nought! Prov. 3, 9 f. 4, 8 (19, 20 לְמַעַן). 20, 22 * (so Mark 11, 24 וִיהִי . . . הַאֲמִינוּ). Cf. Gen. 30, 28†. 34, 12†.

And without וְ:—Ex. 7, 9 * ' take thy rod and cast it to the ground, יְהִי *let it become* a serpent!' but as this is the object aimed at by the two preceding actions, we may also render, *that it may become.* 18, 19 שְׁמַע אִיעָצְךָ. Ps. 50, 15. 51, 16 (*that* my

---

[1] Compare Ewald, *Gramm. Arab.* § 732; Wright, ii. §§ 13, 17.

[2] Comp. Ps. 37, 27 (§ 65). Jer. 25, 5. 35, 15. Job 22, 21.

[3] In the instances marked * or †, the presence of the voluntative is indicated by the form.

[4] Compare above, §§ 62, 64 *Obs.*, where indeed such of the instances as relate to a definite individual act might also have been placed.

tongue may sing). 118, 19. 119, 17 (=*so* or *then* shall I live,
although without וְ). Pr. 3, 7 f.* תְּהִי. 2 Chr. 25, 8 כִּי אִם־בֹּא
אַתָּה ... יַכְשִׁילְךָ הָאֱלֹהִים but go thou (=if thou go) ..., God
will make thee to stumble.

(3) *The double jussive:*—Isa. 41, 28 וָאֵרֶא וְאֵין אִישׁ and
suppose (*if*) I looked, there was no man. Ps. 104, 20 * תָּשֶׁת
חֹשֶׁךְ וִיהִי לָיְלָה =*if* or *when* thou makest darkness, then it is
night. Pr. 20, 25 יָלַע (see p. 104, *n.* 2) let a man cry hastily,
It is sacred, and afterwards he will have to enquire into his
vows! (to see whether he can free himself from them: in *v.*
25[b] understand וִיהִי). Job 22, 28[a]*. (But cf. p. 216, *n.* 4.)

And without וְ:—2 Ki. 6, 27 (notice אַל in the protasis:
the sense of the passage is, however, far from certain).
Ps. 146, 4 (but cf. p. 189, *n.* 2). 147, 18[b]. Job 10, 16 f.* 11, 17
תָּעֻפָה כַּבֹּקֶר תִּהְיֶה: *suppose* it dark (but cf. p. 51, *note*), 'twill
become like the morning. 20, 24. Cf. 2 Sa. 18, 22 וִיהִי מָה
אָרֻצָה־נָּא גַם־אָנִי well, come what may, *I* too will run.

(4) Once or twice only is the jussive followed by an imperative:—Ps. 45, 12 (with וְ). Job 15, 17.

153. Lastly, some passages must be noted in which the
thought is *virtually* hypothetical; although this is in no way
indicated by its syntactical dress:—

Pr. 11, 2 בָּא זָדוֹן וַיָּבֹא קָלוֹן lit. 'pride *has come and* shame
goes on to come,' i.e. follows it in any given case: this compound *general truth* (§ 12) is equivalent in meaning, though
not in form, to the *explicit* hypothetical construction '*if* or
when pride cometh, then cometh shame' (cf. 18, 3[a]). So 11, 8.
25, 4 (where we must not be tempted by the English idiom to
treat הֲגוֹ imperatively, as *v.* 5, which the following וַיֵּצֵא forbids:
the *inf. abs.* is here a substitute for the *perfect*). Job 3, 25[a].
9, 20[b]. 23, 13: וְנַפְשׁוֹ אִוְּתָה וַיָּעַשׂ and his soul desireth (a thing),
and he doeth (it)[1]. 29, 11 for the ear heard me, and it blessed

---

[1] *Paraphrased* in A.V., R.V., by 'and what his soul desireth, even
that he doeth.'

me (=for *when* the ear heard me, *then* it blessed me, R.V.: A. V. *does not render the* כִּי)[1]. These passages throw light upon Ex. 20, 25[b] for thou hast lifted up thy tool upon it וַתְּחַלְלֶהָ and polluted it! =for *if* thou lift up thy tool upon it, thou hast polluted it. Cf. Ps. 39, 12 וַתִּמֶם . . . יִסַּרְתָּ thou correctest *and* makest (=*when* thou dost correct, thou makest, A. V.) his beauty to consume away etc. Add also Ps. 37, 10[b] (where ו cannot be consecutive on account of the position of the tone: contrast Pr. 3, 24). Job 7, 8[b]. 27, 19[b].

154. Often this *hypothetical* perfect, as it may be termed, is followed by the impf. ἀσυνδέτως (cf. p. 33): thus Amos 3, 8 a lion *hath roared*, who shall not be afraid? (i. e. *supposing* it have roared). Job 7, 20 חָטָאתִי *have I sinned* (repeated 35, 6 with אִם: that the perfect is hypothetical is, of course, further clear from the whole tenour of Job's argument), what do I do to thee? 4, 2 and 21 (after an interrog., anomalously). 19, 4. 21, 31. 23, 10. 24, 24. Lev. 15, 3. Pr. 19, 24. 22, 29[2]: cf. Hos. 9, 6.

More rarely it is succeeded by another perfect, as Pr. 24, 10. 26, 15. 27, 12 (contrast 22, 3): once by an imperative, 25, 16.

155. Only very seldom do we meet with what seems like one of the hypothetical constructions noticed above, with the *omission* of the conditional particle:—Josh. 22, 18. Neh. 1, 8; Isa. 26, 10 (§ 136 γ); Lev. 10, 19 וְאָכַלְתִּי and had I eaten,

---

[1] The difficult passage Job 22, 29 cited here in my previous editions (For they are depressed, וַתֹּאמֶר גֵּוָה and thou sayest, Up!=if they are depressed, thou art quickly reassured), I am inclined now, on account of the doubtful meaning which this construction assigns to גֵּאוה, to take with Hitzig, 'When they have humbled thee (cf. Pr. 25, 7), and thou sayest (= complainest), Pride, he will save him that is lowly of eyes' (i.e. thyself),—if thou art humble, God will defend thee, when the proud seek to bring thee down: cf. Dan. 4, 34.

[2] Pr. 6, 22. Nah. 1, 12[b] the first pf. is connected with what precedes by the weak *waw* (as Ps. 37, 10).

would it be good in the eyes of Yahweh? Nu. 12, 14 (cf.
§ 144).

Obs. Whether it is permissible to explain Hos. 8, 12. Ps. 40, 6 by
means of the principle of § 152 is doubtful, as nowhere does the *pf.*
appear in the apodosis. The sequence in Isa. 58, 10 (which is passed
over too lightly by the commentators) is no less unique : still, if Pr.
31, 6 f. Mic. 6, 14 (with ולא and impf. in apod.) can be referred rightly
to § 152. 2 and 3 respectively, they may perhaps justify its being treated
similarly.

APPENDIX I.

The Circumstantial Clause.

156. THE term *circumstantial*, or, as the German word[1] is sometimes though perhaps less expressively rendered, *descriptive clause*, is one which constantly meets the student in the commentaries and grammars of modern scholars: and formulating as it does a characteristic usage of the language, its introduction has been of great service in the rational exposition of Hebrew syntax. It corresponds on the whole to what in the classical languages is generally termed the *secondary predicate*. Any word or words expressive of some fact *subordinate to the main course of the narrative*, or descriptive of some circumstance attaching or appertaining to the action denoted by the principal verb, may form a circumstantial clause or secondary predicate: an adverb, a genitive or ablative absolute, a participle or other word in apposition to the subject—all of which *qualify* the main action by assigning the *concomitant conditions* under which it took place, be they modal, causal, or temporal—are familiar instances. But Hebrew has no signs for cases, no past or future participle, a limited development of adverbs or adjectives, and is weak in special words corresponding to conjunctions like ὡς, ἐπεί, quum etc.: in what way, then, is it able to give expression to

---

[1] *Zustandsatz*, also *Umstandsatz*. With the whole of what follows compare generally Ewald, §§ 306 ᶜ, 341, who, however, seems disposed to extend the principle of the circumstantial clause beyond legitimate limits, to cases where its application becomes unreal.

these subordinate details, which, although secondary, form still such an important factor in all continued narrative?

157. Already in the preceding pages, while considering the various mutual relations to one another of the different clauses which together constitute a complete sentence, we have more than once had occasion to notice how in Hebrew, to a much greater extent than in many other languages, these relations take the form of simple *co-ordination*: in other words, that, instead of the logical relation which each part bears to the whole being explicitly indicated, it is frequently left to be inferred by the reader for himself with just such help as he may be able to obtain from a change of position, or an alteration in the modulation of the voice. Now a similar method is employed for the expression of those circumstantial clauses which modern idiom usually marks more distinctly[1]. The words expressing them are simply *thrown into the sentence,* being either entirely disconnected with what precedes or joined to it only by ן—with a change, however, of the usual order of the words, whereby the construction with ·ן, expressive of the smooth and unbroken succession of events one after another, is naturally abandoned, as being alien to the relation that has now to be represented, and the *subject* of the circumstantial clause *placed first.* In consequence of the subject thus standing conspicuously in the foreground, the reader's attention is suddenly arrested, and directed pointedly to it: he is thus made aware that it is the writer's wish to lay special stress upon it as about to be contrasted, in respect of the predicate following, either with

---

[1] In early Greek we not unfrequently observe the same phenomenon : thus Il. vi. 148 ἔαρος δ' ἐπιγίγνεται ὥρη, which is logically subordinate to the preceding clause ἄλλα δέ θ' ὕλη Τηλεθόωσα φύει, of which it determines the moment of occurrence : grammatically, however, it is *co*-ordinated with it. So xiv. 417. xvi. 825. xvii. 302 μινυνθάδιος δέ οἱ αἰὼν Ἔπλετο (והוא קצר ימים), 572. xviii. 247 f. xxi. 364. xxii. 27 ἀρίζηλοι δέ οἱ αὐγαὶ Φαίνονται, his beams *shining* brightly.

some *other* subject mentioned before, or else with the same
subject under a *different* aspect (i.e. with a different predicate)
previously mentioned or implied. The contrast may at times
be less perceptible, and so possibly be thought not to exist:
but this is no more than happens with μέν . . . δέ in Greek,
which always mark an antithesis of some sort or other, however evanescent it may sometimes appear. For instance,
1 Ki. 19, 19 'and he went thence and found Elisha, וְהוּא חֹרֵשׁ
and *he* (was) ploughing:' this is equivalent to 'while he was
ploughing,' where it will be observed that the italics for *he*
are abandoned: so soon as the circumstantial clause is expressed by a conjunction, there is not generally any further
need to emphasize the subject, the particular relation which
the emphasis was intended to bring out being now represented sufficiently by the connecting particle.

As to the verb (if there be one) following the subject, it
will naturally fall into the pf., impf., or partcp., according to
the character of the circumstance to be described and its
relation in point of time to the action denoted by the verb
in the primary sentence.

158. In the translation of circumstantial clauses there is
considerable scope for variety. Sometimes the וֹ may be
rendered most simply and naturally *and*—the subordinate
position of the fact thus introduced being manifest from the
sense of the passage; but at other times it will be better,
precisely as in the case of the participle in Greek or Latin,
to make the meaning more evident by the adoption of some
circumlocution such as *if, when, although, as, since,* etc., as
the context requires.

159. Let us first consider some instances in which the conjunction appears:—Gen. 18, 12 וַאדֹנִי זָקֵן *and* my lord *is old*
=my lord *being old.* 16. 18 ואברהם היו יהיה *seeing that* (A.V.)
Abraham etc. 19, 1. 24, 56 וַיהוָֹה הִצְלִיחַ דַּרְכִּי *and* (=*since*)
Yahweh hath prospered my journey. 28, 12 וְרֹאשׁוֹ מַגִּיעַ the
top thereof *reaching* to heaven. Nu. 16, 11[b] *since* or *for* what

are we . . .? (justifying עַל יִ״ : so Ex. 16, 7). 24, 18 וְיִשְׂרָאֵל
עֹשֶׂה חַיִל *while that* Israel doeth valiantly. Dt. 4, 11 (cf. Jud.
8, 11[b]). 28, 32 וְעֵינֶיךָ רֹאוֹת. 32, 31 *and* our enemies are judges
(i.e. our own enemies *admitting* it). Ruth 1, 21 why call ye
me Naomi וַיהוָה עָנָה בִי *when* or *seeing* Yahweh hath testified
against me? Josh. 3, 14 וְהַכֹּהֲנִים *the priests being* before the
people. 15[b] (may be most conveniently placed in a paren-
thesis: LXX ὁ δὲ Ἰορδάνης ἐπληροῦτο· δέ being used as Thuc.
i. 93. 4 ὑπῆρκτο δὲ κ. τ. λ., or as in the phrases σημεῖον δέ· δῆλον
δέ· i. 11. 2 etc.). 8, 11[b] (cf. 1 Sa. 17, 3). Ps. 35, 5[b]. 6[b]. Hos.
6, 4[b] *and*=since (or *for*, A.V.). Job 33, 19 Qrê *while* or
though the multitude of his bones is in vigour.

Gen. 11, 4 וְרֹאשׁוֹ בַשָּׁמַיִם=*with* its top in the heavens. 24, 10
al. בְּיָדוֹ . . . וְ=*with* . . . in his hand. 25, 26 וְיָדוֹ אֹחֶזֶת בַּעֲקֵב עֵשָׂו
=*with* his hand taking hold etc. 44, 26 וְאָחִינוּ הַקָּטֹן אֵינֶנּוּ אִתָּנוּ.
Dt. 9, 15[b]. Isa. 35, 10. 43, 8 וְעֵינַיִם יֵשׁ *although* they have
eyes. 60, 11 וּמַלְכֵיהֶם נְהוּגִים. Ps. 28, 3 וְרָעָה בִּלְבָבָם *while* or
though mischief is in their hearts. 55, 22[a]. 64, 7. Pr. 3, 28
וְיֵשׁ אִתָּךְ: *it being* by thee. 12, 9. 15, 16.

A circumstantial clause begins but seldom with any word
other than the subject, unless it be one adapted for, or de-
manding, a prominent position: Dt. 19, 6 וְלוֹ אֵין מִשְׁפַּט־מָוֶת
whereas . . ., A.V. Josh. 22, 25. 2 Sa. 13, 18 וְעָלֶיהָ כְתֹנֶת פַּסִּים.
16, 1 וַעֲלֵיהֶם מָאתַיִם לֶחֶם. 2 Ki. 10, 2 וְאִתְּכֶם. Isa. 3, 7. 6, 6
וּבְיָדוֹ. 23, 15 Del. וְנִשְׁכַּחַת (ptcp.[1] cf. Ez. 9, 8, p. 90 *n.*). Amos
7, 7. Ps. 60, 13 ; and with the emphatic word לֹא, 1 Sa. 20, 2
וְלֹא יִגְלֶה אֶת אָזְנִי *without* disclosing it to me. Isa. 45, 4. 5 *when*
or *though* thou didst not know me. Ps. 44, 18 *though* we had
not forgotten him. 139, 16. Job 9, 5. 24, 22 וְלֹא יַאֲמִין בַּחַיִּין
while (or *though*) despairing of life. 42, 3 *though* I understood

---

[1] Taken by some (e. g. Dillm., Stade, § 410[a], Anm. 1) as an irregular
perf. However, if ונשכחת were the *first* statement introduced by
והיה ביום ההוא, the second (. . . מקץ) would naturally be introduced
by ו, which is not the case.

not. Often also in such phrases as וְאֵין מַצִּיל Ps. 7, 3 al.
וְאֵין מַחֲרִיד *without any to frighten* Lev. 26, 6 al. וְאֵין קֹבֵר 2 Ki.
9, 10. Pr. 28, 1 ואין רֹדף. Qoh. 4, 8 ואין שני *without* a second.

160. The most instructive and noticeable instances, however, are those in which a *personal pronoun* forms the subject
of the circumstantial clause: where this is the case, it is often
even more impracticable than before to elicit a suitable or
intelligible meaning without resolving the Hebrew idiom into
some relatival or participial construction. Thus Gen. 15, 2
what wilt thou give me, ואנכי הולך ערירי=*seeing* I go hence
childless? 18, 8 והוא עֹמֵד עליהם=*as* he was standing beside
them. 27 ואנכי עפר ואפר=*though* I am dust and ashes. 20, 3
וְהִוא בְּעֻלַת בָּעַל׃=*for* she is married to a husband. 24, 31
why dost thou stand without, ואנכי פניתי=*when* I have prepared the house? 62 וְהוּא יֹשֵׁב *as* or *for* he was dwelling
(assigning a *reason*, entirely different from וַיֵּשֶׁב 25, 11, where
the וֹ introduces a new and independent statement). 37, 2
וְהוּא נַעַר *he being* a lad (*while yet* a lad, LXX ὢν νέος). Ex. 23, 9
ואתם ידעתם for *ye* know. 33, 12 thou sayest to me, Bring up
this people, ואתה לא הודעתני *without having* told me etc. Josh.
17, 14 why hast thou given me only a single lot, ואני עם רב
seeing I am a great people? (cf. 1 Sa. 18, 23). Jud. 3, 26 and
Ehud escaped וְהוּא עָבַר *he having passed over* etc. (not the
mere addition of a fresh fact like וַיַּעֲבֹר, but the justification
of the preceding נִמְלָט). 4, 21 וְהוּא־נִרְדָּם (pf.) *he having* fallen
fast asleep. 16, 31 *after having* judged. 1 Ki. 1, 41 וְהֵם כִּלּוּ
they having finished. 2 Ki. 5, 18. Isa. 49, 21 ואני שכולה וגלמודה.
53, 4 ואנחנו חשבנהו *although* we (mistakenly) deemed him
stricken, smitten of God, and afflicted (viz. as a judgment
for his own sins). 7 נִגַּשׂ וְהוּא נַעֲנֶה (where the unemphatic ʻand
he was afflicted' is obviously an insufficient rendering of
והוא נענה: the words must signify either ʻ*he being* (already)
afflicted,' or (Delitzsch, Dillm.; cf. R. V.) ʻthough suffering
himself to be afflicted,' ʻthough he humbled himself' (cf. Ex.

10, 3) : only in this way is a contrast with נגש secured). 12
והוא . . . נשא *though* he bare[1]. Hos. 3, 1 *although* they turn.
Ps. 50, 17 (in contrast to *v.* 16). 55, 22ᵇ והמה פתחות *being* (in
reality) drawn swords. Job 21, 22 והוא רמים ישפוט *while* or
when HE judges those that are on high. 22, 18 *when* HE (of
whom they had used the language quoted in *v.* 17) *had* all
the time filled their houses with prosperity.

Obs. It must not, however, be supposed that *all* sentences framed
like ושאול אמר are circumstantial clauses : emphasis or the love of
variety causes sometimes this form to be adopted in preference to ויאמר
שאול; especially noticeable are those cases where, when statements
have to be made respecting *two* subjects, the first having been introduced by ·ַו, the second is thrown into relief against the first by *the
subject being placed before the verb.* This variation is the Hebrew
equivalent to μὲν . . . δὲ of the Greeks: in English the antithesis is
not indicated by anything further than a slightly emphasized pronunciation.

Thus Gen. 4, 2 And Abel was (or rather became—היה is ἐγίγνετο,
γίγνεται much more than ἦν, ἐστὶ) a shepherd, וקין היה but Cain was
(became and continued to be) a tiller of ground. 3 f. 6, 8. 8, 5. 10, 8.
13. 15 (facts about the personages named *v.* 6, and so contrasted among
each other). 11, 3ᵇ. 13, 12. 18, 33.

Similarly when something has to be stated about a *new* subject, that
subject is sometimes put first, though by no means exclusively, as Gen.
11, 12. 14 (contrast 13. 15), but in the exactly similar sentences 16. 18
etc. we have ·ַו: then 27ᵇ והרן הוליד. 13, 14. 14, 18 etc.

A third case in which the same order of words is observed is for
the purpose of introducing the mention of a new state of things, or
new situation, which, while preparatory to what is to succeed, is in no
immediate connexion with the preceding portion of the narrative.
Those instances in which the fresh fact is one that is *anterior* to the
point at which the main narrative has arrived, have been already
adverted to and explained p. 84, where also an obvious reason was
assigned for the abandonment upon such occasions of the more usual
construction with ·ַו. Although, however, the new statement is intro-

---

[1] Not 'and he bare' (A. V.), which must have been וַיִּשָּׂא: the point
is that he was numbered with transgressors, *although* actually so far
from being one himself that he had even borne the sin of others.

ductory, and accordingly in a certain sense subordinate, to what follows, yet the subordination is not sufficient to create a formal circumstantial clause ; moreover, the clause in question precedes instead of following the sentence it is supposed to qualify : in fact the change of form merely marks the commencement of a new thread which is afterwards interwoven with the narrative as a whole. The deviation from the usual style of progression, and also the significance of the new one adopted in its place, may be appropriately indicated in translation by the employment of *now*. Thus, in addition to the passages cited p. 84, see Gen. 16, 1 *now* Sarai, Abram's wife, had borne him no son (contrast 11, 30). 37, 3 *now* Israel loved. 39, 1. 43, 1. Ex. 13, 21. Josh. 13, 1.

The preceding remarks apply with no less force to those cases in which the subject is a *pronoun*, to sentences, for example, of a type so common in the Psalms, beginning with ואני, ואתה etc. Although, in thus inserting the pronoun, it is always the intention of the writer to mark it as being in *some* way specially emphatic—either as denoting a *different* subject, which is to be contrasted with a previous one, or as introducing a fresh and emphatic statement about the *same* subject— yet the clause in which it appears need not of necessity be *subordinate* to what has preceded : its importance may render it *parallel* and *co-ordinate*, and in this case it cannot, of course, be regarded as a circum- stantial clause. Thus Gen. 33, 3 *he himself* (in opposition to the persons named *v.* 2). 42, 8 ('but *they*'). 23 LXX αὐτοὶ δὲ οὐκ ᾔδεισαν ὅτι ἀκούει (שֹׁמֵעַ *was* hearing) Ἰωσήφ. 49, 19[b] (a fresh thought in con- trast to 19[a]). 20[b] (pointing back emphatically to the subject אשר). Jud. 4, 3. 13, 5 (and *he*—however others may fail—will etc. : cf. Gen. 16, 12. Matth. 1, 21 αὐτὸς γὰρ σώσει κ.τ.λ.). 18, 27. 1 Ki. 1, 13 *he* (and no one else : so *vv.* 24. 30. 35). 2, 8. 19, 4 (opposed to נערו). Isa. 1, 2 והם (sons !). Ps. 2, 6 but *I* (however ye may rage). 5, 8. 9, 9. 13, 6. 31, 7[b] (in contrast to השמרים). 15. 23. 37, 5. 106, 43 והמה ימרו but *they* (nevertheless, in spite of יציל) kept rebelling.

The presence of the pronoun should always be noted in Hebrew, though it is sometimes difficult, without a careful study of the context, to discern the motive which prompted its insertion : let the reader examine for himself, with the view to discover in each instance what the motive may have been, the following passages :—Gen. 41, 15. Ex. 28, 5. Jud. 11, 35. 2 Sa. 19, 33 (see 17, 27). 1 Ki. 22, 32. 2 Ki. 4, 40. 12, 6. 19, 37. Ps. 109, 25. Isa. 24, 14[1].

---

[1] The pronoun is also expressed sometimes (as one of my reviewers has pointed out) in *responses*, where although no special stress rests

In the same way sentences introduced by וְהִנֵּה form in general such
an integral part of the narrative that they can hardly with fairness
be termed circumstantial clauses : certainly they often indicate, a state
of things either already completed (*pf.*), continuing (*part.*), or about to
commence (*impf.*), but the manner of their introduction by the particle
הנה, and their occurrence usually after some verb of *seeing, ascertaining,
perceiving*, shews that the stress lies not so much on the mere circumstance as such, but on *the impression it produces* upon the principal
subject.   The construction with הִנֵּה is preferred to that with ·וַ for two
reasons : 1. to mark the occurrence of an event more or less startling
or noticeable for the subject; 2. to indicate with greater precision than
is possible by ·וַ alone the relation as regards time of the new event to
what precedes it in the sentence—whether, for instance, it is antecedent
or simultaneous.

Thus Gen. 8, 13 and he looked *and behold* the face of the ground
חרבו *had become* dry (LXX ἐξέλιπε· had the writer used ויחרבו, the
meaning would have been ambiguous, as the drying would have been
naturally supposed to *succeed* the act of looking). 37, 7. 9 (observe the
variations of tense). 42, 27. Dt. 9, 13 I see this people, *and behold* it is
a stiff-necked people. Jud. 3, 25. 2 Ki. 2, 11 and often.

161.   But clauses expressing a subordinate thought occur
also without וַ : thus (1) Gen. 12, 8 and pitched his tent there
בֵּית־אֵל מִיָּם וְהָעַי מִקֶּדֶם Bethel *being* on the west etc. 1 Sa. 26,
13 רַב הַמָּקוֹם בֵּינֵיהֶם; and in such phrases as אֵם עַל בָּנִים Gen.
32, 12; פֶּה אֶחָד Nu. 14, 14; עַיִן בְּעַיִן 32, 31; פָּנִים אֶל פָּנִים
with one mouth Josh. 9, 2. 1 Ki. 22, 13; קוֹל גָּדוֹל *with* a loud
voice 1 Ki. 8, 55; כַּף רְמִיָּה *with* a slack hand Pr. 10, 4;
שְׁכֶם אֶחָד Zeph. 3, 9; Dt. 5, 5 אָנֹכִי עֹמֵד *me stante*. Isa. 26, 16

---

upon it, a slight prominence is evidently not unsuitable, as Jud. 6, 18.
11, 9 : add 2 Sa. 3, 13. 1 Ki. 2, 18.

I take this opportunity of putting together some passages in which
the pronoun (emphatic) *follows* the verb : Ex. 18, 19. 22. 26. Jud. 8, 23.
15, 12. 1 Sa. 17, 56. 20, 8. 22, 18. 23, 22 כִּי עֵרֹם יְעָרִים הוּא (so Ex. 4,
14). 2 Sa. 12, 28 פֶּן אֶלְכֹּד אֲנִי 17, 15. Isa. 20, 6 (so 2 Ki.
10, 4). 43, 26. Jer. 15, 19. 17, 18 (so Ps. 109, 28). 21, 5 (so Lev. 20, 5.
26, 32). Ez. 16, 60. 62. Dt. 5, 24.   But in the *late* Heb. of Qohéleth, אֲנִי
is often so used with hardly any emphasis, merely to mark the stages in
the author's meditations (as 1, 16. 2, 1. 11. 12. 13. 15. 18. 20) : cf. Del.
p. 207, or C. H. H. Wright, *Ecclesiastes*, p. 488 f.

מוּסָרְךָ לָמוֹ *when* thy chastisement is towards them. 60, 9. Ps. 32, 8 I will give counsel עָלֶיךָ עֵינִי *with* mine eye upon thee. 64, 9 and they (indef.[1]) made each (of them) [=they were made, cf. 63, 11 יַגִּירֻהוּ] to stumble, עָלֵימוֹ לְשׁוֹנָם their own tongue *being* against them. Job 20, 25[b] (Hitz. Del.; Dillm.).

(2) With a participial determination of the subject[2] as the secondary predicate : Nu. 16, 27 יָצְאוּ נִצָּבִים came forth *stationed* (or *so as to be*[3] stationed). Jud. 1, 7. 8, 4 (cf. Ex. 26, 5[b]). Isa. 33, 1 כַּהֲתִמְךָ שׁוֹדֵד lit. when thou finishest *as* a devastator. 36, 22 came קְרוּעֵי בְגָדִים lit. *as* men torn of garments. Jer. 2, 27. 17, 25 רֹכְבִים . . . וּבָאוּ shall enter *riding* (accus.). 23, 5 וּמָלַךְ מֶלֶךְ and shall reign *as* king (cf. 37, 1). 17. 41, 6. 43, 2. Ps. 7, 3. 78, 4 etc.; and preceding the verb, Gen. 49, 11. Ex. 13, 18 וַחֲמֻשִׁים עָלוּ. Isa. 57, 19 *creating* the fruit of the lips, ' Peace, peace,' saith Yahweh etc. (i. e. *as* one who gives human lips the occasion to praise him, Yahweh now promises peace to Israel). Ps. 10, 10 Kt. (וְדָכָה). 56, 2. 92, 14 LXX πεφυτευμένοι . . . ἐξανθήσουσιν. Pr. 20, 14[b] Del. Ez. 36, 35[b].

(3) The same principle with substantives or adjectives : Gen. 37, 35 אָרֵד . . . אָבֵל I shall go down . . . *as* one mourning. Lev. 20, 20 עֲרִירִים יָמֻתוּ. Dt. 4, 27 וְנִשְׁאַרְתֶּם מְתֵי מִסְפָּר ye shall be left *as* few in number. 9, 3 אֵשׁ אֹכְלָה. Ru. 1, 21 מְלֵאָה. 1 Sa. 2, 33 יָמוּתוּ אֲנָשִׁים shall die *as* men (but LXX בְּחֶרֶב אֲנָשִׁים, probably rightly). 3, 2 הֵחֵלּוּ כֵהוֹת lit. began *as* dim ones= began to be dim (unusual : cf. above, Isa. 33, 1). 2 Sa. 19, 21 באתי היום ראשון I am come this day *as* a first one etc. Job

---

[1] From the Semitic point of view הַמַּכְשִׁילִים : see the writer's note on 1 Sa. 16, 4 ; Ges.-Kautzsch, § 144. 3[d] Rem.

[2] Which *we* should regard instinctively as in *apposition* with the subj. : inasmuch as Arabic, however, in (2) and (3), not less than in (1), would employ regularly the *accusative* (defining the *state* of the subj. or obj., whilst the act is taking place : Wright, ii. pp. 123, 125, 129, 213, ed. 2), no doubt the instances in Hebrew should be conceived as implicitly in the same case : cf. Del. on Hab. 2, 15 ; Aug. Müller, § 415 (who cites also Gen. 9, 20); Ewald, § 279 ; Ges.-K., §§ 118. 5 ; 120. 1[a].

[3] Cf. Qor. 4, 18, and Del. on Ps. 68, 31 (text and sense doubtful).

15, 7 הֲרִאישׁוֹן אָדָם תִּוָּלֵד lit. wast thou *as a first one* born (to be) a man? (accus. of product, Ges.-K. § 121. 2 Rem. 1). 19, 25 וְאַחֲרוֹן עַל עָפָר יָקוּם and *as one coming after me* (and so able to vindicate my innocence) shall he stand up upon the dust. 24, 5 פְּרָאִים יָצְאוּ go forth *as* wild asses. 10[b] וְרֵעֵבִים נָשְׂאוּ עֹמֶר. 27, 19. 31, 26 וְיָרֵחַ יָקָר הֹלֵךְ and the moon moving *as* a bright one (=brightly). 41, 7 shut up together חוֹתָם צָר *as* a close seal. Isa. 21, 8 וַיִּקְרָא אַרְיֵה and he cried *as* a lion. 22, 18 כַּדּוּר. 24, 22 shall be gathered with a gathering אַסִּיר *as* captives[1]. 65, 20 the youth shall die בֶּן מֵאָה שָׁנָה *when* a hundred years old (cf. Gen. 17, 12). Ps. 11, 1 צִפּוֹר[2]. Similarly 2 Ki. 5, 2 וַאֲרָם יָצְאוּ גְדוּדִים went forth *as* marauding bands. Jer. 31, 8 קָהָל גָּדוֹל יָשׁוּבוּ הֵנָּה shall return hither *as* a great company (cf. 1 Ki. 8, 65). Zech. 2, 8 פְּרָזוֹת תֵּשֵׁב יְרוּשָׁלִַם shall sit (poet.=be inhabited) *as* open villages[3].

Obs. 1. This construction of the ptcp. is not so frequent as might be expected, in one large class of cases its place being filled by the 'gerundial' inf. :—לֵאמֹר =λέγων (but Arab. قَائِلًٰ *as* one saying,—accus.). Only very seldom when standing alone is it preceded by וְ: 2 Sa. 13, 20. 1 Ki. 7, 7. Hab. 2, 10. Ps. 55, 20 (on 22, 29, see § 135. 6).

Obs. 2. Still rarer is the use of the participle to describe the contemporaneous condition of the *object* of a verb or preposition : see, however, 1 Chr. 12, 1 עַל עָצוּר. 2 Ki. 10, 6 מִגְדָּלִים. 19, 2 וַיִּשְׁלַח. לְצִקְלַג עוֹד עָצוּר. 2 Ki. 10, 6 מִגְדָּלִים מְתַכְּסִים .... Neh. 6, 17. In such cases (except after words like רָאָה, הִשִּׂיג, שָׁמַע, as Ex. 2, 11. 5, 20 (cf. 19). 14, 9. 23, 4) it is usual to prefix the pronoun (§ 160).

The ptcp. is found referring to a *genitive*, Gen. 3, 8 קוֹל י״י מִתְהַלֵּךְ the sound of Yahweh (lit.) *as* (or *while*) walking (accus.) in the garden. 4, 12. Cant. 5, 2 קוֹל דּוֹדִי דוֹפֵק (comp. Del. on these passages), and similarly elsewhere ; also (though this is of an exceptional character) Jer. 44, 26

---

[1] But אֹסֶף הָאַסִּיר (Weir), or אֲסֵפַת אַסִּיר would be more usual (Is. 33, 4 ; Lev. 26, 36. Is. 45, 17. Jer. 22, 19. 30, 14. Ez. 16, 38. 22, 20).

[2] Unless הַר כְּמוֹ צִפּוֹר should be here read.

[3] See parallels in Arabic to several of the above examples in Wright, l. c. §§ 44[c] (with the Remarks), 74. Strictly, also, the predicate after היה should be conceived (like that of كَانَ) as an accus., היה נַעַר, for instance, signifying properly 'existed *as* a youth' = Engl. 'was a youth.'

בפי כל איש יהודה אומר[1]: and to a *suffix*, 1 Ki. 14, 6 באה. Ps. 69, 4 *as* I wait (LXX ingeniously מִיַחַל [and so Targ.], as 58, 6 מְחָבָם). Job 25, 2; cf. Ps. 107, 5. Job 9, 4. 26, 7-9 (to נגדו, *v*. 6). Isa. 44, 20. (Comp. Ewald, *Gramm. Arab.* ii. pp. 47, 267 *bottom*.)

162. Now suppose the idea expressed by the participle has to be *negatived*, how is this accomplished? לא is not used with the ptcp. except on the rarest occasions[2]: אין, involving the addition of the pron. suffix, would be here too periphrastic to be suitable: nothing remains, therefore, but to have recourse to *the finite verb*, either tense being chosen, as the sense may demand[3].

Thus Lev. 1, 17 לא יבדיל *without* dividing it. Ps. 17, 3. 26, 1 (cf. § 34 *end*). Job 8, 12 עוֹדֶנּוּ בְאִבּוֹ לֹא יִקָּטֵף *without* being plucked off[4]. 29, 24 לא יאמינו *when* or *if* they lacked confidence. 31, 34 וָאֶדֹּם לֹא־אֵצֵא פתח=*not going* out. Also in לא תֵדַע יָדַע, לא *without his* or *thy knowing*, i.e. unexpectedly, Isa. 47, 11[b]. Ps. 35, 8. Pr. 5, 6: cf. with וְ, § 159 *end*.

The *perfect* used similarly affords the only means by which our past partcp. active can be represented in Hebrew: Gen. 44, 4 לא הרחיקו (subordinate to יצאו את העיר) *without having* gone far. Ex. 34, 28. Lev. 13, 23 לא פשתה *without having* spread. Nu. 30, 12 לא הניא. Dt. 21, 1 *it not being* known. Job 9, 25[b].

163. But the same use of the verb ἀσυνδέτως is likewise found even where there is no negative:—

---

[1] Cf. 2 Sa. 12, 21 בעבור הילד חי on account of the lad *while* alive [comp. Jer. 14, 4 because of the earth (which) is dismayed (pf.)]. 18, 14 בלב אבשלם עורנו חי LXX ἔτι αὐτοῦ ζῶντος.

[2] It negatives it as an *attributive*, Jer. 2, 2 לא זרועה. 18, 15 (so בלי 2 Sa. 1, 21. Hos. 7, 8); as a *predicate*, 4, 22. 2 Sa. 3, 34. Ps. 38, 15. Job 12, 3 לא נופל אנכי (more pointed than אינני נופל; cf. Ex. 4, 10: Ewald, § 320[b]). Ez. 4, 14. 22, 24. Dt. 28, 61 (בלי Ps. 19, 4), and very anomalously Nu. 35, 23. Zeph. 3, 5. 1 Ki. 10, 21.

[3] Even as an attributive, the ptcp. must be *continued* by the finite verb, if a negative is involved: Ps. 78, 39. Ex. 34, 7.

[4] Cf. Nu. 11, 33 טרם יכרת (the construction of the entire verse is similar).

Gen. 21, 14 and gave it to Hagar, שָׂם *having placed* it on
her shoulder. 44, 12 הֵחֵל LXX excellently ἀρξάμενος. 48, 14.
Dt. 33, 21[b]. Josh. 11, 12. Jud. 6, 19 שָׂם. 20, 31 הנתקו. 1 Ki. 7,
51 ויבא ... את הכלים נתן וג׳ and he brought in the vessels ...,
placing them etc. 11, 27. 13, 18 (ψευσάμενος αὐτῷ). 18, 6 (cf.
Nu. 11, 32). Isa. 29, 13 (notice the accents, comparing p. 106,
n. 3). Jer. 20, 15; Ps. 7, 7. 57, 4 חָרֻף, 71, 3. 119, 126 הֵפֵרוּ
תורתך (reason for 126[a]).

And in the impf., expressing sometimes concomitance,
sometimes a consequence :—Ex. 8, 5[b]. 7[b]. Nu. 14, 3 *so that*
or *while* our children will be a prey. Isa. 5, 11 *while* wine
enflameth them. 27, 9 לא יקומו. 60, 11 לא יסגרו. Jer. 4, 7[b].
30 *beautifying* thyself in vain. 13, 16 Kt. ישית. 15, 19. 16, 6
etc. Ps. 103, 5. Job 11, 18[b]. 30, 28 קַמְתִּי בַקָּהָל אֲשַׁוֵּעַ surrexi
in contione *lamentaturus*[1], Del.

Obs. Add also the ἀσύνδετα, Num. 21, 30 וַנִּירָם אָבַד חֶשְׁבּוֹן. Ez.
17, 4[b]. 19, 3. 5. 6. 12. Job 16, 8[a]; with an impf. 1 Sa. 13, 17. 18, 5
ויצא דוד ... ישכיל=went forth ..., *doing* wisely. Isa. 42, 14 (cf. § 34
end). Jer. 15, 6 את נטשת אתי ... אחור תלכי. Ps. 50, 20
תשב באחיך; in the future, Ez. 5, 2 תשאני אל רוח תרכיבני; Job 30, 22 תדבר.
ולקחת ... תכה. 24, 11 תחם. Isa. 3, 26[b] ונקתה לארץ תשב=and she
shall be emptied, *sitting* on the ground. 29, 4 ושפלת מארץ תדברי;
and, where the first verb is a subsidiary one, 1 Sa. 20, 19 וְשִׁלַּשְׁתָּ תרד מאד
(read תִּפָּקֵד *shalt be missed* with LXX : תֵּרֵד is not an idea that would
be qualified by מאד). 20 (if LXX אֲשַׁלֵּשׁ for שלשת be correct).

Occasionally the impf. is subordinated to a previous verb with a syntactical freedom better known in Arabic or Syriac: Isa. 42, 21 יהוה
חפץ ... יגדיל תורה ויאדיר Yahweh was pleased ... *that he should*
make the teaching great and glorious. Job 19, 3 לא תבשו תהכרו
לי (1. תהכרו). 32, 22 לא ידעתי אֲכַנֶּה=I know not *how to* give flattering
titles. Lam. 4, 14 לא יוכלו יִגָּעוּ they are unable *to* touch (cf. Nu. 22, 6).
Is. 47, 1[b]=5[b] לא תוסיפי יקראו לך (Wright, ii. § 8[d]: Matth. 8, 28 Pesh.

---

[1] Cf. 16, 8[b] ויקם בי כחשי בפני יענה and my leanness riseth up against
me, *that it may answer* (or *answering*) in my face. 24, 14. Ps. 88, 11.
102, 14, likewise (as Del. remarks) after קם. Comp. the Arabic usage,
Wright, ii. § 8[d, e], and below, p. 244, towards the bottom.

such that no man إِلَّا رُجُلاً وَهُوَ= نَعَمُ يُكَبَّ ; Luke 18, 13 إِلَّا رُجُلاً وَهُوَ; ; نَامِ I know not *how to build*, cited by Nöldeke, *Syr. Gramm.* § 267 : but more commonly with **؟**): Hebrew, in such cases (except when it throws the two verbs into the *same* tense, Hos. 1, 6. 5, 11. 6, 4. 9, 9. Jer. 13, 18), prefers almost invariably the infinitive.

Peculiar also is the union by ו in Gen. 30, 27 (·ו). 47, 6 (cf. Job 23, 3 knew *so that* I might find him). Ct. 2, 3. Esth. 8, 6 (consec., p. 130).

164. The secondary predicate is often expressed by a short clause consisting of בְּלִי, לֹא, אֵין, followed by a subst., which may be attached to either a subst. or a verb: so for instance the phrase אֵין מִסְפָּר *without number*, Joel 1, 6. al. (with וְ Ps. 104, 25. 105, 34: cf. 72, 12. Job 5, 9, and וְלֹא 29, 12); Gen. 31, 50. Ex. 21, 11: אֵין כָּסֶף. 1 Ki. 22, 1 they continued three years אין מלחמה. Isa. 47, 1 אֵין כִּסֵּא. Hos. 7, 11 יוֹנָה פוֹתָה אֵין לֵב. Ps. 88, 5 like a man אֵין אֱיָל *without* strength. Pr. 25, 28 עִיר פְּרוּצָה אין חומה. Lam. 5, 3 Kt. Job 8, 11. 24, 10 naked, they walk up and down (Pi'el) בְּלִי לְבוּשׁ *without* covering. 33, 9. 34, 6 (cf. Ps. 59, 5). 24 יְרֹעַ כַּבִּירִים לֹא חֵקֶר he breaketh in pieces the mighty *without inquisition;* 12, 24 בתהו לֹא דרך in the *pathless* waste. 26, 2 זְרֹעַ לֹא־עֹז the arm *without* strength. 38, 26ᵃ לְהַמְטִיר עַל־אֶרֶץ לֹא־אִישׁ. 2 Sa. 23, 4 a morning לֹא עָבוֹת *without* clouds (or, idiomatically, *a cloudless* morning). This use of בלי and לֹא, however, is confined to poetry, except in 1 Chr. 2, 30. 32 וימת לא בנים (Ewald, § 286ᵍ).

Obs. בבלי and בלא are met with occasionally in prose (as well as poetry), but not באין (often in Prov.): ואין is, however, more common than אין alone. The Chronicler has several times לאין (*in the condition of*[1] *no* ... = *without*), but in a manner peculiar to himself.

165. In almost all the preceding examples, the circumstantial clause has been *appended* to the principal sentence: we have, however, already met with a few instances in which a participial clause was prefixed (§ 161), and we shall soon

---

[1] The לְ of norm or state, as in לבטח, etc.: Ewald, § 217ᵈ.

find that such a position is by no means uncommon, or confined to the participle alone.

If we compare a sentence such as 1 Ki. 13, 20 with one
like *v.* 23, we shall at once see that the participial clause
הֵם יֹשְׁבִים in the former is, in position and force, the precise
counterpart of the adverbial clause אַחֲרֵי אָכְלוֹ וג' in the latter;
and that like it, it notifies a circumstance strictly subordinate
to the main narrative, in a manner exactly reproducible in
Greek by the use of the gen. abs. (LXX καὶ ἐγένετο αὐτῶν
καθημένων κ.τ.λ.). The participle as thus used is frequent,
especially in the historical books: from the analogy of the
corresponding expressions in the classical languages, it may
be appropriately termed *the participle absolute*[1].

Thus Gen. 42, 35 and it came to pass, הֵם מְרִיקִים *as they
were emptying* their sacks, that they found etc. 2 Ki. 2, 11
וַיְהִי הֵמָּה הֹלְכִים ... 8, 5 LXX αὐτοῦ ἐξηγουμένου. If
it is required to express *past* time, the perfect naturally takes
the place of the participle :—Gen. 27, 30 and it came to pass,
אַךְ יָצֹא יָצָא יַעֲקֹב Jacob *having* only just gone out, that Esau
his brother came in. Josh. 4, 18 נִתְּקוּ. 2 Ki. 12, 7[b]. And
add Gen. 15, 17 וַיְהִי הַשֶּׁמֶשׁ בָּאָה, a passage in which the
perfect makes it evident (quite apart from considerations of
gender) that ויהי must not be taken closely with השמש : rather
'and it came to pass, *the sun having gone down*.' Compare
also Gen. 24, 15. 2 Ki. 8, 21 וַיְהִי הוּא קָם לַיְלָה וַיַּכֶּה[2]. 20, 4.
Jer. 37, 13. 1 Chr. 15, 29.

Obs. It should, however, be noted that in several of the passages last
cited, the accents closely unite ויהי to the word following, so that at
least by the punctuators they were probably understood differently: thus
Gen. 24, 15 וַיְהִי־הוּא. 2 Ki. 8, 21 (like וַיְהִי בֻנֹה Gen. 4, 17). 20, 4
and Isaiah was—he had not gone out etc. (cf. Isa. 22, 7 *and there were*
thy choicest valleys—they were filled with chariots). Cf. § 121. *Obs.* 2.

---

[1] Cf. p. 147 *note*, and § 126.

[2] In the parallel, 2 Chr. 21, 9 הוּא is omitted, and the passage can only
be naturally understood according to § 135. 5.

The analogous construction in the future is found Josh. 22, 18. 1 Ki. 18, 12.

166. In the passages cited the participle clearly constitutes a circumstantial clause. The instances in which no וַיְהִי precedes, such as 1 Ki. 14, 17 הִיא בָאָה וְהַנַּעַר מֵת, or Gen. 44, 3 הַבֹּקֶר אוֹר וְהָאֲנָשִׁים שֻׁלְּחוּ, stand upon a different footing. Here the temporal clause is no longer *subordinate* to the main description (וַיְהִי כְּבֹאָהּ וַיָּמָת הַנַּעַר): it is *parallel* to it, and *co*-ordinate. As a rule, it is true, a time-determination takes a secondary position; but where it is desired to confer some additional vividness upon the description, instead of being treated as a passing detail, it is made a prominent and independent feature in the picture.

167. In fact, it may be observed, even in the classical languages, that time-determinations do not always occupy a subordinate position: in graphic or elevated writing particularly they are often placed on one and the same level with the rest of the narrative. A few instances are worth citing:—Il. xix. 1–3. Dem. *de cor.* § 218 ἑσπέρα μὲν γὰρ ἦν, ἧκε δ' ἀγγέλλων τις ὡς τοὺς πρυτάνεις ὡς Ἐλάτεια κατείληπται· how much fuller and richer the picture, than if the orator had simply said, ἑσπέρας γὰρ ἦκεν ἀγγέλλων τις κ.τ.λ., or employed a word like ἐπειδή ! Soph. Phil. 354 ff. ἦν δ' ἦμαρ ἤδη δεύτερον πλέοντί μοι Κἀγὼ πικρὸν Σίγειον οὐρίῳ πλάτῃ Κατηγόμην. Thuc. i. 50. 6 ἤδη δ' ἦν ὀψὲ καὶ ἐπεπαιώνιστο αὐτοῖς ὡς ἐς ἐπίπλουν καὶ οἱ Κορίνθιοι ἐξαπίνης πρύμναν ἐκρούοντο· iv. 69. 3. Hdt. iii. 108 *end.* iv. 181. 5 μεσαμβρίη τέ ἐστι, καὶ τὸ κάρτα γίγνεται ψυχρόν, 'it is noon, and the water becomes quite cold.' 6 παρέρχονταί τε μέσαι νύκτες καὶ ψύχεται μέχρι ἐς ἠῶ. Liv. xliii. 4 'vixdum ad consulem se pervenisse, *et* audisse oppidum expugnatum' etc. Verg. Georg. ii. 80 Conington, 'nec longum tempus, *et* ingens Exiit ad caelum ramis felicibus arbos.' Aen. iii. 9 and often.

168. But it will still, perhaps, be asked, If this be all, why the peculiar form assumed in the passages in question, which in others becomes even more striking still, as 1 Sa. 9, 11 [1] הֲמָה עֹלִים . . . וְהֵמָּה מָצְאוּ ? why, if nothing more was intended by the writer, was he not satisfied with the more simple and obvious form וַיַּעֲלוּ . . . וַיִּמְצָאוּ ? (cf. § 149 *n.*) The answer is evident. Such a form, being wholly devoid of emphasis, would not have suited his purpose. He wishes to mark as vividly as he can the time at which a given event took place, *with reference to another event.* In order to do this, he makes the latter prominent, by *elevating* it from the lower position it commonly holds, and causing it to *confront* the former as conspicuously and decidedly as the language will permit. In the passages from the Iliad and Demosthenes this antithetical relation is indicated by the μὲν . . . δέ: in Hebrew it can only be expressed by the position of the two subjects—both, contrary to the usual custom (at least with nouns) by which the *verb* stands first, being placed in the foreground. Thus in היא באה והנער מת two actions belonging to *different* subjects, in המה עלים והמה מצאו two actions of the *same* subject are thrown into strong contrast with each other: and the special relation which they are intended to bear to one another is made keenly palpable.

169. We may now collect the principal passages in which this very idiomatic and forcible construction is employed:— Gen. 38, 25 הוּא מוּצֵאת וְהִיא שָׁלְחָה she *was being* brought forth, when she sent etc. (A.V. 'when she was brought forth, she sent,' which though expressing the *general* sense of the original, does not bring before the mind, with equal clearness, the picture הוא מוצאת, upon which the writer dwells). Jud. 18, 3 המה עם בית מיכה והמה הכירו וג'; and with a change of subject, 19, 11. 1 Sa. 20, 36 הנער רץ והוא ירה. 2 Sa. 20, 8. 1 Ki. 14, 17. 2 Ki. 2, 23. 4, 5 [2].

---

[1] Cf. Hdt. iii. 76. 2 ἔν τε δὴ τῇ ὁδῷ μέσῃ στείχοντες ἐγίνοντο, καὶ τὰ περὶ Πρηξάσπεα γεγονότα ἐπυνθάνοντο.

[2] What are we to do with 10, 12 f. הוא בית עקר הרעים...ויהוא מצא,

We find עוֹד in the first clause, Gen. 29, 9 עוֹדֶנּוּ מְדַבֵּר וְרָחֵל
בָּאָה he was still speaking, *when* Rachel entered in. Nu. 11, 33
(hence, only varied in expression, Ps. 78, 30 f.: cf. in *form*
also Job 8, 12 ... וּלְפָנֵי ... עוֹדֶנּוּ). 1 Ki. 1, 22. 42 (cf. of future
time *v.* 14). 2 Ki. 6, 33. Dan. 9, 20 f.; and וְהִנֵּה in the second
clause. 1 Sa. 9, 14 הֵמָּה בָאִים ... וְהִנֵּה שְׁמוּאֵל יֹצֵא לִקְרָאתָם.
17, 23. Job 1, 18ᵇ–19.

If the sense demands it, a *perfect* may of course stand in
the first clause:—Gen. 19, 23 הַשֶּׁמֶשׁ יָצָא עַל הָאָרֶץ וְלוֹט בָּא צֹעֲרָה.
44, 3. 4 הֵם יָצְאוּ וְיוֹסֵף אָמַר they had gone out of the city, *and*
(or *when*) Joseph said. Jud. 3, 24 וְהוּא יָצָא וַעֲבָדָיו בָּאוּ now *he*
had gone out, when his servants came in. 15, 14 הוּא בָא עַד
לֶחִי וּפְלִשְׁתִּים הֵרִיעוּ לִקְרָאתוֹ. 18, 22. 20, 39 f. 2 Sa. 2, 24 al.;
cf. also Gen. 7, 6. 19, 4. 24, 45, and above, § 128 [1].

---

where the pronoun *followed* by the subject to which it refers is unparalleled? I venture to think that for וַיְהוּא we ought to read וְהוּא:
the change is very slight, and would bring the passage into complete
conformity with Jud. 18, 3. 1 Sa. 9, 11 etc.

[1] Ewald adds Jud. 7, 19. 2 Sa. 11, 4, in both places neglecting the
athnach, and supposing the second clause to be introduced exceptionally by וְ. Of 2 Sam., also, he says, 'das *part.* dem sinne nach beinahe
schon einem *part. perf.* im Griechischen entspricht:' but if the author
had intended to convey such an idea of past time, he would assuredly
have written וְהִיא שָׁבָה. הִיא הִתְקַדְּשָׁה מִטֻּמְאָתָהּ וְהִיא שָׁבָה. וְהִיא מִתְקַדֶּשֶׁת can
only be rendered ' *as* (or *while*) she purified herself from her unclean-
ness:' compare the writer's note *ad loc.*

From § 161 *Obs.* 2 it will be plain that the idiomatic equivalent of
καὶ ἐλιθοβόλουν τὸν Στέφανον ἐπικαλούμενον is וַיִּסְקְלוּ אֶת־סְטֶ׳ וְהוּא
קֹרֵא: so Luke 4, 1 וְהוּא מָלֵא (after מִן הַיַּרְדֵּן). 35 לֹא הֵרַע־לוֹ מְאוּמָה
(§ 163). Compare the renderings in Delitzsch's version.

APPENDIX II.

On the Use of the Jussive Form.

170. THE use of the modal forms in Hebrew, particularly of the jussive, presents great difficulties to the grammarian. These difficulties would certainly in great measure vanish, if it could be legitimately supposed that the modal forms were destitute of any special significance, being assumed for 'euphony' or as 'poetical licences' etc., or (in the case of the cohortative *-ah*) being merely 'paragogic;' that, consequently, their presence might be disregarded, and the tenses translated, if need be, in the manner of mere imperfects. But the multitude of instances occurring in the Old Testament, in which the meaning of these forms is clear and unambiguous, forbids such a supposition,—at least unless we are prepared to shew that a particular author wrote incorrectly, or adopted some local style, or else that he lived during a period at which the forms in question had lost[1] their customary significance. We are seldom in a position which enables us to do this: the result is, that grammarians have been driven sometimes to the adoption of strange expedients in order to overcome the disagreement existing between the meaning apparently forced upon them by the form, and that which the context seems to demand.

171. Before proceeding further, however, it will be desirable to give a synopsis of the passages in which the difficulty

---

[1] The same suggestion is made by Olshausen, § 257[a], p. 571: the forms in question, however, occur frequently in passages which are not so late as to make such a supposition probable.

is most seriously felt, including a few which, though they have
been cited elsewhere[1], are still worth some reconsideration.

18 יֵצֶב. Dt. 32, 8 וַתְּהִי. Lev. 15, 24 כִּי יַבְעֶר־אִישׁ Ex. 22, 14
Ez. וַיְּ. 63, 3 וְאַחְזֹק. 42, 6 אוֹ יַחְזַק. 27, 5 יֵשׁב. Isa. 12, 1 תֵּשִׁי.
14, 7 וַיַּעַל. Hos. 6, 1 יְ. 11, 4 וְאַט. Joel 2, 20 וַתַּעַל. Mic. 3, 4
יַכְרֵת. 12, 4 יַמְטֵר. Ps. 11, 6 וַיֵּט ... וְיָשֵׂם. Zeph. 2, 13 וְיַסְתֵּר.
85, 14 תַּשְׁלֵג. 68, 15 יָאְמֶם. 58, 5 יְדַבֵּר. 47, 4 יַדְרֵךְ. 25, 9
15, 33 וַתָּשֶׂם. Job 13, 27 וְיַצֵּב. 15, 25 יָתֵר. Pr. 12, 26 וְיָשֵׂם.
יְהִי ... וַיְמַטֵּר. 20, 23 יַחְזַק. 12 יְהִי. 18, 9 תָּלֹן ... וְ. 17, 2 וְיִשְׁלָךְ.
26 יָרַע. 28 יָגֵל. 23, 9 וְלֹא אָחַז: 11 וְלֹא אָט: 24, 14 יְהִי ... וְ.
25 וְיָשֵׂם. 27, 8 כִּי יֵשֵׁל. 22 וְיִשְׁלָךְ. 33, 11 יָשֵׂם. 21 יָכֵל. 27 יָשֵׁר.
34, 29 וַיַּסְתֵּר. 37 וַיֶּרֶב. 36, 14 תָּמֹת. 15 וְיָגֵל. 38, 24 יָפֵץ. 39, 26
Qoh. 12, 7 עַד יָשְׁקִיף וַיֵּרֶא. Lam. 3, 50 יַגֵּשׁ. 40, 19 יַאַבְרֵנֶץ
16 וַיֵּשׁב. 10 and 28 וְתִחְיֶ. 11, 4 וְתִחְיֶ. Dan. 8, 12 וַתַּשְׁלֵךְ. וַיֵּשׁב.
וַיַּעַשׂ. 17 וְיָשֵׂם. 18 and 19 וְיֵשֶׁב. 25 וְיֵעֹר. 30 וַיָּבֶן; occasionally
also after לֹא (§ 50 a, *Obs.*).

172. The passages here collected are in many ways very
dissimilar; and the reader should examine each separately
by itself. In some, for instance, there is no reason why the
verbs should not be understood strictly as jussives: so Zeph.
2, 13 (§ 50). Ps. 11, 6. 12, 4 (where there is nothing to
suggest a historical reference, above, § 84). Others, as
Lev. 15. Ez. 14 (who separates himself *that he should* cherish
his idols in his heart). Lam. 3, 50. Job 24, 25, in all of which
the infin. with לְ might be substituted for the jussive and וְ
without appreciable alteration in sense (cf. § 64, and Job 9, 33
where, as Del. remarks, יָשֵׁת is equivalent in meaning to
לָשִׁית), may be referred to § 62. The difficulty lies rather
with those which, as it seems, involve merely the statement
of a fact, and in which, therefore, the verb is jussive in form
only, and not in meaning. One solution here proposed is
that ·וְ is omitted, or replaced by וְ. This is adopted by Ewald,

---

[1] Cf. §§ 50 a, 58, 84, 121 *Obs.*, 155 *Obs.*

§§ 233ᵃ, 343ᵇ, and Dillmann (on Job 33, 21), and is extended
by Hitzig (see his notes on Ps. 8, 7. 11, 6 etc.) so as to
include even cases like Ps. 58, 5 (for וַיֵּאָטְמוּ, וְ being the
continuation of the attributive חֵרֵשׁ : cf. § 76 *a*), and 68,
15 (וְ following a time-determination, according to § 127 β).
Böttcher, on the other hand, adhering to the idea of a real
jussive, ii. p. 183, goes so far as to affirm that this mood may
express ' das übel empfundene *muss* des fremden Eigenwillens
Ij. xiii. 27. xxxiii. 11. xxiv. 14. xxxiv. 37 :' but how such a
reversal of its ordinary meaning is possible, it is as difficult
to comprehend as in the case of the cohortative, §§ 51–53.
The former solution is doubtless correct in principle, at least
so far as regards the omission of וְ, though it is somewhat far-
fetched to have recourse to it for Ps. 58 and 68; its truth has
been already recognized, § 83, and it only remains to enquire
whether any more specific ground can be alleged for the choice
of the apocopated form in preference to the ordinary imperfect.

173. It may be observed in most of the instances in
question that the abbreviated form stands at the *beginning of
a clause.* Now this is just the position that would be occupied
by the same form if it were preceded by וְ: it seems allowable
therefore to suppose that (e.g.) יָשֵׂם was retained primarily as
a reminiscence of the normal וַיָּשֶׂם. At the same time, from
the manner in which it was used with וְ, the shorter form
must have become strongly associated with the idea of a
connexion with what precedes; and the desire to preserve
some expression of this suggests itself as another motive
contributing probably towards its retention. But, when it
stands later in the sentence, where וְ would be out of place,
and where it was no longer the Hebrew custom to give
formal expression to that connexion, the impf. appears in its
usual form: e.g. Job 13, 27 וְתָשֵׂם, but 23, 6 יָשֵׂם; 18, 9 יֶחֱזַק,
but 8, 15 יַחֲזִיק; 34, 29 וְיַסְתֵּר, but וְהוּא יַשְׁקִט, the connexion
with וְ being broken by the emphatic הוּא. This explanation
may be accepted as satisfactory for those cases in which the

shorter form is found without a preceding וְ (§ 84 β)[1]: in other
words, יַחְתֹּ, for instance (Job 18, 9), may be regarded as a
poetical abbreviation of וַיַחְתֹּ: but even then, we must beware
of applying it to cases where the reference is to the future, or
where for any other reason וַ could not have stood (e.g. Job
24, 25, where evidently וַיָּשֵׂם could not follow מִי יַכְזִיבֵנִי).

174. On the other hand, where the shorter form occurs,
preceded by וְ (§ 84 a), it must be admitted to be doubtful
whether the punctuation represents a genuine tradition, and
whether וַ (or וְ with the *indicative* mood) should not be
restored. The preference for וְ (p. 98 *top*) must be attributed,
it is probable, not to the original authors, but to the *punctuators*. In some cases the punctuators have apparently
followed a false analogy, in others they seem to have been
guided by a false exegesis. The frequent use of the jussive
form (as a *voluntative*) with וְ appears to have led the Mas-
sorites (who probably had an imperfect sense of the true
force of the jussive form) to adopt mechanically the same
punctuation for cases to which it was not properly applicable.
Thus in Pr. 15, 25 we should in all probability vocalize וְיַצֵּב,
in Job 13, 27 וְתָשֵׂם (or וְתָשֶׂם)[2]. 15, 33 וַיִּשְׁלַח. 20, 23 וַיַּמְטֵר
(unless יְהִי . . . יַמְטֵר may be referred to § 152). 27, 22 וַיִּשְׁלַח.
34, 37 וְיֶרֶב. In Ps. 85, 14[3]. Mic. 3, 4. Job 34, 29. Qoh. 12, 7
the *defectiva scriptio* has most probably occasioned the incorrect vocalization; and we shall hardly be wrong in
reading וְיָשֵׁב, וְיִסְתֵּר, וְיָשֵׂם (cf. b תָשׁוּב . . . וְ)[4]. Elsewhere the

---

[1] As Ps. 25, 9. 47, 4. Job 18, 9. 12. 20, 23 יהי. 26. 28. 33, 11. 21. 27.
Hos. 6, 1. In several of these cases the form is part of the consonantal
text, and does not depend merely on the punctuation. But Pr. 12, 26
(where ו would be out of place) we ought no doubt to punctuate (with
Hitz., Strack) יָתֵר, probably also (with Del. as well) מִרְעֵהוּ ('spieth
out his pasture').

[2] Comp. Dillmann, *Hiob* (ed. 2), 1891, *ad loc.*

[3] The jussive sense, suggested § 58, seems hardly probable here.

[4] Qoh. 10, 20. 12, 4 the ordinary vocalization ויקום, יַגִּיד is preferable
grammatically to the Massoretic reading (Baer) ויקום, יַגִּד.

anomaly appears to be due to false exegesis. Thus Isa. 12, 1
יָשֹׁב *followed* by וּתְנַחֲמֵנִי can hardly be translated except as a
prayer (cf. 55, 7. Jud. 7, 3. Ps. 71, 21), and this, no doubt,
is the sense intended by the punctuation (comp. the fut. of
the Targ.[1]); the *past* sense, which the context requires, would
seem to call for וַתְּנַחֲמֵנִי (cf. Ps. 90, 3 וַתֹּאמֶר ... תָּשֵׁב). 42, 6 is
analogous to Hos. 11, 4 : in both these passages the vocalization with וְ commends itself, as that intended by the original
authors (followed in Hosea by a bare impf., as Jer. 15, 6,
§ 163 *Obs.*)[2]. And Isa. 63, 3 וְיֵז is almost certainly a mis-
punctuation for וַיֵז[3] (observe the following *perfect*, אֶגְאַלְתִּי),
originating in the two preceding verbs being referred incorrectly to the future[4]. So Dan. 8, 12 וַתַּשְׁלֵךְ.

Obs. Ps. 58, 5 a sense of the connexion between the relative clause
and its antecedent may perhaps, through an indistinctly felt analogy
with the connexion expressed by וְ·, have determined the punctuation
יַאְםֵ: Dt. 32, 8. Ps. 68, 15 the original vocalization was probably
תַּשְׁלֵג, יַצֵּב. The same may be supposed to have been the case with the
four instances after לֹא (§ 50 *a, Obs.*): while in 2 Sa. 18, 14 the use of
the cohort. אֲחִילָה may be accounted for by the preceding לֹא having
been viewed as specially negativing כֵּן. And Job 27, 8 it is probable
(provided the text be otherwise correct) that we should punctuate,
as Dillm. (ed. 2) suggests, יֵשַׁל or יָשֹׁל.

175. Of the remaining passages, Isa. 27, 5 receives light

---

[1] וכדו יתוב רוגזך מיני ותרחם עלי.

[2] With Isa. 42, 6 comp. the *past* tenses in the parallel 49, 2.

[3] So Cheyne (crit. note), Dillm., R. V. (and of course, correspondingly, וָאֲדֻרְכֵם, וָאֲרַמְּסֵם, *vv.* 5. 6 וָאָבֵּים, וָאֶשְׁתּוּמֵם, etc.).

[4] 'In order to preclude the supposition that the deliverance was
already past,' Luzzatto, as cited by G. F. Moore, *Theol. Lit.-zeitung*,
1887, col. 292 ('Edom' being interpreted by Jewish exegesis of Rome,
or, more generally, of the imperial Christian power). Probably, also,
in several of the other passages cited § 84 *a* the original vocalization
was with *waw* consec. Comp. Moore, *l.c.*, who observes that in Isa.
51, 2 this is the sense expressed by the older Jewish tradition, as represented by LXX and Targ., but that the intention of the punctuation, on
the contrary, is to interpret the verbs (incorrectly) as futures (hence
וַאֲבָרְכֵהוּ וְאַרְבֵּהוּ instead of וָ'רָ'). So 48, 3ᵃ we should expect naturally

from an Arabic idiom[1], '*or else let* him take hold of my strong-hold'='*unless* he take hold' (Germ. 'es *sei* denn dass man meinen schuz ergriffe'); Dt. 32, 18 תְּשִׁי must of course come from שָׁיָה (like יְחִי from חיה): as, however, the Semitic languages know only נָשָׁה and שָׁהָה (=سها Qor. 51, 11) in the sense of *forget*, it is probable that the text is incorrect, and that we should, with Olsh. p. 511 and Aug. Müller, restore תִּשֶׁה. Job 17, 2 is doubtless '*so that* mine eye *resteth*' (§ 62), which *from the connexion* is equivalent to 'and my eye *must rest:*' 23, 9. 11. 24, 14 appear to be isolated examples of *tmesis* (cf. § 85); 36, 14, see § 64 *Obs.* or § 84 β; Ex. 22, 4 and Job 39, 26 the shorter form may have been chosen by the punctuators on account of the *maqqeph* following[2]; and Job 40, 19 (if the text be sound[3]) A. V. is probably sub-

---

וָאַשְׁמִיעֵם (cf. 3ᵇ וַתָּבֹאנָה), 57, 17 וָאֹכְהוּ and וָאֶקְצֹף (so Dillm.): on 43, 28 see p. 70 *note*. For וָאַשִׂיגֵם Ps. 18, 38 the parallel text 2 Sa. 22, 38 has וָאַשְׁמִידֵם (as it has in *v.* 39 impff. with *waw* consec. for the impff. ἀσυνδέτως of Ps. 18): but here, probably, the more graphic, frequentative sense expressed by the text of Ps. 18, is in both verses original (cf. 38ᵇ. 39ᵃ·ᵝ. 40ᵇ). Elsewhere, also, it is sometimes difficult not to suspect the existing text to be incorrectly vocalized: Job 3, 11, for instance, וְאָנוּעַ would by analogy be וָאָגוּעַ (cf. Gen. 31, 27. Jer. 20, 17 : § 74 *a*), and *v.* 13 וְאֶשְׁקוֹט would be וָאֶשְׁקוֹט (cf. Ex. 9, 15 : § 141). And one wonders why the punctuation of ו is not uniform in (*e. g.*) Ps. 104, 32ᵇ. Job 5, 18ᵃ. 12, 15ᵃ·ᵇ and Job 14, 10. 20ᵃ. 33, 26. So, § 153. 3, it may be doubted whether the explanation of the jussive is not in some cases artificial, and whether we should not read Is. 41 וָאֵרָא, Ps. 104 וַיְהִי (§ 84 β). Pr. 27, 17, as pointed, can hardly be taken except as an *admonition* (Del., Nowack): the affirmative rend. (cf. R. V.) implies in *a* יַחֵד (or יָחֵד, sc. הַמְחָד), and in *b* יָחַד.

[1] Where, however, the *subjunctive* mood is employed (cf. for a similar variation, p. 67 *n.*): Ewald, § 629; Wright, ii. § 15 (6), 'I will certainly kill the unbeliever أَوْ يُسْلِمَ *unless* he become a Muslim.'

[2] On the (false) analogy of וַיֶּגֶד־לָה, וַיֶּחֱזַק־בּוֹ, etc. (cf. Olsh. p. 570). Otherwise König i. 275 (one of the traces of the older formation of Hif'il with *ṣere* instead of *ḥireq*).

[3] The LXX have here πεποιημένον ἐγκαταπαίζεσθαι ὑπὸ τῶν ἀγγέλων

stantially correct, lit. '*let* him that made him *bring* his sword *nigh* to him!' (for none else can do so.)

Obs. Joel 2, 20 ותעל is extremely difficult: the reference being clearly to the future, ו cannot be regarded as a substitute for וְ: the form must, therefore, be that of a real jussive, but this, *after the previous* וצלה באשו, whether it be rendered *and let* ... or *that* ... *may*, seems unsuited to the context. We are almost constrained to suspect an error in the reading; though the excision of וצלה באשו as a gloss, proposed by Merx, perhaps weakens the latter part of the *v.* too much to be probable. In Dan. 11 (where, for the same reason, ו cannot be in place of וְ), in so far as the instances may not be presumed to depend, like 8, 12 (§ 174), upon a false punctuation, we may be content to suppose that the mood was used without any recollection of its distinctive signification[1]. It is strange that Dr. Pusey (*Daniel*, ed. 2, p. 591) should have accepted Ewald's classification, § 343[c], as satisfactory. A distinction ought obviously to be made between such cases as Isa. 19, 20. Ez. 33, 31, where the verb after ו is the simple imperfect, and those like Joel 2, 20, where it is jussive: the former, though less usual, present no real difficulty (see § 134), it is the latter which embarrass us. Dr. Pusey says, 'the condensation of this idiom, the use of the apocopated form, with the simple *and*, shews there is great emphasis in it:' but by what process can a wish or command, such as we know to be signified by the apocopated imperfect, be transformed into a mere expression of emphasis? Certainly the jussive, like the imperative, is sometimes employed in a rhetorical style with brilliancy and effect; but then, as we saw §§ 56–58, it retains its rightful force, and, in fact, would not be effective unless it did retain it: in the instances alleged, however, its proper meaning is taken from it, and a *different* meaning, incompatible with, and *not derivable from*, the meaning borne elsewhere, is substituted in its place. Such a substitution is contrary to all analogy or probability; and it is preferable to acquiesce in a solution which is in agreement with a known principle of language.

αὐτοῦ, which points to a reading הֶעָשׂוּי לְשַׂחֶק בּוֹ 'which is made (for Him) to play with him' (cf. Ps. 104, 26, as understood by Ew., Hitz., Kay, Cheyne, and R.V. *marg.*) for העשו יגש חרבו, which is possibly right: observe that the difference in the *ductus litterarum* is slight.

[1] The Hebrew of the book of Daniel is late; and in other respects also the syntax of ch. 11 is much inferior to that of the usual prophetic style.

APPENDIX III.

On Arabic as Illustrative of Hebrew[1].

176. In few departments of knowledge has the 'comparative' method of enquiry been more fruitful of valuable and interesting results than in the investigation of the phenomena presented by language. What that method is, and, at least in so far as regards the Aryan languages, what some of the more important of the results alluded to are, will be familiar to most English readers from the well-known volumes of Professor Max Müller, or the more recent work of Professor Sayce, in which the principles of Comparative Philology are at once lucidly set forth and abundantly illustrated. A general acquaintance may, therefore, be presupposed with the character, for example, of the cumulative evidence by which the

---

[1] The following appendix (of which the substance appeared first in 1874) is now, strictly speaking, superseded by the late Dr. Wright's admirable *Lectures on the Comparative Grammar of the Semitic Languages* (1890). It has, nevertheless, been deemed expedient to retain it, in the hope that it may prove serviceable to some who have not access to Dr. Wright's more comprehensive volume. Two other works in which particular departments of the same subject may be studied, are (1) P. de Lagarde, *Uebersicht über die im Aramäischen, Arabischen und Hebräischen übliche Bildung der Nomina* (1889), and (2) J. Barth, *Die Nominalbildung in den Semitischen Sprachen* (1889, 1891): cf. Aug. Müller, *ZDMG.* 1891, pp. 221–238. Very valuable contributions to the same subject are also to be found in Nöldeke's *Mandäische Grammatik*, and in the same author's articles and reviews in the *ZDMG.* (and elsewhere), e.g. *ZDMG.* 1883, p. 525 ff. (on verbs ע״ו in Hebrew), 1884, p. 407 ff. (the terminations of the Semitic perfect), 1886, p. 718 ff. (on Friedr. Delitzsch's *Prolegomena*), etc.

direct or collateral genealogical relationship, subsisting between the languages belonging to a given family, may be established, with the nature of the successive modifications a language may undergo, with the laws which regulate the particular and distinctive form assumed in each by the same word, and with the mutual illustration which languages thus allied afford of one another.

177. The same method is, however, no less applicable to the Semitic family of speech than to the Aryan. A merely superficial comparison of the vocabulary and accidence—to say nothing of the syntax—is sufficient to reveal the fact that all the Semitic languages are intimately connected with one another, and that the nations speaking them must, at some period or other, have dwelt together in a common home[1]: more accurate and systematic research shews that none of them can lay claim to *exclusive* priority above the rest, as being the one from which the others are derived (in the same manner, for instance, as the Romance languages are derived from Latin), but that they are the descendants of a deceased ancestor, whose most prominent characteristics, though with different degrees of clearness and purity, they all still reflect. Each after its separation from the parent stock pursued a path of its own, some, as it would seem, through long years preserving almost intact many of the features they originally possessed; others, on the contrary, lopping these off, or else assimilating them, with greater or less rapidity. It is just in virtue of this *uneven development* of language, just in virtue of the fact that what is mutilated and obscured in one language is frequently in another language of the same family retained in a relatively unimpaired condition, and transmitted so into historical times, that the

---

[1] On theories respecting the probable locality of this common home, comp. Nöldeke in the *Encycl. Britannica* (ed. 9), art. 'Semitic Languages,' vol. xxi. p. 642, and Wright, *Compar. Gramm.* ch. 1, p. 5 ff.

explanation of one by the other is still possible, even when the relationship lies no longer in a direct line.

178. Are there, it will be asked, any principles, analogous to those embodied in 'Grimm's Law,' regulating the inter-change of consonants between the different Semitic languages? 'Comparative philology,' writes Professor Sayce[1], 'is based on the recognition that the same word will be represented by different combinations of sounds in a group of allied dialects or languages, and that each combination will be governed by a fixed phonetic law. An English *h*, for example, will answer to a Greek and Latin *k*, an English *t* to a German and a Sanskrit *d*. When once a sound is given in a language, we may know the sounds which must correspond to it in the cognate languages. Now and then, of course, subordinate laws will interfere with the working of the general law: but unless such an interference can be proved, we must never disregard the general law for the sake of an etymological comparison, however tempting. . . . The laws of phonology are as undeviating in their action as the laws of physical science, and where the spelling does not mislead us will display themselves in every word of genuine growth. Even the vowels cannot be changed and shifted arbitrarily.' It follows that the laws of this kind, operative in the Semitic languages, must be determined, if the true relations subsisting between those languages are to be ascertained, and reckless etymologizing avoided. When this has been done, we are in a position, for example, to test the value of a proposed derivation, and may even be able to fix the relationship of an outlying form, as when Lagarde completes the identification, suggested by J. D. Michaelis in 1792, of צָעִיף[2].

---

[1] *Introduction to the Science of Language* (1880), i. p. 303 f.

[2] Admirable as the work of Gesenius in his *Thesaurus* is, the stage which the comparative study of the Semitic languages had reached in the author's lifetime did not always permit him to make his etymological notices fully adequate ; and in his treatment of roots, the expressions

A scientific comparison of the Semitic languages, based upon the necessary systematic classification of the phonetic phenomena presented by them, must be sought in special treatises, such as those named at the beginning of the chapter (p. 219). Two or three illustrations of the results gained by the comparative study of these languages may, however, be given here. Thus the following specimen-lists exhibit, in a tabular form, some important and clearly-established laws, analogous in character to 'Grimm's law' in the Aryan languages: the first is derived chiefly from Lagarde, *Semitica* I (Gött. 1878), pp. 22–27, and shews that *when Heb.* צ *= Aram.* ע, *the Arabic equivalent is* ض[1]. The meaning of this equation of course is, that the sound with which the words cited were originally pronounced by the *common* ancestors of the Arabs, the Arameans, and the Hebrews, in their common home, was gradually modified, after different families or tribes had separated from the common stock, and acquired independent existence, until it was finally fixed to ض in Arabic, צ in Hebrew, and ע in Aramaic[2].

(1) In 'Anlaut:'

عَأْنٌ	= צֹאן	= עֵז, عَنْزُ.
ضَبّ a species of *lizard*	= צָב Lev. 11, 29	= ܟܟܐ.

---

used by him, especially the phrase *vicina radix*, may sometimes tempt the reader to confuse what ought to be kept distinct. The interchange of allied sounds in different dialects must, however, be distinguished from the use of allied sounds—or groups of sounds—to express *allied ideas* in the *same* dialect: e.g. a harder or softer palatal or dental, as סגר and סכר, מזג and מסך, גזז and קצץ, כנס and גנז. These instances shew further how in a language particular sounds go together and determine each other: גז', קץ', כס', for example, but not גצ'. So in Mandaic קמ' becomes regularly גמ'; סמ' becomes צמ'.

[1] And in Ethiopic (if the corresponding word is in use) ፀ.

[2] Words *borrowed* in historical times, by one dialect from another, naturally do not come within the operation of the law: see some examples in the foot-notes.

ضَبَرَ *to gather* in bundles	= צָבַר Gen. 41, 49	= ܟܘܒܪ̈ܐ[1] *corn.* [*dense.*
ضَبَطَ *to guard, hold*	= צבט Ruth 2, 14	= ܚܣܝ[2] ? *be close,*
ضَحِكَ	= צחק	= ܚܣܘ (for ܚܣܡ).
ضَرَّ *to harm*	= צָרַר *be hostile*[3] צָר *adversary*	= עָר *adversary* (Dan. 4, 16[4]).
ضَرَّة *one of two wives*	= צָרָה 1 Sa. 1, 6	= ܟܢܬܐ 1 Sa. 1, 6.
* * *[5]	= צֶמֶר	= ܥܡܪܐ *wool.*
ضَاقَ Qor. 9, 119	= צָק	= ܩܨ, עָק (Isa. 49, 20 Targ.).
ضَأْل *lotus*	= צֶאֱלִים Job 40, 21 f.	= ܩܠܠ[6] βάτος.

Where there is already ע in the root, Syriac avoids the double guttural by substituting ܠ:—

ضِلَع	= צֵלָע	= ܐܠܥܐ[7'](Targ. עֲלָע).
ضَفْدَع	= צְפַרְדֵּעַ	= ܐܘܪܕܥܐ (Targ. עוּרְדְּעָן).
ضَبُع *hyaena*	= צִבְעִים	= ܐܦܥܐ[7''] Sir. 13, 18.
ضعف III *duplicavit,* Qor. 2, 263: ضِعْف 38, 61	= [צעף[7]	= ܐܠܦܐ[7''] *double,* Isa. 40, 2.
* * *	= צִרְעָה *hornet*	= אוּרְעִיתָא Ex. 23, 28 Ps.-Jon. (ערעיתא Onq.).

---

[1] The *roots*, not the particular word or form cited, are compared.

[2] Nöldeke, *Mand. Gramm.* p. 43.

[3] But צָרַר *to bind* = ضَرَّ = Aram. צְרַר, one of the many examples of roots distinct in Arabic, but confused in Hebrew. See below, p. 230 f., as well as several of the following foot-notes.

[4] Unless I am mistaken, not found elsewhere in Aramaic, except (if the text be correct) as a *borrowed* word in the late Hebrew of Ps. 139 (*v.* 20). On 1 Sa. 28, 16 see the writer's note *ad loc.*

[5] Eth. ዐምር:

[6] Löw, *Aramäische Pflanzennamen* (1881), p. 275 f.

[7] Whence צָעִיף Gen. 24, 65, properly, as Lagarde shews, some *square* garment. The adv. ܚܦܐܝܬ occurs 2 Cor. 1, 15.

(2) In 'Inlaut:'

رَقَا = רָצָה = ڣـكـل.

وَضَا *nituit, emicuit* [1]   = יָצָא = ڣـكـل, יָצָא (of plants
ወፅአ: *to go forth* }   springing forth).

وَضَع *deposuit* = יצע = * * *

حِضْن, ሕፅን: *bosom* = חֹצֶן = ڡـنـل (for ڡـحـنـل, ڡـنـل) [2].

(3) In 'Auslaut:'

أَرْض = אֶרֶץ = ڣـكـل [''].

بَيْضَة *ovum* = בֵיצָה = ܒܥܟܠ.

حمض = חָמֵץ = ܚܡܥ, ܣܦܥ, חֲמַע Ex. 12,
       34. 39.

ربض = רבץ = ڣـكـل Gen. 29, 2 Targ.
       and Pesh. [3]

رَض = רָצַץ = أَب Isa. 36, 6.

مَرِض *aeger fuit* = מרץ [4] = ܡܝܚ [5].

* * * = מיץ, מוץ = ܡܚ *agitavit* (lac).

فَض *divulsit* = פצץ = ڣـس (أَفَّ) [''] Isa. 59, 5
       for (בקעו).

قَبَض *prehensit* = קָבַץ = ܡܟܒ [5] *to fix*.

And with avoidance of the double guttural:—

عَرَض *contigit* = * * * = أَب (ألَف) [''] (Targ. עֲרַע).

عِفَة [6] = עֲע = אָע.

مَخَض *concussit* = מָחַץ = ܡܚܣܠ (ܡܚܣ) [7] (for ܡܚܣ).

---

[1] Comp. צמח, in Syriac *splenduit* (ܘܝܚ܌ܡܚܣ = ἀπαύγασμα, Heb. 1, 3),
but in Heb. and the Aramaic of the Targums, *germinavit*. See also
Ges. *Thes.* p. 56ᵃ.

[2] Cf. Hoffmann, *ZDMG.* 1878, p. 753.

[3] And, as a *borrowed* Aramaism, in the late Ps. 139 (*v.* 3). (The
Hebrew verb רבע, Lev. 18, 23. 19, 19. 20, 16, unless it can be supposed
to be a technical loan-word—cf. the *Afˁel* in Aramaic (Gen. 36, 24
Ps.-Jon.)—must have a different origin.)

[4] Job 16, 3. 1 Ki. 2, 8. Mic. 2, 10.

[5] Nöldeke, *ZDMG.* 1878, p. 406.   [6] Nöldeke, l.c.

[7] מָחָא and מָחַץ (Isa. 55, 2. Ps. 98, 8; ימחאו כף Ez. 25, 6 יען מחאך יד)

Instances, however, also occur of the series ‫و‬ = ‫ﭫ‬ = ‫ض‬; as
‫ضمد‬, ‫צמד‬ ‫رمد;‬ ‫نقض,‬ ‫נפץ‬, ‫نفّ‬ : and ‫حزن‬[1] occurs by the
side of ‫(وفد‬, ‫سعد‬ beside ‫سعده‬, ‫فو‬ (Ps. 74, 14 for ‫(רצץ‬
beside ‫رضّ‬. Examples of the frequent ‫و‬ = ‫ﭫ‬ = ‫ص‬ need not
be given.

Another series is ‫ﻁ‬ = ‫צ‬ = ‫ﭫ‬: thus—

(1) ‫ظبى‬ *dorcas* = ‫ﻃﺒﻴﺎ‬, ‫טַבְיָא‬ 2 Sa. 1, = ‫צְבִי‬.[2]
19

‫ظهيرة‬*noon-day*,Qor. = ‫ﻃﻴﻬﺮﺍ‬, ‫טִיהֲרָא‬ = ‫צָהֳרַיִם‬.
24, 57: cf. ‫ظاهر‬ *conspicuus*, 34, 16

* * * = ‫(ﺻﻮﻑ‬) ‫ﺻﻮﻑ‬(Dt. 11, = ‫צוּף‬.
4)

‫ظلّ‬ *shade* = ‫ﻃﻼ‬ = ‫צֵל (צְלָלִים)‬.[3]

‫ظلع‬ = ‫טְלַע‬ Gen. 32, 32 = ‫צָלַע‬ *to halt.*
Onq. and Ps.-Jon.

‫ظلم‬ *to oppress* = ‫ﻃﻠﻢ‬, ‫טְלַם‬ = * * *[4]

‫ظمى‬ = * * * = ‫צָמֵא‬.

‫ظعن‬ *to break up,* = ‫ﻃﻌﻦ‬ *sustulit* = ‫צָעַן‬ Isa. 33, 20.
move quarters, Qor. 16, 82

will therefore be the same word, the former being the genuine Hebrew
form, the latter of Aramaic origin ; but passing into Hebrew by different channels, they acquired different significations, as in English *bench*
and *bank*, *ditch* and *dyke*, *channel* and *canal*, etc. (see further illustrations in Max Müller's *Lectures on the Science of Language*, second
series, Lect. vi (ed. 1891, p. 335 ff.).

[1] Disputed by G. Hoffmann, *ZDMG.* 1878, p. 762, on account of the
meaning. See, however, Payne Smith, *Thes. Syr.*, col. 2996.

[2] But ‫צבי‬ *delight, ornament,* is from √ ‫צבה‬ = ‫ﺻﺒﺎ‬ = ‫ﺻﺒﺎ‬ *to be inclined towards.*

[3] ‫צלל‬ Neh. 3, 15 is an Aramaism : see 1 Ki. 6, 9. 7, 3 Pesh. And ‫צלל‬
tinnivit = ‫ﺻﻠ‬ = ‫ﺻﻞّ‬.

[4] The Heb. ‫צלם‬ = Aram. ‫צלמא‬ is from √‫צלם‬ = Arab. ‫ﺻﻠﻢ‬ *to cut
off* or *out* (Nöldeke, *ZDMG.* 1886, p. 733). ‫ﺻﻨﻢ‬ *image* (compared in
my former edition) appears to be a loan-word from the Aram. ‫צלמא‬:
see Sig. Fränkel, *Die Aramäischen Fremdwörter im Arabischen*, 1886,
p. 273.

ظُفْر *nail*   = ܛܦܪܐ   = ¹.צִפֹּרֶן

(2) عَظُم *to be strong,*   = * * *   = עָצֹם ,עָצַם².
عَظِيم *mighty,* Qor. 2, 256

عَظْم *bone*   = ܟܪܥܐ *thigh,* Gen.   = עֶצֶם.
       32, 32. Nu. 5, 21 al.

نَظَر *inspexit*   = נְטַר³ *to keep, observe*   = נָצַר⁴.

(3) حَفِظَ *be attentive to* = ܣܩܝܒ *assiduous*   = חָפֵץ⁵.

    * * *   = ܦܨܐ   = רָץ.

وَعَظَ *monuit*   = יְעַט   = יָעַץ.

قَيَّظَ   = קָיִט Dan. 2, 35   = קַיִץ⁶.

A third not less important series (passing by ز = ܙ = ז) is
ذ = ܕ = ז :—

(1) ذِئْب   = ܕܐܒܐ   = זְאֵב.

---

¹ But צִפּוֹר *bird* = عُصْفُور, prob. from √ صَفَر *to whistle* (said esp. of a bird). And צְפִירָה *garland* (Isa. 28, 5) is from √ ضَفَر *to plait* or *braid* (the corresponding word in Arabic ضَفِيرَة signifies *a plait of hair*).

² But עצם *to close tight,* Isa. 29, 10. 33, 15 = عصم.

³ נטר *to keep* (a vineyard), Cant. 1, 6. 8, 11 f., is most probably an idiom of North Palestine (cf. Del.), the dialect of which appears to have been slightly tinged by Aramaisms (comp. the writer's *Introduction to the Literature of the O. T.,* 1891, p. 421 f.) : but נטר in the sense of *keeping anger* must be connected, it seems, with a different root, the more original and literal signification being preserved in the *derivative* מַטָּרָה (as in מִדְבָּר, אַלְמָה, תִּקְוָה *cord,* צִיּוּן and other words). نَاطُور is confessedly—Fränkel, *Fremdwörter,* p. 138—a loan-word from the Aramaic : is the case the same with the verb نَطَر *to keep a vineyard,* Saad. Isa. 1, 8 ?)

⁴ But נֵצֶר *a shoot* is from √ نَضَر *nituit, laete viruit.*

⁵ Friedrich Delitzsch, *Prolegomena eines neuen Hebr.-Aram. Wörter-buchs zum A. T.* (1886), p. 168, endorsed by Nöldeke, *ZDMG.* 1886, p. 742. חָפַץ in Job 40, 17 (יחפץ זנבו כמו ארז) *to stiffen* or *straighten down* is thus a distinct word (cf. p. 230 f.) = Arab. خَفَض *to depress, lower* (e. g. wings, Qor. 15, 88. 17, 25).

⁶ But קֵץ *end,* in spite of the play in Amos 8, 2, is from קצץ = قَصّ *to cut off.*

ذُبَاب = وُحُدا = זְבוּב.

ذَبَحَ = وَحَ = זָבַח.

ذُو, ذَاتَ, ذَا = דִּי, דָּא, דֵּין = זֹאת, זֶה, זֹה.

ذَهَبْ = وَهَدا = זָהָב.

ذَابَ = דּוּב, وُت Ps. 78, 20 = זוּב.

ذَحْلٌ *rancour,* = דְּחֵל *to fear* = זָחַל Job 32, 6[1].
malevolence

ذَكَرَ = وَكَ = זָכַר.

ذَكَرْ = وَمَدُا = זָכָר.

ذَنَبْ = דַּנְבָּא, وُهنحدا = זָנָב.

ذَقَنْ = وُمَندا = זָקָן.

ذَرَا = דְּרָא, وُوُ = זָרָה[2].

ذِرَاعْ = وُوُحدا = זְרוֹעַ.

أُذُنْ (2) = אוּדְנָא, (وُولُ = אֹזֶן.

بَذَرَ = בְּדַר, حَوُو = בוּר.

كَذَبَ = صَحَت = כָּזָב.

حَذَا *ex adverso* = חַדְיָא, صَمُحدا = חָזֶה[3] *breast.*
fuit: حِذَاءٌ *res alteri opposita*

* * * = נְדָא 2 Ki. 9, 33 Tg. = נָזָה *to spirt* (ib.)[4]
نَتَ Isa. 63, 3 Pesh.

---

[1] But זחל *to creep* = זְחַל = زَحَلَ *to withdraw, lag behind* (Nöld. *l.c.* p. 741). (The words sometimes undergo slight modifications of meaning in the different languages.)

[2] But זרע *seed* = وَهَدا = زرع.

[3] חזה *to see* is Aram. חזא.

[4] But יַזֶּה Isa. 52, 15, if the text be sound, can hardly mean anything except *cause to leap, startle* (Ges. Del. Dillm. R.V. *marg.*, etc.: cf. the writer's *Isaiah, his Life and Times*, p. 153), and will thus be a different word, from נזה = Arab. نَزَا *to leap.* Delitzsch, in his note on the passage, confuses the two roots, נזה = נדא = [نذا], and נזה = [נזא] = نزا. See more fully G. F. Moore, in the *Journal of Biblical Literature* (Boston, U.S.A., 1890, p. 216 ff.), whose objections, however (p. 221),

وَدَعَ *to flow*	= דִּיעֲתָא *sweat*	= זֵעָה‎, יֶזַע‎.
(3) أَخَذَ	= ?אָמ‎	= אֲחַז‎.
إِذَا ,إِذْ	= אֱדַיִן Dan. 2, 15	= אֲוַי ,אָו‎.
عَاذَ Qor. 23, 99	= * * *	= עוּ (עוז)[1] *to take refuge.*

A fourth series is ث = ܠ = שׁ, the original lisped dental becoming in Hebrew a simple sibilant :—

(1) ثَبَرَ *to destroy*	= ܬܒܪ	= שָׁבַר *to break.*
ثَدْىٰ *breast*	= ܬܕܐ	= שַׁד (for שַׁדְיֿ‎).
ثَابَ *to return*[2]	= תָּב	= שָׁב‎.
ثَوْر *bullock*	= תור‎, ܬܘܪ	= שׁוֹר‎.
ثَكِلَ *be bereaved*	= תכול	= שָׁכֹל‎.
ثَلْج *snow*	= תלגא	= שֶׁלֶג‎.
ثَلَاث *three*	= תְּלָת‎, ܬܠܬ	= שָׁלֹש‎.
ثَمّ *there*	= ܬܡܢ	= שָׁם‎.
ثَمَانٍ *eight*	= ܬܡܢܝܐ	= שְׁמֹנֶה[3].
ثَنَى *to repeat*	= ܬܢܐ	= שָׁנָה 1 Sa. 26, 8[4].
ثَقِفَ *to attain to, overcome, seize*	= ܬܩܦ *to be strong*	= * * *[5]

---

against the rendering 'startle' are hardly strong enough to authorize correction of the text: נצח Isa. 63, 3. 6, for instance (from √ نفخ *to sprinkle*), cannot be the same word as the נצח which occurs elsewhere in the O. T.: and there are other similar ἅπαξ εἰρημένα in Hebrew (e.g. שׂחר *to charm*, Isa. 47, 11 ; חפץ Job 40, 17, above, p. 226).

[1] עוז *to be strong* = Arab. عَزّ‎.

[2] But ثَابَ *to be converted*, is a theological term, *borrowed* (as the ت shews) as a loan-word from the Aramaic: cf. Fränkel, *l.c.* p. 83; H. Hirschfeld, *Beiträge zur Erklärung des Ḳorân* (1886), p. 39.

[3] שָׁמֵן *fat* = ܫܡܝܢ = سمن‎. [4] But שׁנה *year* = ܫܢܐ = سنة‎.

[5] The Hebrew equivalent, if it existed, would by law be שׁקף. It follows that תקף and its derivatives, where they occur in the Hebrew of the O. T. (Job 14, 20. 15, 24. Qoh. 4, 12. 6, 10. Esth. 9, 29. 10, 2. Dan. 11, 17), are not genuine Hebrew words, but borrowed from the Aramaic.

اِثْنَانِ *two*	= תְּרֵין, לٔٮۮ	= שְׁנַיִם.
ثُعَالَة *fox*	= תַּעְלָא	= שׁוּעָל.
ثَعْلَب *fox*	= * * *	= שעלבים.
ثَغْر *gap, opening*	= תְּרַע *gate*	= שַׁעַר.
ثَقُل *to be weighty*	= תקל *to weigh*	= שקל.
ثَرَى *to be moist*	= תְּרָא Nu. 6, 3 Ps.-Jon.	= [שרה], whence מִשְׁרָה Nu. 6, 3[1].
(2) * * *	= עֲתַר	= עשר *to be rich.*
وثب (dialect.)	= יתב	= ישב *to sit.*
مثل *to liken*	= מְתַל	= משל.
أثِم *to be guilty*	= * * * [2]	= אשם.
أنثَى *woman*	= אִתְּתָא	= אִשָּׁה (for אנשה)[3].
إثر *footstep*	= אֲתַר *place*	= אַשּׁוּר.
(3) ? [4]	= בְּהֵת	= בּוּשׁ.
* * *	= בְּרוֹתָא	= ברוש *cypress*[5].
جَدَث *sepulchre* (Qor. 54, 7)	= * * *	= גדיש Job 21, 32[6].
حَدَث *to renew*	=	= חֲדַשׁ.

[1] Cf. Pesh. (ib.). The word is not derived from שרה = Aram. שרא *to loosen:* see Fränkel, p. xii. (The statement in the *Journal of Philology*, xi. p. 205, based upon Gesenius, must be corrected accordingly.)

[2] The genuine Aramaic equivalent would be אתם. אשמא of the Targums is not therefore a true Aramaic word, but a loan-word from the Hebrew of the O. T.

[3] Not connected etymologically with אֱנוֹשׁ, אֲנָשִׁים = the ܣ, س, in Aramaic and Arabic, as against the ل, ث, shew that the sibilant in אנוש is different in origin from that in אשה. It is even scarcely possible for אִישׁ (with its long vowel), however parallel in usage, to be akin etymologically with אִשָּׁה.

[4] Comp. Nöld. *ZDMG.* 1886, pp. 157, 741.

[5] ברותים Cant. 1, 17 (unless the ת be due to textual error) must be another of the Aramaizing forms found in this poem.

[6] Different from גדיש *sheaf,* and possibly to be read גָּדֵשׁ.

حَرَثَ	= תַרַת ,אَ² (rare)	= חרש *to cut in* (usu. *to plough*)[1].
وَرَثَ *to inherit*	= יְרִית	= ירש.
لَيْثَ *lion*	= לִיתָא	= ליש.
بُرْغُوثَ *flea*	= ڤَةُؤَاُحُلَا	= פרעש[2].

Etymologies which offend against the established laws which a language follows, however plausible superficially they may appear to be, should always be viewed with suspicion[3]. 'Etymology,' to quote again Prof. Sayce's words[4], 'is not a plaything for the amusement of the ignorant and untrained; it is a serious and difficult study, not to be attempted without much preparation and previous research.' The etymologist who aspires to something better than reckless guessing, must both be thoroughly trained in the principles of scientific philology, and possess a sound practical acquaintance with the language (or languages) with which he deals.

Instances of roots, distinct in Arabic, but confused, either in themselves or in their derivatives, in Hebrew, have been referred to in some of the notes on the preceding pages: the following are additional examples of the same peculiarity:—

(1) חבל *to bind* (whence הֶבֶל *cord*)=حَبَلَ, but חבל *to be corrupt* = خَبِلَ *to be unsound;* חטב *to gather fire-wood*[5] = حَطَبَ,

---

[1] But חרש *to be dumb* = خَرِسَ.

[2] See further, on the subject of the preceding pages, Wright, *l.c.* Chap. iv; Fränkel, *Fremdwörter*, pp. xii–xiv; W. R. Smith, *Journ. of Phil.*, xvi. p. 74.

[3] Thus the proposed explanation of Βοσορ (2 Pet. 2, 15) as בצור, 'an Aramaic equivalent for the Hebrew בעור, the letters ע and צ being (as often) interchanged' (*Speaker's Comm.* i. p. 739), exactly inverts the relation actually subsisting between the two languages. And the explanation of שמואל as *Heard of God* contradicts one of the widest inductions of which the records of the Hebrew language are susceptible; comp. the writer's note on 1 Sa. 1, 20.

[4] *L.c.* p. 349.

[5] Not connected with חצב: cf. on the signification Wetzstein, *ap.* Delitzsch on Ps. 144, 12.

but חָטַב *to have dark stripes* (Pr. 7, 16. Ps. 144, 12) = خَطِب ;
to be of a dusky colour; חָלָב *milk* = حَلَب, but חֵלֶב *fat* = خِلْب ;
חָלָל *profane* (open to all, common), הֵחֵל, חִלֵּל, חָלִיל, *to begin*
(open), from √ حَلّ *to loosen, be open* (licuit), but חָלָל *wounded,*
חוֹלֵל *to pierce,* from √ حَلّ *perforavit;* חמר *to be red* (whence
חֲמוֹר *ass*) = أَحْمَر *red,* حِمَار *ass,* but חמר *to ferment* = خَمَر,
חֶמֶר (poet.) *wine* = خَمْر ; חנן *to shew pity* = حَنّ, but Job 19, 17
(prob.) = خَنّ (conj. x) *to be loathsome;* חפר *to dig* = حَفَر, but
חפר *to be ashamed* = خَفِر *to be bashful;* החרים from خَرَم *to shut
off, seclude,* but חָרוּם *slit-nosed,* from خَرَم *to cleave* (cf. أَخْرَم
slit-eared).   (2) עוה (Isa. 21, 3 al.) *to bend, twist* = عَوَى, but עוה
to go astray, act erringly (2 Sa. 24, 17 al.), the root of עָוֺן
iniquity, = غَوَى ; עֱוִיל Job 16, 11 = עַוָּל (cf. Dillmann) *unrighteous,*
from عَال *to decline, especially from right* (cf. עָוֶל, עַוְלָה), but
עֱוִיל *young child* (ib. 19, 28. 21, 11) from غَال *to give suck* (cf.
עוּל, עֲלוֹת); עטה *to grasp* (Isa. 22, 17) = عَطَا, but עטה *to cover
התעלל *to occupy, amuse oneself* (see Fleischer ap.
Delitzsch, on Isa. 3, 4, ed. 3), from √ عَلّ, but עלל *to enter*
(common in Aram.) = غَلّ (hence על *yoke* = غُلّ); עָפָר *dust* =
عَفَر, but עֹפֶר *fawn* = غُفْر ; עָרֵב *to be sweet, pleasing,* no doubt
akin to عَرِب *alacer, lubens fuit,* but עֹרֵב *raven* = غُرَاب (cf.
غَرِب *niger fuit*), עֶרֶב *evening,* from غَرَب *occidit* (sol),
place of sunset, מערב *west* = مَغْرَب ; אֶצְבַּע *finger* = أَصْبَع, but
צבע *to dip, dye* (whence צָבוּעַ, צֶבַע) = صَبَع.   (3) חָצֵר *court,*
from حَصَر *to enclose,* but חָצִיר *grass,* from خَضِر *to be green;* צוּר,
צוּרָה *form* = صُورَة, صُورَوْا, but צוּר *rock* = صُوَّان ; צרח *to shout* =
صَرَخ, but צריח *underground chamber* = ضَرِيح ; רִצְפָּה *pavement,*
רָצוּף (Cant. 3, 10) *fitted together* (in mosaic fashion), from
√ رَصَف *to arrange side by side* (e.g. stones), but רִצְפָּה, רֶצֶף,
heated stones = رَضْف (id.).   (4) פרש (Mic. 3, 3. Lam. 4, 4) *to
cleave, divide, distribute* (strictly פרס, as Isa. 58, 7. Jer. 16, 7) =

فرس *to tear*[1], but פרשׂ *to spread out* = فرش; שְׁבָבִים *splinters*
(Hos. 8, 6), from √ سَبّ *to cut*, but שָׁבִיב *flame* (Job 18, 5),
from √ شَبّ *to blaze;* שֶׁרֶד *a style,* cf. سِرَادٌ a kind of *needle,*
but שָׂרִיד *fugitive,* from √شَرَد شَرَدَ *to escape.*

Obs. The same phenomenon is far from uncommon in other languages: thus *to blow* (of the wind) = Anglo-Saxon *blâwan;* (of a flower)
= A.S. *blôwan: last* (verb) = A.S. *gelæstan; last* (adj.) = *latost; last*
(burden) = *hlæst; last* (mould for making shoes) = *lâst: to lie* (repose) =
licgan; (speak untruth) = *leôgan :* French *son* = both *suum* and *sonum :*
neuf = both *novem* and *novum: louer* (to praise), from *laudare, louer* (to
let), from *locare: νέω to spin* = Sanskrit *nah, νέω to swim* = Sk. *snu,*
νέομαι to come = Sk. *nas.* See Max Müller's *Lectures,* second series,
Lect. vi (ed. 1891, p. 358 ff.).

179. Although our immediate object is but a narrow one,
being the illustration, not of the Hebrew language as a whole,
but only of the verb (under certain aspects) by Arabic, yet in
order to accomplish this satisfactorily, it will be desirable to
make our way sure by defining more closely the relation in
which these two languages stand towards each other. If
Arabic were altogether a *younger* language than Hebrew,
i.e. if it represented a more recent stratification, an ulterior
stage beyond that at which Hebrew had arrived, it would be
chimerical to expect it to throw much light upon the latter :
we do not, as a rule, look to French or Italian to elucidate
Latin, and we should not, in the case assumed, look to
Arabic to elucidate Hebrew. If, however, notwithstanding
the difference of date, Arabic exhibits particular formations
in a more original condition than Hebrew, then such a
course would be the natural one to adopt, and our expecta-
tions would not be disappointed. And this is, in fact, the
case. Arabic is, in many respects, *an older language than
Hebrew:* speaking roughly and without intending the analogy
to be pressed in detail, we may say that Hebrew bears the

---

[1] See Nöldeke's interesting study on פרשׂ, פרס, and פְּרַס Dan. 5, 25 in
the *Zeitschr. für Assyriologie,* 1886, p. 414 ff.

same sort of relation to Arabic that English does to German. Consider in what manner German often lights up an obscure corner in English: I do not, of course, mean to imply that it presents us with the constituent factors of our own language in their ultimate and original form, but it reduces our irregularities to rule, it exhibits what with us is fragmentary, residuary, or imperfect, as parts of a complete and systematic whole. Various rare or antiquated forms, provincialisms, the peculiarities connected with the use of the auxiliaries, may be taken as examples. What is the meaning of *worth* in the line, 'Woe worth the day, woe worth the hour?' It is plain that it cannot be used in its ordinary acceptation as a substantive or an adjective: but our own language offers us nothing with which it can be connected or identified. In English the word is, in fact, the only survivor of a once numerous family: separated from its kindred, its meaning, and even what part of speech it is, has become totally forgotten. But in German the whole family still exists in the shape of a verb, complete in all its parts, and forming an integral element in the language. Thus the irregularity ceases to be irregular: the fragment at once falls into its proper place, as a part in a living whole, and as such re-assumes the signification which had well-nigh been irrecoverably lost[1]. And, similarly, it is often possible in Arabic to trace the entire stratification of which Hebrew has preserved nothing more than a few remains scattered here and there, which, *taken by themselves*, can never be adequately explained.

180. The assertion, however, that Arabic is an older language than Hebrew will excite, probably, the reader's surprise. It will appear to him, in the literal sense of the word, preposterous, thus to invert the natural order of things: he will deem it incredible that such an ancient language

---

[1] Earle, *Philology of the English Tongue*, § 283.

should be younger and less primitive than one which does not enter the field of history for more than 1500 years after a period at which the former is known from authentic records to have flourished. And yet such an opinion is not so incredible or improbable as it may at first sight appear. If, for instance, as competent and independent authorities affirm, there are parts of Arabia in which the language of the Qor'an may be heard in unaltered purity at the present day, if, therefore, the Arabic language has remained unchanged during the last 1200 years, may it not have continued in the same manner comparatively unchanged during an indefinite period previously? Were not the tranquil and secluded habits of the Arab tribes (whose motto might well have been the words להם לבדם נתנה הארץ ולא עבר זר בתוכם) eminently calculated to preserve the integrity of their language, while the migratory and unsettled life of the early Hebrews, to say nothing of their depression and subjugation in a foreign land, the effects of which cannot but have been strongly impressed upon their language, would tend in just the opposite direction? May not Hebrew then, so to speak, be a language which is *prematurely old*, while Arabic, under the influence of favourable external conditions, retained till a much later date the vigour and luxuriance of its youth?

Obs. It may also be recollected that there are other instances in which, of two languages belonging to the same family, the one which historically is known only as the later, may nevertheless contain many elements more primitive than any to be found in the other. For example, compare Latin with Greek. Greek appears as a fully developed language long before the date of the earliest records written in Latin (inscriptions of about 250 B.C.): yet comparative philology teaches us that Latin is in more respects than one an *older* language than Greek— it retains the older forms, which in Greek have gradually given way, and receded from sight. Thus the digamma (ϝ), which the metre proves to have existed at the time when the Homeric poems were composed, before long vanished from the language : in Latin the corresponding sound (v) was retained to the end (*vinum, vicus, video,* etc.). Similarly, where in Greek we have only the aspirate, Latin retains the earlier

sibilant: cf. ἕ, ἕξ, ἕπτα, ὅλος, ἵστημι with *se, sex, septem, salvus, sisto*.
Numerous instances may also be found in the case- and person-endings.
In Greek σ was regularly dropped between two vowels, in Latin it was
retained, at least under another form: accordingly in gene*r*is, musa*r*um,
we hear the representative of the σ which had already disappeared even
in the oldest Greek forms, γένεος (for *γενε-σ-ος) and μουσάων. Passing
to the verb, we have here *s*um by the side of εἰμί (for *ἐσμί, Sk. *ásmi*),
e*s* by the side of εἶ (i.e. *ἐσί, cf. ἐσσί, Sk. *ási*), e*r*am by the side of ἦν,
in Homer ἔην (i.e. *ἔσην), siem (for es-iem) by the side of εἴην (i.e.
*ἐσίην): in *legit* the *t* is preserved which has vanished from λέγει (for
*λέγετι), though it re-appears in λέγεται, and in verbs in -μι takes the
form of σ: *legimus* and *legunt*, like the dialectic λέγομες, λέγοντι, are
older than λέγομεν, λέγουσι (for λέγονσι, i.e. λέγοντι), and *legentem*,
like *matrem* and *decem*, is older than λέγοντα, μητέρα, and δέκα (Sk.
mātáram, daśan). These examples, shewing as they do that numerous
forms still existed in Latin centuries after they had been lost or materially modified in Greek, form an interesting parallel to some of the
instances cited above from Arabic as compared with Hebrew.

181. But we are not confined to probable reasoning: the
presence of the older form in Arabic admits frequently of
direct demonstration. Let us take two or three of the more
obvious cases. In Hebrew the consonant following the
article is regularly doubled: we may indeed surmise from
analogy that the duplication conceals some letter which once
formed part of the article; but what that letter may have
been, the Hebrew language itself does not afford the mate-
rials even for a plausible conjecture. In Arabic the hidden
letter is obvious. There the article is 'al, in which the *l* is
never assimilated in writing with the following consonant, and
not in pronunciation except when the latter is a sibilant,
dental, or liquid. Thus 'almalku=הַמֶּלֶךְ: 'ashshamsu=הַשֶּׁמֶשׁ.
Now it is inconceivable that 'almalku can have arisen out of
hammélekh by disintegration: Hebrew itself tells us that
מִצְפּוֹן, מִדַּבֵּר, נָתַתָּ are posterior to מִן־צִפּוֹן, מתדבר, נתנת: it is
accordingly evident that Arabic has preserved the older un-
assimilated form which in Hebrew regularly suffered assimilation. Exactly the same relation between the two languages

is observable in 'anta, 'antum by the side of אַתָּה, אַתֶּם. Again in ה‍ָ several originally distinct terminations have become merged : this can be shewn inferentially from Hebrew itself, but in Arabic these terminations are still distinguishable. In all feminine nouns such as מְדִינָה, the *h* represents an original *th*, dropped in ordinary pronunciation, but reappearing[1] in *st. constr.* and before a suffix מְדִינַת, מְדִינָתִי[2]: in Arabic the *t* is written regularly, *medînatun*, city (where *n* is the so-called 'nunation,' and *u* marks the nominative case). Similarly כָּתְבָה was once *katabath*, as we see from the form assumed before a suffix וּנְבְתַּם (cf. also the sporadic forms עָשָׂת, אָזְלַת, הִרְצָת, etc.): accordingly in Arabic we have regularly, as 3 *fem.*, *katabat*. In verbs ל״ה, the ה stands for an older י or ו, which must indeed be presupposed for such forms as גָּלוּי,

---

[1] So in French the *t* of *habet*, *amat*, lost in *il a*, *il aime*, becomes audible again in *a-t-il? aime-t-il?* Ἔδειξα is in Sk. *adiksham*, and the liquid with which the Greek word must once have terminated is seen in the middle ἐδειξά-μ-ην.

[2] Retained in Phoenician, all but uniformly (Schröder, *Phön. Gramm.* p. 170), and likewise in Moabitish (see *Notes on Samuel*, p. lxxxvi ff.). In Hebrew, also, it is preserved in certain proper names (some doubtless of Canaanitish origin), as בָּשְׂמַת Gen. 26, 34. 1 Ki. 4, 15 ; מַחְלָת Gen. 28, 9. 2 Chr. 11, 18 ; אֲחֻזַּת Gen. 26, 26; בְּכוֹרַת 1 Sa. 9, 1 ; also גָּלְיָת and גְּנֻבַת: more often in names of places, as אֵילַת Dt. 2, 8 ; בְּזֶקַת Josh. 15, 39 ; גִּבְעַת 18, 28 ; דִּבְרַת 19, 12. 21, 28 ; צָרְעַת 1 Ki. 17, 9 : further, with a long vowel, שִׁמְעָת 2 Ki. 12, 22 ; שָׁמְרַת 1 Chr. 8, 21 ; מִכְמְתָת Josh. 16, 6 ; לִבְנָת 19, 26 ; בַּעֲלַת 19, 44 ; אֶפְרָת Gen. 48, 7 ; עַיָּת Isa. 10, 28 ; חֲמָת often. Add also the rare poetical forms נַחֲלַת Ps. 16, 6 ; עֶזְרָת 60, 13 = 108, 13; שְׁנָת 132, 4 (see Del. ed. 3 or 4); and the archaic זִמְרָת Ex. 15, 2 'my strength *and a song* is Yah,'—the supposition that י of the suffix may have dropped out is rendered improbable by the recurrence of exactly the same form Isa. 12, 2. Ps. 118, 14 : at the same time it is *possible* (Böttcher, i. p. 241) that the older language, dispensing with superfluous letters, intended the י of the next word to do double duty, so that the whole would read וְזִמְרָתְיָהּ. The suggestion that the names ending in ת‍ָ are apocopated from ה‍ָ‍ָ (Hupf.) is not necessary, or supported by analogy. Cf. Ges.-Kautzsch, § 80. 2, rem. 2[a, b].

חָסָיָה, יַרְבִּיוּן, אָתָיו, and the derivatives רְאִי, נִקָּיוֹן : in Arabic the weak consonant is often visible to the eye (though quiescent when the vowel immediately preceding it is *a*), as رَأَى *ra'a^y* = ראה, أَتَى *ata^y* = אתה, نَقِيَ *naqiya* = נקה.

At the commencement of a word Hebrew evinces a strong dislike to the presence of ו, a letter for which Arabic has almost as marked a preference: thus for ירשׁ, ישׁע, ילד, we find *walada, wasi'a, waritha;* in which of the two languages now has the change taken place? Hebrew itself will answer this question. By the side of יָלַד we find יֵלֵד, נוֹלַד, הוֹלִיד (cf. הִתְוַדַּע), where it is impossible to account for the ו except by supposing it to have been the original letter which in ילד was modified into י owing to a peculiarity of Hebrew pronunciation: the opposite assumption cannot be made, because no assignable reason exists for an original י to be changed into ו so soon as it ceases to begin a word. More than this, the Arabic *'awlada* shews us the uncontracted form of הוֹלִיד: as in *'aw, qawlun, maw'idun* (مَوْعِد), for אוֹ, קוֹל, מוֹעֵד etc., the waw retains its consonantal value, and *aw* (which is obviously the earlier form) has not yet become *ô*.

182. Having thus by a variety of instances, all pointing in the same direction, established our right to treat Arabic forms as more primitive than the corresponding forms in Hebrew, we may go further, and adopt the same opinion, without hesitation, in cases which might seem inconclusive if considered by themselves, but which, in the light of those instances, will not admit of explanation by any different hypothesis. It is a characteristic of languages which occupy towards one another the relation here shewn to subsist between Arabic and Hebrew, that isolated or sporadic forms in the one correspond to forms of regular occurrence in the other. Now for אַתְּ, לָךְ, קָטַלְתְּ, we find occasionally a K'tib קטלתי, לכי, אתי (2 Kings 4, 2. 7. 16. 23. Ruth 3, 3. 4 al.), and in Arabic this *yod* is the regular mark of the 2nd *fem. sing.,*

as *'anti, laki* (Qor. 3, 32), *qatalti:* accordingly it is plain that
i was the original vowel (cf. also תִּקְטְלִי), which in Hebrew,
gradually becoming inaudible, was ultimately omitted in
writing, except in the cases alluded to, and before a suffix
where like the *th*, § 181, it naturally reappears (קְטַלְתִּינִי)[1].
In the same way, there can be hardly any doubt that the rare
terminations ‍וֹ—, ‍ִי—, ‍וֹ—, sometimes affixed to words in *st.
constr.* (Olshausen, §§ 107, 123; Ges.-Kautzsch, § 90.2, 3)[2], are
relics of ancient case-endings—petrified survivals[3], meaning-
less in Hebrew, full of meaning in Arabic and in the primitive
language from which Arabic and Hebrew are both equally
sprung.   The case is similar with ‍הָ—, which, with names of
places, was still felt to retain a definite import (expressing
motion towards), but in לַיְלָה regularly (cf. ἡ νύχθα in modern
Greek), חָרְסָה Jud. 14, 18 (which cannot be simply *feminines*,
if only on account of the tone) is a perpetuation of the old
accusative-ending -*an*, though with loss of its particular sig-

---

[1] In Syriac the *yod* is written, but not pronounced: ܟ݁ܬܰܒ̈ܝ (ܝܰܒ̈,
ܡܶ̈ܠܰܝ. Syriac likewise sides with Arabic in some of the other
points enumerated: cf. ܠܰܝ (ܝܰܠ, ܝܰܠܳܐ, ܩܳܛܠܰܐ (3 *fem.*), (ܝܰܠ/ܟ݁ܡ,
ܬܰܡܠܟ̈ܝ, ܡܶܛܪ̈ܬܗ. In the Aram. ܗܳܐ, הֲוָא (=Heb. היה), we see
the older ו, which is also retained in the name יהוה.

[2] The ‍וֹ— of the nomin. is found, not only in compound proper names,
as פְּנוּאֵל *face of God*, שְׁמוּאֵל *name of God*, רְעוּאֵל etc., מְתוּשָׁאֵל *man of
God* (שׁ being the relative pron.=Assyr. *sha*), מְתוּשֶׁלַח, but also most
probably (if the reading be correct) in בְּכֹרוּ 1 Chr. 8, 38=9, 44, in מַלִיכוּ
Neh. 12, 14 Qrê, and certainly in גַּשְׁמוּ, the 'Arabian,' Neh. 6, 6: in
illustration of this *foreign* name, may be cited the numerous Nabataean
proper names (Euting, *Nabatäische Inschriften*, 1885, pp. 73, 90–92),
ending regularly in ו (e.g. גִּלְחֹמוּ, מַלְכוּ, הַגְרוּ, מַקִימוּ, וַהְבוּ, כַּהִילוּ,
etc.).   See also Philippi, *St. Constr.* p. 132; Blau, *Zur Althebräischen
Sprachkunde*, in Merx' *Archiv*, i. (1870), p. 352.—Ewald's explanation
of the forms referred to, *Lb.* § 211ᵃ, is not probable: it is criticized at
length by Philippi, *l.c.* p. 104 ff.

[3] Most of the infinitive forms, in Greek and Latin, are the petrified
cases of abstract nouns—whether locatives or datives: Sayce, *Introd.*
i. 430, ii. 144; Curtius, *The Greek Verb*, p. 344 (Engl. Tr.).

nification[1]. And this leads us to the subject which immediately concerns us. Exactly as בַּיְתָה corresponds to بَيْتًا *baytan*, so אֶקְטְלָה corresponds to the Arabic 'energetic' اَقْتُلَنْ (also اَقْتُلَنَّ) *'aqtulan* (also *'aqtulanna*).

Obs. On הָ— it may further be remarked that it clings likewise to a few geographical names, Dt. 10, 7 Gudgódah, and in the fem. Num. 33, 22 f. Keheláthah ; 33 f. Yotbáthah ; Josh. 19, 43 and Jud. 14, 1. 5 Timnáthah ; Mic. 5, 1 Ephráthah. It is to be recognized also in the poetical by-forms (in all of which the tone is similar) אֵימָתָה Ex. 15, 16 ; יְשׁוּעָתָה Ps. 3, 3. 80, 3. Jon. 2, 10 ; סוּפָתָה Hos. 8, 7 ; עַוְלָתָה 10, 13 (also Ez. 28, 15. Ps. 125, 3 ; עֹלָתָה Ps. 92, 16. Job 5, 16) ; עֶזְרָתָה Ps. 44, 27. 63, 8. 94, 17. The view that these are 'double feminines' is an extraordinary one, and is rightly abandoned in Ges.-Kautzsch, § 90, 2, rem.[a, b] ; they agree precisely in form with עַזָּתָה *to Gaza*, הַגִּבְעָתָה *to Gibeah*, and the only question is whether they are actual archaisms

---

[1] This will not surprise us any more than the manner in which, after the declensions, as such, were given up in the Romance languages, the noun still continued to be designated by a form derived not from the Latin nominative, but from the *accusative :* thus in French we have *rien, raison, murs, maux,* from *rem, rationem, muros, malos ; le, les, mon, mes,* from *illum, illos, meum, meos,* etc. Respecting this selection of the accusative, see further Brachet's *Historical French Grammar* (Kitchin's translation), pp. 88–96, where it is likewise shewn how, in isolated instances, as in *fils,* the nominative was preserved : in French, then, by a strange reversal of what might have been anticipated, the nominative was the exceptional form ; in Hebrew, on the other hand, this peculiarity fell to the share of the accusative as well. ' In modern Arabic the oblique form of the plural (*-în*) has everywhere superseded the direct form (*ûn*),' Wright, *Arabic Grammar,* i. § 347, rem. *b :* cf. Philippi, *St. Constr.* p. 143 ff.

In classical Arabic the noun is declined as follows :—

	SINGULAR.	DUAL.	PLURAL.
N.	*kâtibun =* (כְּתָב)	*kâtibâni*	*kâtibûna.*
G. D.	*kâtibin*	}	}
A.	*kâtiban*	*kâtibaini*	*kâtibîna.*

The coincidence of the Hebrew dual and plural with the *oblique* cases in Arabic is remarkable, and cannot be purely accidental.

which held their place in the language, or whether they are *affected* archaisms framed at will by particular poets. For those at any rate which are isolated (as עֲיָפָתָה Job 10, 22[1]) or are met with only in later writers (צָרָתָה Ps. 120, 1'; and the masc. הַפֵּוְתָה 116, 15; נַחֲלָה *torrent* 124, 4), the latter alternative is decidedly the more probable: the use of '—, Ps. 113, 5-9. 114, 8. 123, 1 (see Delitzsch, Introd. to Ps. 113; Ges.-Kautzsch, § 90. 3[a]), shews to what an extent the later poets loved these quaint forms. But the termination may here and there have been employed with its proper force, as in Ps. 80, 3 לכה (חושה לעזרתי cf. 38, 23) קומה עֶזְרָתָה לנו 44, 27; וְלִישׁוּעָתָה), and perhaps also 63, 8. 94, 17.

183. To the reader who is unacquainted with Arabic, the force of this comparison will be rendered more palpable if it be explained that in that language the imperfect tense possesses four distinct modal forms, each marked by its own termination, viz. the indicative, the subjunctive, the jussive, and the energetic. Thus from *qatala* (= קָטַל) we get—

	INDIC.	SUBJ.	JUSSIVE.	ENERGETIC.
1 sing.	*'aqtulu*	*'aqtula*	*'aqtul*	*'aqtulan* (or -*anna*).
3 pl. masc.	*yaqtulûna*	*yaqtulû*	*yaqtulû*	*yaqtulun* (or -*unna*).

In *yaqtulûna* the source of the *n* in יִקְטְלוּן immediately discloses itself: like modern Arabic, Hebrew, as a rule, discarded the final syllable -*na;* it was not, however, disused altogether, but kept its place as a fuller and more significant form, adapted to round a period, or give to a word some slight additional force[2]. With the subjunctive we are not here further concerned: but the two remaining moods have

---

[1] But המזמתה Jer. 11, 15 is corrupt (see R.V. *marg.*, or *QPB*[3]): read with LXX המומה הַנְדָרִים for המומתה הרבים (with יעברו מעליך רעתך).

[2] Particulars respecting its occurrence may be found in Böttcher, § 930: the instances are also collected *in extenso* by König, *Alttestamentliche Studien*, ii. (Berlin, 1839) [a comparison of the style and language of Dt. with that of Jerem.], p. 165 ff. See more briefly the author's *Notes on Samuel*, on 1 Sa. 2, 15.

both left in Hebrew indelible marks of their presence, in a manner which declares that they must once have been more uniformly and extensively recognizable than is now the case: marks which it is the more important to observe, since, *as the usage of the language shews*, they still retained a distinctive meaning. As regards the jussive, nothing need be added to what has been already said (§§ 44, 151 *Obs.*). With respect to the energetic, which, like the jussive, is used indiscriminately with *all* the persons, a reference to the examples given below, p. 245, will shew that its use is by no means limited to the expression of a strongly-felt purpose or desire, but that it is employed much more widely, to convey, for instance, an emphatic command, or to add a general emphasis to the assertion of a future fact—it being a matter of indifference whether this fact is *desired* by the speaker or not: and the reader will not unnaturally wonder why, when its signification is so broad and comprehensive in Arabic, any difficulty should be felt in conceding a similar scope to the Hebrew cohortative. *A priori*, to be sure, the cohortative, so far as can be seen, might have been employed with the same range of meaning as the energetic: it is only actual examination which, fixing narrower limits for the vast majority of passages in which it occurs, forbids us to exceed them for the two or three isolated occasions upon which its predominant sense seems out of place.

Obs. In many—perhaps most—of the cases where Arabic makes use of the energetic, Hebrew would, in fact, avail itself of a totally different construction, viz. the *infinitive absolute* prefixed to the verb—a construction which imparts similar emphasis to the sentiment expressed, and of which it is almost impossible not to be spontaneously reminded, as one contemplates the Arabic energetic. Not only do the two idioms agree in other respects, but, singularly enough, the infinitive absolute is frequently found after אִם (e.g. Ex. 15, 26. 21, 5. 22, 3. 11 f. 22. Lev. 7, 18. 13, 7. 27, 10. 13), precisely as the energetic occurs after إِلَّا. Will it, then, be thought too bold to conjecture that the wider and more general functions which this form continued to exercise in Arabic, were in Hebrew superseded by the rise of a new idiom, of genuine native growth, which gradually absorbed all except one? that in this way the termination *-an* or *-anna*, from having been once capable of a more varied application, came ultimately to be definitely restricted to the single function with which we are familiar? Both idioms subserving upon the whole the same objects, after the inf. abs. had established itself in the language, they would speedily come into collision; it would be felt, however, that the two were not needed together, and by a division of labour the language would gain in both definiteness and force.

184. The opinion that Hebrew exhibits in germ the grammatical forms which appear in a more developed form in Arabic, cannot be sustained; and though it has had its advocates[1], is now deservedly abandoned by scholars. It need only be added that in adopting the view, which has been accepted and exemplified in the preceding pages, there are, of course, two errors to be guarded against: one, that of imagining Hebrew to be *derived from* Arabic; the other, that of concluding *everything* exhibited by the classical Arabic to have originated in primitive Semitic times. The true state of the case is rather this: Hebrew and Arabic, with the other Semitic languages, are the *collateral* descendants of the old Semitic stock, among which Arabic appears upon the whole to have preserved the greatest resemblance to the parent tongue: but this by no means excludes the possibility, and, indeed, the probability, of Arabic itself, after its separation from the other languages, developing particular forms and constructions peculiar to itself alone.

Obs. So Nöldeke, the highest living authority on the philology of the Semitic languages, writes (*Encyclopaedia Britannica*, ed. 9, art. 'Semitic languages,' p. 641 f.) :—' But just as it is now recognized with ever-increasing clearness that Sanskrit is far from having retained in such a degree as was even lately supposed the characteristics of primitive Indo-

---

[1] Comp., for instance, Renan, *Histoire Générale des Langues Sémitiques,* pp. 424, 425 (ed. 1863), or the *Dict. of the Bible* (ed. 1), art. 'Shemitic languages and writing,' § 32 (1863).

European speech, so in the domain of the Semitic tongues we can assign to Arabic only a relative antiquity. It is true that in Arabic very many features are preserved more faithfully than in the cognate languages,— for instance, nearly all the original abundance of consonants, the short vowels in open syllables, particularly in the interior of words, and many grammatical distinctions, which in the other languages are more or less obscured. But on the other hand, Arabic has coined, simply from analogy, a great number of forms, which, owing to their extreme simplicity, seem at the first glance to be primitive, but which, nevertheless, are only modifications of the primitive forms; whilst perhaps the other Semitic languages exhibit modifications of a different kind.' And (p. 646) 'with regard to grammatical forms, Hebrew has lost much that is still preserved in Arabic[1]: but the greater richness of Arabic is in part the result of later development[2].'

185. Turning now from structure to function, we may collect a few illustrations of the more noticeable significations that are borne by the two tenses.

§ 13. See Wright, ii. 1e, and cf. Qor. 3, 75. 108. 6, 31. 7, 69.

§ 14. Ewald, *Gramm. Arab.* ii. p. 347 : 'Usus perfecti de re futurâ in Korano latius patet, videturque mihi vestigia quaedam hebraei perfecti cum ו relativo servare.' The use alluded to is, I believe, confined to those descriptions of the 'Hour' of resurrection, or the future life, with which the Qor'an abounds ; and though at times the perfect appears in the neighbourhood of other perfects without *waw*

---

[1] It is noteworthy that, as Gesenius long ago remarked (Pref. to his *Lehrgebäude der hebr. Sprache*, 1817, p. vii), the modern *popular* Arabic often agrees with Hebrew against the classical or *literary* Arabic, many grammatical forms existing in the written language having in the popular language dropped out of use, precisely as happened in Hebrew : for some illustrations of this, see Wright, *Arabic Gramm.* i. §§ 90 *end*, 185 rem. *e*, 308 *end* (as well as different passages in his *Compar. Grammar*); Philippi, *Wesen und Ursprung des St. Constr.*, 1871, p. 145 ff.

[2] See further, on the same subject, Philippi, *Wesen und Ursprung des St. Constr.* passim, especially pp. 124, 142–151, with Nöldeke's review of it in the *Gött. Gel. Anzeigen*, June, 1871, p. 881. Nöldeke gives it as his opinion that the presence of vowel-terminations in old Semitic, as germs of the Arabic cases, is very probable : he only demurs to the supposition that as yet they had definitely begun to fulfil the functions of the three cases as such.

(e.g. 6, 22–31. 7, 35–49), yet it is so much more frequently found surrounded by *imperfects* (in a future sense) as to make it difficult to avoid accepting Ewald's conclusion. The list given by Ewald by no means exhausts the instances which might be found : two or three examples will, however, be sufficient for our present purpose. 11, 11. 100 he (Pharaoh) will head his people on the day of resurrection *fa'awradahum* (as though וְהוֹרִידֵם), *and lead them down* into the fire. 14, 24–28 *and they will* come forth to God altogether, *and he will* say etc. 25, 27 and one day will the heavens be cleft *and the angels be sent down* descending. 44, 54–56. 50, 19–30. 78, 19 f.

§ 17. Qor. 7, 87. 11, 35 إِنْ شَآءَ si *voluerit*. 45. 83 as for thy (Lot's) wife, on her shall light what *will have lighted* on them. 109 abiding in it as long as the heavens and earth *shall have lasted*, except thy Lord *shall have willed* otherwise. 42, 43 ; after حَتَّى *until*, 6, 31.

§ 19. Cf. Qor. 3, 138. 159. 7, 149. 10, 52.

§ 27. Various instances of the *inceptive* force of the imperfect :—
3, 42 he only saith to a thing, Be, فَيَكُونُ *and it is ;* so 52. 19, 36 (cf. Ps. 33, 9). 7, 98. 11, 40 وَيَصْنَعُ and he *went on* to build the ark. 18, 40 وَيَقُولُ. 20, 41. 58, 9 ; after إِذْ (=אז), 3, 120 إِذْ تَقُولُ *then* thou *wentest on* to say ; after ثُمَّ (cf. שם), 3, 22. 40, 69. 58, 9, cf. 11, 77. 21, 12. Also 7, 114. 26, 44 and Moses cast down his rod, فَإِذَا هِيَ تَلْقَفُ and behold IT *began devouring* their inventions. 11, 44 وَهِيَ تَجْرِى and IT *began to* move.

3, 39 when they *were casting* lots. 145. 147 when ye *were coming* up the height. 21, 78 when they *were giving* judgment. 40, 10.

The inceptive force of the tense is also conspicuously displayed when it follows a verb in the past for the purpose of indicating the intention or object with which the action was performed; as 3, 117. 6, 25 when they come to thee *to dispute* with thee. 7, 72. 10, 3 then ascended his throne *yudabbiru* to rule all things. 42, 9 ; cf. 3, 158. 34, 43 al., and Wright, ii. § 8d. With יוֹם אוֹלֵד בּוֹ, cf. 19, 15 *yawma yamûtu* (= יוֹם יָמוּת) the day he would die on.

§ 34. Wright, ii. § 8e ; Qor. 7, 84 and sit not in every road *menacing and misleading* (both indic.). 11, 80. Compare also Steinthal, *Charac- teristik*, p. 267.

§§ 44–46. On the energetic, see Wright, ii. § 19. Unlike the Hebrew cohortative, it is used freely in *all* the persons ; the nature of its intensifying influence will be clear from the examples:—Qor. 3, 75 surely (لَ) *ye shall* believe in him ! 194 *la'ukaffiranna* (= כַּפֵּר אֲכַפְּרָה) surely I will forgive you your evil deeds ! 6, 12 he *will* surely gather you together for the day of resurrection. 14 *do not be* of the 'associators' [i.e. the Christians]! 35, 80 *do not be* one of the ignorant! 77 surely, if my Lord doth not guide me, surely *I shall be* of the people that err! 7, 5 surely *we will ask!* 121 surely *I will* crucify you! And after إمّا *if at all, whether:* 6, 67 and *if* Satan *cause thee to forget* (= ואם נשׁה ינשׁך השׂטן=), etc. 19, 26 (=אם ראה תראי); 7, 33. 199. 10, 47 (cf. 40, 77) *whether* we *let thee see* some of the things with which we threaten them, or (أو) *take thee* to ourselves, to us is their return. 43, 40 f.

§§ 122–129. The use of the Arabic ف *fa,* as illustrating the employment of ו to introduce the apodosis or the predicate, was already appealed to by the mediaeval Jewish grammarians and commentators (e.g. by Ibn Ezra, frequently[1]). Examples may readily be found: thus with ורעו *know then,* Ps. 4, 4, compare Qor. 3, 14 O our Lord! we have indeed believed, *so* forgive us our sins! 44 I come to you with a sign from your Lord; *so* fear God and obey me: behold God is my Lord and your Lord; *therefore* serve him! 89 God is truthful; follow, *then* etc.

With the instances in §§ 123, 127, compare (α) 3, 49. 50 as to those who believe, *them* (ﻓ) he will pay their reward. 26, 75–77.

(β) 6, 72 in the day that he saith, Be, *then* it is! 16, 87 and when they shall have seen the punishment, *then* it will not be lightened off them. 26, 80. 43, 50. 50, 39 in the night, *then* praise him! (in Hebrew, with of course the perfect, ובלילה ושׁבּחתּו.)

(γ) 3, 118 (14, 14 f.) upon God, *there* (ﻓ) let the believer trust! 10, 59 in the grace of God and in his mercy, *why,* in this, *this* let them rejoice! 16, 53 فَإِيَّايَ فَارْهَبُونِ *so* me, *me* revere! 42, 14; constantly after من *whoso,* as 3, 70 whoever has been true to his engagement, and fears God, *why* (ﻓ), surely God loveth those that fear him. 76. 88. 45, 14 whoever does right, *falinafsihi* (ולנפשׂו) *'tis* for his own soul; after *whatever,* 42, 8. 34; in the apod. after *if,* 40, 22; after *whether* . . . *or* . . ., 10, 47. 40, 77.

---

[1] See his Comm. on Gen. 22, 4. Ex. 9, 21. Lev. 7, 16. Is. 48, 7. Zech. 14, 17 (§ 124), etc. Comp. W. Bacher, *Abraham Ibn Esra als Grammatiker,* Strassburg, 1882, p. 138 f.

APPENDIX IV.

On the Principle of Apposition in Hebrew.

Note. The following pages, which lay no claim to independent research, are based on the two papers of Professor Fleischer, 'Ueber einige Arten der Nominalapposition im Arabischen,' in the *Berichte über die Verhandlungen der Kön. Sächs. Ges. der Wissenschaften zu Leipzig*, 1856, pp. 1–14; 1862, pp. 10–66 (reprinted in his *Kleinere Schriften*, ii. 1, 1888, pp. 1–74); and on those parts of Philippi's monograph on the Status Constructus (Weimar, 1871) in which the same subject is treated with more immediate reference to Hebrew. The object of Fleischer's first paper was to correct certain mis-statements in the Grammars of De Sacy and Ewald: it provoked (as might have been anticipated) a characteristic reply from the last-named scholar in the *GGAN*. 1857, pp. 97–112: and the second paper accordingly defends *in extenso*, with a profusion of illustrative examples, the principles laid down more briefly in the first. The dispute between the two great grammarians turned, however, not so much upon the facts (though doubtless these were not duly estimated, and in part also overlooked by Ewald) as upon the relative priority, in the class of instances under discussion, of the *st. constr.* and apposition, Ewald contending in favour of the former, and regarding apposition as a breaking up of the older and stricter union of words, and the last resource of a decaying tongue, while Fleischer maintained that, where idioms defining the relations between words with precision and smoothness, are found side by side with simpler and rougher constructions in which those relations are only noted in their broader outline, presumption is in favour of the priority of the latter. The *principle* of apposition, however, is not confined even to late Hebrew, so that Fleischer's position seems to be more in accordance with analogy, and is accepted without hesitation by Philippi (p. 90 f.).—It is convenient sometimes to use the term *Annexion* (= إِضَافَة) to denote the *st. constr.* relation.

The main principles here explained were also, it is worth adding, recognized long ago in their bearing on Hebrew syntax by the late Professor Lee, of Cambridge: see his *Hebr. Gr.* (1832), §§ 219. 1–3, 220.

186. Apposition, in the widest sense of the term, is the combination of the two parts of a 'simple judgment' into a complex idea[1]. Every apposition, therefore, presupposes the possibility of a correlative predication, and any peculiarity in the nature of the one will but reflect a corresponding peculiarity in the nature of the other. For example, such expressions as 'man born of a woman,' Ἰωάννης ὁ βαπτίζων, imply, and may be derived from, the propositions 'man is born of a woman,' Ἰωάννης ἦν ὁ βαπτίζων. Of course instances like these, which merely view a single subject under two aspects, are not the peculiar property of any language: but the Semitic languages extend the principle much beyond what would be in harmony with our mode of thinking; they bring two terms into parallel juxtaposition in order to form a *single conception*, in cases where we should introduce a preposition, or substitute an adjective, as the more precise 'exponent' of the relation subsisting between them. The principal cases fall under two heads, which may be considered in order.

In Arabic, the material of which an object is composed is often not conceived under the form of an attribute or quality belonging to it (a *golden* crown): it is regarded as the *genus* or class to which the object is to be referred, and which is specified by being appended to the object named, as its closer definition (*the crown, the gold;* or *a crown, gold*). In this example, the *crown* is the principal idea, to which *gold* stands in *explanatory apposition*[2]: the crown is first indicated generally, and its nature is then more closely described by

---

[1] *Berichte*, 1862, p. 12.

[2] In the technical language of the grammarians it forms a بيان : see Dr. Wright's *Arabic Grammar*, ii. § 94, p. 248 (ed. 2, 1875). But two other constructions are likewise admissible : *a crown of* (مـن) *gold*, and *a crown of gold* (the *st. constr.*).

the mention of the class to which it belongs, the understanding combining the two ideas thus thrown down side by side into the logical unit which we express by the words *the* (or *a*) *golden crown*. Let this be distinguished from the other form of apposition, *a pound, gold;* here the first word marks a weight, measure, or number, and the second is described as the *Permutative*[1] of the first; and here, moreover, the measure, apart from the thing measured, being but an impalpable magnitude, it is the second, not the first word, which is the principal idea.

187. The form which the predicate assumes is determined similarly. Terms expressing *distinctly* its relation to the subject, such as *consists of, contains, extends over, measures, weighs*, etc., are avoided: an article *is* the material of which it is composed, the whole *is* its parts, the genus *is* its species, the thing weighed *is* the weight, etc. Or, to pass to concrete instances (selected out of a large number collected by Fleischer from Arabic authors), 'their garments *are* silk' (Qor. 35, 30), 'each house *is* [not, *is of*] five stories,' 'Memphis *was* aqueducts and dams,' 'potash *is* many kinds,' 'the crocodile *is* ten cubits,' 'the waters of the Nile in such and such a year *were* (= rose) five cubits,' 'the pilgrimage *is* (= lasts) some months' (Qor. 2, 193): in all these instances the predicate is in the *nominative*, and it follows that a simple relation of *Identity* must be affirmed between it and the subject. The idiom admits of imitation in English, more or less close, and sometimes quite naturally: Mecca was at that time *all* saltwort and thorns, the field was one mass of bloom, 'the poop was beaten gold, ... the oars were silver:' still, in Arabic at any rate, it must have been in too constant use to imply quite the emphasis which its rarity gives it in our own language, or which is made still plainer by the addition of 'all.'

---

[1] بدل: so called because the idea of the empty measure is *exchanged*, as the sentence advances, for that of the thing measured (*ibid.* § 94 rem. *b;* § 139 rem. *b*).

188. By aid of these principles, a multitude of constructions occurring in the O. T. receive at once a natural and
sufficient explanation : the harshness and abruptness, as it
seems to us, may not indeed be removed, but this is now
seen to constitute no difficulty to the Semitic mode of thought.
From our point of view, the simplest test of a legitimate
apposition will be (§ 186) its capability of being transposed
into a proposition in which a relation of identity between
subj. and pred. can be conceived ; and in fact all the examples,
it may be observed, will bear this transposition. Now (1)
just as Arabic says الصَّنَمُ الذَّهَبُ *the image, the gold,* so in
Hebrew we have Ex. 39, 17 הָעֲבֹתֹת הַזָּהָב; 2 Ki. 16, 17 הַבָּקָר
הַנְּחֹשֶׁת: these are both cases of apposition, 'the cords, the
gold' = *the golden cords;* 'the oxen, the brass' = *the brazen
oxen:* not only is there no necessity to postulate an ellipse,
'the cords (even the cords) of gold[1],' but Arabic usage altogether prohibits it[2]. Further examples: 1 Sa. 2, 13 the fork,
the three prongs = *the three-pronged fork.* Zech. 4, 10 האבן
הבדיל the plumb-stone; further, Gen. 6, 17. 7, 6[3]. Nu. 7, 13.
Jer. 52, 20. 1 Chr. 15, 19 מְצִלְתַּיִם נְחֹשֶׁת; and somewhat more
freely, to denote, not the actual substance of which an object
consists, but a physical or material characteristic displayed
by it, Jer. 31, 40 וכל־העמק הפגרים והדשן all the valley, the
corpses and the ashes[4]. Ez. 22, 18 סיגים כסף היו they are
become *silver-dross* (the first word in English qualifying the
second, so that the order is reversed). Ex. 22, 30 בשר בשדה

---

[1] As is done e.g. by Kalisch, § 87, 10. Ewald, § 290ᵉ, less probably,
regards these as cases of dissolution of the *st. constr.,* brought about by
the article prefixed to the first word.

[2] Fleischer shews that annexion is not here allowable.

[3] Unless (as has been supposed) מים in these two passages be a gloss,
explanatory of מבול.

[4] As predicate, 'the valley was corpses and ashes,' like 'Memphis
was aqueducts.' With §§ 188–192 comp. generally Wright, § 136ᵃ;
Ew. § 287ʰ.

טרפה flesh in the field, that which is torn = *torn flesh* (cf. Jer. 41, 8). 24, 5 and 1 Sa. 11, 15 זְבָחִים שְׁלָמִים (elsewhere זבחי שלמים). Dt. 3, 5. 16, 21 אשרה כל עץ = an Ashérah (of) any wood. Isa. 3, 24 מעשה מקשה. Ez. 43, 21 אֶת־הַפַּר הַחַטָּאת the bullock, the sin-offering (usually פַּר־הֹחחטאת). Ps. 68, 17 mountains, peaks[1] = *peaked mountains*. Cant. 8, 2 אַשְׁקְךָ מִיַּיִן הָרֶקַח I will give thee to drink of wine, spiced mixture[1] = *spiced wine*[2].

(2) To these correspond, in the predicative form, Ex. 9, 31 השערה אביב והפשתה גבעל the barley *was ears*, and the flax *was bloom*. Jer. 24, 2 one basket *was* good figs etc.[3] Ez. 41, 22 הַמִּזְבֵּחַ עֵץ. Gen. 1, 2 the earth *was* an emptiness and waste. 14, 10 the vale *was* pits[4], pits of slime. Isa. 5, 12 and their feast *is* harp and lute etc. 30, 33 מְדֻרָתָהּ אֵשׁ וְעֵצִים. 65, 4 וּפָרַק פִּגֻּלִים כְּלֵיהֶם. Ps. 23, 5 כּוֹסִי רְוָיָה my cup *is an overflowing*. 45, 9 all thy garments *are* myrrh. Ezra 10, 13 והעת גשמים the season *was* showers. Jer. 2, 28 thy gods *are* the number of thy cities[5].

189. It is but an extension of this usage (though, as it would seem, more liberally employed in Hebrew than in Arabic[6]) when terms denoting other than material attributes are treated similarly. Thus (1) Josh. 16, 9 הֶעָרִים הַמֻּבְדָּלוֹת the cities, the separations = the separate cities[7]. Ps. 120, 3

---

[1] Embracing in a complex idea the subj. and pred. of the proposi-tions, ' the mountains *were* peaks,' ' the wine *was* spiced mixture.'

[2] Lee (§ 219) explains similarly Ez. 34, 20 *lit.* sheep, fatness. But no doubt בְּרִיאָה (cf. *v.* 3), or at least בְּרִיָה (Olsh. p. 327), should be restored.

[3] Cf. ' all the district was figs, vines, and olives ' (*Ber.* 1862, p. 34).

[4] The first בארות a *suspended st. constr.*, like Ps. 78, 9: Ew. § 289c.

[5] Cf. ' their woes are the number of the sand ' (*Ber.* 1862, p. 39).

[6] On '*adlun*, and some other words originally substantives (comp. in Hebrew מיטב, which is only in the later language, Ps. 109, 8. Eccl. 5, 1, treated as an adj., and declined), see *Berichte*, 1856, p. 5; Wright, ii. § 94 rem. *b*.

[7] But possibly הַמֻּבְדָּלוֹת (pt. Hof.) should here be read: cf. the verb Hif.) in Dt. 4, 41. 19, 2. 7.

לְשׁוֹן רְמִיָּה O tongue, deceitfulness! 1 Ki. 22, 27 and Isa. 30, 20 מַיִם לַחַץ water, affliction (i. e. water given in such scant measure, as itself to betoken affliction). Zech. 1, 13 words, consolations = *consoling words.* Ex. 30, 23 בְּשָׂמִים רֹאשׁ = *choice* spices. Pr. 22, 21[b] אֲמָרִים אֱמֶת. Ps. 60, 5 יַיִן תַּרְעֵלָה wine, staggering (the staggering being conceived as conveyed by the wine) = wine of staggering. Jer. 25, 15 הַיַּיִן הַחֵמָה.

(2) Gen. 11, 1 the whole earth was שָׂפָה אֶחָת. Ex. 17, 12 וַיְהִי יָדָיו אֱמוּנָה and his hands were *firmness* (= were firm). Isa. 19, 11 (perhaps) עֵצָה. 27, 10 the city is בָּדָד *solitariness.* 30, 7 רַהַב הֵם שֶׁבֶת Rahab (Egypt), they are *utter indolence* (lit. *a sitting still*). Jer. 48, 38 כֻּלֹּה מִסְפֵּד. Ez. 2, 8 אַל־תְּהִי־מֶרִי be not *rebelliousness*[1]. 16, 7 וְאַתְּ עֵרֹם וְעֶרְיָה. Ps. 19, 10 מִשְׁפְּטֵי יהוה אֱמֶת. 25, 10. 35, 6. 55, 22 his heart is *war.* 88, 19 מְיֻדָּעַי מַחְשָׁךְ (if the rendering of Hitz. and R.V. *marg.* be right). 89, 48 (M. T.) זְכָר אֲנִי מֶה־חָלֶד = remember *quantilli sim aevi.* 92, 9 וְאַתָּה מָרוֹם and thou art *loftiness* (cf. 10, 5 מִשְׁפָּטֶיךָ מָרוֹם). 109, 4 (an extreme case) וַאֲנִי תְפִלָּה[2]. 110, 3 thy people is נְדָבוֹת (*all*) *freewillingness.* 120, 7 אֲנִי שָׁלוֹם[3]. Pr. 8, 30 וָאֶהְיֶה שַׁעֲשֻׁעִים and I was (*all*) *delight.* Job 8, 9 for we are *yesterday* (2 Sa. 15, 20 כִּי תְמוֹל בֹּאֶךָ). 22, 12 is not God *the height of heaven?* 23, 2 גַּם־הַיּוֹם מְרִי שִׂחִי (unless מַר should be here read: cf. 7, 11). 26, 13 בְּרוּחוֹ שָׁמַיִם שִׁפְרָה by his breath the heavens are *brightness.* Dan. 9, 23[2] כִּי חֲמוּדוֹת אַתָּה. Qoh. 2, 23.

---

[1] A passage which shews that in itself כִּי מֶרִי הֵמָּה Ez. 2, 7 is quite a legitimate construction: still LXX, Targ. Pesh. and 21 MSS. have here בֵּית מֶרִי, which is in agreement with Ez.'s general usage (e. g. 2, 5. 6. 3, 9. 26. 27), and is probably correct. (So 44, 6 read with LXX, Targ. Corn. וְאָמַרְתָּ אֶל בֵּית הַמֶּרִי.)

[2] Where to supply אִישׁ (Kimchi, *Michlol*, 51[a] ed. Lyck, 1862, and others) is unnecessary and wrong.

[3] So elsewhere with this word, as 1 Sa. 25, 6 וְאַתָּה שָׁלוֹם וּבֵיתְךָ שָׁלוֹם. 2 Sa. 17, 3 כָּל־הָעָם יִהְיֶה שָׁלוֹם. Pr. 3, 17 כָּל־נְתִיבוֹתֶיהָ שָׁלוֹם. Job 5, 24 וְיָדַעְתָּ כִּי שָׁלוֹם אָהֳלֶךָ (comp. Del., who shews why שָׁלוֹם cannot be an 'adverbial accus.:' also Ewald, § 296[b] *end*). 21, 9 בָּתֵּיהֶם שָׁלוֹם; and elsewhere.

Obs. Other cases of an abstract word used as predicate : Gen. 49, 4
(implicitly). 1 Sa. 22, 23 מִשְׁמֶ֫רֶת; 21, 6. Isa. 23, 18 and frequently
קֹ֫דֶשׁ[1]; Ez. 27, 36 בַּלָּהוֹת הָיִית thou art become *terrors,* which throws
light on 26, 21 בלהות אתנך, and 16, 38 ונתתיך דם חמה וקנאה (after
a verb of *making*): cf. the phrases עשה פ' כלה *to make* any one *an
utter end,* i.e. to exterminate him ; *to make* any one (all) *neck,* or
shoulder (Ex. 23, 27. Ps. 21, 13), i.e. to make them shew only their
backs in flight.

190. The same tendency to express a compound idea
by two terms standing in apposition may be traced in other
cases, not of the same distinctive character as those which
have been already discussed. It is doubtless, for instance,
the explanation of those constructions in which analogy
would lead us to expect the *st. constr.,* but in which we find
in fact the *st. abs.*—with or without the article. Thus, in
expressions indicating locality, Nu. 21, 14 אֶת־הַנְּחָלִים אַרְנוֹן
(see Dillmann). 34, 2 הארץ כנען. 1 Sa. 4, 1 הָאֶ֫בֶן הָעֵ֫זֶר the
stone Help (5, 1. 7, 12, however, the *st. constr.* אבן העזר is
used). 1 Ki. 16, 24 הָהָר שֹׁמְרוֹן (but הַר צִיון, הַר גרזים, etc.).
1 Chr. 5, 9 הַנָּהָר פְּרָת (usually נְהַר פְּרָת). Further, 2 Sa. 10, 7
הַצָּבָא הַגִּבֹּרִים the host, (even) the mighty men. 1 Ki. 16, 21
העם ישראל (so Josh. 8, 33. Ezra 9, 1). 2 Ki. 7, 13 Kt.
הֶהָמוֹן ישראל (Qrê הֲמוֹן ישראל, omitting the art., as just below,
in the same verse). Jer. 8, 5 העם הזה ירושלם[2]. La. 2, 13
בְּחִיל גבורי O daughter, Jerusalem[3]. 2 Chr. 13, 3 הַבַּת ירושלם
מלחמה. 14, 8. Ezra 2, 62 their book, the registered (perhaps
the *title* of the record). Neh. 7, 5. Dan. 8, 13.

Obs. So the infin. after היום, Ex. 9, 18. 2 Sa. 19, 25 ; cf. 2 Chr. 8, 16.
But it is too bold to extend this principle to Isa. 22, 17 הנה יהוה מטלטלך

---

[1] Comp. in proper names יוֹכָ֫בֶד Yah is *honour,* יוֹעֶ֫זֶר Yah is *help,*
יְהוֹשׁוּעַ Yah is *opulence,* which are different from the *verbal* types
יִשְׁמָעֵאל, יְהוֹשָׁפָט, etc.

[2] Where, however, LXX do not recognize ירושלם: probably rightly.

[3] Unless this be one of the anomalous cases of the art. in *st. constr.*
(Ewald, § 290[d]; Ges.-Kautzsch, § 127 rem. 4). Elsewhere, even as a
vocative, there occurs regularly בת ציון, בת ירושלם, etc.

שלשלה גבר (as was done formerly by Delitzsch) : גבר must either be a voc. (Hitz. Ew. Cheyne, Dillm. R.V. *marg.*), or belongs to § 161. 3 (Ges. Del. ed. 4¹, R.V.). It is difficult also to follow Philippi (p. 86) in referring here Josh. 3, 14 הָאָרוֹן הַבְּרִית, 8, 11 הָעָם הַמִּלְחָמָה : in the former passage, the original text had probably only הארון, הברית being added by a subsequent editor or redactor (cf. 1 Sa. 4, 3–5 LXX and Heb., with the author's note); in the latter, there may have stood originally either simply העם (as *v.* 10 : so Dillm.), or עַם־הַמלחמה (as *vv.* 1. 3. 10, 7. 11, 7), העם having been written in error by a scribe, who did not see what was to follow, through the influence of *v.* 10 (twice).

Philippi would account similarly for בְּכָתֵף פלשתים Isa. 11, 14; but here it can hardly be doubted that Nöldeke is right (*GGA.* 1871, p. 896) in regarding the punctuation בְּכָתֵף as embodying *a particular interpretation*, that, namely, which is already found in the Targ. (כְּתַף חַד) and is followed by Rashi, according to which בְּכָתֵף is taken, not in connexion with פלשתים, but, like שכם אחד Zeph. 3, 9, and ܟܐܦ ܣܡ in Syriac, as a metaphorical expression = 'with one consent.' The same interpretation is also given of שכמה, Hos. 6, 9 (Tg. Rashi, Kimchi, A. V.); but there, no less than here, the absence of the crucial אֶחָד seems decisive against it. If, however, we abandon this interpretation, and connect כתף with פלשתים, we must abandon also the punctuation which embodies it, and read the usual *st. constr.* form בְּכֶתֶף. A similar instance is afforded by 5, 30 : here the old interpretation of צַר וָאוֹר וג', still traceable in the characteristic paraphrase of the Targ., is 'moon and sun are darkened' etc., and this is represented both by the accentuation and the *qameṣ* under ו, coupling together צר ואור : but if that interpretation be given up, both the accents and the punctuation must be modified likewise. So 2, 20 לחפר פרות the punctuation is meant probably to express the sense *to dig holes* (cf. Kimchi): *to the moles* must be read לַחֲפַרְפָּרוֹת. See further 43, 28 (p. 70 *n.*), and the passages cited from the same book in § 174 : also Ps. 10, 8. 10 (where the *points* express the sense, 'thy host,' and 'the host of the grieved ones'). Qoh. 3, 21 (the pronouns היא, which would be altogether out of place, if הָעֹלה and הירדת had the *art.*, but which are required—see Nu. 13, 18–20—if the ה be the interrogative, shew that the punctuation is incorrect, and that the rendering of R.V. must be adopted : see

---

¹ Where, however, the reference to מים ברכים and 30, 20 seems to be no longer in place, illustrating, as it does, the now discarded explanation of ed. 3.

Delitzsch or Wright). 5, 17 (the *reviʿa*, with accompanying pausal form, at אֲנִי, expresses a false interpunction : see Del.).

Other apparent instances, also, deviate too widely from the normal usage of the language to be due to anything but textual corruption : so Josh. 13, 5 הארץ הגבלי (cf. Dillmann). 1 Sa. 1, 1 הרמתים צופים (where the text, if only on account of the *masc.* ptcp., cannot be correct : read, after LXX, צוּפִי *a Zuphite*—cf. 9, 5—for צופים, and see more fully the writer's note *ad loc.*). 2 Sa. 20, 23 כל הצבא ישראל (read simply כל הצבא : see 8, 16). Ez. 45, 16 כל העם הארץ (omit הארץ with LXX, Cornill). And in 2 Sa. 24, 5 הנחל הגד is not to be rendered, with R.V., 'the valley of Gad :' the text of the first part of the verse must be emended, with Wellh. and Lucian's recension of the LXX, to ויחלו מערוער ומן העיר וג': the whole will then read : 'And they began from Aroer and from the city that is in the midst of the torrent-valley (same expression as Dt. 2, 36. Josh. 13, 9. 16), *towards Gad*' etc. In Jer. 32, 12 also it is doubtful whether הספר המקנה can be rightly explained as 'the deed, the purchase' = the purchase-deed : *vv.* 11. 14 we find the normal ספר המקנה, and in *v.* 12 for את הספר המקנה LXX have simply καὶ ἔδωκα αὐτὸ (comp. Stade in the *ZATW.* 1885, pp. 175–8). Jud. 8, 32 עָפְרָה אבי העזרי must no doubt be corrected to עָפְרָת אבי העזרי, exactly as 6, 24 : observe that ἐν Ἐφραθα Ἀβιεσδρι of the LXX presupposes a final ת. אָבֵל in the compounds אָבֵל מצרים, אָבֵל כרמים, אָבֵל השטים, אָבֵל בית מעכה, אָבֵל מחולה, seems (if the punctuation be correct) to have retained anomalously the longer vowel in the *st. constr.*[1]: the same may have been the case in שָׁוֵה קריתים Gen. 14, 5 (cf. שָׁוֵה alone *v.* 17). בְּאֵרֹת in בארת בני יעקן Dt. 10, 6 may be the *st. constr.*: see Gen. 26, 18.

191. A *double* determination by both a following genitive and a prefixed article is as a rule eschewed in Hebrew; though it is met with occasionally (Ewald, § 290[d]; Ges.-Kautzsch, § 127 rem. 4), particularly in the later language. The following passages, however, in which, it will be noticed, the *st. constr.* is dependent not on the consonants but only on the vowel-points, are otherwise in such com-

---

[1] The *nature* of the second term in these instances is opposed to Philippi's view that they may be cases of apposition : the French ' Maison Orléans ' etc., which he compares, are derived from a different family of languages, and cannot be regarded as really parallel.

plete analogy with some of those just cited, that it is difficult
not to believe that the punctuation is in error, and that the
st. abs. should be restored: 2 Ki. 16, 14 where הַמִּזְבֵּחַ הַנְּחֹשֶׁת
would be in conformity with הַבָּקָר הַנְּחֹשֶׁת, *v.* 17 (§ 188. 1);
Ex. 39, 27 read הַכֻּתֳּנֹת שֵׁשׁ (§ 193 or § 195).

Obs. 1. But Jud. 16, 14 הַיָתֵד הָאֶרֶג the corruption is probably deeper:
comp. G. F. Moore in the *American Oriental Society's Proceedings,*
Oct. 1889, p. clxxvi ff. (who cancels היתד as a gloss): and Jer. 25, 26
כָל־הַמַּמְלָכוֹת הָאָרֶץ אֲשֶׁר עַל פְּנֵי הָאֲדָמָה we must evidently read כָל־
הַמַּמְלָכוֹת (without הארץ), with LXX; notice the tautology of the
existing text.

Obs. 2. 2 Ki. 23, 17 the last words belong to ויקרא, not to עשית; and
if הַמִּזְבֵּחַ be read, they run quite naturally 'against the altar *in* Bethel;'
cf. 1 Ki. 13, 4: the preposition is, of course, not necessary with a *compound* proper name, for the purpose of expressing locality: see e.g.
2 Sa. 2, 32 אֲשֶׁר בֵּית לֶחֶם which was *in* Bethlehem (but בְּחֶבְרוֹן), 2 Ki.
10, 29 בֵּית־אֵל *at* Bethel (but בְּדָן)[1]. So Gen. 31, 13 אָנֹכִי הָאֵל בֵּיתְאֵל
may be understood as · 'I am the God *at* Bethel,'—i.e. the God who
appeared to thee at Bethel. In accordance with the same principle
Nu. 22, 5 הַנָּהָר אֶרֶץ בְּנֵי־עַמּוֹ is naturally 'the river *in* the land of'
etc.: comp. 2 Sa. 17, 26 ...אֶרֶץ הַגִּלְעָד. ויחן. In Ez. 47, 15 הַדֶּרֶךְ חֶתְלֹן,
חתלן might possibly be an accus. of direction after הדרך; but the
occurrence in 48, 1 of the normal דֶּרֶךְ חֶתְלֹן makes it probable, in view
of the notoriously incorrect state of the text of Ezekiel, that דרך חתלן
should be read likewise here. Elsewhere it must remain uncertain
whether we have anomalous cases of the art. with the *st. constr.*, or
whether the art. is due to corruption of the text: so, for instance,
Jer. 38, 6 הַבּוֹר מַלְכִּיָּהוּ בֶן־הַמֶּלֶךְ. Ez. 46, 19 הַלְּשָׁכוֹת הַקֹּדֶשׁ (see the
usual form in 42, 13). 2 Ki. 16, 17ª. For הַמֶּלֶךְ אַשּׁוּר Isa. 36, 8. 16 the
parallel text 2 Ki. 18, 23. 31 has correctly מֶלֶךְ אַשּׁוּר; and for הַגֶּפֶן
שִׂבְמָה Jer. 48, 32 there is found in the fundamental passage Isa. 16, 9
the regular גֶּפֶן שִׂבְמָה (the explanation as *accus. loci,* suggested by

---

[1] Similarly בֵּית י״י *in* the house of Yahweh, 2 Ki. 11, 3. 15 and constantly, בֵּית־אָבִיךְ Gen. 24, 23, פֶּתַח הָאֹהֶל *at* the entrance of the tent,
Gen. 18, 1. 10 etc., but בְּבֵיתוֹ,בְּבֵיתִי, etc. The note in the *Speaker's
Comm.* ii. p. 545 is doubly wrong. But we do not find שִׁלֹה, שֹׁמְרוֹן,
etc., unless a verb of *motion* has preceded (as 1 Sa. 1, 25): cf. the
writer's note on 1 Sa. 2, 29.

Philippi, p. 38 f., would be very harsh, and not in accordance with usage).
On some other passages, see Ges.-Kautzsch, § 127 rem. 4.

192. The same principle regulates the use of terms specifying weight, number, or measure :—

(1) Ex. 27, 16 מָסָךְ עֶשְׂרִים אַמָּה a veil, *twenty cubits.* 29, 40. 30, 24 שֶׁמֶן זַיִת הִין olive oil, a hin. Nu. 15, 4–7. 2 Sa. 24, 24 כֶּסֶף שְׁקָלִים חֲמִשִּׁים. 1 Chr. 22, 14 זָהָב. 2 Chr. 4, 2 a line, thirty in cubits. Ez. 40, 5. 47, 4 מַיִם בִּרְכַּיִם[1] *waters, knees,* in our idiom, waters reaching to the knees. Similar are Nu. 9, 20 יָמִים מִסְפָּר[2]. Neh. 2, 12 אֲנָשִׁים מְעַט. Isa. 10, 7 גּוֹיִם לֹא מְעָט. Gen. 41, 1. 2 Sa. 13, 23 al. שְׁנָתַיִם יָמִים two years, time. Dan. 10, 2 שְׁלֹשָׁה שָׁבֻעִים יָמִים. 3[3]: Jud. 19, 2 יָמִים אַרְבָּעָה חֳדָשִׁים (where the order is reversed). Here, however, in Hebrew the *st. constr.* may be used, which is not permissible in Arabic[4]: 1 Ki. 7, 10 אֲבָנֵי עֶשֶׂר אַמּוֹת stones of 10 cubits. Dt. 4, 27 מְתֵי מִסְפָּר.

(2) As predicate: Ez. 45, 11 the bath and the ephah *shall be* one size[5]. 2 Chr. 3, 4 the porch *was* 20 cubits. 11. Gen. 47, 9 מְעַט. Dt. 33, 6 וִיהִי מְתָיו מִסְפָּר and let his men be *a number!* (i.e. numerable, few). Isa. 10, 19 מִסְפָּר יִהְיוּ.

193. There are two cases, however, which though they may at first sight appear similar to these, are in fact different : (I) when the first member of the pair is definite, the second indefinite ; (II) where the measure, or weight, *precedes* the thing measured or weighed.

I. Let us take as an example 1 Chr. 28, 18 הַכְּרוּבִים זָהָב.

---

[1] Cf. 'he is from me the length (Nom.) of a spear' (*Ber.* 1862, p. 51).

[2] Cf. Qor. 18, 10 سِنِينَ عَدَدًا years, a number [here, *numerous* years] (*ib.* p. 39). So in Syriac ܟܟܠܐ ܡܢܝ̈ܢܐ, ܡܬܡܚ̈ܝܐ ܟܝܢܐ.

[3] Hence, no doubt, חֹדֶשׁ יָמִים, יֶרַח יָמִים, though regarded in itself יָמִים might be a genitive, are to be explained similarly.

[4] 'A cord *of* a cubit' cannot be said in Arabic: only 'a cord, a cubit' (*ib.* p. 31: see the illustrations, pp. 39, 50 f.).

[5] Cf. 'an image, the size (Nom.) of a man' (*ib.* p. 57).

This must not be rendered 'the cherubim of gold;' זהב is an accus. of limitation, defining more precisely the nature of the cherubim (called technically *temyíz*), just as in Arabic خَاتَمٌ حَدِيدًا (or اَلْخَاتَمُ), a (or the) ring *as regards* or *in* iron[1]. Examples of this idiom from Ex. 25 ff. are doubtful, as the words there are mostly under the government of a preceding עשה, or similar word; but it must be recognized in some passages which, though apparently simple, have in fact caused much perplexity to grammarians, viz. Ps. 71, 7 מַחְסִי עֹז; 2 Sa. 22, 33 מָעוּזִּי חָיִל; Hab. 3, 8; Ez. 16, 27 דַּרְכֵּךְ זִמָּה; Lev. 6, 3 מִדּוֹ בַד, where the first word is defined by a pronominal suffix. In the first place, though Hebrew alone would not enable us to affirm it, these cannot be rendered (as some commentators have supposed) as if they involved a *double* annexion,—'my refuge *of* strength' etc. It is a general rule, writes Fleischer[2], in all the Semitic languages, that when a word is in the *st. constr.* with a following genitive, 'its capacity to govern as a noun (seine nominale Rectionskraft) is thereby so exhausted that under no conditions can it govern a *second* genitive in a different direction.' Accordingly, 'my iron shield' in Arabic can never be expressed by 'my shield of iron' (gen.), but only either in apposition 'my shield, the iron,' or, with the defining accus., 'my shield, in iron:' an example translated literally into Greek, runs ἔνεγκε πρὸς αὐτὸν τὸν θώρακά μου τὴν σίδηρον. It follows that עֹז, זִמָּה, etc. must be regarded as either in apposition, or as accusatives: the circumstance that they are all indeterminate (not מחסי העז) is in favour of the latter supposition,—my refuge *as to* or *for* strength, thy way *for* or *in* wickedness[3].

Obs. Lev. 26, 42 בריתי יעקב and Jer. 33, 20 בריתי היום are probably similar: 'my covenant—Jacob,' 'my covenant—the day,' בריתי being

---

[1] Philippi, p. 39; Wright, ii. p. 136. Comp. Dan. 11, 8 (Bevan).

[2] *Berichte*, 1856, p. 10; cf. Philippi, p. 14.

[3] So also Lee (§ 220. 3), citing in addition Lam. 4, 17.

determined *obliquely*, so to say, by the adjuncts יעקב and היום respectively: Ewald indeed (§ 211ᵇ) compares מלאתי משפט etc.; but the
personal pron. seems desiderated. Delitzsch, in his note on 2 Sa. 22
(at the end of Ps. 18, p. 203, ed. 4), adopting Nägelsbach's remark that
in certain cases the type מַחֲסִי עֹז for the usual מַחֲסֶה עָזִּי must have
been a logical necessity, suggests that this transposition of the pron.
suffix to the *nomen regens* may have been adopted thence into the
syntaxis ornata; but have we any evidence that those cases were
sufficiently numerous to give rise to the *tendency* to transpose which
this explanation presupposes? Was not what to us appears to be a
logical necessity avoided in Hebrew by an innate difference both of conception and expression?

In אֹיְבַי שֶׁקֶר Ps. 35, 19. 69, 5; שֹׂנְאַי שֶׁקֶר 38, 20, שקר is unquestionably an adverbial accus. *in falsehood* = falsely: cf. 119, 86. Ez.
13, 22, and the frequent رَغَبًا *greedily*, ظُلْمًا *oppressively*, in the Qor'an.
The view that it may be a genitive, expressed in the earlier editions
of Delitzsch's commentary, is in his two last (1873 and 1883) entirely
abandoned. The ptcp. with a suffix is followed by other adjuncts of an
adverbial nature, 17, 9 בנפש; 35, 19ᵇ חנם.

194. II. This case exemplifies the second type of apposition, referred to in § 186, 'a pound, gold,' in which, the first
term denoting merely the unfilled measure, the term which
follows it is the one of primary import. Here, however,
though Arabic very often makes use of apposition, it does
not do so exclusively: the article measured may be specified
by being placed in the accus. (a pound *as to* or *in* gold)[1];
and here also annexion (which was not allowable in a former
case, § 192) may take the place of apposition, in Arabic no
less than in Hebrew. But, as Hebrew does not mark the
case-endings, where the *st. constr.* is not employed, it must
remain uncertain whether the object measured was conceived
in apposition, or as an accus. of limitation: there are analogies which perhaps favour the latter[2].

---

[1] Wright, ii. §§ 44ᵉ, rem. *c*, p. 136; 94, rem. *b:* Lee, § 219. 1 *note*.

[2] Examples of the acc. of respect are numerous, Ewald, 281ᶜ, 283ᵃ :
Job 15, 10 כביר מאניך ימים. Ez. 45, 14 הנת השמן (though these two
words agree badly with the context, and are probably a gloss: cf.
Smend, Cornill) is, however, a clear case of apposition.

Instances are very frequent: Gen. 18, 6 שָׁלֹשׁ סְאִים קֶמַח 3 seáhs, meal (or, *in* meal). Ex. 9, 8 מְלֹא חָפְנֵיכֶם פִּיחַ כִּבְשָׁן. 28, 17 (¹מְלֹא בֵיתוֹ כֶסֶף (so Nu. 22, 18 מְלֹא הָעֹמֶר מָן 16, 32. עֲשִׂרֹן סֹלֶת (39, 10 ארבעים טורים אבן טורי אבן). 29, 40 a tenth (of an ephah), fine meal. Nu. 5, 15 עשירית האיפה קמח. Ruth 2, 17 איפה שערים an ephah, barley. 1 Ki. 18, 32 סָאתַיִם זֶרַע. 2 Ki. 3, 4 100,000 אֵילִים צֶמֶר 100,000 rams, wool (i.e. their fleeces). 5, 17 כִּכְּרַיִם כָּסֶף; and 23 מַשָּׂא צֶמֶד פְּרָדִים אֲדָמָה. often after שקלים, etc., and שקל being omitted) עֶשְׂרִים כָּסֶף. Cf. 2 Sa. 24, 13 שֶׁבַע שָׁנִים רָעָב. A similar usage prevails in the case of מִשְׁנֶה, Gen. 43, 15 משנה כסף. Dt. 15, 18 (but some edd. read here משנה). Jer. 17, 18 וּמִשְׁנֶה שִׁבָּרוֹן שָׁבְרֵם.

The construction of *numerals* falls under the same general principles: שלשה, חמשה, etc. are substantives and construed as such: שלשה בנים *lit.* a triad, sons (apposition), and so עֶשְׂרִים שקלים 20 *shekels;* but עֶשְׂרִים שָׁנָה 20 *in* years (accus.[2], שנה being indeterminate).

Obs. The principles of Semitic syntax thus established have a bearing on the much controverted passage Ps. 45, 7 כִּסְאֲךָ אֱלֹהִים עוֹלָם וָעֶד. In addition to the ordinary rendering, 'Thy throne, O God, is for ever and ever,' three others have been proposed: (1) 'Thy throne is God for ever and ever,' (2) 'Thy throne of God (or, Thy God's throne, i. e. Thy divinely established throne) is' etc. (Ges. *Jes.* i. p. 365). (3) 'Thy throne is God's throne (cf. 1 Chr. 29, 23) for ever and ever' (Ibn Ezra; Kimchi, *Michlol*, 51ᵃ; Ges. *Thes.*; Ewald; Hitz.). The first of these, being felt to include an unsuitable comparison, has found few supporters in modern times[3]: and Gesenius' supposition, implied in (2),

---

[1] An exact parallel is afforded by Qor. 3, 85 there shall not be accepted from one of them (מלא הארץ זהב=) مِلْءُ الأَرْضِ ذَهَبٌ *the fulness of the earth, gold,* where another reading is the *accus.* ذَهَبًا *'in* gold.' On the Syriac usage, Nöldeke, *Syr. Gramm.* (1880), § 214.

[2] So always in Arabic for numerals between 11-99 (Wright, § 99): cf. Philippi, p. 89, and see Aug. Müller, *Schulgramm.* § 468 f.

[3] See against it, most recently, Cheyne, *Bampton Lectures* 1889, p. 182.

that כסא is followed by two genitives in different relations, is exactly
what is declared by Fleischer (cited § 193) to be inadmissible. But
even (3) does not appear to be more tenable : the predicate, in the
parallel instances (§ 188), is conceived always *in the nominative, not
in the genitive;* so that the insertion of 'throne of' is plainly unauthor-
ized. Can, however, 'Thy throne is God' be understood, on the
analogy of the examples in § 189, to mean 'Thy throne is divine'
(rather, perhaps, 'godly,' Mal. 2, 15)? All these examples, it was
shewn, presuppose a relation of *identity* between the subject and the
attribute predicated of it ; and though it may be convenient to translate
in English by an adjective, this translation is justified, not by having
recourse to an ellipse, but by *the tacit assumption of that relation.* The
ideas of *God* and *throne*, however, are so dissimilar, that it does not
seem possible to class this passage in the same category. It is indeed
urged by Hitzig that while עולם occurs frequently enough as an *indirect*
predicate, only לעולם is used as the *direct* predicate : thus 10, 16 Yahweh reigneth עולם, but 106, 1 his mercy לעולם *is* for ever, Lam. 5, 19
כסאך להדור ודור. The observation is an acute one, and (I believe)
correct : still, as we saw, words denoting time do stand as predicate,
and as such are identified with the subject ; can it be said that 'Thy
throne is עולם' differs, so far as form is concerned, from 'we are תמול,'
Job 8, 9? At least, the identification of a divine throne with eternity
seems easier than that of God with a human throne. Cf. Ps. 52, 3 חסר
אל כל־היום. 2 Chr. 12, 15[b].

Olshausen, admitting that Ez. 41, 22 etc. (§ 188. 2) are 'altogether
different,' but yet feeling the difficulty of עולם, suggested that a *verb*
had fallen out, and gives choice of four (בנה, הקים, כונן, הכין), one
of which might be prefixed to כסאך : but this would render the first
verse-half rather heavy, and Lagarde's סָעַד for ועד (*Proph. Chald.*
p. XLVII) is rhythmically preferable (see Ps. 89, 2). The proposal,
which has also been made, to omit אלהים as a gloss, would surely leave
the first clause singularly weak[1].

195. The analogy of the primary predicate is followed
also by the *tertiary* predicate. Just as Hebrew says 'the
altar *was* stone,' so it says, not 'he made the altar *of* stone,'
but 'he made the altar, stone.' This is different from the
inverted order, which also occurs, 'he made the stones an

---

[1] For other suggestions on the passage, see Cheyne, *The Book of
Psalms* (1888), pp. 127, 384 ; and *Bampton Lectures*, p. 182.

altar:' in the former 'he made the altar' is the chief thought, and is a complete sentence in itself; the material is specified by being appended to the term 'altar' in apposition: in the latter the 'stones' are the principal idea, and the sentence is only completed by the addition of the word 'altar.'

(1) Examples are frequent:—Gen. 2, 7 וַיַּעַשׂ אֵת הָאָדָם עָפָר מִן הָאָרֶץ and he made man, dust from the earth. Ex. 20, 25 לֹא תִבְנֶה אֶתְהֶן גָּזִית thou shalt not build them (of) hewn-stone. 25, 28. 26, 14. 15. 27, 1. 1 Ki. 7, 15. 27. Our idiom would here regularly insert *of*. And with the principal predicate *before* the verb:—Ex. 26, 1 וְאֶת־הַמִּשְׁכָּן תַּעֲשֶׂה עֶשֶׂר יְרִיעוֹת. 29. 28, 39ᵇ. 38, 3 כָּל כֵּלָיו עָשָׂה נְחֹשֶׁת all its vessels he made (of) copper.

When, however, the material is to be particularly specified, that naturally stands first: Ex. 25, 18 and thou shalt make two cherubim, gold; (here follow the closer directions) מִקְשָׁה תַּעֲשֶׂה אֹתָם *beaten work* shalt thou make them. 29ᵇ. 39. 26, 1ᵇ. 7ᵇ. 31ᵇ. Dt. 27, 6 אֲבָנִים שְׁלֵמוֹת תִּבְנֶה אֶת מִזְבַּח י״י. Isa. 50, 3.

(2) In all the preceding instances the verb goes closely with the *object made*, in those which follow it goes primarily with the *material*:—Gen. 28, 18 וַיָּשֶׂם אֹתָהּ מַצֵּבָה. Ex. 12, 39 and they baked the dough עֻגֹּת מַצּוֹת (into) unleavened cakes. 30, 25 וְעָשִׂיתָ אֹתוֹ שֶׁמֶן and thou shalt make it (into) holy anointing oil. 32, 4. Lev. 24, 5. Nu. 17, 3. 4 and they beat them out (into) a covering for the altar. 1 Ki. 18, 32 וַיִּבֶן אֶת הָאֲבָנִים מִזְבֵּחַ. Jer. 5, 22. 18, 4. Hos. 4, 8 their silver (which) עָשׂוּ עֲצַבִּים they made (into) idols. Amos 4, 13 עֹשֶׂה שַׁחַר עֵיפָה *lit.* maker of the dawn darkness. Isa. 50, 2ᵇ. 51, 10.

With the material or substance which is the *object* of the action preceding the verb:—Mic. 1, 7 עֲצַבֶּיהָ אָשִׂים שְׁמָמָה. 4, 13 וְקַרְנֵךְ אָשִׂים בַּרְזֶל and thy horn I will make iron. Isa. 26, 1 salvation maketh he (to be) walls and bulwark. Ps. 91, 9. Job 28, 2 וְאֶבֶן יָצוּק נְחוּשָׁה and stone one melteth (into) copper. Also Ez. 35, 4 עָרֶיךָ חָרְבָּה אָשִׂים. Amos 5, 8 יוֹם לַיְלָה הֶחֱשִׁיךְ day

he darkeneth (to) night (cf. with לְ, Job 17, 12 לַיְלָה לְיוֹם
יָשִׂימוּ).

And with that which is the *result* of the action preceding
the verb:—1 Ki. 11, 34 כִּי נָשִׂיא אֲשִׁתֶנּוּ. Ps. 39, 6 טְפָחוֹת נָתַתָּה
יָמַי. 89, 28 etc. Isa. 26, 18 *lit.* salvations (i.e. saved and safe)
we could not make the land (cf. *v.* 7 יָשָׁר תְּפַלֵּס מַעְגַּל צַדִּיק
(into) an even one dost thou level the path of the just): cf.
Ps. 58, 9 like a snail תֶּמֶס יַהֲלֹךְ that passeth away into slime;
and with a passive verb, Isa. 24, 12 וּשְׁאִיָּה יֻכַּת שָׁעַר and into
ruins is the gate broken. Job 22, 16 נָהָר יוּצַק יְסוֹדָם (into) a
stream is melted their foundation.

Obs. I have multiplied examples here on account of their bearing on
Ps. 104, 4 עֹשֶׂה מַלְאָכָיו רוּחוֹת מְשָׁרְתָיו אֵשׁ לֹהֵט. Of these words two
renderings, it will be clear, are quite legitimate: (1) 'maketh his messengers *of winds*, his ministers *of flaming fire*' (Del. Cheyne); Ex. 25, 28
(37, 15. 28) would then be a precise *formal* parallel, וְעָשִׂיתָ אֶת הַבַּדִּים
עֲצֵי שִׁטִּים, and the meaning would be that winds and fire are the
elements of which the messengers are formed; and (2) 'maketh his
angels *to be* winds, his messengers *to be* flaming fire' (LXX. Dr. Kay),
i.e. transforms them into winds and fire (arrays them 'with the out-
ward properties of physical phenomena') [the Targ., less literally,
'making his messengers (אִזְגַּדּוֹהִי not his *angels*) *swift as* wind, his
ministers *strong as* the glowing fire']. Can the words, however, be
rendered, (3) 'who maketh his messengers the winds, his ministers
the flaming fire?' Do they express not that God makes his messengers
of winds, or transforms them (upon occasion) into winds, but that he
uses the winds in his service? There is unquestionably much authority
for this view: it was adopted without hesitation or remark by Rashi
(עוֹשֶׂה אֶת הָרוּחוֹת שְׁלוּחָיו), Ibn Ezra (quoting Ps. 148, 8), Kimchi;
and among moderns by Ewald, Hitz., Hupf.: it is also strongly commended by the general purport of the Psalm, which (as is well drawn
out by Dean (now Bishop) Perowne, in a paper in the *Expositor*, Dec.
1878, p. 461) is to shew how the various *natural* agents are appropriated to different uses by the Creator. This, the same paper further
tells us, was so strongly felt by the late Bishop Thirlwall, that nothing
but the 'irresistible compulsion of a grammatical necessity,' derived
from the order of the words, forced him to reject the rendering proposed: the Dean himself felt similarly until a comparison of Isa.
37, 26. 60, 18[b] led him to think the difficulty might be overcome.

Where authorities are thus divided an opinion must be offered with diffidence : still *presumption* appears to me to be unfavourable to (3). Let us vary the phrase in Micah with the view of producing one as parallel as possible to the one before us.   הַשָּׂם קַרְנָיו בַּרְזֶל would be a good Hebrew expression (cf. Ps. 69, 12 ואתנה לבושי שק. 147, 14 השם גבולך שלום): the *horns* would be the primary idea, and the object of the sentence would be to state that they were of iron : had the intention been to express that the iron was made into horns, the instances (2) above (p. 261) seem to shew that the order would have been השם. Job 31, 24. השם בשר זרועו. Jer. 17, 5   18, 12.   104, 3.   ברזל קרניו: 38, 9 בשומו ענן לבושו. Isa. 54, 12 ושמתי כדכד שמשותיך (where the following clauses with ל can have no retrospective bearing on the construction of the first) would then be similar.   If the analogy here suggested be just, it cannot but confirm the doubts entertained by Bishop Thirlwall against the rendering 'maketh the winds his messengers' etc. : would not the word *maketh*, also, in this expression, implying application only, and not constitution, be the equivalent of שם rather than עשה?   Isa. 37, 26 the strong term להשאות limits far more than עשה the sense of what follows : 60, 18ᵇ וקראת ישועה חומותיך the *definiteness* of חומותיך as compared with ישועה causes it to be naturally taken as the primary object ; and in fact the same definiteness must be felt to give מלאכיו an analogous position in relation to רוחות.   Nor would 60, 17ᵇ, which might also be appealed to, be more decisive : the rendering of this passage given by A.V., Hitz., Dr. Kay, and R.V. cannot be shewn to be insufficient.

After all does the first rendering, 'Who maketh his messengers of winds, his ministers of flaming fire,' afford such an inadequate sense? Though it may not state it so directly as 'who maketh the winds his messengers etc.,' does it not still clearly imply that the winds and fire are the personified instruments executing the Divine purpose, and accordingly express substantially that appropriation of natural agents which Dean Perowne rightly desiderates?

APPENDIX V.

1. *The Casus Pendens.*

196. In prose and poetry alike, terseness and simplicity are the notes of Hebrew style. A sentence may indeed be prolonged indefinitely, when its different parts are connected merely by *and* (Dt. 8, 12–17. 24, 1–4. Jer. 13, 13); but otherwise, if it be at all involved, it speedily becomes unwieldy[1]. One of the secrets therefore of writing a lucid and classical Hebrew style is to break up a sentence into manageable subdivisions. In poetry each verse must have its own rhythmical scheme: it must be articulated, rhythmically and logically, into well-defined clauses; each of these must as a rule not consist of more than three or four words; and if for the sake of breadth or variety, a clause contains more, it should be such as to admit naturally of a pause in the course of it (Ps. 27, 4. 42, 5. 65, 10). It follows from this that a piece of modern English poetry, for instance, can seldom be rendered literally into Hebrew; its long sentences must be transformed so as to be capable of distribution into parallel clauses; and the abundance of epithets which in our eyes add richness and beauty, but which are incompatible with the light movement of a Hebrew lyric, must be sacrificed, and expressions chosen which, while brief, suggest them more or less by implication. Similar principles regulate the

---

[1] Instances of such sentences first become frequent in the latest Hebrew style, especially in Chronicles, Esther, and Daniel.

style of Hebrew prose. Sentences must be connected in the simplest manner possible: co-ordination must often take the place of subordination (pp. 157 *n.*, 186 f.): a series of conditional clauses must be relieved by והיה (§ 121), and a phrase like ἵνα ὅταν ἔλθῃ (Luke 14, 10) must be rendered, not by והיה כבוא … ואמר, but either ואמר … למען יבא or למען כאשר יבא (comp. Dt. 8, 12 f. R.V. and Heb.).

197. One of the commonest and most characteristic artifices of which Hebrew avails itself for the purpose of avoiding an unwieldy sentence is the *casus pendens* (in Arabic, the nominative). This possesses more advantages than one: not only does it give the subject (or object) a prominent place at the beginning, and ease the body of the sentence by permitting a light pronominal suffix to take its place: but it further rounds the sentence off, and gives it an ending upon which the voice may suitably rest (e.g. Job 29, 16 וריב אלמנה אחקרהו. Ps. 90, 17 ומעשה ידינו כוננהו).

The following are the principal types:—

(1) Gen. 28, 13 the land which thou liest upon, לך אתננה to thee will I give it and to thy seed (substitute אֶתֵּן for אתננה, and it will be found that, *however the words be arranged*, the sentence will lose either in neatness or expressiveness, or both). 26, 15. Dt. 2, 23. 7, 15. 14, 27. Josh. 9, 12 (אתו) this our bread—hot did we provide it from our houses, when etc. 2 Ki. 1, 4. 10, 29. Isa. 1, 7 אדמתכם זרים אוכלים אותה. 9, 1 (balance and parallelism far better preserved than by על יושבי … אור נגה:). 15, 7ᵇ. 26, 11 accents (very harsh: Ew. Dillm. construe as R.V. *marg.*). 42, 3. 53, 4. 59, 12ᵇ. Jer. 36, 14. Ez. 32, 7. 8. Ps. 125, 5. 145, 6. 147, 20. Job 17, 15 (ורוח כְּהָה מִי יִשָּׁאֶנָּה ותקותי מי ישורנה (so Jer. 2, 24. Pr. 18, 14).

(2) Slightly different are Gen. 17, 15. 34, 8 שכם בני חשקה בכור שורו הדר לו. 17, 33. הצור תמים פעלו. Dt. 32, 4 נפשו … 2 Sa. 21, 5 f. 23, 6 ובליעל כקוץ מֻנָד כֻּלָּהַם but worthless men— as thorns driven away are all of them. Ps. 10, 5. 15 וָרָע. 11, 4

(2 Chr. 16, 9). 18, 31 הָאֵל תמים דרכו. 46, 5. 89, 3. 90, 10.
104, 17. 125, 2. Isa. 11, 10 (cf. Ez. 10, 11ᵇ). 13, 17. 15, 5ᵇ.
16, 4 Del. R.V.[1] 19, 17 Hitz. Ch. (accentuating אותה אליו
יִפְחָד). 27, 2 the vineyard of wine—ענו לה sing ye of it! 32, 7
וכלי כליו רעים. 34, 3. 41, 29. 65, 25. Jer. 49, 21. Hos. 9, 8.
1 Sa. 2, 10. 1 Chr. 23, 14. 2 Chr. 15, 1. 20, 14; after a partcp.
1 Sa. 3, 11. Pr. 11, 26. 14, 21ᵇ. 16, 20ᵇ (see also p. 147, *n.* 2)[2].

Often also with אֵינֶנּוּ and עוֹדֶנּוּ, as Gen. 42, 13 והאחד איננו.
ואהל רשעים איננו. Job 8, 22 יוסף איננו ושמעון איננו 42, 36
(much superior rhythmically to ואין אהל רשעים). Ps. 104, 35
והוא 44, 14 ואברהם עודנו עומד. Gen. 18, 22 ורשעים עוד אינם;
עודנו שם. Nu. 11, 33. 1 Sa. 13, 7 ושאול עודנו בגלגל.

(3) Jud. 17, 5 והאיש מיכה לו בית אלהים. Lev. 7, 7. 33. Pr.
24, 8. Job 22, 8 ואיש זרוע לו הארץ.

(4) With a personal pronoun as subject, Gen. 17, 4 ואני
אתה (Isa. 59, 21) הנה בריתי אתך. 24, 27. 48, 7. 49, 8 Judah!
יודוך אחיך *thou*—thy brethren shall praise thee. Dt. 18, 14ᵇ.
1 Sa. 12, 23. Ez. 4, 12 (30, 18). 9, 10. 33, 17ᵇ. Job 21, 4.
1 Chr. 22, 7. 28, 2.　So ואני הנני Gen. 9, 9 etc.

(5) Gen. 42, 11 all of us—sons of one man are we.
2 Sa. 5, 1.

(6) The casus pendens is sometimes marked as the object,
by את being prefixed: Gen. 13, 15. 21, 13. 1 Sa. 25, 29ᵇ.
Lev. 3, 4. Isa. 51, 22. Ez. 16, 58; גם אותו הכוהו 2 Ki. 9, 27;
Gen. 47, 21. 1 Sa. 9, 13ᵇ for *him* just to-day—ye will find
him.

Instances in which the predicate is introduced by וְ or וַ
will be found §§ 123 *a*, 127 *a*.

Obs. 1. The same principle with לֹ, 1 Sa. 9, 20. 2 Sa. 6, 23. Josh.
17, 3. Qoh. 1, 11 : בֹ, Neh. 9, 29. Ps. 35, 8 ; עַל, Jer. 50, 21. Ez. 1, 26ᵇ;
מִן, Gen. 2, 17. These examples differ from those cited § 123 *Obs.*, as

---

[1] Unless, as is done by LXX, R.V. *marg.*, and most moderns, we
should read נָדְּחֵי מוֹאָב for נִדְּחֵי מוֹאָב.

[2] This use of the casus pendens is very common in Rabbinical Hebrew,
e.g. in the Mishnah, *passim.*

will be clear if a couple be compared : ' in his iniquity which he hath done בו ימות, *in it* shall he die,' here the stress falls evidently upon בו; but in ובמשפטיך חטאו־בם ' and against thy statutes, they have sinned against them,' the emphasis is rather on the entire thought.

Obs. 2. Sometimes the subject, instead of being represented by a pronoun, is repeated, or replaced by an equivalent or alternative expression : Lev. 4, 11 f. את כל הפר, referring back to all the parts named separately in *v.* 11 : והוציא, § 123 *a*). 7, 19[b] והבשר כל טהור יאכל בשר and the flesh—every one that is clean shall eat flesh. 17, 3 f. (לאיש ההוא resumed by איש איש אשר . . .). 18, 9 (20, 6, § 123 *a*). 22, 22 (אלה). 23, 2 (מועדי). 25, 44 (עבד ואמה at the end, referring back to עבדך ואמתך). 27, 32. Nu. 14, 7 (lightening the sentence by making הארץ alone, without the relative clause, the *immediate* subject of the predication : so Jer. 27, 8 הגוי). 31, 35. 1 Ki. 10, 28[b]. The reference back is looser, Ez. 1, 13. 10, 10. 22. Hos. 8, 13 ; Jer. 44, 16. Dan. 1, 20 (see § 127 γ).

Isa. 1, 13[b] is to be explained on the same principle, ' new moon and sabbath, the calling a convocation—I cannot away with them ' would be what analogy would lead us to expect; but the prophet heightens the effect of his words by substituting for *them*, a fresh object of his indignation און ועצרה. Jer. 13, 27 is rhythmically similar: ' thine adulteries, thy neighings, the lewdness of thy whoredom—upon the hills in the field have I seen thy abominations ! ' the last word שקוציך pointing back to, and resuming, 'נאופיך וגו. Comp. 6, 2. Dt. 32, 14[b]

Isa. 49, 19, the original subject 'חרבותיך וגו, as the sentence advances, is left in suspense, and ' replaced by *thou,* the subject of 'תצרי (Hitz.).

198. If this use of the casus pendens be borne in mind, it will enable us to understand in what sense the assertion is true that the *copula* is expressed by the pron. of the 3rd person. Of course the mere juxtaposition of subj. and pred. —the latter as a rule standing first—is sufficient in Hebrew for predication, e. g. Gen. 3, 6 כִּי טוֹב הָעֵץ. 4, 13 גָּדוֹל עֲוֹנִי מִנְּשׂוֹא : of what nature, then, are the instances in which the pronoun is employed as well? Two cases must be distinguished : those, viz., in which the pronoun is *interposed* between the subj. and pred., and those in which it *follows* the predicate. Let us take the latter case first. Such a sentence as ' these men are at peace with us ' could be expressed by שְׁלֵמִים אִתָּנוּ

הָאֲנָשִׁים הָאֵלֶּה שְׁלֵמִים Gen. 34, 21 : but the form הָאנשׁים האלה
הֵם אִתָּנוּ, lit. 'these men—they are at peace with us,' is at
once less cumbrous and less abrupt: the subj. moreover has
greater prominence, and at the same time the pred., still
preceding הם as before it preceded האנשׁים, is not entirely
deprived of emphasis. The pronoun, however, does not
express the copula: שלמים הם אתנו *they are at peace with us*
implies the copula, and is a complete sentence in itself, and
the pred. שלמים is only referred to האנשים האלה by these
words being prefixed as a casus pendens. The advantage of
such a form when the subj. consists of a long relative clause
will be evident. Gen. 30, 33. 31, 16 all the wealth which
etc. לָנוּ הוּא וּלְבָנֵינוּ *it is ours and our children's* (how stiff the
sentence would be if it read כי לנו ולבנינו כל העשר וגו'). 43.
41, 25 the dream of Pharaoh, אחד הוא *it is one.* 45, 20. 47, 6.
48, 5 (לי הם). Ex. 3, 5ᵇ. 16, 36. 32, 16. Nu. 11, 7. 13, 3. Dt.
1, 17. 4, 24. Josh. 5, 15. 6, 19. 22, 14ᵇ. 2 Sa. 21, 2 (after
לא). Isa. 1, 13. 41, 22 (Gen. 23, 15 Nu. 16, 11). 49, 21 but
these—אֵיפֹה הֵם where were they? Qoh. 3, 15; with a partcp.
Ps. 50, 6 for God—he is about to judge. Mic. 7, 3. Jer. 6, 28.
Cf. in Aram. Dan. 2, 28 דנה הוא . . . חלמך.

Obs. 1. So after אֲשֶׁר in *negative* sentences, Gen. 7, 2 ומן הבהמה
אשר לא טהורה הוא. 17, 12 אשר לא מזרעך הוא. Nu. 17, 5. Dt. 17, 15
אשר לא אחיך הוא. 20, 15. Jud. 19, 12. 1 Ki. 8, 41 (= 2 Chr. 6, 32).
9, 20 (= 2 Chr. 8, 7). But Ps. 16, 3 אשר בארץ המה is an unparalleled
expression for the *positive* statement, 'who are in the land' (cf. 2 Sa.
7, 9): and we should in all probability read 'the saints אשר בארץ המה
אדירי וג' that are in the land, *they* (§ 199) are the nobles, in whom
(Ges.-K. § 130. 4) is my delight.'

Obs. 2. Zeph. 2, 12 and ye, Cushites—slain of the sword are they!
with a change of person, after the opening vocative, as Mic. 1, 2 = 1 Ki.
22, 28 שִׁמְעוּ עַמִּים כֻּלָּם; and regularly in such cases as Isa. 22, 16.
47, 8. 48, 1. 54, 1 shout, O barren one לא ילדה, *woman that hath* not
borne! cry aloud לא חָלָה (p. 18, *n.*) *woman that hath* not travailed!
11 עֲנִיָּה סֹעֲרָה לֹא נֻחָמָה afflicted, tossed one, *woman that is* not com-
forted! Mic. 3, 9. 2 Ki. 9, 31 השלום זמרי הורג אדניו is it peace, thou
Zimri, *his* (in our idiom, *thy*) master's murderer? Mal. 3, 9.

Ps. 76, 8 אתה נורא אתה *thou*—thou art to be feared (cf. Gen. 37, 30[b]), recalls the Syriac usage : Matth. 26, 73 ܐܢܬ ܡܢܗܘܢ ܐܦ ܘ ܐ݇. John 4, 12. Comp. Jud. 5, 3 אנכי *I*—to Yahweh *I* will sing.

199. The case is different, when the pronoun stands *before* the predicate, which is then mostly (not always, Josh. 22, 22. Pr. 10, 18. 28, 26) definite. Now there is a difference between the definite and indefinite predicate : being defined, the pred. does not merely refer the subj. to a class, it *circumscribes* the class in such a way as to make the subj. identical with it : thus, to say τὸ πνεῦμά ἐστι τὸ ζωοποιοῦν implies that nothing besides can claim that epithet, and a reflex emphasis is accordingly thrown back upon τὸ πνεῦμα. It follows further that, subj. and pred. being co-extensive, the proposition is a convertible one, and it is immaterial which of the two terms is considered to be the subject, though as a rule the one which from its position is the first to be apprehended *definitely* by the mind, will be most naturally so regarded. Now though the *mere* need of separating subj. and pred. in these cases (Ewald, § 297[b]) does not seem a sufficient explanation of the insertion of the pronoun (for, as the otherwise similar instances § 296[a], and above § 135. 7 shew, it could be dispensed with), it will not be difficult after what has been said to conjecture the motives which must have dictated its use : in virtue of its power of resuming and reinforcing the subject (§ 123 *Obs.*[1]), the pronoun at once makes it plain which of the two terms is the subject, and at the same time gives effect to the emphasis which, it has been just shewn, in these cases belongs to it. Observation corroborates the justice of this explanation. If the instances be examined, it will be found that, while they are much less common than those explained in § 198, the pronoun as a

---

[1] Add (from one book) Pr. 6, 32. 11, 28. 13, 13. 21, 29. 22, 9. 24, 12. 28, 26 ; more rarely, where the pred. is a partcp. (undefined), Dt. 31, 3. 1 Sa. 1, 13. Josh. 22, 22.

rule is evidently meant to be emphatic: in a large proportion of cases, consisting of the phrases יהוה הוא האלהים (Dt. 4, 35. 39. 7, 9. 1 Ki. 18, 39 etc.), יהוה הוא העובר, יהוה הוא הַנֹּתֵן לָכֶם, יהוה הוא ההולך לפניכם or לפניך (Dt. 3, 22[1]. 9, 3. 31, 6. 8 al.), this is unmistakeable[2]. Thus יהוה הוא האלהים is 'Yahweh, *He* (and none else) is the God:' Dt. 10, 9. 18, 2 יהוה הוא נחלתו Yahweh, *He* is his inheritance (cf. 10, 17). But the pronoun is not the copula: הוא נחלתו (as 10, 21 הוא תהלתך shews) is a complete sentence; and the pronoun here merely resumes the subj. *with* emphasis, just as when in a different position, § 198, it resumes it *without* emphasis[3]. In both cases alike, then, the copula is not expressed by the pronoun, but is *understood*: in translating, however, it is generally convenient to drop the pronoun, and hence *the substantive verb seems to be its only representative*. Further instances:—
Gen. 2, 14. 19 (הוא resuming the rel. clause *whatever* ...; cf. with a verb 15, 4. 44, 17. Ex. 12, 16. Dt. 1, 30, and often). 9, 18 וְחָם and Ham, *he* was the father etc. 15, 2. 42, 6 ויוסף הוא השליט and Joseph, *he* was the ruler over the land, *he* was the counsellor. Dt. 12, 23 הדם הוא הנפש. Isa. 9, 14. 33, 6. Job 28, 28. Ez. 27, 13. 17. 21 f. (cf. 23, 45. 36, 7). Hos. 11, 5[4]. Cf. Nu. 16, 3 כל העדה כֻּלָּם קדֹשִׁים.

---

[1] Where the stress is on *who* is הנלחם לכם: 4, 24 (§ 198) on the contrary the stress is on *what* Yahweh is, viz. אש אוכלה.

[2] The parallelism in Dt. 9, 3. 31, 3. 8. Jos. 22, 22 (cf. 23, 3 and 5), where הוא is resumptive, first with the ptcp., and afterwards (cf. § 123 *Obs.*) with *the finite verb* (י"י אלהיך הוא העובר לפניך אש אוכלה הוא) י"י הוא יֹדֵעַ וישראל הוא יֵדָע; ישמירם והוא יכניעם לפניך), affords a strong argument against the opinion that הוא in this position was felt merely to do duty for the copula. Cf. also Ps. 100, 3 and 101, 6[b]; Pr. 28, 26[a] and [b].

[3] Albrecht, *ZATW.* 1888, pp. 250-2 does not properly distinguish these two cases.

[4] So ὁ Θεός ἐστιν ὁ ἐνεργῶν = האלהים הוא הפועל. The inserted pronoun doubtless in time lost its distinctive force, and ultimately *became* little more than the copula (cf. the 'pronoun of separation' in Arabic: Wright, ii. § 124); but Neh. 2, 20. 1 Chr. 11, 20 (Ryssel,

Obs. So after אֲשֶׁר in *positive* sentences, chiefly before an adj. or ptcp.; Gen. 9, 3 כל־רמש אשר הוא חי, Lev. 11, 26. 39. Nu. 9, 13 העיר אשר הוא 14, 8. 27. 35, 31. Dt. 20, 20 האיש אשר הוא טהור. עֲשָׂה עִמְּךָ מלחמה 1 Sa. 10, 19. 2 Ki. 25, 19 (∥ Jer. 52, 25 היה for הוא). Jer. 27, 9. Ez. 43, 19. Hag. 1, 9. Ruth 4, 15. Neh. 2, 18. Qoh. 4, 2. 7, 26; and before a verb 2 Ki. 22, 13 (היא omitted in the ∥ 2 Chr. 34, 21). These are probably all the instances that occur. On the same usage in other Semitic languages, comp. the references in the writer's note on 1 Sa. 10, 19.

200. Does הוא do duty for the copula when inserted between אַתָּה or אֲנִי and the predic., as Ps. 44, 5 ?אַתָּה הוא מַלְכִּי Here we must either (with Roorda, § 563, and Delitzsch on Isa. 37, 16) suppose that הוא strengthens the preceding pronoun, as though equivalent to αὐτός—'*thou, he* (and none else), art my king,' or (with Ewald, § 297ᵇ *end*[1]) regard it as anticipating the predicate—'*thou* art *he*—my king.' The rarity with which הוא is appended to a *noun*—Isa. 7, 14 י"י הוא. Nu. 18, 23 הלוי הוא. Esth. 9, 1 stand perhaps alone in O.T.— the difficulty of separating אֲנִי הוּא הַמְדַבֵּר Isa. 52, 6 from אֲנִי הוּא 41, 4. 43, 10. 13[2] etc. and אתה הוא Ps. 102, 28 (where הוא is, of course, predicate), and the analogous . . . מִי הוא (if not . . . אלה הם as well), where the pronoun cannot be accounted for except on the assumption that it is anticipatory, favour the latter supposition. The other instances are 2 Sa. 7, 28 אנכי אנכי הוא. אתה הוא האלהים. Isa. 37, 16. 43, 25 מֹחֶה פשעיך. 51, 9. 10. 12. Jer. 14, 22. 29, 23ᵇ Kt. (Ew. Keil

---

p. 63) do not differ from Gen. 24, 7. 2 Sa. 14, 19ᵇ: Esth. 2, 14 הוא is required on account of the partcp.; and אתה הוא Neh. 9, 7 is by no means *peculiar* to the latest books. With the use of the pronoun to signify the presence of the subject, Lev. 13, 4 (noted on the same page), comp. 1 Sa. 20, 33 (though the text is here doubtful). Isa. 36, 21. Jer. 50, 15. 25. 51, 6. 11; cf. Mic. 2, 3, and perhaps Job 32, 8 (or § 201. 1?).

[1] So *Gramm. Arab.* § 657; and Aug. Müller, § 499.

[2] Where *I am he* (sc. that I have ever been) = 'I am the same,' predicating the identity of an individual with himself: but whether הוא can predicate the identity of *different* individuals, as many commentators suppose on Job 3, 19, must be regarded as exceedingly doubtful.

etc.). Neh. 9, 6. 2 Chr. 20, 6. So in Aram. Dan. 2, 38 אנתה
את הוא אלהא חֲיֵי .Gen. 16, 13 Onq .5, 13 .הוא ראשה די דהבא
כולא. Ps. 71, 5 את הוא סוברי.

Obs. 1. 1 Chr. 21, 17. Ez. 38, 17 also, הוא is clearly predicate. The
change of person which follows in these passages (κατὰ σύνεσιν) is very
unusual : Jer. 49, 12 ואתה הוא נקה תנקה may, however, perhaps offer
a parallel[1]—the relative being omitted (§ 201. 2); see also Jud. 13, 11.
Neh. 9, 7 (cf. Nu. 22, 30); and cf. in Syriac, Wright, *Apocr. Acts of
Apostles*, pp. 179, 12. 180, 3. 198, 11 al. ; *Acta Pelagiae*, pp. 3, 20. 8, 7.

Obs. 2. Ezra 5, 11 (Aram.). . . . אנחנו המו is quite in accordance
with the Syriac usage, Luke 22, 67 ܐܸܢ݇ܬ ܗ݂ܘ ܡܫܝܼܚܵܐ if *thou art
the Christ.* 70, and often. Matth. 5, 13 ܐܲܢ݇ܬܘܿܢ ܐܸܢ݇ܘܿܢ ܡܸܠܚܵܐ
ye are the salt of the earth (Nöldeke, § 312 D).

201. (1) Another class of cases, however, though a small
one, exists, in which the predicate standing first, the pronoun
is found before the *subject :* Isa. 51, 19 שְׁתַּיִם הנה קראתיך. Pr.
30, 24. 29. Cant. 6, 8. 9 אחת היא יונתי. Lam. 1, 18 'צדיק הוא י'',
cf. 1 Chr. 9, 26 (המה). How these are to be understood, will
appear from a comparison of Pr. 6, 16. 30, 15. 18, cf. 1 Sa.
6, 9 : the pronoun in all alike is an imperfect anticipation of
the subject, which in the former is completed by the *noun*
following, just as in the latter it is completed by the relative
clause following : ' four things are they, the little ones of the
earth' is quite parallel to 'three things are they, (which) are
too wonderful for me,' 'three things are they, (which) be not
satisfied,' 'an accident is it, (that) hath befallen us[2].'

Obs. The pronoun anticipates the subj. rather differently, Ez. 11, 15.
21, 16. And may not Isa. 10, 5 וממה הוא בירם ועמי be most easily
construed similarly? the order, and (in the Hebrew) the rhythm, of
' and a staff is it in their hand, mine indignation' closely resembles that
of ' to us is it given, the land, for a possession.'

(2) The pronoun is used very similarly after מי :—Gen.
27, 33 מי אפוא הוא הצד ציד *who* then is *he*—the one that

---

[1] Otherwise Ewald, § 314ᵃ (*du selbst*), Delitzsch (*l. c.*): cf. the
' enclitic' ܘ݂ܗܘ, Nöldeke, *Syr. Gramm.* § 221.

[2] So also probably Qoh. 6, 10 and that which he, even man, is, is
known (Delitzsch, Nowack).

hunted venison? Ps. 24, 10 מִי הוּא זֶה מֶלֶךְ הַכָּבוֹד[1]; elsewhere with the finite verb, the relative being omitted, Isa. 50, 9 מִי אַתָּה (cf. 60, 8 הוּא יַרְשִׁיעֵנִי). 1 Sa. 26, 14 מִי אֵלֶּה כָעָב תְּעוּפֶינָה. Job 4, 7 מִי הוּא נָקִי אָבָד *who* is *he* (that) perished innocent (§ 161. 3)? 13, 19 מִי הוּא יָרִיב עִמָּדִי, al.; and in the plural, Gen. 21, 29. Zech. 1, 9. 4, 5 מָה הֵמָּה אֵלֶּה *what* are *they*—these? = what are these? With זֶה, Jer. 30, 21. Comp. Ewald, § 325ª.

(3) It is found, thirdly, in the formulae ... אֵלֶּה הֵם and (in the sing.) ... זֶה הוּא. The first of these, if Noldius is to be trusted, occurs only Gen. 25, 16. Lev. 23, 2 אֵלֶּה הֵם מוֹעֲדֵי י״י. Nu. 3, 20. 21. 27. 33. 1 Sa. 4, 8. 1 Chr. 1, 31. 8, 6. 12, 15, the construction without הֵם being far more common (Gen. 36, 5. 12 etc.). In 1 Sa. 4, אֵלֶּה has a disjunctive accent, and the pronoun following seems intended to give it emphasis—'these—*they* (= eben diese) are the gods which smote' etc. (cf. 2 Chr. 28, 23); but the other passages are different, and אֵלֶּה is apparently devoid of any particular stress, so that it is most natural to regard הֵם, as הוּא above, to be merely anticipatory. If this explanation be rejected, it can only be supposed that, though originally הֵם had an independent emphasis, this was in course of time lost, and the combination used without regard to it[2].

Of ... זֶה הוּא, the only examples are 1 Chr. 22, 1. Qoh. 1, 17; but it is frequent in post-Biblical Hebrew (where the two words even coalesce into one זֶהוּ). Qoh. 2, 23 גַּם זֶה הֶבֶל הוּא. 4, 8ᵇ. 5, 18ᵇ. 6, 2ᵇ (in all which the order is different) belong rather to § 198; so also 1, 10 (disregarding accents).

Obs. In Aramaic, comp. (1) Dan. 2, 9 חֲדָא הִיא דָתְכוֹן. Gen. 18, 25 קָיָים הֻוא יְהוָה. 2 Sa. 2, 27. 4, 9 and often קוּשְׁטָא אִינוּן דִּינָךְ Onq. מִבְּנֵי יְהוּדָאֵי הוּא דֵין Dt. 30, 12 Jerus. לָא בִשְׁמַיָּא הִיא אוֹרַיְתָא Ex. 2, 6. מָה דְחִילִין הִינוּן 66, 3. טָב הוּא חַסְדָךְ 63, 4. אַן הוּא אֱלָהָךְ Ps. 42, 4

---

[1] מִי הוּא made more pointed by the enclitic זֶה, as מִי alone, *v.* 8. Jer. 49, 19 al.

[2] Cf. in Arabic Qor. 3, 8, cited by Dr. Wright, ii. § 124.

עוֹבְדָךְ ;(2) Dan. 3, 15[b] ... וּמֵן הוּא אֱלָהּ דִּי . Ezra 5, 4 ; (3) Dan. 4, 27
הֲלָא דָא הִיא בָּבֶל רַבְּתָא . Ex. 14, 25 Onq. דָּא הִיא גְּבוּרְתָּא דִּי ; and see
Ps. 119, 84 Pesh. . . . ܐܝܟ ܡܦܩ, and Nöldeke, *Syr. Gr.* § 311.
Similarly in the Mishnah, as *Aboth* 2, 1 אֵיזוֹ הִיא דֶּרֶךְ יְשָׁרָה שֶׁיָּבֹר לוֹ
הָאָדָם; 2, 16 נֶאֱמָן הוּא בַּעַל מְלַאכְתְּךָ שֶׁיְּשַׁלֶּם־לְךָ שְׂכַר פְּעֻלָּתֶךָ, etc.

2. *Some Uses of the Infinitive with Lamed.*

202. The use of the infinitive with יֵשׁ and אֵין does not
differ substantially from the corresponding Greek construction
with ἔστιν and οὐκ ἔστιν respectively : the one affirms, the
other denies, the action indicated by the verb, not as a
particular past or future occurrence, but (in virtue of the
signification of the inf. and לְ) as an intention capable of
execution *in the abstract :* i.e. its possibility generally.

(1) 2 Sa. 14, 19 אִם אֵשׁ לְהֵמִין if *it is possible to go* to the
right hand or to the left of all that the king has said ! 21, 4.
2 Ki. 4, 13 הֲיֵשׁ לְדַבֶּר־לָךְ *can (I) speak* for thee to the king?
2 Chr. 25, 9 ; but the usage only becomes frequent later :
Hag. 1, 6 (*ter*). Esth. 4, 2 אֵין לָבוֹא. 8, 8. Ezra 9, 15. 1 Chr.
23, 26 וְגַם לַלְוִיִּם אֵין לָשֵׂאת for the Levites also *it was not* (i.e.
they had not) to bear. 2 Chr. 5, 11 אֵין לִשְׁמוֹר לְמַחְלְקוֹת *it was
not* possible to keep the courses. 20, 6[1] וְאֵין עִמְּךָ לְהִתְיַצֵּב none
can stand in conflict with thee (עִם as Ps. 94, 16). 22, 9. 35, 15
(had no need), cf. *v.* 3. Qoh. 3, 14. Without לְ, Ps. 40, 6
אֵין עֲרֹךְ אֵלֶיךָ *there is no comparing* unto thee, οὐκ ἔστι παραβάλ-
λειν σοί, and, as the text stands, Job 34, 18[2] : cf. Ez. 18, 3.

---

[1] But 14, 10 is different : there is none *with thee* (=*beside* or *like
thee :* cf. Ps. 73, 25) to help (and decide : cf. Lev. 26, 12. 33) between
the mighty and (him that hath) no strength (constr. of כֹּחַ לְאֵין as
לְאֵין אוֹנִים Isa. 40, 29). Comp. Ruth 4, 4.

[2] But the *inf. c.* alone, without either אֵין or לְ (§ 204 *end* , is very
much opposed to analogy ; and it is better either to punctuate הָאֹמֵר
(*inf. abs.*, as Job 40, 2. Jer. 7, 9 : Ew. § 328[a]), or to read (with LXX,
Vulg., Ew., Dillm., al.) הָאֹמֵר.

(2) Where לֹא is found instead of אֵין, it denies more absolutely, and categorically, אין implying that though the attempt to do the act would be folly, still it might be made, but לֹא implying that the conditions are such that it would be (or actually was) out of the question altogether:—Jud. 1, 19 כִּי לֹא לְהוֹרִישׁ ... (where אין would not have been strong enough). Amos 6, 10 *there is no* mentioning the name etc. (for dread of the consequences). 1 Chr. 5, 1 וְלֹא לְהִתְיַחֵשׂ לַבְּכֹרָה and he *could not be* reckoned for the birthright. 15, 2 לֹא לָשֵׂאת (*must* not); and in Aramaic, Dan. 6, 9 דִּי לָא לְהַשְׁנָיָה. Ezra 6, 8.

203. With the substantive verb, the inf. with ל expresses naturally the idea of *destination*:—Nu. 8, 11 וְהָיוּ לַעֲבֹד. 24, 22 יִהְיֶה לְבָעֵר Qáyin shall be *for consuming*. Dt. 31, 17. Isa. 5, 5. 6, 13. 37, 26; cf. 44, 15. 2 Ki. 16, 15[b]; and with a passive verb, Ez. 30, 16 לְהִבָּקֵעַ. Scarcely different is מָה לַעֲשׂוֹת *quid est faciendum ?* Isa. 5, 4. 2 Ki. 4, 13. 2 Chr. 25, 9 al.

204. This usage may lead us on to the so-called 'periphrastic future.' Here the inf. with ל, expressing as usual a direction, tendency, or aim, forms the sole predicate: the subject, as a rule, stands first so as to engage the mind, the purpose which is postulated for it follows; and thus the idea arises of an inevitable sequence, or obligation, though not one of a formal and pronounced character, which is expressed in Hebrew by other means[1]. Hos. 9, 13 ואפרים להוציא להורג בניו and Ephraim *is for bringing forth* his sons to the slayer, —or as this is the entire scope and object in regard to which Ephraim is here considered—*is to* or *must* bring forth. Isa. 10, 32 yet to-day (such is his haste) בנב לעמד in Nob *is he for* tarrying, or *must* he tarry. 38, 20 י״י להושיעני *is ready to*

---

[1] By the addition of על (on the analogy of עָלַי אֱלֹהִים נְדָרֶיךָ, Ps. 56, 13); as 2 Sa. 18, 11 וְעָלַי לָתֶת לְךָ and it would have been *incumbent upon* me to give thee. Neh. 13, 13. Ezra 10, 12 (Baer) כדבריך עלינו לעשות; or of ל, Mic. 3, 1. 2 Chr. 13, 5. 20, 17. 26, 18: 1 Sa. 23, 20 וְלָנוּ הַסְגִּירוֹ and it shall be our place (*or* for us) to deliver him etc.

save me, A.V. Jer. 51, 49[1]. Hab. 1, 17[2]. Ps. 32, 9. 49, 15 and their form לְבַלּוֹת שְׁאוֹל *is for* the wasting away of She'ol[3] = must She'ol waste away. 62, 10. Pr. 18, 24. 19, 8 a man of understanding למצא טוב *will be finding* prosperity. 20, 25 *will have to* enquire. Job 30, 6 בערוץ נחלים לִשְׁכֹּן *must* they dwell (R.V.). 1 Chr. 22, 5 לבנות לי"י להגדיל למעלה *must be* built to Yahweh so as to shew greatness exceedingly etc. Ezra 10, 12 (Hahn) כדבריך עלינו לעשות: Qoh. 3, 15.

More rarely of past time :—2 Sa. 4, 10 אֲשֶׁר לְתִתִּי לוֹ cui *dandum erat mihi.* 2 Ki. 13, 19 לְהַכּוֹת *percutiendum erat* quinquies aut sexies; and after an *implied* injunction 1 Chr. 9, 25. 2 Chr. 8, 13 (cf. Gen. 42, 25); and, more freely, 11, 22 כי להמליכו for (it was his purpose) to make him king. 12, 12 ולא להשחית and *was no longer for* destroying utterly[4]. 26, 5 ויהי לדרש and he *set himself* (A.V.) to seek etc. 36, 19 : cf. 28, 23. Also Gen. 15, 12. Josh. 2, 5 and the gate *was about to be* shut.

In a question:—Gen. 30, 15 וְלָקַחַת and art thou for taking? Esth. 7, 8 הגם לכבוש את המלכה עמי בבית. 2 Chr. 19, 2 הלרשע לעזר wilt thou help the *wicked?* cf. Ex. 2, 14 with אומר.

Obs. 1. Isa. 44, 14 לִכְרָת־לוֹ, if the reading be correct, must be also added, 'a man *prepares to*—or *must*—hew him cedars;' for it can scarcely be supposed that this is an isolated example of a real impf. in ל, such as is met with in Ezra and Daniel (להוא, להון, להוין,), in the Targ. of Ps.-Jon. Ex. 22, 24 (להוי), in the Talmud (e.g. דליתנו, *ut dent*, לזלו *eant*, דלשמעו, דליקומו, לימרו, דלייתו *ut afferant*, etc.), in Mandaic (Nöldeke, *Mand. Gramm.* §§ 166, 196), and also, as it

---

[1] 'Yea, Babylon must fall' (Ew., Hitz., Graf): but Rashi paraphrases היתה לנפול בה חללי ישראל; and similarly Kimchi, A.V.

[2] Where Del. remarks that (e.g.) לעשות may have the signification of either *est facturus, est faciendum, est faciendo,*—the tense of the subst. verb (which is implied in the construction itself) being determined naturally by the connexion.

[3] Construction as Ex. 17, 1. 2 Sa. 16, 2 לאכול הנערים for the eating of the young men. 19, 20[b].

[4] Comp. the use of ל ולא, 28, 21. 1 Chr. 21, 17.

would seem, in Assyrian[1]. On this, in addition to the references given
by Dr. Pusey, *Lectures on Daniel*, pp. 49, 623 (ed. 3), see Dietrich,
Abhandlungen (1846), pp. 182, 186, and Lowe, *Fragment of Talmud
Babli* (Cambridge, 1879), p. 1 ff., who shews, by instances, that it has
no distinctively jussive force, but that, as Nöldeke says, both in Mandaic and in the Talmud, it interchanges freely with the form in נ,
without any difference in signification. Indeed, the impf. in ל seems to
be but a phonetic variation of that in נ, and should doubtless be
altogether disconnected from the Rabbinical infin. with ל (see *Obs.* 2),
although, as the two are apt to approximate closely both in usage
and form—comp. e.g. Dukes, *Blumenlese*, No. 44 (p. 96), 465 (fut.),
599, 601, 662 (infin.)—they have been supposed by some to have a
common origin[2]. (On the forms in Ezr. Dan., comp. also A. A. Bevan,
Commentary on the Book of Daniel, 1892, p. 35 f.)

Obs. 2. This usage is employed freely in later Hebrew ; e.g. *Aboth*
4, 22 Jost or Strack (31 Taylor) הילודים למות והמתים להחיות והחיים
לידון the born *are to* die, and the dead *are to* revive, and the living *are
to* be judged ; and in such formulae as תַּלְמוּד לוֹמַר the Scripture *means
to* say, *Kerithoth* 9, 6 and often ; איכא למימר *numquid dicendum?*
ליחוש *timendum* est, ליתני *docendum* erat, את לן לימא *dicas* nobis *tu*,
לומר לך *dicam* tibi, כחצות למימר ליה למה why *was he* (obliged) *to*
say כחצות ? ואיפיכא וליעביד *et agendum* erat inverso modo (Dietrich,
l.c., p. 184 f.). Cf. the common לומר לו היה he *ought to have* said.

205. Another usage of the inf. and ל is to be connected
with that *gerundial* use of this idiom, which is well known
(Ewald, 280^d : 1 Sa. 12, 17. 14, 33 lo, the people are sinning
לֶאֱכֹל *so as to eat = in eating* with the blood. 20, 20 *so as to*

---

[1] It is hardly doubtful, however, that Ewald, Cheyne, Delitzsch
(ed. 4), and Dillmann, are right in treating לכרת as simply an error of
transcription for יכרת or כָּרַת.

[2] In some of the passages in which this form is cited as a future, it
seems, from the construction, to be really an *infin.*: thus Ex. 10, 28
Jer. למלך שמע להוי ולא לממות צבא הוא ; Fürst, *Perlenschnüre*, p. 44,
39 (=Esth. 1, 2 Targ. II) after וכא (p. 43, 26 is למהוי). p. 62, 4
פקידא אנא ולהוא...קדמך רעוא יהא. Instances of the inf. Qal
without מ are met with occasionally in Aramaic : Ezra 5, 13 לבנא.
Gen. 9, 14 Onq. בעננותי. 49, 6 קטול (absol.). Lev. 13, 7 Ps.-Jon. הלוכי.
Ps. 105, 14 לטלומיהון, 109, 23 בצליותיה. Cant. 1, 8 למחי; in the
Talm. לוכל נכנסין intrant ad edendum, לימא etc., and להוי itself,
Dukes, No. 662 להוי מחתרא בחד אמתא תירום תפיש.

aim, or *aiming*, at a mark. 36. 1 Chr. 22, 5 לְהַגְדִּיל); its use,
viz. after a particle of comparison, where the sense *so as to*
merges into that of *in respect of*. Gen. 3, 22 ye shall be as one
of us לָדַ֫עַת *so as to know* etc., which does not differ from *in
respect of knowing* good and evil. 41, 19 לָרֹע[1]. Pr. 26, 2 כִצִּפּוֹר
לָנוּד כַּדְּרוֹר לָעוּף (cf. 25, 3). 2 Sa. 14, 25 now as Absalom there
was no man fair in Israel לְהַלֵּל מְאֹד—either, *for praising*
(= to be praised) exceedingly, LXX αἰνετὸς σφόδρα, or *in
respect of* praising. Isa. 21, 1 כְּסוּפוֹת בַּנֶּגֶב לַחֲלוֹף as whirlwinds
in the South (Gen. 12, 9 R.V. *marg.*) *for*, or *in respect of*,
sweeping through. Ez. 38, 9. 16. 1 Chr. 12, 8 כַּצְּבָאִים עַל הֶהָרִים
לְמַהֵר.

206. The inf. with לְ also appears in continuation of a
finite verb, the particular sense to be assigned to it being
determined by the mood of that verb, but implying generally
the presence of some aim or purpose :—Ex. 32, 29 מִלְאוּ יֶדְכֶם
הַיּוֹם לַיהוה . . . וְלָתֵת עֲלֵיכֶם הַיּוֹם בְּרָכָה fill your hand (i. e. con-
secrate yourselves, 2 Chr. 29, 31) this day unto Yahweh, . . .
and *be for placing* upon yourselves a blessing (i.e. and act so
that a blessing may be bestowed upon you). Lev. 10, 10. 11
(cf. R.V. *marg.*[2]); 1 Sa. 8, 12 וְלָשׂוּם (after a fut.). 1 Chr. 6, 34.
12, 33. 2 Chr. 2, 8 (continuing וַשְׁלַח, *v.* 7). 7, 17. 30, 9 *and
will be for* returning; Amos 8, 4 ye panters after the needy
וְלַשְׁבִּית *and* (that are) *for making* (or *that would make*) to fail
the poor of the land. Isa. 44, 28[3]. 56, 6[4]. Ps. 104, 21 (all
after the ptcp.); Jer. 17, 10[3]. 19, 12[3] (continuing אֶעֱשֶׂה). 44,
14. 19; Ez. 13, 22 וּלְחַזֵּק (continuing הַכְאוֹת). Job 34, 8[b5]. Ps.

---

[1] Cf. Ex. 24, 10 as heaven itself לָטֹ֫הַר *for* brightness.

[2] But the construction is here somewhat forced; and it is possible
that these two verses do not stand in their original context.

[3] The rendering 'even' (A.V., R.V.) in these passages and in Qoh.
9, 1 does not represent properly the force of the Hebrew.

[4] At least the accents and the parallelism suggest that וְלַאֲהָבָה is
the continuation of הֲבִלּוּים rather than of לְשָׁרְתוֹ.

[5] If וְלָלֶכֶת be treated, as is done by Ew., Del., R.V., as parallel to
וָאֵרַח rather than to לְחֶבְרָה.

25, 14. 109, 16 וְנִכְאָה לֵבָב לָמוּתת and *is for slaying* etc. Qoh.
7, 25 (Delitzsch, Nowack, R.V.). 9, 1 וְלַבּוּר[1] (after וָנַתְתִּי).
Whether 1 Chr. 10, 13. Neh. 8, 13 belong here is doubtful[2].

Obs. Only once thus, of *past* time, in an earlier author, 1 Sa. 14, 21ᵇ
now the Hebrews had been to the Philistines as aforetime (cf. 2, 27.
19, 7. 2 Sa. 19, 29), in that they went up with them to the camp,
וגם המה להיות and they also *were for being* with Israel. But the *v.*
seems clearly meant to describe, not a purpose or preparation, but a
fact; and though a sense of the former is evanescent in some of the
passages where the inf. and ל is used by the Chronicler (§ 204), this
must not be assumed as a matter of course in an early writer. In point
of fact LXX. Pesh. (perhaps), Vulg. for סביב וגם המה read סבבו גם
המה (Targ. *adds* תבו); and this on the whole, though it involves the
insertion of אשר after העברים (οἱ ὄντες LXX), seems preferable: 'and
the Hebrews, who were etc. . . . , *they also turned* (2 Sa. 3, 12) to be
with Israel:' cf. *v.* 22.

207. Occasionally the ל introduces the inf. merely as the
object of a verb:—Isa. 5, 2 וַיְקַו לַעֲשׂוֹת עֲנָבִים. Esth. 4, 13 think
not *te evasuram esse.* 1 Chr. 29, 17.

3.　*Order of Words.*

208. The following illustrations of variations in the order
of words (noted briefly by Ewald, § 309ᵃ) may be useful :—

(1) *Object, verb, subject.* This, the effect of which is to throw
emphasis on the object, is fairly frequent; and examples
from two or three books will be sufficient: 1 Sa. 2, 19 וּמְעִיל
אֹתִי שְׁלַח י"י 17, 36. 25, 43. 28, 7, 14. 15, 1. קָטֹן תַּעֲשֶׂה־לּוּ אִמּוֹ
18ᵇ. 19ᵇ. 1 Ki. 14, 11. Isa. 6, 5ᵇ כִּי אֶת הַמֶּלֶךְ י"י צְבָאוֹת רָאוּ
עֵינָי 9, 7. 26, 9ᵇ. 40, 19. 64, 1. Ps. 11, 5ᵇ. 139, 16 גָּלְמִי רָאוּ
עֵינֶיךָ. Job 5, 2. 14, 19. 15, 30.

(2) *Object, subject, verb.* This is exceedingly rare, except
with the participle, when it is the usual order :—2 Ki. 5, 13.

---

[1] Unless the true reading be that of LXX, Pesh. (so Bickell) וְלִבִּי רָאָה
(cf. 1, 16), which is very possible, as the meaning of בּוּר is doubtful.
Grätz conjectured וְלָתוּר (1, 13. 2, 3. 7, 25).

[2] With §§ 202–206, comp. Ewald, 237ᶜ, 295ᶠ, 351ᵒ.

Isa. 5, 17. 28, 17[b] וסתר מים ישטפו. Jer. 34, 5[b]. 49, 11. Ps. 51, 5. Pr. 5, 2[b] ודעת שפתיך ינצרו. 5. Qoh. 12, 14: but with the ptcp., Gen. 37, 16 את אחי אנכי מבקש. 41, 9. Jud. 9, 36. 14, 4. 2 Ki. 6, 22. Jer. 1, 11. 7, 19 האתי הם מכעיסים. 45, 4. 51, 6 al.

(3) *Subject, object, verb.* Here the subject is followed immediately by the object, with which it has no *direct* connexion; a break, often reflected in the accentuation, is thus produced, which by inviting a pause almost gives to the subject the prominence of a *casus pendens :* at the same time, in prose, a poetical colouring is conferred upon the phrase by the verb being transferred to the end, while in poetry the monotony of two similarly constructed parallel clauses may be avoided:—Gen. 17, 9 ואתה בריתי תשמר. 23, 6[b] (איש לא יכלה קברו would have been a little dull). Jud. 17, 6. Lev. 7, 18[c]. 21, 10 (allows stress to rest on ראשו and בגדיו). 13. 26, 8. 1 Sa. 20, 20 ואני (unless the reading of LXX, § 163 *Obs.*, is to be here preferred). Isa. 3, 17. 11, 8[b]. 13, 18. 17, 5. 26, 19. 30, 24. 32, 8 ונדיב נדיבות יעץ but the liberal man—he counselleth liberal things. Ez. 18, 19. 27[b]. 23, 25[b] המה בניך ובנותיך יקחו. 34, 19. 36, 7. Hos. 12, 11. Ps. 6, 10[b]. 10, 14. 11, 5[a]. וְדִבֶּר פיו עם פיו ועיניו את עיניו Jer. 32, 4[b] המה עקבי ישמרו 56, 7. תראינה. 34, 3. 2 Chr. 31, 6, which perhaps justifies the Mas. text of 2 Sam. 17, 27–29.

Obs. A tendency may often be observed in the Aramaic portions of Daniel and Ezra to throw the verb to the end. With the place of the *infin.* in Isa. 42, 24. 49, 6 ונצירי ישראל להשיב comp. Dt. 28, 56 ורדמם לשום Jud. 9, 24. אשר לא נסתה כף רגלה הצג. Neh. 10, 37. Esth. 3, 13[b] = 8, 11[b]. 2 Chr. 31, 7. 10; and in Aramaic Ezra 4, 22 (שלו object to למעבר). 5, 9. 13. Dan. 2, 16. 18. 3, 16 (פתגם not connected with על דנה, but the obj. to להתבותך: the order in Pesh. is similar). 4, 15 לא יכלין פשרא להודעותני. 5, 8. 15[b]; 6, 5 seems rather to resemble Lev. 19, 9. 2 Sa. 11, 16. The so-called ' periphrastic future ' has also commonly the same position (§ 204).

(4) *Verb, object, subject.* This order emphasizes, as Ewald says, the subject at the end :—Gen. 21, 7 היניקה בנים שרה. Nu. 5, 23. 19, 7. 18. Jud. 12, 11. 13. 1 Sa. 15, 33. 1 Ki. 8,

63^b. 19, 10. Isa. 19, 13 התעו את מצרים פנת שבטיה. Jer. 31, 2.
36, 9. 24. 48, 4. Jon. 3, 8. Ez. 23, 47. Ps. 34, 22 ; otherwise
rare, except when the object is the light pronominal אֹתוֹ, אֹתָם,
etc. ; Ex. 12, 6. Jer. 3, 11 (נפשה). 49, 16.

4. *On Constructions of the type* יוֹם הַשְּׁבִיעִי[1].

209. As is well known, when a substantive in Hebrew is
defined by the article, an accompanying adj. or partcp. is, as
a rule, defined by it likewise (e.g. הַמָּאוֹר הַגָּדֹל). In post-
Biblical Hebrew (the Mishnah etc.) it became customary in
such cases to *omit* the article before the subst. (as כְּנֶסֶת הַגְּדוֹלָה
the great Synagogue, יֵצֶר הָרַע the evil inclination) ; and the
beginnings of this usage are traceable in the Old Testament.
It may be of interest to collect, and if possible, to analyse the
principal instances that occur.

(1) With an *adjective*. Here, though the cases altogether
are relatively few, the usage appears to have arisen in connexion with familiar words, which were felt to be sufficiently
definite in themselves, without the addition of the article, as
יוֹם, Gen. 1, 31 יוֹם הַשִּׁשִּׁי. 2, 3 את יום השביעי. Ex. 12, 15 מיום
הראשון עד יום השביעי 18. 20, 10 (in the Decalogue) = Dt. 5, 14
את יום השביעי. Lev. 19, 6. 22, 27 ; חָצֵר *court*, 1 Ki. 7, 8 חצר
האחרת the *other* court (see R.V.). 12 חצר הגדולה[2]. 2 Ki. 20, 4
Qrê. Ez. 40, 28 חצר הפנימי. 31 חצר החיצונה ; שער, Ez. 9, 2
שער העליון (so 2 Chr. 23, 20). Zech. 14, 10 שער הראשון ; מבוא,
Jer. 38, 14 מבוא השלישי אשר בבית יהוה,—the last three words

---

[1] The substance of this section appeared originally in the *Journal of
Philology*, xi. (1882), p. 229 f. Comp. also Ew. § 293^a; Ges.-Kautzsch,
§ 126. 5, rem. 1.

[2] The 'great court' was that which enclosed both the Temple and
the official buildings constituting the Palace ; the 'other court' was
that which was entered through this, and which surrounded the actual
residence of the king. Comp. the plan in Stade's *Gesch. des V. Israel*,
i. p. 314 f.

denoting well-known parts of the Palace or Temple[1]: with
words defined by כל (rare), Gen. 1, 21 ... כל נפש החיה הרמשת
(so Lev. 11, 46[a]); ... כל נפש החיה אשר Gen. 9, 10.' Lev. 11,
10; or by a numeral, Gen. 41, 26 שֶׁבַע פָּרֹת הַטֹּבֹת (followed
vv. 26. 27 by the regular idiom)[2]. Nu. 11, 25 שבעים איש
הזקנים: with a proper name, Jud. 14, 3: cases hardly redu-
cible to rule, Lev. 24, 10 את איש הישראלי (cf.—though this
depends only on the punctuation, and is followed immediately
by האיש הָרֹאשׁ—2 Sa. 12, 4 (לְאִישׁ הֶעָשִׁיר). 1 Sa. 6, 18 אָבֵל
19, 22 .רוּחַ הָרָעָה 16, 23 .דרך הטובה 12, 23 (אֶבֶן).(read הגדולה
שמן הטוב 2 Ki. 20, 13 ,(בֹּור הַגֹּרֶן), (read with LXX בור הגדול
(in the ‖ Isa. 39, 2 (השמן הטוב) Jer. 6, 20 קָנֶה הטוב (but Ct. 7,
10 יֵין הַטֹּוב: see Ewald, § 287[b]). 17, 2. Zech. 4, 7 הר הגדול.
Ps. 104, 18 הרים הגבהים ליעלים. Ezra 10, 9 הוא חדש התשיעי
(the only instance with חדש in the O.T.)[3]. Neh. 9, 35[4].

(2) With a *participle:*—where the subst. is a term definite
in itself, as a proper name, Dt. 2, 23 כפתרים היושבים בכפתור,
or limited in virtue of its own character, Jud. 16, 27 כשלשת
עולת .אלפים איש הראים וג'. Ruth 2, 6 (read הַשָּׁבָה[5]). Nu. 28, 6
גוים רבים ...תמיד העשויה. Dan. 9, 26[b], cf. with גוים, Mi. 4, 11
... האמרים. Ez. 2, 3[6]; or by כל, Gen. 1, 21 (so Lev. 11, 46[a]:
see under 1). 28 כָּל־בשר הרומש. 7, 21 כָּל־חַיָּה הָרֹמֶשֶׂת על הארץ

---

[1] But מבוא ,שער ,חצר, יום are everywhere else construed regularly, even in the same phrases, as 1 Ki. 7, 9. Ez. 40, 17. 19, 32. 42, 1
etc., the only exception being the n. pr. חצר התיכון Ez. 47, 16.

[2] Comp. with האלה Gen. 21, 29. On some instances with הזה, cf.
the writer's notes on 1 Sa. 14, 29. 17, 12. 17.

[3] But Dt. 29, 7 (cited by Kautzsch, § 126. 5, rem. 1[a]) שבט המנשי
(so 1 Chr. 26, 32), המנשי is plainly a genitive: cf. Jud. 18, 1. 1 Chr.
23, 14.

[4] But Neh. 3, 6 = 12, 39 שער הישנה, there is doubtless an ellipse of
some subst. before הישנה,—whether העיר, or החומה, or הברכה: cf.
Guthe in the *Zeitschr. des Deutschen Pal.-Vereins*, 1885, p. 279.

[5] See Ew. § 331[b] (1); Ges.-Kautzsch, § 138. 3[b]; or the writer's note
on 1 Sa. 9, 24.

[6] Where, however, אל גוים should probably be omitted with LXX,
Cornill.

עַל הָאָרֶץ. Lev. 11, 46[b] כָּל־נֶפֶשׁ הַשֹּׁרֶצֶת עַל הָאָרֶץ, or a following gen., Ez. 21, 19: other cases, 1 Sa. 25, 10. Jer. 27, 3. 46, 16 =50, 16 חֶרֶב הַיּוֹנָה *the oppressing sword.* Ez. 14, 22[1]. 32, 22 נפלים (so *v.* 24, but *v.* 23 כֻּלָּם חֲלָלִים הַנֹּפְלִים בַּחֶרֶב). Pr. 26, 18. Ps. 119, 21 (if the accentuation be correct): with a passive partcp. Isa. 7, 20 תַּעַר הַשְּׂכִירָה. Jer. 32, 14 אֶת סֵפֶר הַגָּלוּי הַזֶּה Zech. 11, 2 Kt. Ps. 62, 4 נֶדֶר הַדְּחוּיָה; very anomalous (but dependent only on the punctuation) Jud. 21, 19 לִמְסִלָּה הָעֹלָה מִבֵּיתאֵל שְׁכֶמָה[2].

Obs. Although, after a subst. defined by an art., Heb. idiom uses regularly הַזֶּה, הַזֹּאת, הָאֵלֶּה (as הַדָּבָר הַזֶּה, הַדְּבָרִים הָאֵלֶּה)[3], yet after a subst. defined by a *pronom. suffix,* it is to be noticed that the art. is not used: see Gen. 24, 8 וְנִקִּיתָ מִשְּׁבֻעָתִי זֹאת. Dt. 5, 26 לְבָבָם זֶה *this* their heart. 21, 20 בְּנֵנוּ זֶה. Josh. 2, 14 אֵת דְּבָרֵנוּ זֶה. 20. Jud. 6, 14. 2 Chr. 24, 18; Ex. 10, 1 אֶת־דְּבָרַי אֵלֶּה *these* my signs[4]. 11, 8 כָל עֲבָדֶיךָ אֵלֶּה. Dt. 11, 18 אֹתִי אֵלֶּה 1 Ki. 8, 59. 10, 8. 22, 23. 2 Ki. 1, 13. Jer. 31, 21 *end.* Ezra 2, 65. Neh. 6, 14. The only exceptions (if I am not mistaken) are Josh. 2, 17 שְׁבֻעָתֵךְ הַזֶּה, where the *gender* of הֹזֶה is a sufficient indication that the text cannot be sound (cf. Gen. 24, 8 above); and 2 Chr. 1, 10 אֶת־עַמְּךָ הֹזֶה הַגָּדוֹל, where the art. may be due to the influence of the following הַגָּדוֹל.

---

[1] Where, in view of the fact that בנים ובנות are the *objects* of deliverance in *vv.* 16. 18. 20, it seems better to vocalize, with LXX, Pesh., Symm., Vulg., Cornill, הַמּוֹצִיאִים.

[2] In 1 Chr. 25, 23 שַׁעַר הַפֹּנֶה must doubtless be read for שַׁעַר הַפוּנֶה. as in the parallel 2 Ki. 14, 13.

[3] But in Phoenician הַשַּׁעַר זְ, as in Moabitish הַבָּמָת זֹאת: see *Notes on Samuel*, pp. xxviii, xc.

[4] Add Ex. 9, 14, where both the sense and symmetry of the verse are much improved, if, with Hitzig, we read אֵת כָּל מַגֵּפֹתַי אֵלֶּה בָּךְ for אֶת כָּל מ' אֶל לִבְּךָ: cf. the frequency of the same combination, 'thou, thy servants, and thy people,' previously (7, 29. 8, 5. 7. 17. 25).

INDEX I.

∗∗∗ The references are to the sections, except where otherwise marked.
O. = Obs. ; n. = note.

INDEX II.

⁂ The references are to the sections, except where otherwise marked.

O. = Obs.; n. = note.

Leviticus.